Praise for *Jack de Crow*

"a great travel writer and more importantly a great traveller"
—*Sydney Morning Herald*

"not just an adventurer, but an artist, philosopher and keen observer of the world around him"—*The Canberra Times*

"Mackinnon's journey makes a lovely picaresque tale, one dotted with English literary references and wonderful descriptions of the English and European countryside"
—*Good Reading*

"a marvellous adventure, and Mackinnon recounts it with humour and unflagging enthusiasm ... a clever and entirely engaging read"—*The Melbourne Times*

"a wonderful idea for a book – a series of ever bolder improvisations ... undertaken in praise of the spirit of adventure"
—*Times Literary Supplement*

The Unlikely Voyage of Jack de Crow

The Unlikely
Voyage of
JACK de
CROW

A.J. Mackinnon

Black Inc.

Published by Black Inc.,
an imprint of Schwartz Publishing Pty Ltd
37–39 Langridge Street
Collingwood VIC 3066 Australia
email: enquiries@blackincbooks.com
http://www.blackincbooks.com

This is a revised edition of *The Unlikely Voyage of Jack de Crow* by A.J. Mackinnon, first published by Seafarer Books, 102 Redwald Road, Rendlesham, Woodbridge, Suffolk IP12 2TE, UK.

The National Library of Australia Cataloguing-in-Publication entry:

Mackinnon, A. J. (Alexander James), 1963- author.

The unlikely voyage of Jack de Crow / A. J. Mackinnon.

2nd edition.

9781863956659 (paperback)
9781922231611 (ebook)

Mackinnon, A. J. (Alexander James), 1963---Travel.
Jack de Crow (Dinghy)
Sailing--English Channel.
Sailing--Europe.
Sailing--Black Sea.
Voyages and travels.

910

Illustrations and maps by A.J. Mackinnon
Book design by Thomas Deverall

Printed in Australia by Griffin Press. The paper this book is printed on is certified against the Forest Stewardship Council® Standards. Griffin Press holds FSC chain of custody certification SGS-COC-005088. FSC promotes environmentally responsible, socially beneficial and economically viable management of the world's forests.

FSC
www.fsc.org
MIX
Paper from
responsible sources
FSC® C009448

Contents

PART THREE *Into the East*

Part One

Bumping into Places

The Teacher's Thief

> For there is an upstart crow, beautified with our feathers, that
> with his tiger's heart wrapped in a player's hide supposes he is
> as well able to bombast out a blank verse as the best of you.
> —ROBERT GREENE, *A Groat's Worth of Wit*

This is an account of a journey made from North Shropshire in England to Sulina on the Black Sea, sailing and rowing over three thousand miles in a small Mirror dinghy. It was in many ways an accident that it happened at all. I had intended to spend a quiet two weeks travelling the sixty miles or so down to Gloucester on the River Severn. Somehow things got out of hand – a year later I had reached Romania and was still going.

I have many heroes. They are mostly drawn from the world of children's literature, I confess. But the earliest hero I can remember is Doctor Dolittle, that plump and kindly figure who lived in Puddleby-on-the-Marsh and talked to the animals. It was not this last attribute that first entranced me, however. It was the illuminated capital letters at each chapter heading which made a high-pooped, billow-sailed little galleon of each capital 'S,' or turned an 'A' into a frame of leaning palm trees, and, above all, it was the marvellously casual line:

Doctor Dolittle sailed away in a ship with his monkey and his parrot, his pig and his duck, and bumped into Africa.

Bumped into Africa! Here was the way to travel! No timetables, no travel agents, no dreary termini clanging with loudspeaker announcements. No grubby platforms, no passports, no promises of postcards to be sent on safe arrival, just the little ship slipping down the river to the sea. Indeed the chief attributes of all the good Doctor's voyages seemed to be simple enough: a cheerful optimism and a beloved hat, both of which I happened to have. There was clearly nothing stopping me doing the same.

*

I had been working for six years as a teacher in a place called Ellesmere College. This is a minor public school set amid the meres and
meadows of Shropshire – a flat Shire land of grazing cattle and
placid canals where narrowboats glide serenely across the countryside. In the distance rise the first blue hills of Wales, an altogether
wilder and more enchanted land.

Some of that dark Welsh magic must have leaked from those
nearby valleys, seeping across the prosperous plain to lap about the
confines of Ellesmere College. For in my first year there something
happened which has a bearing on all this present tale.

Amid the busy routine of a new term in a new place, there grew
in my mind a faint but persistent daydream, a niggling ambition of
the most childish and unlikely sort: namely, to own a tame crow. To
this day I am not quite sure where such a fancy came from. Perhaps
it was the weight of my academic gown on my shoulders, heavy as
Prospero's cloak, that prompted me to seek out an Ariel of my own.

One does not, of course, share such daydreams readily with others. They have a habit of wilting on contact with outside scrutiny. But
when my oldest friend rang to see how I was settling in to my new
life at Ellesmere, I did confide to him, half jokingly, self-mockingly,
my avian fancy. Well, Rupert has long ago become accustomed to
this sort of thing from me, so after expressing a polite but distant
acknowledgement of my latest daydream, he neatly turned the conversation to more immediate issues such as the quality of school
food, coming holiday dates and whether I'd purchased a car yet.

But perhaps such fancies are not so much wishes as faint psychic
previsions of what will be. For the next day, the very next day, I
received a brief note in my pigeon-hole via the College receptionist:
'Crow arrives Friday next. Prepare.'

Rupert had, within hours of putting down the phone, stumbled
across a tame, slightly injured jackdaw that needed an owner.

The bird arrived in a cat basket in the middle of the House Singing Competition and, from the moment he arrived, divided the
entire College into two camps – those who adored him, and those
who loathed him to the least of his sooty black feathers. The first
camp consisted of the Headmaster's family, the laundry ladies and
me; the second camp was everyone else, who regarded him more as
a Caliban than an Ariel.

I called him Jack de Crow as a pun on the Headmaster's sur-
name, du Croz – though his full name was actually Jack Micawber

The Master Summons His Familiar

Phalacrocorax Magister Mordicorvus de Crow, a wild and marvellous name spun out of some dark, dog-Latin, cobwebby corner of my brain and which defies rational explanation. The Headmaster was, I think, suitably flattered. He did not, after all, dismiss me when his school was systematically plundered by the new arrival.

For Jack de Crow found a wide field of play for his talents at Ellesmere. In the first week he burgled the Bursar's bedroom and stole Mrs Bursar's ruby earring, demolished an important set of exam papers in the office of the Director of Studies, and brought to a halt an important hockey match by sitting on the hockey ball and unpicking all the stitches before he could be shooed away. Week Two ended with the loss of a gold pen and a bunch of keys from my Housemaster's desk, and the steady increase among the students of 'Crow-ate-my-homework'–style excuses. And this was when he was still in less than peak condition.

Once he had recovered, Jack strutted and swooped and thieved his way unchecked around College, taking refuge at times of crisis in the hallowed precincts of the Headmaster's orchard garden under the protection of his kindly namesake. If I stepped outside and raised my arm and called 'Jack, Jack, Jack, Jack!' he would come fluttering down from some lofty chimney-pot to perch on my wrist, much to the consternation of the elderly Chaplain, who was convinced that – as if being Australian wasn't bad enough – I was in league with the Devil. Thus did Jack live out my enchanter's dream.

But then, one day, he was gone. Many of my colleagues breathed a sigh of relief and stopped looking nervously over their shoulders, and even I felt that life might be easier; I had been held largely to blame for Jack's list of crimes. But something ever so slightly magical had faded from the landscape. Time and routine and normality rose to obliterate that first dream-like year in a tangle of timetables and curricula, meetings and lesson plans, sporting fixtures, rehearsals and the slow grinding of the academic year, and the name of Jack Micawber Phalacrocorax Magister Mordicorvus de Crow faded from the memories of men.

Until years later when I decided it was time to move on and Jack de Crow was gloriously revived.

*

Five years had fled by. My feet were itchy and I felt it was time for a grand gesture and a dramatic farewell, and to have lots of people say touching things about me. Finally I hit upon it. The very thing! I decided to leave Ellesmere – not by the Inter-City 10.15 to Birmingham with a suitcase in each hand, not by a lift to the airport checking the whereabouts of my passport every three minutes, not even by hitch-hiking off between the dusty July hedgerows with a cardboard sign outstretched – but, like my dear Doctor Dolittle, by sailing away in a jolly little galleon and seeing what I bumped into on the way.

The Dinghy and the Dreamer

There was a merry passenger,
A messenger, a mariner,
Who built a gilded gondola
To wander in ...

—J.R.R. TOLKIEN, *Errantry*

Just over the fields from Ellesmere College lies a little mere, fringed with tall trees, dotted with ducks and coots and the odd haughty swan, and on Wednesdays and Saturdays, suddenly alive with the skim and swoop of white sails. Here on this strip among the speedwell lie thirty or forty little sailing boats – the fleet of the Whitemere Sailing Club. Here are the gaudy pink and blue of plastic Toppers, constructed seemingly of Lego and Tupperware; the slim white forms of Lasers, half gull and half shark; the tiny wooden Optimists like little floating armchairs. But right at the back of this meadow strip in a corner of the fence, half smothered in thistles and golden ragwort, is the upturned hull of an ancient Mirror dinghy, lowliest and least of the College sailing fleet. Its deep curved wooden hull is a fading, peeling yellow. Its square pram nose is lost in a tangle of blackberry brambles, and out of the dark slit of the centreboard case a dozen spiders battle for supremacy with the scuttling woodlice.

It is a sorry sight, but for all that my heart kicks with nostalgia. A Mirror is to the sailing world what a Volkswagen Beetle is to the world of motoring. Everyone, anywhere, without exception, who has ever sailed a dinghy seems to have learnt the basic skills in one of these gallant little tubs with their distinctive scarlet sails, almost invariably taught by some eccentric great-aunt wearing a big straw hat and calling out 'Swallows and Amazons forever!' with each tack and turn.

People will tell you that the Mirror was first designed in the 1950s in response to a competition initiated by the *Daily Mirror*, but frankly I don't believe it. No, it was clearly designed some time in the 1900s as a joint project between Arthur Ransome and Heath Robinson, with Ernest Shepard chipping in occasionally on the blueprints. Looking down at the familiar lines of this upturned dinghy lying in the hot May sunshine, I am suddenly struck by an odd notion.

'Phil!' I call out to the Master-in-Charge-of-Sailing. 'Does this Mirror float?'

He straightens up from some screw-tightening task on a nearby boat trailer and wades through thistles to join me. We both gaze down at the patchy hull in the hot sunshine.

'Hmm. Not sure. It did once, I assume.'

'When?'

'1946, I think. No, no, I tell a lie. It was before the War, I reckon.'

We turn it over, revealing a patch of sun-starved tendrils and blanched stems, a nest of five fieldmice and eight million woodlice, but, remarkably, a reasonably unscathed interior. I ponder. A good sand down. A tin of paint. A couple of coats of varnish. She might just do.

'Er, Phil, could I borrow her, do you think? Just for a bit. I'm thinking I might take her on a trip when I leave College – sail away in her, even. What do you think?'

Phil gazed out across the blue-silver waters of Whitemere, surrounded on all sides by woods and hilly fields, and stroked his beard.

'Well, yes, of course. Only ...' He sounded doubtful.

'Yes?'

'Well, setting off from here, I don't think you'll get very far. No one's discovered a Northwest Passage out yet. Twice round the mere and I think you'll be getting bored somehow.'

But it was decided. In six weeks' time I would put the newly refurbished Mirror in the nearby Llangollen canal (a more promising through route than Whitemere) and see where I got to – Gloucester near the mouth of the Severn, I thought. Phil, that saintly man, even promised to drive down to wherever I reached and pick my vessel up in a trailer to return it to weedy retirement at Whitemere, leaving me to continue by balloon, elephant, in the belly of a whale or whatever else would avoid the tedium and predictability of International Air Travel.

Meanwhile, there was much work to be done: paint and varnish and sandpaper to be purchased, the Mirror's rigging and sails to be dug out from ancient mothballs in the sailing loft, maps consulted, oars and rowlocks obtained, and a dozen other things, all on top of the end-of-term scramble.

Three weeks went by before I even gave the derelict dinghy another thought, by which time I found that Phil had quietly organised for the boat to be brought up to College, stripped, sanded, varnished and painted, and there she* was, looking as bright and sturdy as a toy duck in buttercup-yellow with her timbers honey-gold inside. The only thing left for me to do was to decide on a name. After three seconds' thought, armed with a pot of gloss black, I painted in wobbly letters on her transom and both sides of the prow the proud appellation *Jack de Crow*.

Just as I had arrived at Ellesmere with a daydream solidifying around me in the form of that notorious bird, so too would I depart it with Jack accompanying me – in a new guise certainly, but still, I suspected, with the same quality of waywardness that had been the original Jack's trademark.

Now is the right time, while I am standing over the dinghy in the warm sunshine waiting for the black paint to dry, to describe a Mirror dinghy for the benefit of those not fortunate enough to have had a nautical Swallows-and-Amazons great-aunt. I comfort myself with the thought that all the classics are unashamedly dull when it comes to describing the minutiae of nautical travel.

Jack de Crow is eleven feet long and four feet wide. Her nose is not pointed like most dinghies, but cut off square, giving her a sturdy, snub-nosed look. There is nothing even remotely aggressive or shark-like about a Mirror. She looks about as streamlined and racy as a toy hippo. The front three feet consist of a flat deck beneath which are two door-less lockers. This is where your aunt stows away bottles of ginger pop and pemmican sandwiches and more serious sailors store spare bits of rope or sail or shackles. It was where I was

---

* Like the boat's avian namesake, *Jack* proved an elusive and tricksy individual from the very start. There was, for example, the question of the vessel's gender. The name Jack and the original bird were, of course, masculine, even aggressively so at times, but as every sailor knows, ships are always 'she.' So which was it to be? He or she? Him or her? Shunning the attractions of an ambiguous and androgynous companion for my trip down the waterways, I soon settled on 'she,' and *Jack de Crow* remains a lady, albeit a rather tomboyish one, to this day.

to stow all my worldly possessions: a space about the size of your average vegetable crisper.

Three broad decks or seats run right around the cockpit, making a Mirror the most sofa-like of all small dinghies to sail, and enabling several First Mates, an Able Seaman and a Ship's Boy to be deployed in relative comfort about the dinghy. Across the middle, however, is a sturdy thwart where a solitary oarsman will sit to row. Slotting into the gunwale on either side to hold the oars are the rowlocks, pronounced 'rollocks,' much to the amusement of the Third Form when attending sailing lessons. (*Yes, alright, settle down, Smithers, settle down ...*)

So much for the dinghy as a mere rowing boat. However, she is primarily a sailing vessel and as such needs a mast, rigging, a centreboard and a rudder.

A Mirror's mast is only ten feet tall, not nearly tall enough to take a full-sized sail, so it makes use of a *gaff*, a long light beam of wood with a hollow groove along its underside into which the thick leading edge of the sail is threaded. It is this gaff that is hauled aloft and when fully erect (*Alright, Smithers, I've warned you once*) projects out another six feet or so above the mast top, providing the necessary height for the sail.

By modern design standards this is a clumsy contraption, but it was ideal for my purposes. Unlike most dinghy sailors out for a quick skim on a local reservoir, I would be encountering bridges, and it is a very rare bridge that is generous enough to allow a fully masted dinghy to sail beneath it with impunity. With the ability, however, to simply lower the gaff and dip the peak and still keep sailing onwards, I was sure that I could escape being mauled by all but the lowest and meanest of the bridge tribe.

We have just hauled up the *mainsail* and noticed that along its bottom edge is a long, heavy and potentially deadly wooden beam, a *boom*. This is what swings about in a gale in a sea-faring film and sweeps hero and villain off into the raging seas to battle it out there once the poop-deck fighting has become tedious. At the outer end is a dangling pulley through which a rope, the *mainsheet*, threads. This then runs through a series of pulleys to end up in the skipper's hand, allowing him to haul in or let out the mainsail with ease. The only thing you need to know about this is that of all the myriad pieces of tackle and equipment on a sailing boat, this is the one that will jam, tangle or catch at every opportunity and cause imminent

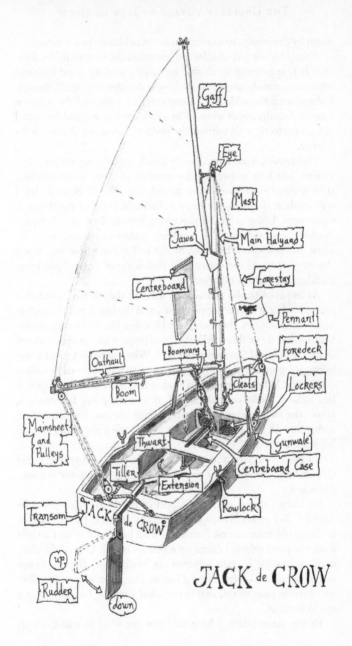

Gaff

Eye

Mast

Jaws

Main Halyard

Centreboard

Forestay

Pennant

Foredeck

Outhaul

Boomvang

Lockers

Boom

Cleats

Mainsheet
and
Pulleys

Thwart

Gunwale

Tiller

Centreboard Case

Extension

Transom

JACK
de CROW

Rowlock

up

Rudder

down

JACK de CROW

11

death by drowning, strangulation or sheer bloody bad temper.

Nearly finished. A smaller sail known as the *jib* runs up the fore-stay. It is apparently invaluable for sailing into the wind for some mysterious aerodynamic reason. Very soon after setting off, though, I abandoned the additional complexity of a jib, and the relevant Law of Aerodynamics went off in a sulk somewhere and *Jack* and I got on perfectly well without its pedantic presence. So much for science.

The *rudder*, I assume, hardly needs explaining unless, dear Reader, you have grown up as a member of some desert-dwelling tribe without even the scantiest knowledge of boats. Nevertheless I will explain that it is the most vulnerable piece of the dinghy's equipment, being prone to ploughing into underwater obstacles, crushing against lock walls, jamming against banks and so on. By some divine mystery, however, by the end of the whole trip, it was the single part of the entire boat that had not needed patching, mending, replacing or discarding.

As opposed to the *centreboard*, a hefty slab of hardwood that seemed to break at every opportunity, and the last item in this over-technical catalogue. The centreboard is a slim but heavy vane of timber that slots down through the hull and projects like an upside-down shark's fin several feet below the keel. When down it provides stability and prevents the dinghy drifting sideways in certain sailing conditions. When drawn up and out of the long centreboard case, it lies around, barks your shins and, if you are going fast enough, allows the foamy brine to well up through the case like a bubbling spring and fill half the dinghy with water before you notice what is happening.

So there you have a Mirror dinghy described. Any questions? (*No, not you, Smithers, put your hand down, I don't want to know. Dismissed.*)

Or rather, that is only one aspect of the Mirror described. In one of C.S. Lewis's Narnia books the children meet a retired star, a silvery old man named Ramandu who has come to rest awhile from the great celestial dance on a remote island. One of the children, on hearing his tale, splutters out in disbelief, 'But Sir, in our land a star is just a huge flaming ball of gas.' Ramandu replies, 'My son, even in your world, that is not what a star is, but only what a star is made of.'

By the same token, I have told you not what *Jack de Crow* is, merely what she was made of. To tell you what that gallant little boat is, I must borrow from the poets and the songs of voyagers everywhere. For *Jack* is all these: a stately Spanish galleon sailing from the isthmus, dipping through the tropics by the palm-green shores – Tom Bombadil's cockle-boat, otter-nudged and swan-drawn up the Withywindle as the day draws down – a gilded barge bearing King Pellinore to Flanders in Malory's romance – or the magic flying Viking ship of a forgotten childhood story. He is Madog of the Dead Boat in his dark coracle beneath the shadow of the Welsh Bridge – Captain Cook's *Endeavour* sailing into Botany Bay in the bright, banksia-scented sunshine – or even that other little Mirror many years ago in which a small boy sailed between lonely isles on a lake in the Snowy Mountains, dreaming of Doctor Dolittle, treasure maps, pith helmets and the rivers of old England where I knew I would one day voyage.

Departure and Dismay

> Farewell, happy fields,
> Where joy forever dwells; hail, horrors!
> —MILTON, *Paradise Lost*

Clop, creak, splosh.
  Clop, creak, splosh.
  Clop, creak, RAM, tangle, splosh.
  I was off.

It was a mild, golden evening, the second day of September. Some hours earlier I had trailered the good ship *Jack de Crow* over to the canal at Colemere Woods. Here a little redbrick bridge carries a farm track over the canal where it runs between Yell Wood and a wide field running up to a gentle horizon. In summer this field is a Monet's palette of scarlet poppies and sky-blue linseed, and one large solitary oak tree tops the rise, a lonely giant against the sky. But this evening fifty or so of my friends and colleagues and a handful of students thronged the bridge, each with a glass in hand, and cheered as my dear friend Debbie officially christened the boat with a bottle of home-made hawthorn brandy. This clear amber liquid I had distilled some years previously from hawthorn blossom, collected one sunny May afternoon on the banks of Whitemere, and it had been from the very start utterly undrinkable. It was good to find an appropriate use for it at last.

Debbie had dressed superbly for the occasion in an Edwardian outfit and her short speech was touching and apt, but she was clearly unfamiliar with the usual protocol of ship-launching. Instead of the customary shattering of the bottle on the prow, for reasons she has yet adequately to explain, she uncorked the bottle and proceeded to pour the rancid fermenting liquor *into* the dinghy, liberally scattering it over thwart and deck and rucksack. Three thousand dancing midges dropped like confetti out of the air over a fifty-foot radius, the merry throng on the bridge above us reeled back clutching their throats, and I half expected to see the newly varnished deck start to bubble and peel like frying bacon as the hawthorn brandy got to work on the timbers.

Nevertheless, *Jack de Crow* slid down the bank and into the canal and bobbed, a buoyant little vessel impatient to be off. All my fare-wells had been said, all my worldly goods stowed, the mast and rig-ging lay in a long neat bundle down one side, the oars were in their rowlocks and the light was fading. It was time to go.

Clop, creak, splosh.
Clop, creak, splosh.
Clop, creak, splosh.
Clop, creak, splosh.

And the last the good folk of Ellesmere College saw of me was a small pith-helmeted figure rowing away into the shadowy blue dusk beneath the beech trees, a silver V of ripples at the bow diminishing to nothing until a bend of the woody canal hid me from sight and I was gone.

The drama of the occasion – the rowing off into the sunset, the gloomy woods and blue shadows, a setting for *A Midsummer Night's Dream* – all of this had been exactly as I intended. But as the silence closed about me, I suddenly felt flat and rather tired. A romantic gesture it had been, and I had been playing the star role – but it was a real farewell too, with all that entails. From tonight I was, quite literally, homeless. Nor did I have a new job to go to. I had left behind six years of familiarity and friendship and ease, and I had only the vaguest notion of where I was going. As the dusk deepened to darkness, the water about me became a black mirror etched only with fine silver-point, fine as nettle-hairs. Somewhere an early owl hooted. Under my very bows something turned with a *clop* and sent rings of light rippling across the canal waters, silver on Indian ink.

For all the beauty, a sense of desolation seemed to rise like a mist from the waters beneath me and the dark pool of Blakemere on my left. Midges whined in my ears; my hands upon the oars were already slippery with sweat and the dinghy seemed to skid from tangled bank to bank as I made my unsteady progress down the dark tunnel of trees. It also occurred to me, somewhat more pro-saically, that in all the glamour of planning for this departure I had forgotten to find out how to row. It is not as easy as it looks, not by a long chalk.

It was with some relief and feeling a little foolish that I emerged into a clearer stretch of the canal running between two fields. The sky was now fully dark, a lovely deep Prussian blue spangled with warm stars, and as I reached the junction where the short arm turns right towards Ellesmere Town, the main canal wound away to the left, inlaid with the reflecting constellations. All the magic of the crossroads rose up to meet me in the neat foursquare signpost that glimmered white at the junction. 'The road goes ever on and on,' I murmured to myself, thinking of Bilbo slipping away to Wilderland in the dusk. It dispelled the last clinging webs of Blakemere's dark spell, the smell of weed and stagnant water. Happier now and with a sort of calm excitement, I turned my dinghy westward and rowed away into the night.

That evening I rowed only another mile or so and curled up on the towpath under a little humpbacked bridge carrying a disused farm lane between two fields. Snug in my sleeping bag and my head pillowed on a fleecy jacket, I lay awake awhile listening to the night noises around me: the breezy rustle of dry leaves in the sloe hedge, the distant bark of a dogfox, the cough of a nearby cow.

Just beyond that far hedge were the playing fields of the College, and just up the hill my friends were settling down for the night in their cosy apartments, high in some redbrick tower or grey-gabled wing. In ten short minutes I could walk there and knock on any of a dozen doors for a late-night whisky or mug of coffee. I could even beg a bed for the night instead of this damp and lonely towpath. *Perhaps I will,* I thought. *One more night. One more evening of warmth and companionship. They'll understand. I've had three farewell parties already, so a fourth won't matter, surely. That cow is coming closer. I don't want cow-cough all over me. Better start tomorrow. Debbie could christen the boat with something a little less noxious this time. Properly.* Cough, cough … Rustle … Snore.

*

I woke with a start. The sky was an early morning grey, a brambling was singing in the hedge above me, and the grass was pearled over with dew. In the next field a flock of blackheaded gulls was pecking over the newly ploughed soil, occasionally rising into the air in a swirling, white-flaked cloud before settling again further on. Now, looking back on that scene, can I recall a bulkier shape among them, perhaps? A different bill? No …? No … it's no good. If there *was* an albatross among those gulls, I never noticed it. There was certainly nothing whatsoever to indicate that the next eighteen hours were to be the most disastrous of my life.

My plan, as far as I had one, was this. On consulting the Shrewsbury Ordnance Survey Map (OS 126) a few days earlier, I had been pleased to note that the Shropshire Union Canal that ran past Ellesmere wound its way westward for a few miles and then forked. The right-hand branch turned northward towards Llangollen via a spectacular aqueduct and several long tunnels, but the southern branch lolloped along in a less dramatic fashion towards Welshpool and the Breidden Hills. There at Welshpool, the canal ran parallel to the upper reaches of the River Severn, separated only by a strip of road. Once I had made it to there (two hours? three hours?), it would surely be the work of a minute to commandeer some loitering youths, the yeomanry of Welshpool, and haul *Jack de Crow* the twenty feet or so between the canal and the river. As I saw it, that would be the only major obstacle between me and the Bristol Channel. Once on the broad bosom of the rolling Severn, I'd probably be in Bristol by tea-time the next day.

I had been sitting in the White Lion Antique Shop and Tea Rooms the previous day, my OS map spread before me, cheerfully telling anyone who would listen of my proposed route, when a grubby figure slurping tea in the corner spoke up.

'Ellesmere to Welshpool, ye say, young maister? Along that theer thicky canal? Ee, but ye'll 'ave a deal o' moither gittin' a boat beyond Maesbury on that bit o' water, that ye will. Arrr.'

A little miffed at this interruption to what had been turning into a splendid account of the coming voyage to a group of admiring customers (as long as I kept talking, they kept buying me cinnamon tea-cakes), I turned and replied in the sort of confident tones that Phineas Fogg himself might have used to address a doubting crony in the Athenaeum.

'My good man, we're not talking about a common barge or motor launch here. Though you may be right in pointing out the limitations of such craft, my *Jack de Crow* can go anywhere, Sir. La! She is a pioneering vessel, Sir, a feather-light, flat-bottomed skiff whose very delight is those winding waterways, those reedy backwaters closed to the world and its dog. I think you need not worry on that account, Sir!'

'Ahrr well,' said the rustic cynic in the corner. 'Suit yerself. All

Oi knows is that Oi graze my goats on that theer stretch o' the canal. Still you'm knows best, Oi'm sure. Marnin'!'

And off he stomped.

A second, closer scrutiny of the OS map among the teacups did reveal that yes, beyond Maesbury Marsh the solid pale-blue line indicating the canal did seem to thin out a little ... in fact, became distinctly dotted ... and I might have to revise my route.

Damn.

Some of my audience were losing faith in my abilities as an explorer and beginning to drift away, so I had to make up my mind quickly. Ah yes, here. This thin blue thread on the map. The very thing. Perfect.

'I *will*, gentlemen,' I rapped out, snapping all attention back to me, 'be taking the ship down ...'

Yes? Yes?

(A nifty flourish of a handy teaspoon.)

'... the Morda Brook.'

Gasp!

That'll show 'em, I thought. The Morda Brook. So that was the plan. A breezy sail down the canal to Maesbury Marsh, where surely some ox-eyed yokel would be standing by to await orders; a quick lift and heave of the featherweight skiff into the limpid waters of the Morda Brook; and an easy ride on the current down to the Vyrnwy River and the cottage of a friend and colleague, Keith, who would expect me for a gin and tonic and early supper that evening.

A plan beautiful for its spontaneity, simplicity and utterly deluded optimism.

*

After two hours of rowing in good spirits between banks heavy with ripe blackberries, I came to Frankton Locks, a series of three locks stepping down a long decline of about six hundred yards. I was mildly apprehensive about how *Jack* and I would be greeted here. I had no idea whether small unpowered vessels were allowed through them. There was also an uneasy thought in my mind concerning licences. Did I need one? Surely not for such a harmless little tub. So it was with a few well-rehearsed winning smiles and persuasive banter that I approached the first of the three locks.

'Ah,' said I to the red-haired lock-keeper who appeared. He had watery blue eyes and a complexion the colour of brick-dust. 'There's no problem, I assume, in taking this little fellow down the locks, is there?'

'Yep.'

'Ah. Meaning "Yep, I can"?'

'No. Meaning "Yep, there's a problem." No unpowered boats in the locks, I'm afraid. Sorry.'

'I've got oars,' I said brightly, waggling them at him.

'Sorry,' he said, and turned on his heel.

I had a brief but miserable vision of rowing back to the College, poking my head round the Common Room door and saying, 'Hi! Remember me! The Traveller returns. Brilliant trip. I'll tell you all about it one day. Meanwhile, anyone got an Inter-City timetable I could borrow?'

This I quickly dispelled and hurried after the lock-keeper.

'Um, hello, sorry. Me again.'

A blank look.

'Chap with the dinghy, yes? Look, there's a barge coming along now. What if I get towed through? Is that okay?'

Red looked me up and down, looked at *Jack de Crow* wallowing hopefully beside me, and made up his mind.

'Nope. Sorry. No towing.'

Right, right. *Right.*

I took a deep breath, and hurried after him once more.

'Okay. Here's what I'll have to do. I'll empty her of all her luggage, remove the bundled rigging and somehow lift her out of the canal. Then I will drag her bodily down the towpath to beyond the lowest lock. I assume there's no serious objection to that?'

There followed a few seconds of teeth-sucking cogitation and, finally, grudging agreement.

'But if you start cutting up the towpath,' he added, 'I'll have to ask you to stop. We can't have British Waterways property damaged, you know.'

By now I was beginning to suspect that Mr Ginger-mop was not fully behind my project. The suspicion was confirmed when, after I had removed the luggage, the rigging, the oars and all extraneous weight, it came time to lift bodily the entire dinghy up the sheer three feet of concrete canal bank onto the towpath; a two-man-and-a-small-crane job if ever there was one.

'Right,' I called to Mr Stickler-for-the-Rules, who'd been sitting on a nearby bollard lighting up a pipe. 'I'm ready.'

'Ready? For what?'

'I wonder if you could possibly help me to lift ... it's a bit tricky for one person, you see, and ...'

'Oh no. Can't do that, I'm afraid. Not my job, see. Can't get involved.'

And he took another contented puff on his pipe.

Flinging *sotto voce* a few happy statistics about tongue cancer and pipe smokers over my shoulder, I set to hauling the boat out of the water. The method I adopted was to haul up *Jack*'s bows as far as I could until the dinghy's keel was resting on the concrete lip of the canal, her rear two-thirds sloping sharply down into the water. Then, putting all my weight on the front third and ignoring the ominous cracking sounds of grinding timber from her keel, I levered the stern up level until the boat was horizontally hanging out seven feet over the water. Finally, I pivoted the whole boat around parallel to the canal and safely onto the towpath.

This method brought on only the mildest of hernias and was one I had occasion to use later, so I was actually very grateful to Mr Carrot for his passive encouragement to develop a solo technique. That gratitude does not extend, however, to his next piece of churlishness.

I started to haul *Jack* down the towpath, a long and mercifully grassy slope of about six hundred metres, but by a third of the way down I was reduced to a sobbing wreck. I recalled my conversation in the tea shop. Feather-light skiff? *Hah!* Light-winged dryad of the waterways? *Pshaw!* Bobbish little jollyboat? *Phooey!* She felt as if she were constructed of solid plutonium, and was about as draggable on dry land as a dead dugong. The fact that it had begun to drizzle did not improve my spirits.

Just then, when I was picturing in my mind's eye the warmth, comfort and grace of a British Rail Inter-City second-class carriage, there came a friendly call: 'Need a hand, mate?'

Two burly workmen scraping some windowpanes on a refurbished lock-side cottage had watched my painful progress down the towpath and decided I needed help. I directed one to take the prow and the other to join me in carrying the stern, and with a quick heave-ho we had covered the next fifty yards in a matter of seconds. In two minutes more I would be afloat and on my merry way again, a free spirit, a lissom Ariel, a bird of ...

'OY!'

The call floated down the towpath from the top lock where the lock-keeper was standing beckoning to the two workmen to drop what they were doing and come immediately.

They did.

They returned.

'Sorry mate,' they intoned together. 'The boss says we're not to get involved, and we have to get back to work on 'is window frames. Sorry. Good luck, though,' and off they trudged to the cottage.

Ah. I see. So when the lock-keeper said he couldn't get involved, he clearly didn't include in his policy of non-involvement the act of telling *other* people not to get involved. Right-o.

One dreary hour later, I was back on the water at last, with all my gear re-stowed. The canal lay before me in a featureless three-mile stretch across the waste of Rednal Flats, and I set off, sculling into a thin drizzle borne on a stiffening headwind. There is, as I had realised the evening before, an art to rowing, and it was an art that I did not in fact possess. My progress that day across the Rednal Flats was a sorry zigzag of crashes and curses from bank to bank, the oars flailing ineffectually in the rowlocks and my back and arms beginning to ache abominably. I spent more time trying to extricate myself from bankside vegetation than in forward motion and I began seriously to doubt the wisdom of the whole foolish venture.

Another miserable doubt was looming. The map showed three thick black chevrons across the blue line of the canal, a symbol I would come to loathe in the months to come: namely, another flight of locks a mile or so ahead. Aston Locks, three of them spread over more than a kilometre. Would I encounter another officious lock-keeper? And what really were the rules about rowing boats in locks? Would I find this impasse all the way down the Severn? If so, I may as well give up now, sink the dinghy in this hellish canal and sneak off to a train station somewhere. I could always sit in a rented bed-sit in Bournemouth for six months and make up fictitious letters to all my friends about my wonderful nautical adventures. It has been done before. Yes (*heave, slosh, crunch*), that's what (*heave, swing, jam*) I would do (*heave, thud, rustle*).

Then we were at Aston Locks, and there was a smiling, cheery-looking man in the standard British Waterways green uniform.

'Now look,' I started up defiantly. 'Dinghies. Rowing boats. Are they allowed in canal locks or not? Because – '

'Oh, aye. No problem there, boyo.'

Pause. Welsh. Has possibly misunderstood.

'You mean, unaccompanied, just on their own?'

'Oooh yes. Don't see why not. They're boats, after all. Got to get down somehow, isn't it?'

Another pause.

'I'm sorry. Are you telling me that this boat, unpowered as it is – '

'Unpowered? No. You've got oars there, boyo. That's powered in my book.'

'And this is legal, is it? Right down the Severn as well?'

'Oh yes, isn't it. All over England and Wales, far as I know.'

'And so, let me get this quite clear. I, meaning *me*, could take *this* boat, *Jack de Crow*, down through *these* three locks, unaccompanied? Yes?'

He looked at me cheerfully, encouragingly, kindly.

'Oooh yes. No problem. After April, next year. Out of use since 1956, see. But come April and they'll be like new pins. Cheerio!'

*

The newly developed Mackinnon 'Swing and Hernia' method of removing a dinghy single-handedly from a canal came into its own that afternoon. Three times I unloaded the boat, three times dragged her an inch per heave across gravel, boulders, marsh and broken concrete to send her scraping once more into the black and stagnant waters of the Aston Lock flight. I started to calculate that considering the distance she'd done overland since leaving Ellesmere, I'd have done better to equip her with a set of sturdy wheels rather than oars. Perhaps I could convert the wretched thing into a sort of caravan and save an awful lot of trouble all round.

And even when we finally reached the open canal again beyond the third lock, it was difficult to tell where land stopped and water began. The passage narrowed to a humid green lane, only a boat's width, between towering bulrushes and creeper-clad alders, making every stroke of the oars a frantic struggle akin to beating anacondas to death every five feet. The lurid green of duckweed grew so thickly that it looked as though I were ploughing across a velvety bowling lawn, leaving an inky black trail behind me. But all this was like the Spanish Main when compared with what was to come.

*

The Morda Brook, despite my breezy assertion in the White Lion Tea Rooms, is by no stretch of the imagination a navigable waterway, but it was my only route out. So it was that at the reedy deadend of the canal I hauled *Jack de Crow* out of the water for the fifth time that day and dragged her a hundred yards down a narrow lane to slide her over the ford and into the dank, black waters of the least navigable stretch of water in Britain.

The Morda Brook, oh the Morda, the moist and morbid Morda, the Morda of my nightmares. Actually, no, at first, it was quite fun. Once away from the ford, the brook turned into a sparkling stream, cutting between high clay banks lined with alder and overhanging willow, little more than five feet wide in most places. I soon found that the easiest way to proceed was to stand in the boat and pole or paddle my way along with a single oar in the manner of a Venetian gondolier – albeit a rather muddy, leaf-plastered one – and be carried onward by the steady chattering current beneath the keel. Every five minutes or so I would have to leap out into the shin-deep waters to drag *Jack* bodily over a bar of shingle or round a particularly tight bend, but the change from the monotonous slog of rowing was a welcome relief.

There was a lightening of the air as well. The afternoon had turned golden and blue; high white clouds were tinged by the westering sun and for the first time that day I felt touched by a sense of adventure and high spirits. This was exploring if you like! Occasionally there was a greater obstacle to overcome: a black, many-clawed alder tree that swept its low branches down over the stream's surface and had to be worked around, or a half-submerged log that needed heaving aside. But these were merely grist to the mill and added to my growing elation.

All the time as I progressed, the banks of the Morda reared higher about me until I was alone in a narrow world of dark water and steep clay sides clothed in wild mint and Himalayan balsam. This last is a wonderfully triffid-like plant with a complicated pink flower rather like a snapdragon smelling of peaches. The seed pod – a tightly sprung contraption – explodes at the lightest touch into a tangle of curlicues sending hard black seeds like buckshot shooting in every direction. With every stroke of my paddle, half a dozen of these pods would instantly recoil with a soft splitting pop and the decks of my little galleon would rattle with tiny cannon-shot, and the air would grow yet heavier with the drowsy scent of peach balm.

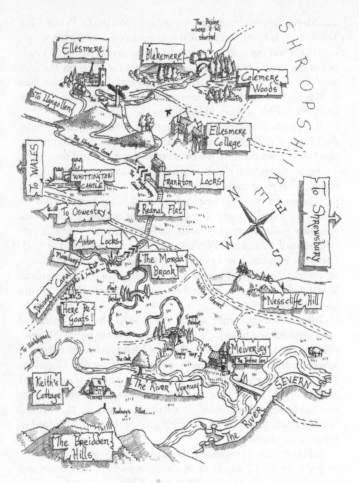

Colemere Woods to the Severn

Night was falling, the gold faded from the landscape and white stars began to glimmer out in the clear evening blue, and what with the meandering wriggles of the brook I had no idea what distance I had covered. I knew that there was an old road bridge only half a mile up from the confluence of the Morda and the wider Vyrnwy. I knew also that Keith's cottage where I was bound that night (and where even now a sparkling, clinking, lemon-sliced gin and tonic would be waiting) was only a mile or so across the fields from the Vyrnwy in the hamlet of Rhos Common. So when I poled around a sharp bend and saw the last gleam of twilight making a perfect disc beneath the arch of a bridge ahead, I breathed a heartfelt sigh and calculated that I would be sitting down to supper within the half-hour.

I paddled onwards beneath the bridge's black arch and round the next bend where surely the waters would suddenly widen into ...

Well, alright. Around the next bend then, surely, to find the infant Morda meet her bigger sister, the graceful Vyrnwy, just about ...

Hmm. Perhaps a little further than I thought, until yes – clearly the current was slowing up as one would expect of a tributary mere yards before curving round one final bank to find ...

Damn.

Better consult the map.

Too dark. Better find the torch.

Too dark to do that either.

Make mental note: leave torch handy in future.

Ah, here's the torch. Where is map? Ah, here.

Make mental note: keep map in waterproof cover in future.

Unfold soggy map. Tears soggily into five pieces.

Make mental note: buy sticky-tape.

Find relevant section. Yes, as I thought. There *is* a bridge just five hundred yards up from Vyrnwy. So where has blasted Vyrnwy disappeared to? Stupid map.

Make mental note: write stiff letter of complaint to Royal Ordinance Survey Office.

Sudden horrid idea. Check map again ... Damn, damn, damn, damn, damn! There are *two* bridges – the one I have just passed which is only an inch on the map away from Maesbury, and then the second bridge more than four inches on the map – six miles – to go from here. Only *then* comes the Vyrnwy, the cottage at Rhos Common and the gin.

There was nothing for it but to keep battling on downstream. So on I went. Unseen willow branches raked across my face and clutched at the dinghy's gunwale. Grounding on to a shallow bed would have me stepping out, not onto an ankle-deep shoal of sand, but into a thigh-deep sludge of black mud. Log jams and barbed-wire tangles occurred round every bend and the mosquitoes rose in whining clouds about my head undeterred even by the lingering vitriolic fumes of the hawthorn brandy. At last after four black hours of this thrashing, hacking, blind progress, I bumped my way under the second bridge and knew that this time, truly, honestly, the Vyrnwy was only five hundred yards downstream – and beyond that, the lighted windows and warm welcome of Keith's cottage.

'*Sing ho! for the life of a bear,*' I sang, '*Sing ho! for the life of a bear,*' and all of a sudden the stars above seemed extra sparkly and silver in the black night sky. But the Morda Brook, that spiteful, black-hearted witch of a stream, knowing she was about to lose me forever, had one or two last tricks to play.

Sweeping under a low alder tree the boat caught for the hundredth time that day in an overhanging bough, as black and scratchy and crooked as only an alder branch can be. More impatient than ever now that the end was so near, I levered the dinghy forward with all my might using the oar and heard a most satisfying splintering crack of wood as the boat groaned, strained and then shot clear into a broad starry pool, trailing broken branches and twigs on all sides.

'*Hah! hah! hah! Hee! hee! hee!*

Alder witch, you can't catch me!' I sang in happy delirium.

'*Alder witch, I'm Jack de Crow,*

I break your bones, and off I go!' I burbled to myself as I leant over to clear the debris that draped around the gunwales and the rowlocks.

Rowlocks?

Rowlock. Singular.

Gunwale. Singular.

In the pitch dark my groping hands felt the awful truth. The splintering crunch I had heard as I tore free of the alder had not been the tree's branches breaking; it had been the entire starboard rowlock ripping away and taking a two-foot section of the gunwale along with it. My blind fingers felt the smooth, sturdy woodwork end in a splintered mass and groped hopelessly for the cold metal horseshoe of the rowlock. Gone. Torn away. Lying, presumably, in the black depths of the pool beneath that malicious alder's water-logged roots, while its niggly twigs and arid leaves hissed out in the sudden night breeze a mocking lullaby:

Jack de Crow! Jack de Crow!
You won't get far if you cannot row.
Crippled Crow, don't mock me,
The Witch of Morda, the Alder Tree!

Too weary and numb to consider the consequences of having lost the power to row properly (except round and round in very small circles), I drifted on around the final bend ... and into the final trap.

Here, only a hundred yards upstream from where the Morda lost itself in the greater Vyrnwy, the brook narrowed into a sheer-sided gully between cliffs of slippery clay and thick nettles rearing twenty feet either side in a near-vertical slope. Across the stream at this point stretched a taut, black, double-twisted strand of barbed wire, as rigid and unyielding as an iron bar. This lay one foot above the water from bank to bank, attached either end to solid ancient willow stumps, so old and immovable that the wire had grown deep into the bark and become part of the stump itself. It was a dinghy trap, and utterly impassable.

In the blanketing darkness I tried blindly dunking the dinghy low enough in the water to scrape beneath the wire, but to no avail. Even at her lowest the boat had a foot and a half of freeboard. I considered hauling her *over* the rigid wire, but between the sheer banks there was not the slightest foothold for me to stand on to perform this operation, and a prodding oar confirmed my suspicion that the stream at this point was over six feet deep. Another approach was needed: technology.

In the midnight blackness I rummaged around in the half-ton of leaf mould, mud and debris that filled the bottom of the dinghy and located my Leatherman tool, a wonderfully useful parting gift from the Common Room, and equipped with, among other things, a sturdy pair of wire-cutters. However, twenty minutes of straining with sweat-slippery and blistered hands to snip through the wire resulted only in a sudden twang, a plop and suddenly empty hands. The torch revealed the wire still uncut but the Leatherman nowhere to be seen – another trophy claimed by the Morda Brook.

It was at this point that I made my first sensible decision of the day. I was cold, hungry and exhausted, I was only one mile – two at the most – from Keith's cottage, and he had been expecting me since five o'clock. It was now nearly eleven, I guessed, and if I hurried I might catch him before he gave up waiting and retired to bed.

The boat would go nowhere in the night – in fact, would probably still be there for the next few millennia – and I could leave the problems for the morning and broad daylight. A saunter by starlight across open fields while I was still relatively dry and cheerful, and all would be well.

Leaving most of my things in the boat, I scrambled up the nettle-grown bank (what were a few stings when salvation was so near at hand?) and identified, with some relief, the lights of Rhos Common across the flat plain, no more than six fields away.

'*Ah! First the gin, I think, Keith, thank you,*' I murmured as I tripped my way across the first starlit pasture.

'*And if you could perhaps be running a hot bath while I drink this? Good chap,*' as I negotiated a stile into the next field.

'*Now, supper. We'll start with soup, ox-tail if possible, Keith,*' (avoid cow-pats) '*and move swiftly on to … let's see now … smoked salmon? Excellent!*' (Head for gap in hedge.) '*But meanwhile, a warm, fluffy towel and a Noel Coward dressing gown embroidered with Chinese dragons, if you would be so kind.*' (Those lights were distinctly closer.) '*Ah. Thank you.*'

I strode across the open flat meadow towards the distant lights. One of them, I reckoned, I could even identify as Keith's kitchen window …

I stopped dead.

I had to.

At my feet the meadow ended abruptly in a cliff that dropped twenty feet into the broad, starlit waters of a gleaming river. A wide river. A swift, deep river. A totally unfordable river. The long sought-after Vyrnwy River, lying between me and the bright, hazy dream of Keith's cottage.

I do not remember much after that. Possibly I fainted. Possibly I was overcome by a black, Berserker rage blotting out all conscious action for the next hour.

Only snatches come back to me. I remember a furious stamping stride back across the fields – a hasty, but painful, plunge back down the nettled bank into the oil-black waters of the Morda. I remember sinking immediately over my head down, down, till I found the oozy bottom – then, on hastily resurfacing, cracking my head so hard on the keel of the dinghy underwater that everything went swimmy. I remember that somehow, incredibly, and possibly helped by a blind, bitter, bloodyminded rage, I managed to heave that dinghy up onto the barbed-wire strand from underneath, surfacing from below and scraping her over the rusty strand in three great hoicks while the barbs gouged out deep grooves in the hull. I remember the sudden rush of elation as I realised *Jack* was over at last, and the floundering, clay-splattering manoeuvre that got me out of the water and into the dinghy like an epileptic seal, hardly heeding the long sound of ripping cloth as the barbed wire shredded my trouser-leg from knee to cuff. Then the short paddle around the final bend and out onto the broad bosom of the Vyrnwy, the delirious attempt to row to the opposite bank with only one oar and wondering vaguely why the stars were spinning so crazily in circles above me.

Finally there came the blessed scrunch of keel on fine shingle and the half-hearted tug of *Jack*'s nose up onto the little beach by a spreading oak, followed by the determination to just walk away, walk away and never, *ever* come back.

It wasn't over yet. While waltzing deliriously through the middle of a wide meadow, I felt a sharp jolt as though someone had flung a pebble and caught me on the funny-bone. I also seemed unable to move forward, try as I might.

Ping! The jolt came again. An invisible bolt out of the darkness. And still I was rooted to the turf.

Ping! A sling-shot to the nerves again. In English folklore there is a phenomenon called a 'stray sod,' a patch of grass enchanted by the faeries to bewitch and bewilder any mortal careless enough to stumble upon it. I had clearly found one, put there – possibly – by the same malicious wight who had designed the Morda Brook.

Ping!

It took me some twenty seconds and five more shocks to realise that I was standing up against an electric fence in the darkness. I am sure it was only the additional amps that gave me the energy to get to Keith's at all.

And so this long and weary chapter comes to a close. At half-past midnight, I clawed at the cottage window like some hideous swamp creature and startled Keith into a near heart attack. He opened the door to a gibbering, mud-oozing wreck, Jenny Greenteeth's husband, my face peppered with nettle rash, my head garlanded with alder twigs, willow bark and leaf mould. Never so weary, never so in woe, bedabbled with the dew and torn with briers, I stood swaying in the doorway. One trouser leg flapped open to reveal a gashed and bloody calf and the hands held up in supplication were a mass of cuts and blisters beneath the grime. One eye was swollen and closed where a hail of Himalayan balsam seeds had scored a direct hit, and a puddle of silt, river water and fresh liquid cow dung was spreading at my feet. I was still twitching every four seconds as the last of the amps chased one another playfully through my nervous system.

'Any chance of a gin?' I chirruped, before pitching headlong into the hallway and onto the floral carpet.

'Ice and lemon, please. I'll have it here on the floor. Thanks.'

Sails and Stained-Glass

Never in his life had he seen a river before – this sleek, sinuous, full-bodied animal, chasing and chuckling, gripping things with a gurgle and leaving them with a laugh, to fling itself on fresh playmates that shook themselves free, and were caught and held again. All was a-shake and a-shiver – glints and gleams and sparkles, rustle and swirl, chatter and bubble.
— KENNETH GRAHAME, *The Wind in the Willows*

Day Two.

Day Two?!

Day Two was not going to be remotely like Day One if I could help it – nor were Days Three, Four, Five and through to Eternity.

Rules would have to be made, and as I awoke and went through the cheerful ritual of waking up properly, I listed them.

Rule 1. Stop before nightfall. Never, ever sail after dark again.

Rule 2. Stick only to waterways marked clearly as thick pale-blue lines on the map. Thin dark-blue lines are mere culverts, brooks and drainage ditches and not to be considered as even remotely navigable.

Rule 3. Consult map carefully and often.

Rule 4. Stay dry.

I said my heartfelt thanks to Keith and apologised for the six inches of rich river silt in the bottom of his bath. Then I walked back across the meadows to see what could be done about *Jack de Crow*.

As far as I knew, I was returning to a half-wrecked dinghy full of sodden luggage, with a large section of her gunwale missing, one rowlock irretrievably lost, my Leatherman multi-tool likewise full fathom five at the bottom of the Morda Brook, and therefore any chance of repairing the damage gone with it. But the day was warm, the fields were wide and peaceful, and I felt like Mole hurrying for the first time, the sunshine hot on his fur, across the Great Meadow for his life-changing appointment with the River.

And besides, I had my four Rules, my four sensible, well-considered, easy-to-keep rules. Especially the last one. I liked that one. *Stay dry.*

When I reached the Vyrnwy's bank and the little shingle beach by the spreading oak tree where I'd pulled *Jack* up the night before, I decided suddenly on a Fifth Rule.

Rule 5. Tie the dinghy up each night. Firmly.

Jack had vanished.

Same shingle beach. Same massy oak. Same broad bend. No *Jack*.

Day Two was already beginning to look a lot like Day One.

So tired and careless had I been last night that I had done barely more than hoist her bows onto the shingle. Now, on an extra six inches of floodwater, she was gone.

I found her half-an-hour later a mile downstream, caught in a tangle of osiers and willow in midstream. Rule 4. flickered tauntingly through my mind for a few seconds and then I stripped off and plunged in.

Swimming down to *Jack* was easy. Boarding her was accomplished by the epileptic seal method again. Rowing her back upstream against the considerable current with only one oar was a task that would have challenged Odysseus. My resemblance to that voyaging hero was emphasised by the fact that, just as he is depicted on all those Greek vases, I too was stark naked. It was indeed fortunate that this stretch of the Vyrnwy meanders through wide flat water-meadows empty of all but placidly grazing Friesians and the odd heron, none of whom took the slightest interest in the naked, pith-helmeted gentleman rowing in tight circles in a little yellow dinghy.

It was sheer bad luck, however, that a small party of canoeists consisting of three young women should choose that morning to be out practising their craft on the river, on their way from the Llanymynech Bridge to lunch downstream at the Tontine Inn at Melverley. It is a pleasant but dullish run, this stretch, and does not generally afford the canoeist much in the way of interest to look at. But I think there are three people now who may disagree with me on that score. All I will say is that despite my cheery wave and smile – and my attempts to use my pith helmet in the style of the classical fig-leaf – this small party did not seem inclined to stop and chew the fat or pass the time of day. I cannot think why.

Once they had paddled on, I somehow managed to zigzag *Jack* ashore, climb back into my clothes and start setting things to rights. Strange though it sounds, I cannot think of a time when I have been more content, as slowly through the long noon tide, there on the warm grass under a wide sky, surrounded by miles of empty, lonely fields, *Jack* and I thoroughly sorted ourselves out.

Firstly, I found to my relief that the splintered-off section of the gunwale holding the rowlock had fallen, not into the brook as I had thought, but into the dinghy. Secondly, likewise, my Leatherman was lying buried in the half-ton of debris in the bilges and had not fallen overboard last night. The Morda had only been teasing.

I hauled *Jack* up and spent an hour shovelling out the twigs, the weeds, the leaves, the balsam seeds and alder cones, the clay and silt and shingle that had collected in her yesterday. Then, propping her on her beam ends with an oar, I sluiced her out from stem to stern with the bailer full of water. Finally, I wiped her down inside and out with a big sponge until she was gleaming clean again.

Meanwhile, I had unpacked all my luggage – soon every grassy tussock and thistle clump was draped with underwear, shirts, socks and pyjamas drying in the hot sun, so that the meadow looked like Mrs Tiggywinkle's washing day.

I assessed the damage to the hull from yesterday's overland expeditions and found, to my surprise, that apart from a good many scrapes and gouges in the canary-yellow paintwork, the hull remained watertight.

The main damage was topside, especially that awful broken gunwale. This is a stout thickened length of wood running right around the rim of the boat, making a sort of solid lip to the hull. At the point where the rowlock sits on either side, it broadens out in a D-shaped curve to allow a hole to be drilled down through it. Into this hole drops the pin of the rowlock, enabling an oar to be manoeuvred. It was this section of the gunwale that had snapped away and now needed to be fixed before I could hope to proceed.

I am no carpenter. When in woodwork lessons at school other boys were knocking up drop-leaf coffee tables and walnut roll-top bureaux to take home to their adoring parents, I was struggling to produce a breadboard. A breadboard, I should add, was only distinguishable from a slab of chipboard by its bevelled edges. I hadn't even managed those. What I really needed was some proper wood glue. But unless I was to manufacture some by boiling up cow dung and willow sap, I would have to do without. Instead I looked closely for the first time at the extraneous fittings dotted about the decking of *Jack de Crow*. In its heady days of racing back before the war no doubt it had flaunted all manner of fancy rigging – staysails and spinnakers and what-not – and all these had demanded various eyelets, cleats and runners that were now obsolete, each one sporting a pair of perfectly serviceable screws.

I spent the next couple of hours removing obsolete fittings and with my Leatherman screwing the smashed section of gunwale back into place as a temporary repair job. It would certainly do until I got to Shrewsbury where there was a chandlery and boat-repair workshop.

I made a thorough check of all the rigging. Mast, gaff, boom, sails, halyards, sheets and stays, all needed untangling and unfurling and shaking out of the remarkable amount of river vegetation that had found its way even into the centre of the tightly rolled sails. Once I had finished, I felt that I now knew every inch of the little ship. The whole exercise had forced *Jack* and myself into a more intimate acquaintance, and when I relaunched her, I felt she had become in some sense truly mine. We had survived our first major ordeal together, and though both battle-scarred, we were now ready to set our faces downstream with hopes high and heads unbowed, to take whatever adventure might befall as we journeyed into the wide blue southern yonder.

*

I aimed that afternoon to reach the tiny magpie-and-thatch church of Melverley, set amid its smoky yews. The afternoon continued fine and the steep-sided Breidden Hills, rearing vertically from the plain in three lofty peaks, swung to all points of the horizon as the Vyrnwy meandered in broad loops between buttercup meadows. These three hills seen from afar resembled an illustration on the dust jacket of an old book of fairy tales: The King of the Golden Mountain or The Enchanted Giant. In fact, there was something giant-like about the way the blue, sun-crowned mass seemed to tip-toe silently about the landscape, now straight ahead, now peering over my shoulder, now retreating coyly behind a nearby copse of oaks.

That night at Melverley I dined in the Tontine Inn. I sat down, placed my beloved pith helmet on the table beside me and started to order the grilled chicken and a green salad. The waitress-barmaid, somewhat to my surprise, on seeing the pith helmet broke off in mid-order, clapped a hand to her mouth and ran off into the kitchens. She soon emerged behind the bar dragging the chef with her, and with much muffled giggling and whispering pointed me out in the corner, only to collapse into giggles again. The chef gave me a long amused stare, shook his head and vanished kitchenwards. After a minute or so, back came the waitress clearly attempting to control her mirth, and I'd got as far as telling her that I preferred my salad without dressing when she shrieked, 'No dressing!' and collapsed again with a barely stifled snort of laughter that threatened to choke her as she ran for the door.

A pith helmet is, I admit, an eccentric piece of headgear to wear about the highways and byways of Britain, but that is partly its purpose. There is nothing wrong with a little harmless idiocy to put people off their guard before they find themselves talked into lifting a dinghy over twenty metres of towpath or doling out a free meal to a stranger. But I had not yet encountered a reaction quite so extreme as this at the sight of my headgear. At last an older woman appeared. She was clearly the landlady, presumably taking over from the mirth-struck waitress who, one could only pray, was suffering a choking fit somewhere far from medical aid. She approached the table, glanced at the hat, smirked, but completed taking the order.

'… and afterwards, the Black Forest Gateau, thank you.'

'Certainly sir. Um …?' She paused.

'Yes?'

'If you don't mind me asking, sir, but do you by chance have a rowing dinghy?'

'Well, yes, I do actually. But how did you – '

'A *yellow* rowing dinghy, by any chance?'

'Yes, yellow,' I replied, wondering where this was leading.

'Ah,' said she. 'Good.' She nodded. Then she leaned over and whispered reassuringly in my ear. 'They're a bit old-fashioned hereabouts, see, pet. Me, I'm broad-minded as they come, but all the same, I think you was right to put on a suit of clothes before you came in here tonight. Anything to drink then?'

It was clear that my three lady canoeists had made it to the Tontine for lunch. And equally clear what the main topic of conversation had been over the sherry trifle. But, with luck, a good current and a following wind I could be over the border and into Worcestershire before the news hit the *Shropshire Star* the next day. An early night that night, and an early start on the morrow, and they'd never catch me.

*

Day Three. (You see, we are getting on quicker now.)

Less than a mile from the Tontine Inn, the River Vyrnwy flows into the River Severn, the longest river in Britain and my highway from here to the sea some two hundred miles away. Once onto this relatively broad thoroughfare, it would be time to start doing things in earnest. I would hoist the sail.

I rowed in to a little beach of shingle and spent half-an-hour unwrapping the mast and rigging from its neatly furled bundle, stepping the mast and attaching the long wire stays to their three respective fittings – port beam, starboard beam and prow. Once these were adjusted and tautened, the mast stood proudly erect and *Jack* already looked more like a sailing ship than a common rowboat.

Soon the rudder was in place, the sheets were clear and I was ready to hoist the scarlet mainsail. Even many months later, when I was hauling up the sail for the thousandth time, I could not help thrilling to the sudden bellying out of the red canvas, the sail's peak soaring into place against a bright sky in three swift, easy glides, the clunk of the main pulley lifting free of the gunwales and the smooth run of the mainsheet as the boom swings fully out. There is always the faint, stirring lilt of the Onedin Line music as the sail goes up, the ghostly drift of sea spray on the high bows, and it always took me a second or two to realise that I was not in fact a Bristol clipper heading out into the Atlantic in the last century, but a small dinghy on inland waters about to ram a coot's nest again.

Once a boat is sailing she is alive, and every time those halyards hoist the peak to the heavens with a gentle breeze following, there is a resurrection of sorts. I once saw a sick and dying horse lying in a stable-yard, an ungainly, sweat-darkened tangle of inert legs and neck and hooves on the dusty cobbles. Then the vet stepped back having administered an injection. In ten seconds, with barely a twitch between near-death and full consciousness, the horse rolled, unfolded its legs and shook itself upright in one swift movement and was off, skimming across the field in a gliding canter. The sudden sail-shaking resurrection of *Jack de Crow* that morning on the upper Severn was as heart-thumpingly beautiful as that.

The weary *creak-thud* of the oars was now replaced by that loveliest of all sounds, the light rippling music of water on the wooden drum of the hull. I could sit in the dinghy facing the way I was travelling rather than in the neck-craning posture of the oarsman who must travel through life backwards. The sheets were easing and flexing as the light breeze nudged the mainsail out; the tiller thrummed beneath my fingers, gently tugging to one side as it should but kept in check by my steering hand.

Wonderful it was, but the hazards remained. Though I had been sailing on and off since I was five, I had still to learn the importance of *not* letting go of the tiller. In a dinghy, if you remove your hand from the tiller for so much as half a second, the rudder swings out of control, the boom takes a murderous lurch at you and you find yourself ramming your vessel into a willow tree. The willow tree on this first of many such occasions, a mile or so above Shrawardine, was a particularly clingy specimen and managed to get its green-grey twiggy fingers thoroughly enmeshed in the stays and halyards before I knew where I was.

After several minutes of carefully trying to wiggle the boat free, snapping off a twig here, bending back a bough there, I gradually became aware of a presence six feet above me on the bank.

A bull.

It stamped. It snorted. It pawed the ground, sending great sods of turf and soil down the steep bank and into the dinghy. It had a shiny, spittle-covered brass nose ring. It had two mad, little piggy eyes that turned to two spinning red spiral discs as its temper grew. It tossed its massive head and stubby horns in frustrated rage at being unable to find a way down the bank to gore me to death. For a minute I wondered why my presence seemed to enrage it so. Then I realised that with every attempt to shake the red sail free, despite making ineffective bull-soothing noises, I was flapping a bright red piece of cloth in its face. I may as well have had a thousand cheering Spaniards in the background, worn a frilly shirt and been shouting *Olé*.

Eventually the last willow twig snapped away. Wiping sweat and bull-spittle from my ashen face, I pushed away from the bank and out into the current once more. The westerly breeze blowing down from the Welsh hills behind me filled the sail, *Jack* gave a shake and a ruffle as if to say 'Concentrate, Sandy! Concentrate,' and we were on our way once more. Two miles later the bull's bellowing had faded over the fields and I had stopped shaking enough to think about lunch.

*

The God of Spontaneous Lunch Offers was not slow in manifesting his bounty. Since escaping the bull I had bowled merrily along and was approaching Shrawardine and its overgrown castle mound clothed in fading dog's mercury when a voice hailed me from the bank.

'Twenty years I've been on this river,' it barked, 'and I've never seen a sail. Come and have lunch!' Well, my friends say I'm slow at many things, but when it comes to free lunch invitations my reactions are those of an electrocuted stoat. I put the tiller over, gybed neatly and came to a graceful halt on a grassy bank below a wall bright with purple aubretia and snow-in-summer. At the top of this wall on a sunny terrace sat my host, an iron-browed gentleman with a gammy leg, reclining in a garden chair. He introduced himself as Kiril Gray and waved me towards the French windows behind him.

'In there, on the right. Kitchen. Cold roast beef. Bread. Help yourself. And bring another bottle of red out, would you?'

A few minutes later, I was out again in the September sunshine, a roast beef and horseradish sandwich the size of a Bible in one hand and a goblet of superb red wine in the other. We chatted of this and that, Mr Gray snapping out shrewd questions about my plans hereon and expressing a gruff admiration for my courage.

'Courage?' I queried. 'Why do you say that?'

Suddenly I was worried.

'Ever been to Ironbridge Gorge, hmm? And before that there's Shrewsbury Weir, of course. Didn't they tell you? Ah well, you'll find out soon enough,' he murmured. A silence, while I swirled the wine in the glass, watching the sun make a bright ruby in its dark heart. It was very peaceful ...

'Isn't that gorgeous?' I said. 'That colour – it's like a garnet, or the colour you get in old stained-glass.'

'Funny you should say that. My wife's not here at present. She's putting a new window in Shrewsbury Abbey today. Won't be back till late. More wine?'

'Yes please.' I held out my glass. 'A window? In the Abbey?'

'That's right. Jane Gray by name. May've heard of her. Quite well known actually. Makes stained-glass.'

Ah. I had a vision of Mrs Gray, a little faded perhaps, a Parish Worthy, busy over her retirement hobby with some Make-It-Yourself Craft Kit, piecing together garish glass kingfishers or improbably coloured autumnal sprays in circular frames for polite neighbours to hang in their front-parlour windows. At this very moment, I thought, the Rector of Shrewsbury Abbey was diplomatically accepting some well-meant offering in coloured perspex ('*I call it my Rainbow Prayer, vicar*') and wondering where he could best lose it in some dark side aisle or dusty apse.

'Care to see her workshop?'

'Lovely,' I enthused, and considered launching into how, too, my mother kept herself busy making Victorian Christmas decorations, silk flowers and ceramic kittens for the parish jumble sale. The moment I saw the workshops, however, and a portfolio of Mrs Jane Gray's work, I realised that she and my mother were in very different leagues. The glasswork was magnificent. Photographs and designs for vast windows all around the country spilled into my lap: castles, cathedrals, cenotaphs, museums, and such a blaze of saints and angels, swords, lilies, fountains and flames, glowing like jewels … and these were only the photographs. How they must look in real life, with God's good sunlight transmuting into sapphire and garnet, honey-gold and cool amethyst, I could only imagine. I determined there and then to stop at Shrewsbury Abbey as I sailed past in the next day or two and see the new window in its place. But talking of Shrewsbury, if I wanted to make it there by nightfall I had best be off, so making my farewells to my grim, ironic host ('*Best of luck! Regards to the Weir.*') I hurried down to the dinghy, hoisted sail once more and rippled on my way.

I was immensely grateful, not just for the slabs of roast beef, horseradish and wholewheat bread settling comfortably into my belly, nor for the ambrosial wine sloshing rosily into my bloodstream, but for the chance kindness of a stranger, the spontaneous call across the river at the sight of my red sail that was to set the pattern for the next three thousand miles.

Mr Gray was the first to be warmed by the sight of *Jack de Crow* and to respond so encouragingly; the first of many to send a small part of himself winging down the river with me into the wide lands beyond. And if this sounds uncommonly like an epitaph, then I'm afraid to say that, in fact, it is. Mr Kiril Gray died three days later, but not before receiving a postcard from a pith-helmeted stranger downriver, assuring him of a successful outcome with Shrewsbury Weir and the Ironbridge Gorge, about which he had remained so disturbingly tight-lipped, with only his shrewd eyes gleaming with amusement.

*

The river by this time had become a deep, beautiful dark green running between rich pastures and glossy rhododendron woods and every now and then overlooked by some gracious manor house across shaven lawns. Horses grazed in the meadows and white Charolais cattle browsed beneath spreading chestnut trees, knee deep in the late summer grass.

As there was still a fair following breeze, I had the sail out full and was beginning to relax into the way of things. I found it was possible to sit down low in the stern, my back propped for comfort against my folded life jacket (such a useful thing; I had been right to bring one) and steering the tiller with an idle elbow. The nice thing about running downwind as opposed to tacking into it is how calm and gentle and sunny things appear. With both the current and the breeze going my way on this sunny afternoon, there is no alarming gurgle of water racing under the keel, no pushy wind tugging fitfully at the sails, nothing in fact to indicate that I am moving at all, except for the smooth retreating glide of the distant banks.

Until I stop dead, that is.

I had closed my eyes for a moment, my face upturned to the warming sun, identifying the sweet trill of what I thought was possibly a skylark somewhere above me in the pure serene, when BANG! something clutched at the centreboard, held it fast. The placid green waters of the Severn, seemingly so dreamy a second before, became an inexorable muscle of torrent sluicing past the bows as *Jack* turned side-on to the current. The breeze that had lulled me along now ripped off its benign mask and revealed itself as a bullying braggart, pushing, pushing, *pushing* the sail over until the dinghy was heeling at forty-five degrees and water was pouring over the submerged gunwale.

Whatever had snagged the centreboard beneath the boat was still holding it fast, and any minute now the wind and current would capsize me completely. The orderly sheets and lines had been transformed into a snarled tangle of sodden ropes in the bottom of the boat. The jammed mainsheet was holding the sail hauled in, rather than safely spilling the wind. The life jacket was half overboard, clearly making a bid for shore and leaving me to sink or swim.

I tried pulling up the centreboard, but it was firmly stuck. With an almighty heave and a horrid gouging sound, up it came like a cork from a bottle. I reeled backwards, sprawling into the flooded bottom of the dinghy, while the flying centreboard did a graceful somersault into the air before landing with a crack across my ribs.

I lay for a few seconds, wild-eyed and breathing hard. Floating ropes and a foot of river water sloshed gently about my buttocks as I glared up at the sky and listened to the river rippling on the hull. But all was calm again, instantly, miraculously, the moment *Jack* was freed from the grip of that underwater claw. Now that we were once again going with the elements, the Severn was murmuring its silken whispers under the keel, and the faintest of breezes was saying with some surprise:

'Us? Violent? The dear old river and I? No, you must have been dreaming, old son. We're your friends.'

Jack may have been fooled by these blandishments but not I. As the river and dinghy waltzed arm in arm down the long curling ribbon of water, I sat ramrod-straight, darting suspicious glances from sail to bank, from bank to prow and back to sail, muttering edgily to the odd wayside moorhen, 'Ha! Just try it and see, buster,' as the golden afternoon slipped away and the spires of Shrewsbury town came in sight.

Rapids and Repairs

> But oh! that deep romantic chasm which slanted
> Down the green hill athwart a cedarn cover!
> A savage place; as holy and enchanted
> As e'er beneath a waning moon was haunted
> By woman wailing ...
>
> —COLERIDGE, *Kubla Khan*

I still had five miles to go to Shrewsbury when the breeze died to nothing and I took to the oars once more. But with every stroke the section of gunwale I had screwed into place the day before was slowly working loose. Already the screws were at the cardigan-snagging stage that is a trademark of Mackinnon carpentry.

'Good Lord, is that a Mirror?' a silvery-haired gentleman on the bank called out as I struggled by.

'Yes,' I called back. 'A Mirror. Want to buy one?'

He watched me benignly for half a minute, then spoke again.

'Probably a silly question, old son, but why are you rowing round and round in small circles?'

I explained.

'Ah, now what you need is some wood glue, old boy. And a little expert advice. Pull in here. I may be able to help you.'

And that is how I met Alan Snell, who just happened to have a waterside boat shed at his back, and who just happened to be building a wooden sailing-dinghy in his spare time, and so happened to have wood glue, screws, planes, files, chisels and bags of expertise. He also had rather a nice bottle or two of chardonnay – it seemed that fine wine was becoming a regular feature of these unscheduled riverside stops.

For two hours Alan helped me mend the damaged gunwale and kept refilling my glass, and by the time we had finished the gunwale was as solid as the Rock of Gibraltar, which is more than could be said for the pair of us. As well as gluing, he had taken a strip of steel, drilled screw holes through it, curved it to the shape of the gun-wale's swell and bolted the whole thing on with a reinforcing strip. It is a matter of record that for the rest of the long, long voyage, that gunwale and rowlock never gave the slightest trouble again. It was with blurry words of gratitude that I set off again with both oars pulling strongly once more. The fact that I was still going in circles was, I suspect, entirely due to the third glass of chardonnay.

Shrewsbury lies in a great loop of the Severn and is almost an island. The Romans came and placed a castle at the narrow neck of the isthmus and threw up walls with the river serving as a natural moat. In later centuries the Normans added to the defences, built an abbey, improved the castle, and the town thrived behind its impreg-nable bastions, keeping the enemy hordes at bay for almost a thou-sand years before a major breach in security let in the Town Planners, who wrecked the place.

Still, from the river it remains an attractive town, a mixture of Tudor and Georgian architecture and wide riverside parks. On I rowed, past the Shrewsbury School boathouses in mock Tudor, beneath the gilded blue of the iron tollbridge, and so on to the huge red-stone abbey and my promised stop to see the newly installed Jane Gray window. This depicts St Benedict in lovely neo-mediaeval lines and deep, rich stains, every bit as glorious as I had hoped. For *Jack* and me, there was the sinuous river loop that encircles Shrews-bury, a map in Delft blue glass winding across the bottom of the frame, showing the onward way. An even lovelier window, also by Jane Gray, stood opposite, showing St Winifred crowned with stars and her holy fountain springing in silver-blue arcs at her feet.

By the time I left the abbey, the warm glow of the wine had faded from my veins. This allowed me to row in a relatively straight line but was otherwise a pity, because approaching Shrewsbury Weir I felt in particular need of courage. This is the most fearsome obstacle to navigation in the entire length of the Severn, chiefly because it is not meant to be navigated at all. There is no boat pass, no side chan-nel, no lock – nay, not so much as a fish ladder. It is simply an eight-foot concrete wall built across the river from bank to bank over which the pent-up waters pour in one unbroken, white, roaring fall. At the foot of this thunderous cascade is a great trough of seething foam where the waters roll endlessly back on themselves. This is known to kayakists as a 'stopper,' for the very good reason that it stops things – kayaks, canoes, canoeists and so on, holding them there in an eternal tumble of crushing waters until other things stop as well: breathing, pulse and neural activity, for example. Nothing that goes into this trough ever comes out again. For all anyone knows, there are the whitened bones of Norman soldiers, Tudor suicides and pre-Roman coracle fishermen revolving in an endless whirl at the foot of the weir, held there spinning in a restless watery grave, and soon possibly to be joined by a late twentieth-century dinghy sailor.

To this day, I do not know the proper technique for getting a small dinghy down an eight-foot weir – there must *be* one, surely – but here is the method I invented. I do not recommend it.

1. Moor up well above the weir.

2. Walk along and look at the layout.

3. Blanch slightly.

4. Decide that if and when the boat goes over, one will be somewhere safely on the bank at the time.

5. Rally five or six old-age pensioners who are dozing on park benches nearby.

6. Organise said pensioners into a chain gang to shift entire contents of boat by land to some point below weir.

7. Tie painter, halyard and mainsheet together to make one long, long towrope and attach one end to dinghy.

8. Pause to chivvy back into line one or two pensioners attempting to sneak back to their benches for afternoon doze before job fully done.

9. Hold other end of towrope tightly.

10. Smile bravely.

11. Push dinghy out into midstream with one foot.

12. Walk alongside drifting dinghy on bank clutching rope.

13. Walk more briskly.

14. Trot …

15. Break into panicky gallop …

16. Scream as rope races out through hands, removing most of skin in process.

17. Watch with utter astonishment as dinghy plunges over the fall, breasts the maelstrom unharmed and bobs like a cork over the rolling bones beneath her, laughing all the way.

18. Make short but heart-warming speech of thanks to pensioners, spectators, dogs, ducks, etc. before rowing away downstream using undamaged tips of fingers to hold oars.

Many months after this escapade I read Sam Llewellyn's superbly witty account of a very similar exploit, *The Worst Journey in the Midlands*. His book describes a disastrous attempt to row an ancient dinghy in 1982 from Welshpool to London via the Severn and various Midland canals, and it came as no surprise to discover that we had many experiences in common. The boat-handling pensioners at Shrewsbury Weir were one of them. Do they go there for the weekly exercise, I wonder, or had they just crept cautiously back after a fifteen-year absence reckoning it was now perhaps safe to return to some peaceful riverside dozing?

One of the pensioners there told me, as he limped by clutching my sleeping bag, that he too had set off down the Severn in just such a boat many long years ago. 'Really?' I enquired eagerly. (Perhaps I wasn't so foolhardy after all.) 'Where did you get to? What happened?'

'I got as far as Stourport and was hit by a tanker,' he replied, shaking his head sadly. 'Sank, of course.' He sighed. 'The leg's never been the same since …'

Right.

Below Shrewsbury the river runs swiftly and strongly again in several more loops, and by mid-afternoon a good breeze had sprung up that stiffened to a fair wind over the next few hours, a wind that whipped steely ripples from the river's surface and sent silver-white squalls among the osier leaves.

I will not dwell on the horrible half-hour I spent jammed firmly in yet another riverside willow's branches while the greeny current attempted to suck the keel out from under me. I will pass lightly over the horrid scraping bump as I grounded on the shingle bank below old Atcham Bridge. This is, apparently, where all the drowned bodies end up – those released by the weir, that is. Legend tells of a mermaid that dwells in the deep pools by Atcham, and the story is perpetuated by the fine inn of that name that stands by the double bridge there. More modern tales tell of a giant eel that also lives in the umbrous shadows of the arches. Year by year it grows in stature, feeding on corpses and cockle-boats, defying all attempts to capture it. In the minds of local anglers it has now assumed the proportions of Jormungander the World Serpent. It would not surprise me to learn that the two tales, of mermaid and monster eel, are of equal antiquity – and veracity.

I skimmed on downriver and, just as dusk was falling, saw that the stream divided into two on either side of a thickly wooded island. Which way to go? Where was the main channel? Wind and current were bearing me swiftly on and I had no way of telling the safer route. Just then a flash of blue skimmed out low across the water and zipped down the left-hand channel. A kingfisher! An omen! I have always loved these jewel-like birds – who does not? – not only for their sapphire and flame-orange plumage, but for all the myths and magic that fly with them. First to fly from the Ark, legend has it, the kingfisher flew up and drenched its then drab feathers in the dazzling hues of the first rainbow. Such a symbol of summer days and cloudless skies, old bestiaries claim that it lays its eggs on the silken surface of the sea when it is glassy calm. Such days of tranquillity are known therefore as 'Halcyon days' after the kingfisher's Greek name. I have always made a connection, too, between this secretive bird and the equally elusive Fisher King, mysterious keeper of the Grail in his hidden River Kingdom. Thus it was that with the whirring spark of turquoise leading me down the eastern channel, I silently thanked the gods and steered after my bright guide into the dark tunnel of trees.

Whenever a river is interrupted or split by any obstacle, the current either side intensifies to become a mill race, and this was the case now. It was almost pitch black under the crowding trees, and the channel narrowed to a dark, wrangling torrent that swept over submerged logs and around out-thrust tree-roots. Down came the sail in a flurry. I managed to bundle it safely away out of reach of the ripping branches overhead, and turned quickly to my oars. My raw, rope-burnt hands flinched on the timber of the oar handles, but I was in control again. Then, to my horror, I saw what lay ahead. At the further end of the tunnel of trees, a huge fallen pine tree lay clear across the channel from island to bank, seemingly damming the entire stream. Even from here I could see the long, wicked spikes of pale snapped-off branches, a deadly *cheval de frise* ready to impale me if I were swept down onto them. Aghast, I spun the boat to face back upstream and started to row ... oh so slowly ... back up the wrangling channel. At first I thought I was making headway, but soon I realised that it was no good. The current was so strong that even straining at the oars with cracking muscles I was still being swept down like a leaf on the flood. Only at the very last minute I saw that the left-hand end of the felled trunk was submerged – there the waters sluiced through in a gleaming black-glass muscle of water. I changed tactics and paddled furiously to the left bank to squeeze through the gap, and with only inches to spare brushed by those deadly spikes that jutted out from the main trunk in every direction. With a dark hollow gurgle *Jack* was through.

But I found I had relaxed too soon. The boat stopped with a jolt. After a second or two of violent heeling, there came an almighty crack from somewhere under the keel, and *Jack* drifted on once more.

The centreboard. I had left the damned centreboard down *again*, and now it sounded as though it might be damaged on yet another underwater obstacle.

I tried pulling it up, but it was stuck fast. There was nothing for it. Just as I drifted clear of the lower end of the island, a sloping shelf of mud and shingle appeared on the left bank. Moreover, the lights of a cottage shone out in the dusk a mere fifty yards up the hill. I turned towards the beach, rowed as far in as I could before I felt the centreboard grating on the river bed, and, resigning myself to the fourth wetting in four days, hopped overboard into waist-deep water. Tilting the whole boat over to see her keel, I could see the problem. The centreboard had been smacked hard side-on and had split right across at the point where it protruded from the keel. Rather than breaking away completely, it still hung on by half its splintered thickness, but these splinters were preventing it being drawn up.

A major amputation was called for. A few hefty heaves snapped the damaged centreboard completely in two, allowed me to beach the boat properly and collapse sobbing onto the grassy bank in muddy despair. This boating adventure wasn't turning out quite as I had envisaged. I couldn't recall Jerome K. Jerome leaving a trail of vital components in splintery heaps all the way down the Thames. Ratty had not spent his summer days eschewing the delights of pic-nickery for yet another visit to Harry the Stoat's lumber yard. And in all the fairy tales I knew, chirpy little kingfishers did not lead innocent travellers into death traps and then vanish sniggering.

After lying on the grass for ten minutes feeling thoroughly sorry for myself, I trudged up to the cottage I had spotted earlier, trying out different opening lines in my head.

Excuse me, do you have an open fire and require fuel? I have just delivered a whole stack of firewood to the bottom of your garden in the form of a small, useless dinghy. It will need chopping up, of course. Savagely.

Or ...

Hello, you don't know me, I am a complete stranger and very possibly a raving lunatic. May I take my trousers off in your front room and drink your whisky?

I knocked on the door and was greeted by a pleasant-looking man with greying hair.

'Er ...' I began.

'Good Lord, it's Mackinnon, isn't it? Sandy Mackinnon?'

'Er ...?' I continued. I'd never seen this man in my life.

'Yes, from Ellesmere College. Well, well. You don't know me, but I used to have sons there, and I've been back quite a bit and seen you around. Come in!'

'Er ...'

'So what can I do for you? Lord, you're soaking, come in and take your trousers off. Whisky?'

'Er ...'

'Excuse the mess, won't you. I've just been knocking together a few odds and ends in my workshop. Carpentry, you know. Bit of a hobby.'

'Er ... funny you should mention that ...'

*

Those of you who are sickened by this unfailing tendency to thrive on the kindness of strangers will be mollified to hear that I did not in fact batten hungrily onto this particular one's kindness. Before I could work out the order in which I would take advantage of his various offers of help, I found out where I was – Wroxeter. Beneath this tiny hamlet lie buried the remains of the largest Roman city yet discovered in Britain. Recent archaeological finds even hint that this may well have been the stronghold of the fifth-century *dux bellorum*, the best contender so far for an historical Arthur, which makes Wroxeter nothing less than Camelot. It seemed that my Fisher King had led me true after all. Under normal circumstances, this fact alone would have accounted for the joy that now flooded over me, but on this night I had another reason for euphoria. Less than a mile from Wroxeter was the house of a family I knew well and it was to them that I could cheerfully turn my leech-like feelers for help and hospitality.

A quick phone call, and I was soon ensconced on my friend Jenny's sofa just up the road, sinking in a sea of her home-made silk cushions embroidered with pomegranates, tropical flowers and coral fish. Once my sorry tale was told, Jenny's husband Henry was dispatched to the work shed and emerged some time later with a brand-new centreboard, which was then varnished and left to dry overnight.

As I continued to tell of the discomforts and trials of the voyage, Jenny would get up, bang about in various cupboards outside and then return to hear the next part of the story. When I had finished, she presented me with an array of goods for the morrow: gardening gloves for the prevention of blisters; plastic map case to prevent my already dilapidated map from crumbling further; large packed lunch of sausage sandwiches, cheese, home-grown apples and chocolate bars; a bottle of white wine in case I got tired of rowing in a straight line; a corkscrew; and, best of all, a big, soft cushion appliquéd with gaudy parakeets to sit on in comfort.

The next morning I learnt that there was to be an additional item. Kate, Jenny's ten-year-old daughter, would accompany me for the next ten miles and be picked up at Buildwas Abbey downstream. A further surprise was in store when we all tripped down to where I'd left *Jack de Crow*, my new centreboard under one arm and the sack full of goodies under the other. There was another centreboard, newly made, leaning against the dinghy. A short note from the friendly cottager of the night before wished me well, was sorry to have missed me that morning, and hoped that his mocked-up centreboard might be of some use. From some nearby willow came the thin tinkling sound of a kingfisher laughing.

Hastily, before anyone else popped out of the woods or hurried across the fields with newly made booms, gaffs, oars, rudders or the like, or just blank cheques and suggestions that I should upgrade to a yacht, Kate and I clambered aboard and *Jack de Crow* set off once more.

As the river approaches Buildwas Abbey above Ironbridge Gorge it runs in broad sweeps between flat green fields which lap against the Wrekin, a steep conical hill dominating the whole plain from Staffordshire to the Welsh border like a brooding giant. At one point on this stretch we sailed around a bend and straight into a flock of Canada geese, who launched themselves into the air in a hurricane of wings. What a flurry and fury all about us, a whirring, wonderful snowstorm of beaks and breasts and wide, wide pinions. It was a phalanx of archangels ascending to the Throne. The gibble-gabble from a hundred outstretched necks, the creak and whoosh of two hundred wings, the spatter of water all around and our scarlet sail breezing along in the middle of it all; this is what I had dreamt of when I first thought of sailing the Severn. Ah! and the breezy air full of drifting grey goose-down afterwards.

After a little while the breeze died, but that didn't matter because I now had a galley slave. Kate, wearing my red and white handkerchief pirate-style on her dark head, manned the oars while I lay back dreaming in the noonday sun, dreaming of this and that, of giants and T.H. White's geese and golden days ahead, and wondering if I could perhaps purchase Kate for a fair price for the remainder of the journey. My idle happiness was tinged only by a minor irritation that for a ten-year-old beginner at rowing she was doing considerably better than I had done.

Alas, at Buildwas Abbey my brief idyll came to a halt as Jenny appeared on the bridge, waving a huge Union Jack pillowcase flag and hooting like a schoolgirl. Once Kate was safely ashore, I turned my nose downstream once more and prepared to face the Ironbridge Gorge.

Ironbridge, tucked away in its steep valley off the main roads, is not very big and I doubt if many people outside the Midlands are more than vaguely aware of its existence. Yet it holds the distinction of being the very birthplace of the Industrial Revolution. An engraving of the Gorge done in the late 1700s looks like the work of a more than usually deranged Hieronymus Bosch: the river banks crumble beneath the weight of factories, shanty-town houses, belching chimneys and sooty wharves. The river itself is clogged with ships and barges, cranes, derricks, steamers and wherries, and on every side are piles of filth: slag heaps, overflowing middens, effluent pipes and broken piles of rubble swarmed over by emaciated people, skeletal and hollow-eyed.

Today, mercifully, it has largely reverted to a steep secluded gorge, though rather too dank and sinister in the dark depths of its waters for my liking. Up the banks swarmed trees clad in thick creeper, a tangle of black bryony and bitter ivy. Autumn seemed more advanced here, the leaves already rotting to dampness on the trees and clogging the stilly waters. Grim verses chased through my mind – *The shadows where the Mewlips dwell are dark and wet as ink* – and I found that I was singing to myself the Twenty-third Psalm. Under the semicircular arch of Telford's Iron Bridge (incidentally, the first to be

Final Farewell

constructed thus) I drifted ghost-like before the faintest of breezes, but was cheered to see a madcap figure standing high above me on the parapet waving that outsized Union Jack again – Jenny, who had raced down in her car for a last sweeping wave. On an impulse I dug into my rucksack for my tin-whistle, and as the great curving tracery drifted astern I played a rousing chorus of *Rule Britannia*. Thinly over the water came Jenny's lusty vocal accompaniment while Kate – no doubt – shrunk back in horrid embarrassment.

But *Rule Britannia* gave way to the melancholy *Tom Bowling* and just before the bridge dwindled to a distant dot, I got in a couple of bars of *Auld Lang Syne*, modulated to a minor key by the mournful echoes and the air of departure. For this was the start of another stage of the adventure. Once the waving figure of Jenny on the bridge had vanished astern, I would know that I really had said goodbye to my old life at Ellesmere. Up until this point I had been charting familiar territory, seeing old haunts and relying on friends, never more than a phone call and a ten-minute drive away. But from here, from now, beyond the Gorge, all was new.

*

I am not yet beyond the Gorge, however. At the bottom of it lie the Jackfield Rapids, a welter of white water some two hundred yards long, thrashing over and between black boulders and jagged rocks. Every weekend the place is gay with kayaks and canoes and their various lycra-clad, fluorescent-helmeted owners, who spend happy afternoons doing impossible things in craft as slim and unstable as a French runner bean. These boats are tough; the odd knock on a boulder at twenty knots is a mere scuff to the tough fibreglass, and as for flipping over – well, that's half the fun.

I, on the other hand, want merely to get beyond the rapids upright, dry and unscathed, and am none too confident about any of these three. *'Fortune Favours the Brave'* runs the Mackinnon motto – though I've always found that, be that as it may, she also favours the prudent, the discreet and the well heeled. I decide to opt for prudence. The plan is to adopt roughly the same method as for the Shrewsbury Weir, though with protective gloves this time. The problem, however, is that here there is no clear towpath for me to amble along, and there are large rocks midstream against which *Jack* might be crushed like an eggshell. Nevertheless, I try.

I slip and stumble among the slimy black boulders on the bank and attempt to control *Jack's* progress on a short lead, but the current keeps jamming her between rocks or spinning her into side eddies and I have to stumble back upstream a few yards to pull her free. Wiry brambles and the low sweep of ash branches jut out over the banks, hampering my slow to-ing and fro-ing. This footling progress is not to last. *Jack*, an altogether more impulsive soul than I, finally grows impatient with my caution and takes off with a swoop down a small cascade. Taking me off guard, the rope tether pulls me from a wobbly boulder, and I dive head-first into the river on the end of the line, towed along like an unsuccessful water-skier who refuses to let go. Here we go again. A rush and roar of foam about my ears, a lungful of Severn water and a cracking blow on the ribs from a submerged boulder; none of these things can divert me from the sudden illuminating thought that if one is planning to take a boat down

England's fiercest rapids, it makes more sense to be actually *in* the boat at the time.

Twenty yards downstream I surface spluttering in a side pool where *Jack* has fetched up on a black rock and is kindly waiting for me. When I have finished spluttering, I sigh. Day Five, fifth wetting. As for my ribs, they are aching abominably. There are more than two-thirds of the rapids below us still to negotiate. At that point, I lose my patience with this whole prudence lark and decide to take *Jack*'s lead. With a silent prayer I hop in, push off and ride the remaining two hundred yards of the rapids as though *Jack* were a Colorado inflatable raft. I believe I close my eyes.

There is a rush and a roar, one or two sweeping ups and downs, several slow waltzing spins and somehow, miraculously, I am through. The rush mutes to a chatter, the chatter to a gentle chuckle, the chuckle to a murmur, and then dreaming silence steals in once more. I am through. The rapids are behind me and I have survived the greatest hurdle of the journey to the sea.

Steam Trains and Smooth Sailing

> I must go down to the seas again, for the call of the
>   running tide
> Is a wild call and a clear call that may not be denied.
> —JOHN MASEFIELD, *Sea-Fever*

I awoke the next day with a light heart. Bridgnorth, approached by river in the slow gold of the evening before, had taken my breath away, even more than the adrenalin rush of the Jackfield Rapids. The town sits on its high red bluff of rock above the deep winding river, topped by the red sandstone tower of St Leonard's and the more elegant green-domed cupola of St Mary's Church. The previous evening I had walked up the steep winding Cartway that zigzagged up between black and white timber cottages and four-square Georgian houses, each with lead-paned windows lamplit from within, looking indescribably homely in the blue dusk. It may have been the arrival by boat rather than car, but I felt I had come to some foreign port, some island kingdom in a fairytale, five days voyaging across chartless seas rather than the charmless forty-minute drive down the A5 motorway. I almost expected the good folk of Bridgnorth to speak in an unknown tongue and use florins or gilders for currency. This elbow-spreading of time and distance was to remain with me throughout the entire voyage, an enchanted gift from *Jack de Crow* to me as we travelled together through these new-made kingdoms.

My heart was light for a more practical reason, too. Most of the disasters that can befall a small dinghy had queued up to occur in the first five days, and *Jack* and I had dealt with them one and all. Having got them out of the way, we proceeded on our journey with a degree of stately calm, with time to enjoy the pleasures of river voyaging.

And pleasures there were aplenty. The day that I sailed away from Bridgnorth I remember as one of ruffled blue water, long straight stretches of river and high white clouds racing across a bright sky on a stiff northerly breeze. *Jack* took me in an almost unbroken run of twenty-six miles, the red sail out full, the water creaming under my bow and the glorious chuckling, rushing music of sailing dinghies everywhere. Reach after reach I sailed, through deep valleys of beech forest, between cliffs of red sandstone, past dreaming meadows where cows grazed peacefully, and all the while deeply, gloriously happy.

At one point an old black steam train burst from an oak wood beside the river in a chuffing cloud of white smoke. A glance at my map showed that this was the Severn Valley railway that takes trippers between Bridgnorth and Bewdley. For the next mile or so we raced together, train and I, down that long sunny stretch of water, red sails against white steam, while all the passengers leant from the carriage windows and waved and cheered. Then with a long drawn-out hoot from the driver, the train drew ahead and vanished around a curve and I was left blinking and wondering if I had dropped straight into an E. Nesbit story.

At another point that day, I encountered another rapid – one I had not been warned about. The valley here had deepened to such an extent that the wind had died to nothing, baffled by the curves of the gorge and the thick beech forest on either side, so I was rowing along but with the sail still set, idly flapping about my head, ready to catch the next breeze. As I rounded a bend and heard the telltale chatter of water over shallow stones I stiffened in alarm … but no. My experience in the Jackfield Rapids had taught me the wisdom of relying on the family motto; it was better to throw caution to the winds and run straight down the middle. Besides, from the sound of them this section of rapids was a mere trickle compared to the Niagaras I had faced already.

There was one problem, though. Ahead was a gaggle of kayaks, ten or so, occupied by small children and an instructor: clearly a school party of beginners learning that there was nothing to be afraid of on the river, that one was always in control, that even in a rapid such as this one need never capsize.

Fortunately they were strung out only halfway across the river, leaving a good twenty-yard gap for me to shoot through so long as I rowed hard across to the other bank starting *now*. A heave at the oars, a slip of the hand, and my left oar somehow flew out of its rowlock and splashed overboard into the river. By the time I'd recovered an upright position it was twelve feet away and I was drifting broadside on, out of control, towards the happy novices in their frail craft.

The Race

It was an aquatic game of skittles, and I was about to score a perfect strike.

As I called out an apologetic 'Um ... er ... hello?' the instructor and his party looked upstream to see a large yellow dinghy in full sail hurtling sideways down the rapid at them. Newly learnt paddle techniques were abandoned as the pink kayaks struggled to splash out of the way in the turbulent waters and a dozen white-faced eight-year-olds suddenly decided to switch to Pony Trekking elective from now on.

There was nothing at all I could do and, as it turned out, only three of the kayaks capsized, surely an invaluable opportunity for the class to experience a real capsize drill. The instructor was even gracious enough to retrieve my truant oar and return it as I swept on down the next bend, though he need not have hurled it at me quite so vigorously. And for once, the pith helmet didn't raise even the faintest of smiles.

Stourport came and went. Ever since my limping pensioner at Shrewsbury Weir had told me about his collision with a tanker at Stourport, I had entertained uneasy doubts about the place. I envisaged it as a vast industrial dockland where liners and freighters jostled for position alongside huge concrete wharves, and a small dinghy was likely to come to an untimely end beneath seventy tons of misdirected scrap iron. I was relieved to find that Stourport was nothing more alarming than a little riverside town whose only pretension to the world of shipping was that here the Severn became officially navigable. White cabin cruisers and motor boats now became frequent sights along the riverbanks, as well as a whole host of mysterious signs and noticeboards with alarming amounts of red-for-danger symbols all over them. No doubt I would find out what they all meant in time ...

And so the journey rolled on, mile after mile, day after day. Upton-upon-Severn was the next night's stop, a model village with a Roundhead history and an extraordinary tower called the Pepperpot, domed in green bronze and almost lighthouse-like in appearance. Next came the abbey town of Tewkesbury, where I lunched in a fish-and-chip shop whose proprietor stood amid all the greasy bustle of his three harassed staff in the kitchen and practised gypsy tunes on his violin. Full of battered fish, I sailed on to a tiny hamlet called Lower Lode where stands a wonderful riverside inn. Here the lawns sweep down to the broad river, horses champ in the cobbled yard behind, and an old ferryman passes the time of day over a mug of tea and talks of eel fishing and tides. For yes, even here, within hearing of the chimes of Tewkesbury Abbey, the river is tidal, though the landscape around looks as rural and land-locked as Shropshire – from this point on I must plan my journeying with the tides in mind.

That night I sit and share my supper with the family Labrador, dine on blackberries picked that day by the innkeeper's wife and, because the inn is fully booked by fishermen down for a competition, I am put up on a camp bed in the skittle-alley. I cannot think of a much pleasanter place to stay, more homely, more relaxed and unconventional, and life takes on that Elysian tint that I had so looked for when I set out. Jerome K. Jerome is probably sitting at the next table.

In the morning seven fishermen and I sit down at a big scrubbed kitchen table for a breakfast out of a bygone age. There is milk in a big cream jug of blue and white china, steaming hot porridge and amber honey dripping through a comb, catching the morning sunlight in its golden net. There follows a cooked platter of fat sausages nearly bursting their skins, mushrooms dropped sizzling from the pan straight onto the plate, and poached fresh farm eggs on buttered toast, and after that more toast with dark, chunky Oxford marmalade and scalding coffee. The burly fishermen are amused and interested by my trip so far, and wish me luck on the remainder of the voyage. Only one thing my breakfast companions say depresses me. Gloucester is apparently only another day's journey downstream, and until this moment Gloucester has been the intended finishing point of my journey, the point at which I have been planning to leave *Jack de Crow* for Philip to pick up, and to rejoin the twentieth century. Gloucester. One more day. A great despondency settles over me and I push away a proffered second helping of toast. I didn't feel I was ending the voyage; I felt that I'd only just begun.

*

I did not make it to Gloucester that night. The wind sprang up from the south-west and drove up the river in a steady head-on gale, so that I was forced to row or tack downstream.

No sailing boat can sail straight into the wind any more than a twig can drift upstream. But with the sails pulled in hard and the centreboard down, a dinghy can sail diagonally into the wind, though no more than 45 degrees. This is called being *close hauled*, and when the boat zigzags from side to side like a bishop on a chessboard it is said to be *tacking* or *beating*.

Out on the broad Atlantic, or even on a fair-sized lake, tacking is part of the fun and challenge of sailing. On a river, only the challenge remains. Firstly, the relative narrowness of the river makes it necessary to be tacking every fifty seconds or so, with all the flurry and weight-shifting and sail-flapping that this entails. Secondly, the wind is famously fickle, shifting direction every few yards depending on whether you are out in mid-river or close in to a bank. When the wind is behind you, these slight shifts make no great difference, but when tacking, they are maddening. Three times on every tack I found myself pinching the wind because it had swung around a little, or clapped in irons under the lee of a cliffy bank and forced to go through the whole tiller-waggling, sail-shaking process of starting up again.

At times that day the wind became so faint and flighty that I gave up trying to sail and decided to row. So ... loosen the main halyard. Lower the gaff and mainsail into the boat, not into the water. Bundle gaff, boom and sail into a long wrapped red sausage. Hold together with two elastic straps. Hoist the whole furled bundle up the mast out of the way. Tie off halyard on the cleat. Haul up centreboard and stow it away on front deck. Pull up the rudder with the drawstring and cleat it. Ship the oars. Start rowing.

No sooner had I done this than the wind would strengthen into a steady, silver gale, smurring the whole reach of the river with pewter ripples and making every oar stroke a futile attempt to hold my position and not be blown upstream.

So I would decide to try sailing again. Then, of course, by the time I had reversed all the above process, the wind would have died down once more.

It was, frankly, heartbreaking. Eventually I pulled in exhausted to a tiny hamlet called Ashlewort. Here a tiny riverside pub nestled next to an ancient grey-steepled church; inside it was cool and quiet, smelling of hassocks and furniture polish and old roses. On the lectern stood a huge spread-eagled Bible open, as I discovered, to Psalm 107. There were the words, *'And those who go down to the sea in ships, And do business on the great waters, They too see the wonders of the Lord upon the deeps.'*

It's nice to have these Divine promptings occasionally but I was beginning to doubt if I would reach the Lord's great waters after all – not unless the Lord could bring Himself to fiddle with the isobars a bit and send me a favourable wind, thank you very much.

*

On the next day, the Lord met me halfway. The wretched southerly died away but was replaced with a flat and cheerless calm, so I rowed the remaining drab miles to Gloucester in a sullen temper. Already the river was clearly tidal, as the mud banks dropped steeply into the turgid waters on either side and roots of osier and willow hung bleached and scum-whitened above a tangle of debris: detergent bottles, polystyrene foam and hairy red waterweed. Beyond Gloucester, the Severn, I had been warned, became utterly unnavigable, running out to sea in a series of wide estuarine loops that were at low tide a maze of mudbanks and shoals or in flood a raging torrent of whirlpools, eddies and maelstroms. In fact, it is the birthplace of one of the oddest tidal phenomena in the world, the Severn Bore. Every year at the spring and autumn tides, the inrush of water up the narrowing bottleneck of the estuary causes a single wave, four feet high, to race up the river, sometimes up to twenty-six miles inland. Spectators gather on the banks to watch this oddity, presumably well equipped with Wellington boots and perhaps even snorkelling gear. I read of one intrepid chap who took a surf-board down one year and rode the crest of this wave all the way up to Tewkesbury, arriving terrified and exhausted along with logs, smashed punts, a chicken shed and one or two corpses that the wave had picked up along the way.

The imminence of the Severn Bore's arrival was one reason I could not even dream of going beyond Gloucester on the river. Besides, a large weir below Gloucester made the river impassable even for tiny craft, there being no lock or boat pass. It really did seem that Gloucester was the end of the line and I would not even have the satisfaction of reaching the sea. So much for bumping into Africa ...

I rather wished for a better terminus. True, the city's cathedral is a jewel of design, a glory of honey-coloured stone and fan-vaulted ceilings, but much of the town centre has gone the way of so many other English cities, spoilt by a rash of sixties blocks built by the Public Lavatory School of Architecture. The old wharves area has been resurrected – though whether designer clothes shops and hippy-hoppy burger bars are an improvement on the tarry bustle of cargo ships and barges, ocean-going yachts and busy tugboats is a moot point. As I stood there gazing out over the wharves and ware-houses, imagining the days when Gloucester was a busy maritime port, a question suddenly occurred to me: how, if the Severn River has been an impassable, unnavigable channel since the Pleistocene Age, did all these clippers and cutters, these barques and barges, these frigates and freighters ever get here in the first place?

The answer, I found, was a little thing called the Sharpness Canal, and I realised the voyage wasn't over yet. I might just be join-ing those Biblical seabound mariners after all.

High Tide to Bristol

There is a tide in the affairs of men,
Which taken at the flood, leads on to fortune;
Omitted, all the voyage of their life
Is bound in shallows and in miseries.
                    —SHAKESPEARE, *Julius Caesar*

The Sharpness Canal runs roughly parallel with the Severn Estuary for sixteen miles from Gloucester to the port of Sharpness on the Bristol Channel. The canal, I was to discover, cuts across flat, wind-bitten fields enlivened only by the occasional lock-keeper's cottage incongruously decorated with classical Doric porticoes, each one resembling a miniature Greek temple. Once at Sharpness you can be lowered to sea-level in an enormous lock and let loose on the Bristol Channel beyond the worst of the mud-flats and vagaries of the Bore. This then was my route, if only to let *Jack de Crow* sniff the salt air and retire with the dignity of knowing she had reached the sea. Then, I told myself firmly, I really *would* have to stop.

I set off from Gloucester on a morning of grey skies and a strong wind that blew unwaveringly from the south-west. After a mile of slogging along through the usual dreary wasteland that fringes every town, between high brick walls, cyclone-wire fences, the backs of warehouses and supermarkets and multiplex cinemas, I had reached the edges of flat fields and pastures – and the point of exhaustion. The wind was too strong to row against. An attempt at hoisting sail had proved what I knew already – that it was far too narrow a canal to make tacking an option. I was on the point of deciding that Ellesmere to Gloucester was a perfectly respectable journey for a small Mirror dinghy to make, and wondering whether trains ran direct to London, when a booming hoot blasted out from astern.

There, steaming down the canal behind me was a huge vessel, a triple-decked party ship on her way down to Sharpness. As I rowed violently to the bank to avoid being run down, the skipper called out, 'Ahoy! Doctor Livingstone! Need a tow, mate?'

Two minutes later I was aboard, a hot coffee was in my hands and *Jack de Crow* was bobbing astern riding the white wake like a champion surfer. It seemed we would reach the sea after all. The vessel was called *King Arthur* (which pleased me), and Terry, the captain, was a black-bearded, twinkly-eyed chap who, had his hair been whiter, would have been advertising Captain Birdseye fish fingers on the telly.

As we ploughed our way along the canal, he regaled me with tales of surly lock-keepers, dopey narrowboat owners and the one-hundred-and-one ways you can die on the inland waterways of Britain. Meanwhile, I was realising a few mistakes of my own. The first was not putting my centreboard down: the speed with which *Jack* was being towed was causing water to bubble up through the centre-board case like the Trevi Fountain and already the dinghy was half full of water. The second mistake was not stowing the oars properly: I had been in such a hurry to clamber aboard before Terry changed his mind that I had left them in their rowlocks and merely balanced on the gunwales. The swooping and bucketing of the dinghy on the stern wash had dislodged them and now they were trailing in the wake, threatening to drop overboard at any time. The third mistake was in being towed at all.

The first thing that happened was that *King Arthur* stopped dead with a sticky slurp. We had struck a mudbank in mid-canal. *Jack*, not concentrating, carried merrily on at her former speed and nose-butted *King Arthur*'s stern with timber-cracking force. Not only that, but the suddenly slackened towline drooped down into the water and threatened to wrap itself around the churning propellers.

This somehow never happened, and *Jack* drifted around to a safer position snuggled up alongside her mother ship – safer, that is, until in an attempt to reverse off the mudbank *King Arthur*'s stern swung heavily in to one side and looked like crushing *Jack*'s ribs between herself and the bank.

Terry seemed cheerfully unconcerned about the potential damage to his ship or mine. He twiddled the wheel and shoved levers to and fro without abating the flow of amusing disaster stories from all corners of navigable Britain. Meanwhile, *King Arthur* churned and wallowed and swung about like a mother sow with *Jack* dangling from her tail. I began to wonder whether Terry had been merely a witness to all these tales of inland shipwreck, or in fact the prime agent of them. They were certainly told in the third person, but then so were Caesar's *Gallic Wars*.

I need not have worried. Terry was as competent as he was kindly, and soon we were on our way again. However, the exercise had been a neat little demonstration of the Dangers of Being Towed, and had covered, I felt, all areas of concern.

One other thing Terry did for me was to turn my two-week jaunt into a year of major voyaging. 'You'll be going through the Channel then to Bristol, I suppose?' he asked breezily.

'What?! Oh no ... I mean ... well, you can't, can you?'

'Don't see why not. Good little boat like that, no problem. You'd have to pick your tide, of course, and your weather, but you'd be alright.'

At first I thought he was joking. Then I wondered if this was how he had acquired so many hilarious boating disasters in his repertoire: by prompting gullible fools like myself to acts of idiocy and then standing back quietly to take notes. (*'Yes, the best way of opening the lock gates is to ram them hard. Standard practice, honestly ... Bristol Channel in a Mirror dinghy? Easy-peasy! Let me get your name spelt correctly for the obituary column.'*) Was he a sort of Iago of the Waterways, encouraging all comers to rash acts of folly while he himself stood neutrally aside? But when we arrived at Sharpness and I said my thanks and farewells, he seemed so confident in my likelihood of going on, so matter-of-fact about the dangers and the ways to minimise them, that before I'd cast off and rowed three strokes, I knew my sights were now set on Bristol.

*

Sharpness is a place of contrasts. On the one hand there are the docks, a huge area of concrete basins, giant steel cranes, hangars and warehouses and ocean-going tankers, all as bleak and grey and businesslike as shipping ports the world over. But, just around the corner from all this, one branch of the canal ends in a secluded basin tucked beneath a gentle hill that shelters it from the salty winds off the Bristol Channel. Here in the clear depths grow waterlilies and globeflowers, and black moorhens dabble about the bankside reeds. A fleet of swans sails on the ruffled blue surface and a dilapidated row of pontoons holds a motley collection of small craft: old motor launches, small yachts, dinghies and punts with fading paintwork.

The hillside above is a rich tangle of blackberry brambles and wind-swept trees with here and there a cottage nestled deep in a garden bright with autumn flowers: dahlias, marigolds, chrysanthemums, all in seasonal burgundies and golds.

At the head of this basin is a thick concrete pier wall, and stepping onto this I was surprised to find that the other side dropped a sheer forty feet onto the sands of the Severn Estuary. The tide was out. Standing there one could look out across a mile of tawny sand-banks and shoals and the curling silver ribbons of water to the opposite shore where rose the green pastures of Wales. To my right, the estuary narrowed into the blueness of distant hills, and to the left, broadened into a sea of sandy waters stretching limitlessly to the southern horizon; a faint smudge of shadow down there was all that could be seen of the two Severn bridges.

I stood for a while gazing at the purple weed tumbled against the foot of the wall forty feet below me, a pair of herring gulls wrangling over a fishy morsel on a nearby pontoon, and at the vast glimmering hazy brightness of air and sea and sand before me ... then turned to go and find someone to talk me out of my newly grown and perfectly idiotic ambition.

*

The running of an important shipping port like Sharpness is a serious business, demanding organisation, a military severity of discipline and an almost Teutonic respect for the Rules. Captain Horatio Eggersley was just the man for the job. His short, plump figure and baby face with a wisp of red hair tufting out on top were belied by the steely-eyed manner in which he tackled his job as Harbourmaster. Thousand-ton grain ships from the Argentine and rusting freighters from Russia were moved about with the tactical precision of chess pieces. Cranes and derricks swung to and fro in a balletic dance at his choreographic command, and the tides rose and fell to within a centimetre of his carefully computed calculations. The very gulls fly in formation within the precincts of Sharpness Harbour.

His reaction to my suggestion that I might take my Mirror dinghy down the Bristol Channel was not entirely unexpected. He fixed me with a long stare to assess my mental state before reaching behind him and pulling from an orderly file a sheaf of documents. We were in his office perched high above the harbour basin.

Computer screens blinked and glowed, charts and timetables covered the walls stuck with little colour-coded pins and the afternoon sunlight glinted on the braid and brass buttons of his uniform. I found myself struggling not to address him as 'Admiral.'

'These may interest you,' he said. 'A few statistics about the Bristol Channel. Tide records. Information on currents. Position and depth of shoals. Prevalent weather conditions. And this,' said he, hauling out a file as thick as a dictionary, 'is a record of shipwrecks, lost vessels and fatalities in the Channel over the last decade alone. Do feel free to browse.'

As he turned back to his desk and rapped a few curt orders into the radio, I flipped the pages. Numbers, figures, graphs swam before my eyes; the only thing that I could take in was how many exclamation marks there seemed to be. As for the file of shipping disasters, well, they were all great big boats surely – huge, unwieldy vessels with deep keels that were bound to catch on the bottom occasionally. Not nimble little craft like *Jack de Crow* with a four-inch draft and the buoyancy of a cork.

'Hmm, yes,' said I, trying to sound thoughtful and wise. 'So these tides …?'

'Second highest in the world,' snapped Captain Eggersley. 'They reach twelve metres or more.'

'Hmm. I see. So that means the current is …?'

'Ten knots in most places. Fifteen under the bridges. Your outboard motor won't have a chance if you have to fight against it.'

'Ah.' Was this a good time to confess that I didn't in fact have a motor?

I confessed.

Captain Eggersley's jaw sagged briefly and then snapped shut again.

'So the whole idea is, I'm sure you realise, out of the question.'

'Um …'

He sighed. He took a deep breath, and then quite kindly and patiently said, 'Look. Let me explain.' Moving over to a wall chart and picking up a pointer, he continued. 'We are here, you see. Now every six and a half hours all this water *here*' (he swept a hand over an area that embraced half the Atlantic) 'tries to race up the ever-narrowing channel of the Severn Estuary and rises TWELVE metres. It comes in at over ten miles an hour, which is four times faster than anything you've been on so far down the river. It is so fast

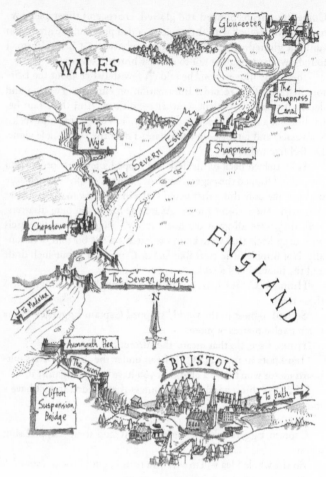

The Severn Estuary

that it actually forms ridges and bumps of water, standing waves in midstream big enough to swamp a boat twice your size. Six hours later the whole process reverses itself but with the added volume of water coming down the Severn itself. This is called "flood tide and ebb tide."'

'Flood tide and ebb tide,' I repeated obediently.

He was into the swing of it now. Sunlight, warm and strong, poured through the wide glass windows looking out onto the estuary under the late afternoon sky. The office was drowsy with the faint hum of computers – a bluebottle fly buzzed sluggishly on the window pane. So peaceful, such a tranquil place to sit awhile dreaming ... Captain Eggersley moved irritably across to the window and dispatched the fly with a glossy copy of *Yachting World*, and I was wide awake once more.

'Now usually between the flooding and the ebbing there are tranquil periods known as high water and slack water. We here, however,' he said proudly, as though he had personally invented the system, 'have virtually no such periods. Ten minutes of still water at the most and the whole lot is on the move again. Now to get to Bristol, which is nine miles inland, you will note here on the chart that a vessel needs to travel *down* the estuary on the ebbing tide for sixteen miles and *up* this other river, the Avon, on the flooding tide. You've got to time it exactly right. If you get swept past Avonmouth on the way down, you'll be in Madeira by tea-time. If, on the other hand, you haven't made it down to the Avon before the tide starts racing in, you'll be in Tewkesbury again – that is, if you haven't sunk on the first shoal, sandbank or navigation buoy that you hit at ten miles an hour in the first five minutes. Now you can see why I'm advising you to give it a miss.'

I considered, frowning a little. It seemed to me that Captain Eggersley was being a trifle pessimistic. Didn't the South Sea Islanders reach New Zealand? Didn't the Vikings sail to Newfoundland? Didn't St Brendan reach America? Didn't Doctor Dolittle bump into Africa?

'Er ...' I said.

'*Look*,' he said firmly, his voice regaining its hard edge. 'I'm a busy man, I've got a lot to do, and when all's said and done, I can't actually stop you. However,' he continued as he took the documents from my hands, 'I am here officially warning you, and most strongly advising you' (he slipped the documents back into the filing cabinet and rammed it shut) 'that to travel from here to Bristol in an unpowered Mirror dinghy is, in my considered opinion, suicide.'

He picked up the thick Shipwrecks and Fatality file and weighed it in his hand. 'Still, high tide here tomorrow will be at 6.26 a.m. sharp. The lock gates will be open between then and 6.47 a.m. I very much hope I will NOT be seeing you then.' He turned to replace the file on a shelf. When he turned back, I looked into his corn-flower blue eyes. They were almost pleading. He sighed, glanced at the file in his hand and replaced it on his desk. 'No point in putting it away then. I expect I'll be adding another report tomorrow. Dismissed.'

*

I am not actually the reckless type. Nor am I a complete fool. I knew that one or two items of equipment were absolutely essential for this hazardous trip on the tidal waters of the Bristol Channel: namely, a chart and an anchor. The little chandlery down by the pontoons and the waterlilies had neither.

So I got out my trusty Ordnance Survey map of the Bristol Channel area, my equally trusty fountain pen, and found a wall chart of the Estuary pinned up in the bar of the Sharpness Working Man's Club. There I copied as well as I could the buoys, the beacon posts, the leading marks and the major shoals onto my own map. As for an anchor, I found an old concrete besser-brick that no one seemed to be using, tied a length of rope around it, and voilà – an emergency brake!

The next morning I woke early and hurried down from my bed and breakfast through the grey dawn to the harbour. I rowed from the little yacht basin around to the main port and into the lock that would lower me gently to the level of the sea. There Captain Eggersley was waiting with two cronies, and all three greeted me with a mournful shaking of their heads.

'I can't dissuade you then?' asked the Captain. I hesitated. I did in fact have one worry. For the past three days the wind had been blowing steadily from the south-west; even now I could see a green flag flapping out from the masthead of a grain ship lying next to the lock. This wind meant I would have to beat all the way down the Channel, and I had been warned that when the wind is blowing against the tide, the turbulence and chop is enormously exaggerated. In addition to this, I was concerned that my navigation skills were not up to keeping clear of the shoals while at the same time zigzagging about the Estuary. The centreboard would have to be down, of course, and this increased the likelihood of sticking on the bottom – my experience with the barbed wire on the Severn above Shrewsbury had already shown me how disastrous that could be even in a mild current. In short, I was uneasy.

'I think I'll be okay.'

'You've got a proper chart of course, haven't you?' asked one of the three. I proudly showed them my specially doctored Ordnance Survey Map. The early morning was damp and I wished I had used something a little more permanent than fountain-pen ink. The head-shaking increased.

'An anchor?' queried the other. I pointed out the besser-block lying on the foredeck and waggled the rope at them playfully. The looks they exchanged spoke volumes. By this time the water level in the lock was dropping, and I and the dinghy were gently descending with it. The three had to crane over the edge of the lock to see me. And still the questions came.

'Food and water? It's a long way to Madeira.' Ah. I hadn't thought of this, but then remembered that somewhere in my bag, I had … ah yes, here it is. A Mars Bar. I held it up for inspection.

'Radio? Compass? Foghorn?' The words came dropping gloomily down the blackened well of the lock as the dinghy descended deeper and deeper, and my spirits dropped with it. 'I've got a tin-whistle,' I called back brightly, but no reply came echoing down from the invisible trio thirty feet above me. The only thing visible now was the rectangle of grey sky and that high green flag, still blowing from the south-west, but drooping even as I watched. The dank black walls and dripping gates rose sheer on every side as I continued to sink. It was like being lowered into a grave.

One last call descended hollowly. The invisible Captain Eggersley was saying: 'Look, I've just consulted the tide tables again. It's the equinox. Today's tides are predicted to be the highest in thirty-six years. Leave it a week and they'll be back to normal. How about it?'

I stared up at the grey sky and that flag, thinking. I was certainly being offered a way out. It was arrogant of me to ignore the concerned and professional advice of these men who dealt with tides and shipping every day of their lives. It was all very well to play this hero game on quiet inland waters – to exaggerate the dangers of bulls and barbed wire, willow trees and weirs, and then laughingly go on my way regardless. It was fine to play the mythical wanderer, pretending that any goldfinch or bright star was an omen, a portent of good fortune to bless me on my way. But here there were no omens, and no belief in any oracle save that of common sense. Was I really wise to venture out onto one of the most treacherous tidal channels in the world, in an unpowered and ill-equipped dinghy, and with a contrary wind to boot?

I glanced up once more at that drooping flag. The wind had now died completely and the flag lay inert. But now, having tried everything in His arsenal to dissuade me, including sending his personal deputy, Captain Eggersley, God finally turned around and said, 'Well then, go on if you're going. Off with you ... and here's a present to help you on your way.' For as I watched, the inert green flag twitched. It twitched again, then fluttered out faintly once more. Within a minute it was bellying out in a fresh wind, a new wind, a wind blowing steadily ... from the north. It was just the wind I needed.

'Well?' came that disembodied voice from the heavens again.

'Open the gates, thank you. I'm on my way.'

*

And after all that, it was easy. I rowed out onto the estuary waters at the very top of the tide, a vast brown-silver stretch of calm waters almost a mile wide, and had my sail hoisted and rudder down in two swift easy moves. The northerly filled the scarlet sail as I reached across to the central channel and then turned south. My makeshift map was spread before me on the decking, the day was warming up, and I sluiced through the sand-coloured waters with enough speed to give me plenty of steerage.

Even once the tide had fully turned and started its long fierce ebb, the impression of tranquillity remained. Drifting with the water, of course, I was not aware of how fast I was actually travelling – only landmarks on the shore could tell me that, and these were so far away that they too crept minutely, serenely, by.

At times I would spot a distant buoy or beacon post and check my home-made map, ticking each one off as I passed it. Sometimes I would notice that two buoys, one behind the other, were shifting oddly in relation to one another and I would realise that the current was carrying me sideways across the main channel while my only apparent motion was forward.

The day grew so warm and the sailing was so easy – lying in the stern, steering with an idle elbow, watching the dreamy glide of the hazy land passing – that I was in more danger of dozing off than anything.

As the first of the two great Severn Bridges approached, I sat up and took notice. I had been warned that the tidal current here was at its fiercest and that I would be reaching this point round about half-tide, the period of maximum flow. There was still a fair following wind, but I shipped the oars into their rowlocks in case I needed extra power. It was only when I was virtually under the giant span, and too close to one of the upright piers for comfort, that I realised the strength and volume of water that was bearing me along. The brown water piled up in a foaming, bulging wave four feet higher on the upstream side of the piers than the surface downstream, and poured in an angry, tawny torrent beneath the mighty bridge. I was swept so swiftly along that the breeze no longer kept my sail bellied out, but let it flap idly as the current bore me quicker than the wind itself. At least here there were no worries about headroom. Far, far overhead a trail of tiny vehicles were on their way to Swansea across that shining span.

The turbulence was worse under the second bridge – below the piers the water churned into a cauldron of eddies and back-currents and muddy-coloured whirlpools that sucked at *Jack*'s keel and tugged alarmingly at the rudder. But so light and buoyant was she that the boiling race could never really get a grip on her shallow hull as it might have done on a larger boat. For all Captain Eggersley's experience and advice, I think I can now claim as true what I had guessed at before: a small dinghy with its lightness and shallow draught was in some ways safer from the shoals and tidal rips than many larger craft.

Not in all ways, however. By one o'clock the wind had died to nothing and I was rowing hard for the shore towards the enormous concrete pier at Avonmouth. The tide, swifter than I had calculated, actually swept me past the pier when I was a mere two hundred yards out from it, and yet it took me another hour of muscle-cracking, back-straining rowing to take me around the end of the pier and into still water. I tied up with shaking, sweaty hands to the rung of a ladder against the pier wall and regarded Captain Eggersley and his pet performing tides with new respect; I had very nearly made that predicted trip to Madeira after all.

The pier at Avonmouth is titanic. From where I moored to the ladder, it was an eighty-foot ascent to the top of the pier. I knew I would have to wait here several hours for the last third of the ebbtide to run out before catching the incoming floodtide up the Avon to Bristol, and I was careful enough not to make the classic mistake of mooring *Jack de Crow* on a short line. If I did so, I would return in two hours to find her dangling down the wall from her painter, fifteen feet above the ebbing tide. No, I left her on a nice long line so that nothing could possibly go wrong. Then I clambered up the wet, barnacled iron ladder to the top of the pier.

I was met by the Harbourmaster of Avonmouth, a relaxed gangling fellow with amused eyes, clearly no relation to Captain Eggersley. 'Ah, well done,' he grinned. 'I was wondering for a while if you'd ever make that last half mile. Come and have some lunch.'

We repaired to his office on the end of the pier, a vast affair of glass and computer screens looking for all the world like a ship's bridge. Here, over sandwiches and coffee, he showed me the electronic instruments for measuring tides, currents and winds, the radio system and the radar screen. 'We've had our eye on you since you left Sharpness – or tried to at least. There's not a lot of metal on your boat, is there? You could sell the design to the Stealth project, no problem.'

He had also rung the Coastguard who had been on full alert, and Captain Eggersley to tell him that the black armbands were no longer needed. Then he turned the topic to football, his son's schooling and life in general. A pleasant two hours passed until a green wavy line on a computer screen told us that the tide had turned and it was time to be on my way.

'You did leave her on a long line, didn't you?' he asked.

'Oh yes,' I replied. 'No worries there.'

And with that and a cheerful thanks for the sandwiches and coffee, I went back along the pier to the ladder-head. I leant cautiously over. Yes, there she was, more than eighty feet below like a tiny yellow toy duck at the foot of that vast wall. She was sitting on grey mud, but even as I watched a swirl of rising water was licking at her bows and soon she would be afloat again.

I clambered gingerly down the iron ladder that plunged away below me, but when I was still fifteen feet above the dinghy, my feeling foot met air. I glanced down, wondering why I could not find the next rung.

Next rung?

There wasn't one. Nor one after that. Nor even after that.

The ladder stopped short just where I had tied the painter two hours previously – between me and *Jack* there was nothing but a sheer drop of black, mud-slimed concrete wall. Clearly the designers of this gargantuan pier had only ever expected gargantuan ships to dock here and had not seen the need for a ladder to descend fully to the muddy ooze.

Sigh ...

I climbed all the way up the ladder again, marched off to the Harbourmaster's office and explained the problem.

'Doesn't reach the bottom? Good Lord, I'd never noticed that before. Deary, deary me. You do have a problem, don't you?'

I marched back to the ladder head and glanced around. Over there was a bundle of old nets and floats and ... yes ... a rope. Back again to the office.

'Yes, old boy. Take what you like. It's all old stuff.'

With a great coil of hairy, slimy, coarse hemp rope over one shoulder, I made my way once more down the ladder. There, some-how, with one hand only (the other being used to cling on to a slip-pery rung) I managed to tie a bulky knot to the lowest rung and then steeled myself to abseil down into the dinghy. At the very last second, just as I'd taken a deep breath to swing into action, I remembered to untie *Jack*'s painter first. (Had I omitted to do this, I'd have had a further two-hour wait in the dinghy until we rose high enough to reach the ladder rung once more.) Holding this painter in my teeth – it tasted of barnacles and salty mud – I launched myself down the abseil rope. I would like to be able to claim that the manoeuvre was executed with the ease and elegance of an SAS-trained marmoset, but honesty compels me to admit that I went down that horrible rope like a bead on a string, serious rope burn only being prevented by the ancient sliminess of the mud that smeared its hairy length. I banged hard into the barnacle-encrusted wall three times as I descended, and believe that I actually let go of the rope for the last six feet, falling in a muddy, shaky heap into the bottom of the dinghy. Luckily, she was now fully afloat. Had she been resting on the mud, my clumsy landing would have surely sent a foot straight through the thin hull. As it was, no damage was done and soon *Jack* and I, muddy but unbowed, made our way around the pier end, waved goodbye to the Harbourmaster behind his glass walls and turned our noses up the Avon for Bristol.

*

The incoming tide swept me up across mud-flats at a steady five knots, with barely an oar stroke needed. In the dazzle of the after-

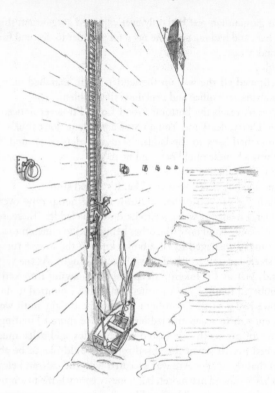

The Ladder Runs Out ...

noon sun, the mud-flats were no longer drab grey but silver-blue as they reflected the wide sky, and they were teeming with bird life. White gulls stood above their own reflections; redshanks and curlews picked daintily over the slabby mud, and flights of duck whirred into the air as I passed. As the channel narrowed and tussocky salt marsh closed in on either side, the odd gaunt heron could be seen poised frozen on the margins – and as the marsh gave way to flat grassy pasture, flocks of green lapwings shrilled and piped and flew with their big rounded wings flopping and rolling and pivoting in the air.

It was splendid. I was on a magic carpet, woven of soft greys and bright silvers, faded sea-greens and blues, a carpet that bore me silently along in the wide, empty afternoon sunshine, as much part of the landscape as the plovers and gulls that inhabited this bewitched no-man's land.

Soon the channel deepened and narrowed to a surprising degree. The teeming mud-flats gave way to mud-cliffs, and these in turn were replaced by black, kelp-covered cliffs of stone. Every now and then I would pass a white house perched on the cliff tops, all curved walls and tiny windows in the manner of a lighthouse. When the tide is fully in, they must squat right at the water's edge, their clean white and blue paintwork reflected in the river, but now they clung high up on the rocks like teeth on unhealthy black gums, thirty feet above the river. At intervals mud-filled creeks would cut down through the rock banks littered with lopsided yachts lolling on the gleaming mud like abandoned toys. In three or four hours' time they would all be dancing at their anchor chains once more, alive and awake.

Later the gorge became steeper and higher still – huge cliffs of orange sandstone above the river; and then there was the historical Clifton Suspension Bridge a hundred feet above me, soaring between its square stone towers; and finally the huge gates of the lock that would take me up forty feet to the floating harbour of Bristol Docks. I had made it, completed the journey from Colemere Woods to Bristol and finished on a note of success and inner contentment – and there was absolutely no question of *Jack* and I parting company just yet.

'How about London?' said *Jack de Crow*.

'London it is,' said I.

Wi' a Hundred Locks an' A' an' A'

Vogue la galère.
(Row on whatever happens)
—RABELAIS, *Gargantua*

Approaching by water, it is easy to believe that Bristol was once regarded as the most elegant city in England. The long harbour snakes for two miles between wharves busy with ships of every description, from tiny sailing dinghies to blunt-nosed tugs, from old schooners to *HMS Great Britain*, moored in splendid retirement. Everywhere you look, someone is doing something on, to or with a boat. Sails are being mended, awnings stitched, engines greased, ropes threaded, narrowboats restored, and a little black Puffing Billy steam engine runs up and down the quayside on narrow rails adding to the air of busy purpose.

On the north side of the harbour rises a long steep ridge, and up this climb the Georgian houses of eighteenth-century Bristol – the fashionable city of Jane Austen's novels – in every elegant shade: cream, rose, pastel golds. This too is the city of Isambard Kingdom Brunel, the great engineer of the nineteenth century who strode about the country with his cigar, knocking up railways and viaducts, tunnels and termini as breezily as a boy playing at sandcastles on the seashore. I was rather hoping his flamboyant shade still haunted the place and would lend me some inspiration; I had a few engineering projects in mind myself.

If I were to continue to London (travelling overland via the Kennet & Avon Canal to the Thames), I would need to conserve funds. This I planned to do by converting *Jack de Crow* into a yacht, so that I could sleep aboard each night.

Well, no, not a yacht, but something more than an open dinghy. To this end I hauled her ashore near a friendly boatyard and over the next three days plunged once more into the baffling world of carpentry.

76

The idea was very simple, and lifted straight from *Coot Club*, one of the Swallows and Amazon books. In it, Tom Dudgeon equips his little dinghy *Titmouse* for sleeping aboard by making an awning that drapes over the boom at night and laces down either side like a tent. This I would do, but whereas Tom slept curled up in the bilges, I planned to make a sort of removable decking, allowing me to lie on a flat platform level with the thwarts. I hit on the idea of constructing some planks that by day would sit lengthways in the bilges under the thwart and replace my old bottom-boards, but by night would fit snugly across the dinghy side by side and create a temporary deck to lie on.

The carpentry involved was basic, but it still took me three days to complete – three days under the open sky and a mercifully warm sun. I was lucky to have the aid of Dave, the taciturn young man who owned the boatyard and kindly lent me the tools and advice I needed, advice such as *'No, that's a screw you're holding. It needs to be inserted with a screwdriver, not a hammer,'* or *'Please never use my best chisel as a screwdriver again or I'll drown you.'*

In the next-door workshop was a blacksmith, and he made me a crutch, a thin pole of iron with a horseshoe-shaped piece of steel on the top. This slotted neatly into the pintel holes where the rudder fitted and would support the end of the boom; the boom then could act like a tent's ridgepole for the awning. The awning itself was a large blue tarpaulin that I took along to a sailmaker's loft overlooking the little Puffing Billy railway and the harbour wharf. Here a girl sewed a strip of Velcro along the front edge and five eyeholes down each side. Through each of these protruded an elastic strap with a hook on the end. When the awning was draped over the boom, the front of the tent was velcroed shut around the mast and the five hooks clipped onto the gunwale, leaving a skirt of tarpaulin dangling outside the dinghy. The back end remained a clear triangle open to the air.

During my three days in Bristol I stayed with an ex-student called Alex. He had only just left school and was in his first week of university, an exciting time of new freedoms and throwing off the shackles of home and school – just when you want a former teacher turning up to stay on your sofa and tell embarrassing school tales to your new flatmates. Alex bore it with his usual exquisite manners and good grace. He is a tall, dreamy, flop-haired lad with all the aggression of a Buddhist gazelle. Oddly enough, every character he

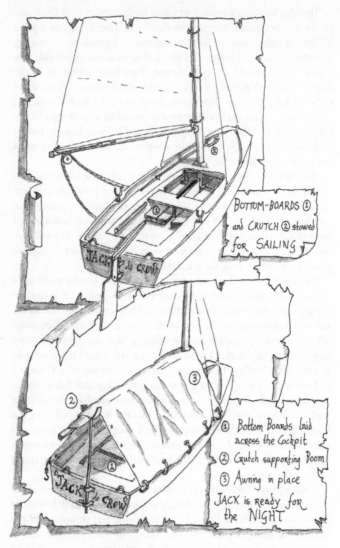

BOTTOM-BOARDS ① and CRUTCH ② stowed for SAILING

① Bottom Boards laid across the Cockpit
② Crutch supporting Boom
③ Awning in place
JACK is ready for the NIGHT

Jack de Crow *by Day and Night*

had played in school drama productions over the last five years had demanded a cold and violent nature. A superb actor; nevertheless I had sometimes had a job to stir him to the necessary heights of bitter rage demanded by each part – threatening to pin his beloved goldfish to the drama noticeboard just before opening night usually did the trick.

When it came time to leave, Alex came down to the dockside, admired my handiwork and presented me with a special bottle of something called Hobgoblin Ale. Then I hoisted sail once more, and *Jack* and I tacked our way up the long harbour, heading inland once more.

*

My love affair with Bristol faded as quickly as the afternoon wind died. Rowing out of the city was a grim business. On and on I rowed as darkness fell, but still I found myself behind Tesco supermarkets or derelict goods stations where wafts of sewage and pungent chemical odours rankled on the damp evening air and drove me on, looking for a mooring place where I would not be asphyxiated as I slept. I was also spurred onwards in my dreary rowing by a gang of youths who jeered from a concrete stairwell. My temptation to stop and give them a short Baden-Powellesque lecture was stifled when they stopped flinging comments and started flinging half-bricks.

By the time I had left the suburbs behind and trees had crowded in on either side, it was pitch dark and I was cursing myself for breaking one of my Rules – the one about never, ever continuing after dark.

Suddenly around a bend ahead there came the blare and tinkle of jazz trombones playing 'New York, New York' at full volume and something resembling the *Louisiana Belle* came steaming down the river, decked out with fairy lights in orange, gold and red. I plunged out of the way to one dark bank and immediately tangled the mast and stays in an overhanging tree while the party boat swept by. Fifty merry, sozzled passengers raised their glasses to the little yellow dinghy crashing up and down in the wake, pinned to the bank by a spotlight beam that blinded the pith-helmeted figure within.

"Allo, Doctor Livingstone,' they happily cried. 'Have a drink! Are you alright there? Gawd, it's Michael Palin. Cheers! Bye,' and those vagabond shoes strayed off down the dark river and left me and *Jack de Crow* filling up with willow twigs and sploshes of water in the choppy wake.

Ten minutes later, eight of which had been spent carefully extricating myself from the twiggy clutches of my captor willow, back she came jazzing away like a full chorus of Seraphim and Cherubim but twice as glittery, and sent me ploughing into another willow to the brassy strains of 'When I'm Sixty Four.'

In the end, however, she turned out to be my saviour. Half-an-hour later in a dark and bosky bend upstream, I found her moored against a section of river bank backed with steep woods, and her whole cargo of happy inebriates piling out into the little waterside garden of a warmly lit house. In the light from the party boat's searchlight I could make out a sturdy pontoon with proper mooring rings and I decided that here was my best chance of a safe place to spend the night. As it turned out, this was the *only* place I could have moored that night in safety. I did not realise until the following morning that this stretch of the river was tidal. Had I tied up to the bank anywhere else, I would have found myself high and dry by midnight, and as likely as not sitting on submerged rocks that would surely hole the dinghy. Mooring to the floating pontoon ensured that I stayed afloat whatever the tide level.

That night was the first spent sleeping aboard. After a meal and a beer or two in the little pub, I crept outside, past a little tinkling fountain and a spotlit statue of Venus knee deep in ferns, and down to the dinghy. Here I set up the awning, put my decking planks in place and unrolled a thin foam mattress. Ten minutes later, to the gentle rocking of the stream and the small rippling night sound of the river, I was fast asleep in my new home.

*

The Avon River winds its way up to Bath to join the Kennet & Avon Canal that would take me over to the Thames. The river widened into a long sunny stretch where a fleet of sailing dinghies were holding a regatta, zigzagging about between reedy banks and wide pastures. There seemed to be two races going on, one among seven or so slim white Lasers, and the other, to my delight, among a fleet of Mirror dinghies, *Jack*'s red-sailed, snub-nosed sisters. I could see the puzzled faces of the other boatmen, frowning as they tried to place me as I sailed up the reach alongside the other racing Mirrors.

As we reached the buoy that marked the limit of the racing

course, one by one my fellow Mirrors neatly rounded it to beat back up to the finish line. I kept sailing, of course, rippling on towards a wooded bend upstream. Faint cries of alarm came from concerned skippers behind me, petulant cries about rounding the buoy and following the correct course ... and something about a bridge. But what cared I for rules and races, buoys and bridges? Let others compete for their tin trophies; I was on my way to the wide world beyond, leaving these tame sailors to shake their heads over the clubhouse coleslaw and ask in wonder, '*Who WAS that pith-helmeted stranger?*'

I should have listened about the bridge, though. Unlike all the bridges encountered on the Severn, this one was a foot too low to allow my mast through, and I spent an awkward ten minutes in a welter of collapsed sail and tangled stays in an attempt to lower the mast and scrape my way upstream beneath the bridge's blackened arch.

Before ever I left Ellesmere, I had rigged up an innovative contraption to allow for this contingency. On a normal Mirror, the three wire stays holding up the mast are bolted firmly to the gunwale by shackles, useful screw devices for such semi-permanent fixtures. However, I had rigged up the forestay to a running pulley system so that by simply releasing a rope I could loosen it off and let it run free, thus allowing the whole mast to lean backwards and, if needs be, lower completely to the deck. I could even haul the mast upright again using only one hand. I was really very proud of my Auto-Pulley-o-matic Ezy-hoist, and I found that the next ninety miles were to justify its presence to the very hilt – they are pretty niggardly in the south-west when it comes to bridge headroom.

Rowing upstream, slight though the current was, was proving to be tedious; I had not realised how much I had been taking for granted the gentle onward flow of the Severn. I found myself singing almost continually to keep up a steady rhythm – old folk-songs, hymns, numbers from musicals – anything to drive me onwards through the water. But always there was something to catch my eye, something to cause me to rest on my oars for a few seconds and make the toil worthwhile: a pair of jays, blue-winged, flying out of an oak copse maybe; the discovery of some skullcap with its indigo flowers hidden beneath a grassy bank; or on one occasion a grass snake gliding across the stream just in front of the bows, so near that I could have leant out and scooped it into the dinghy.

Finally I came to the City of Bath. I rowed on all in a dream into its gracious Georgian heart and came to the graceful curving horse-shoe of the weir below the Pulteney Bridge. Here three cascading steps prevent craft from proceeding further on the Avon River and I must have made an intriguing sight for day-trippers on the bridge, gazing down to watch the oarsmen in the dinghy hanging on his oars and scanning the silver crescents of water ahead for a way forward. Baffled, I paddled around the wide green foaming pool like a confused toy duck until some kindly stranger on the bank pointed back downstream and mouthed the word 'Lock!' above the sweet roar of tumbling waters. Back I rowed a half-mile and there discovered my onward route. Here is the western end of the Kennet & Avon Canal, which rises sharply through six locks to continue its journey across the Wiltshire Downs and so to the east-flowing Thames a hundred miles away.

Bath is as beautiful as the postcards show it, a gem of Georgian elegance in honey-coloured stone. Avenues and arcades spread their amply respectable elbows as luxuriously as after-dinner smokers in a Hogarth painting. Graceful curved facades bask in the sun, tall windows conceal elegant drawing rooms behind rich brocade drapes, and in the spacious squares about the abbey buskers not playing Byrd, Purcell or Elgar are taken quietly away and shot.

The abbey itself is famous for the vast windows of clear glass on every side – its epithet is the Lantern of the West. It is a light, airy building with none of the sombre heaviness of Gloucester and Tewkesbury. I visited also, of course, the famous Roman Baths ... fascinating – or rather, that is what one is supposed to say. But Bath will remain in my mind not as the most important Roman site in Britain, nor the cultural and spiritual centre of the south-west, but as a place where I moored next to a bright garden where a pome-granate tree clambered up a sunny wall, its round fruit as glossy and magical-looking as in an eastern folk tale. It needed a hoopoe or a pair of turtle doves in its William Morris branches of course, but was otherwise perfect. Bath will also be forever the place where I nearly died, dashed to death in the deepest lock in Britain.

Serious Inland Waterway enthusiasts will have been somewhat hurt and puzzled that I have not given some ink and space so far to the joys and terrors of locks. The fact is that even though I had been through twelve or so locks since halfway down the Severn, it was not until the start of the Kennet & Avon Canal that their presence

Paddle

Winch Handle

Boom

Top Pound

Top Gates

Footbridge

Apron

Bollard

Bottom Gates

A LOCK
and its environs

Bottom Pound

began to loom large in my life: larger and more frequently than I would wish on my bitterest enemy.

Canals are artificial rivers but without the flow. Their sheer banks make them a death trap for any badgers or hedgehogs careless enough to topple into them, but otherwise they are charming and picturesque additions to the English countryside. They wind their way along the contours of the land – occasionally ducking through tunnels – on a flat placid level for miles on end; such flat sections of canals are called pounds. Inevitably, however, they must make their way uphill somehow, and it is locks that allow this. A skipper of a boat approaching a lock from downstream finds himself facing a massive pair of black wooden gates, usually decked with hart-stongue, moss and maidenhair ferns sprouting prettily from the woodwork. Once these are opened, the boat glides forward into a narrow compound of concrete walls that rise up to twenty feet above him on either side. The gates behind him are shut fast, some sluices ahead of him (called paddles) are winched open, and water pours into the lock from above, raising the boat higher and higher until he finds himself on the new upper level of the countryside with the next pound stretching away before him. There he discovers that there is a further pair of gates ahead. Once these upper gates are opened, the boat can glide out and continue on its way.

Sounds simple, doesn't it?

'But who is doing all this paddle-opening and gate-shutting?' you may ask. 'If the skipper is steering in and out of the lock, who is it operating the lock itself?'

The usual answer is the skipper's crew, but in cases such as my own, going through a lock consists of the following steps.

1. Moor up and climb ashore 100 yards below lock.

2. Step around nicotine-stained old tramp staggering about on towpath.

3. Go to bottom gates and wind paddles up.

4. Watch water level sink slowly … slowly …

5. Slowly …

6. Until level with bottom pound.

7. Politely agree with horrible tramp that yes, they ought to abolish all the ostriches (…?).

8. Heave and push and haul and strain against long, slippery black-and-white painted beam to open lower gate.

9. Notice 'Wet Paint' sign.

10. Attempt to wipe hands and trousers clean of black and white paint.

11. Wonder where the blazes the lock-keeper is.

12. Assure tramp somewhat shortly that yes, I know I've got paint all over me. No, I don't want your hanky. Or your meths to remove it, thank you very much.

13. Return 100 yards to dinghy.

14. Row dinghy into dank, cavernous lock.

15. Bash into walls while trying to bring dinghy alongside ladder.

16. Holding painter in teeth, start climbing slimy ladder to top of lock.

17. Realise lock is so deep that the painter is not long enough to reach more than halfway up the wall. Damn, damn, damn …

18. Cleverly tie painter to ladder rung with one hand while clinging on with other hand.

19. Finish climbing out of lock.

20. Heave lower gate shut, avoiding paintwork.

21. Winch open paddles in top gate.

22. Wait for water to rise.

23. Wait some more.

24. Wait some more.

25. Realise that water is not rising and that I have committed the cardinal sin of lock operation, i.e. not closing bottom paddles before opening top paddles, thus turning the entire length of the Kennet & Avon Canal into a freely flowing river.

26. Turn to find lock-keeper returned from lunch-break.

27. Listen to irate lecture from lock-keeper about improper use of locks. Tramp nodding sagely over his shoulder, with occasional 'I-told-you-so' headshakes.

28. Hurry to close bottom paddles, bright red.

29. Watch water rise.

30. Quite quickly actually ...

31. Suddenly realise that the ladder rung halfway down where my painter is tied is about to vanish under fifteen feet of rising water.

32. Shin down ladder like steroid-crazed orangutan and struggle to undo knot while water rises.

33. Finally undo knot when it is a foot under churning brown-scummed water full of dead carp.

34. Scramble to top of ladder with soggy painter held in teeth and tie it to bollard.

35. Borrow meths after all to rid mouth of dead-carp taste.

36. As waters rise level with upper pound, heave open top gates.

37. Row dinghy out. Moor up again. Close gates and paddles.

38. Repeat whole process SIX MORE TIMES.

Of course some of the above steps may be omitted if conditions allow, but *Jack* and I went through the whole gamut in that first of the Kennet & Avon locks in Bath: tramp, paintwork and all.

Each lock had its own little surprise to spring on an unwary *Crow*. Some would allow the prow or gaff to catch under a ladder rung as the dinghy ascended and I would have to make a flying leap to free her before she was dunked under and swamped by the rising waters. Others would fill, not by a steady welling up from below the surface but by a sudden horizontal gush of white water from the top-gates that threatened to fill poor *Jack* with half a ton of canal water and rotting badger if she ventured too close under the cascade. All in all, the one hundred and six locks of the K & A kept us very much on our toes.

Sometimes the lock-traversing experience was made delightful by the presence of passers-by and spectators who almost universally wanted to help. This often took the form of well-meant but irritating advice (*'No, no, you'll strain your back if you do it like that. I had an uncle once ...'*) but I remember the very smart lady in a wide-brimmed hat, red as poppies, and a suit more fitted for Ascot than the rigours of lock operating, who insisted on performing the entire procedure herself. I simply sat in the boat and called out instructions from below. This lady took me through not one lock, but three in a row, and after each lock produced a box of Belgian chocolates and rewarded me and herself with one each. She also kept up a constant stream of bright chatter about how jolly it all was, and did I regard myself more as a Captain Hornblower or an Arthur Ransome hero. When she finally waved me goodbye with a beautiful hand begrimed after the third lock, her smart suit crumpled, her hat askew, she called out *'Swallows and Amazons forever!'* Warm-hearted dottiness seems to haunt the waterways of Britain, and my voyage was largely fuelled by the likes of these encounters and kindnesses.

*

Just below Devizes there is a horrible thing known as the Caen Hill Flight. The Flight is a stairway of twenty-nine locks, one after another, stretching over two miles of steady ascent. Narrowboats take about five hours to traverse the flight so must reach the first of the locks by ten o'clock in the morning. After that time, no more vessels are allowed through until the next day. Accordingly, I had carefully set my alarm clock the night before to wake me at 7.30 a.m. This would allow plenty of time to row the few miles to Caen Hill and be there for the ascent. What's more, there was bound to be a queue of narrowboats – I could slip in with one of them, concentrating on keeping *Jack* out from beneath the propellers of my leader vessel while her crew did all that tedious paddle-winding and gate-swinging above me. Thus, remora-like, I would batten on an unwitting host and save myself the back-strain.

It was with a sinking feeling that I woke the next morning with the sun shining brightly on the blue awning, the birds chirruping in a suspiciously mid-morningish sort of way and my alarm clock inexplicably declaring that it was still half past two in the morning. It had stopped.

Not knowing the true time, I dressed, bundled the awning and mattress away and set off rowing up the canal like a demented windmill only to reach the Caen Hill Flight at five minutes past ten. The last boat had just entered the first lock. Not only was I not allowed through that day, but due to a water shortage the flight wouldn't be open again until Monday, two whole days away. I would just have to wait, explained the lock-keeper with an apologetic shrug.

My Herculean feat of overland haulage at the Frankton Locks was not to be considered; not only was the distance just over two miles, but it was also uphill all the way. Unless I had some sort of trailer, I mused. Nearby was a farm, Foxhangers Farm, and off I trotted to see if they had such a thing as a boat trailer which I could borrow for a few hours. They did – and I could – for five pounds ('Deposit?' I enquired brightly. 'No, rental fee,' they replied flatly). The trailer was mine for the day.

Even with a pair of wheels, the haulage operation was no picnic. The dinghy had to be de-rigged, de-masted and emptied of its luggage, and even then seemed to weigh a ton; *Jack* had clearly been putting on weight since Frankton Locks. As I trudged up the long steady incline of the towpath, dragging *Jack* behind me, bystanders stopped and stared; they glanced from me to the canal beside the path and back to me again, and I could see the thought flitting across their worried brows – *Here is a chap on foot pulling a dinghy … NEXT to a canal. I wonder if I ought to point out the obvious?*

No one did, however, so no one received a rabbit chop to the neck, and I continued the long slog uphill, stopping every two minutes as a jellied wreck. But before I was a quarter of the way up the towpath, someone zoomed up on a quad-bike. I recognised him as a man I had encountered the day before, a lock-keeper who had given a very good impersonation of a clinically depressed Kodiak bear with toothache. Your average British Waterways employee, in fact, or such had been my opinion at the time.

He had clearly had a frontal lobotomy since yesterday.

'Want a hand with that?' he enquired cheerfully. 'Go on, hitch her on the back then and I'll take her to the top for yer, Captain. Lovely day, innit?'

Off he whizzed and off I went back down the hill to fetch the rigging. In all, the overland route took just fifteen minutes less than the watery route; the last canal boat for the day was just chugging through the top gates.

*

Devizes was a grey little town, it seemed to me; the skies had clouded over after weeks of bright sunshine. I seem to remember being invited to a fiftieth birthday party for a chap called Ron, but how and why, I have no idea. That evening is lost forever in a bright cider-tinted haze. The following morning I dimly recall trying to install some fenders I had bought the afternoon before – hollow plastic sausages in blue and yellow with loops to be threaded on a length of cord. While I was doing this, I was attacked by a swan.

I have not said much about swan encounters so far, although from Frankton Locks onwards I had been bailing them up, pursuing them, startling them, beating them off with oars or being hissed at by them every two hundred yards. They had rapidly become my least favourite entry in *The Observer's Book of British Birds*. Nobody except me seemed to have noticed, but frankly there were far too many of them. I had been whiling away the hours of rowing by composing in my head a stiff letter to Her Majesty the Queen – who owns every swan in Britain apparently – hinting that a little ruthless swan culling wouldn't be amiss. Clearly this particular swan had added mind-reading to its arsenal of sinister qualities and decided to silence me before such a letter could be sent.

To be attacked by a furious swan when one is balancing low down in a dinghy, one's hands full of fenders and string, and suffering a throbbing, cider-induced hangover, is not an experience I wish to repeat. It is all a nightmare of hissing and huge wings, a nasty orange bill and mad little eyes – a little like being mugged by an enraged archangel. It was only when I managed to grab an oar and take a swipe at it that the wretched bird retired steaming and ruffled to the other bank. Pity poor Leda. I didn't hang around – the fenders could wait. I took off and rowed east as fast as my oars could take me.

*

Out of Devizes the canal enters a quiet empty land of fields and flat pastures. Sedges and bulrushes throng the banks and crowd even into the middle of the canal in places, making the rowing warm work. The grey skies have cleared once more. Nothing stirs in the hot afternoon glare but small flocks of birds – sparrows, chaffinches and a party of long-tailed tits that flitter from hawthorn bush to hawthorn bush in chirruping excitement, or gorge themselves on the blackberries that hang in rich clusters along the bank.

So drowsy is the afternoon and so bountiful the brambles that I spend a happy hour picking blackberries from my dinghy pulled in close to the bank opposite the towpath. Here the crop has remained unharvested by passing picnickers, and the fruit hangs bright and heavy and ripe for the plucking. Soon my pith helmet is full to the brim and my fingers are stained with the sweet purple ink; my bare sun-browned arms too bear the evidence of blackberry picking, the odd white scratch or smear of blood from a thorn that has gone deep. It strikes me with an almost physical blow how lucky I am to be here. The rest of England is at work, pinched into suits and smart shoes in city offices or serving burgers in stifling motorway eateries; bathed in the pallid green glow of computer screens, or directing traffic in a haze of hot exhaust, or sitting in sweltering classrooms trying to lure back 3B's attention from the bright world beyond the window to the dates of the Armada in front of them. And I? I am standing in my shirtsleeves in the hot September sunshine, balancing aboard a buttercup-yellow dinghy, picking blackberries. I am Tom Sawyer playing hookey; Laurie Lee in his rich Slad valley; the boy Arthur in the Forest Sauvage, dreaming of giants. I am Sandy Mackinnon, in fact, aged twelve, picking blackberries in my own beloved valley above Adelaide and the holidays stretching away to the horizon.

*

The Kennet & Avon Canal rises in a series of four more locks from the village of Wootton Rivers. At the first of these I found a narrow-boat moored alongside, also waiting for the go-ahead to proceed. Her name was *Diana* and on board lived John and Di, who within ten minutes of chatting had taken out adoption papers, got me to sign and adopted me as the son they had always wanted.

John was a shortish middle-aged chap with a capable manner and quiet eyes – and selective moments of deafness to Di's steady stream of Cockney badinage. Di herself was a woman with 'land-lady' written right across her broad bosom, hair the peroxide tint of barmaids everywhere, and the sharpness and boldness of wit to match.

Their offer to tow me through the first lock extended to the next three – then 'Why not the tunnel, luv, and since yore 'ere, yoo'l join us for sangwidges, wont 'e, John. John? JOHN? Gor blimey, 'e's switched right orf again, I dunno, 'e'll forget 'is own 'ead one day …'

Over thick, succulent tuna sandwiches eaten on a sunny lockside and followed by homemade coffee cake and mugs of tea, Di expounded on Life. 'It's funny, Sandy, innit, but wot I fink is yer got to *make* time, ain'tcha, uvverwise wots it all abaht, eh?' Here she handed me a mug the size of a small barrel. 'I mean, take kingfishers. *I* see kingfishers, *yoo* see kingfishers, even John 'ere sees kingfishers. But John's sister, now she dahn't see 'em, does she, does she, John, even when there's one right under 'er nose? There's one, I says, right there, but she can't never see 'em cos, like, I don't fink she's got inner peace, if yoo know wot I mean.'

She paused to let out a long sigh. 'I fink inner peace is somefing yer got or somefing yer ain't – yoo got to be special to see kingfishers … sort of all quiet, like.' Three seconds of inner peace would follow, and then we'd be off onto the next topic: Water Voles and the Art of Give-and-Take, for example. She was marvellous.

That evening at Little Bedwyn we moored up on a peaceful grassy bank where white geese grazed in a meadow. As I was setting up the awning for the night, Di came down the towpath and fixed me with a beady eye. 'Now look 'ere, Sandy. I'm not doing this out of charity like – and it's no good saying no 'cos I won't 'ear of it – but yore coming for supper tonight on board *and* yer'll eat wot yer given, and there's the shower there also to use as yer like, orlright? And 'ere's a glass of white to be getting on wiv, okay?'

Well, I'm a timid sort and hardly dared refuse. Of course, I'd have preferred to wander off to a pub in the dark, spend an outrageous sum on a microwaved Chicken Kiev with French Fries and spend the evening reading beer mats – but one must make sacrifices at times. One mustn't be selfish. So I forced myself to have a scaldingly blissful hot shower aboard and ended up choking down Di's honey roast ham, the pease pudding, hot green beans and onion sauce, the chocolate sponge and the selection of fine liqueurs afterwards before deciding that I had been dutiful enough and retired to my little floating bed.

Coming awake on *Jack de Crow* was always lovely – to watch the golden-green reflections of reeds and morning sunshine rippling just half a yard from my feet through the open triangle of tent; to see the faint mist curling off the water and smell wet grass and water mint crushed between *Jack*'s hull and the spiderwebbed bank an arm's length away – these are faint previsions of Heaven. But when on this particular morning it was supplemented by John standing barefooted on the dewy grass in his pyjamas and holding a breakfast tray, it was beyond the dreams of angels. There was a mug of aromatic coffee; buttered toast with scrambled eggs, light as a cloud and sprinkled with black pepper; slices of toast with thick, dark marmalade – and a silver knife and fork winking in the bright sun, wrapped in a flowery napkin. And a note: 'Bon appetit. Get your skates on. We sail in an hour. Di.'

I don't remember exactly how many days *Jack* and I remained firmly attached as adopted waifs to *Diana*'s motherly wing. From the sheer volume of information I learnt about John and Di's life history and philosophies and the amount of superb food pressed on me at every opportunity, I would guess six months, but my diaries seem to indicate two days at most. Meanwhile, on we glided, leaving the wide skies of Wiltshire and down into the thatched-cottage, chocolate-box villages of Berkshire.

*

And so we draw near to the end of the Kennet & Avon Canal where it joins the mighty Thames at Reading. Several days passed in sunny innocence, days in which I rowed beneath a warm sun through a gentle landscape, one feature of which was the little concrete pillboxes every mile or so along the northern bank of the canal – a relic of the Napoleonic War but revived in the Second World War to act as a line of defence against any invasion from the south. It seemed odd at first to think of this quiet pastoral wiggle of water being any sort of military Maginot Line – why, it looked narrow enough to leap across – but I soon realised that to an advancing enemy it would certainly create an obstacle, especially when covered by firepower from these sturdy pillboxes. Nowadays each one is half covered in brambles and periwinkle and used to store fertiliser bags by local farmers, or for less reputable purposes by the young folk of the area.

It was along one such section of the canal that I decided to go bathing. Here the River Kennet ran in and out of the canal at intervals so the water had largely lost its murky dead-rabbit colour and was relatively clean. It was a solitary spot, so I decided that a bit of skinny-dipping would not go amiss. I enjoyed a happy ten seconds snorting and wallowing in the canal before deciding that in the interests of preserving my extremities, I would leave this sort of sub-zero bathing to the Finns. Just as I was hauling myself out of the depths, however, there came a rustle from the hedgerow and out stepped an elderly gentleman with a brace of charming beagles at his side. Clenching my teeth, I lowered myself back into the frigid waters.

Mr Beagle did not seem perturbed by the sight of a blueish torso rising from the canal waters; in fact, he was inclined to chat. After some genial questions, he told me of the annual rowing race that takes place in these parts, the longest of its type in the world. It runs from Devizes to Westminster along the canal with all its locks and then onto the Thames and down to London. The only stipulation is that the boats must be light enough to be carried over the locks, British Waterways not being geared up to cope with the sudden heated rush of a hundred or so excitable contestants. My beagle man went on to explain that many years before, when he had been working at the nearby paper mills, he and some colleagues had constructed a rowing boat out of corrugated cardboard. The resulting vessel had proven to be so portable and light that it had won the celebrated prize … and then had promptly sunk below the Houses of Parliament after being holed by a piece of driftwood the size of a matchbox.

'By golly, it was cold in the river as I remember,' he reminisced, 'and that was only June. Things must've got warmer since then. You certainly seem to be enjoying your dip,' he added before raising his hat politely, calling his dogs and sauntering off down the towpath. That was the last time I tried skinny-dipping in the waterways of England – my extremities have never been quite the same since.

Death and the Dreaming Spires

Slow let us trace the matchless vale of Thames;
Fair winding up to where the Muses haunt ...
          —THOMSON, *Seasons*, 'Summer'

From Reading the Thames flows sixty miles south-eastwards to London, which meant that I could finish my journey in about four days. But as I rowed out onto the broad green river in glittering sunshine there was Caversham Bridge spanning gracefully over its reflected light and shadows, and I thought of all that lay upstream: the villages of Pangbourne and Goring with their willowy lawns and stately riverside manors; the old Roman town of Dorchester-upon-Thames; then Oxford, of course, and all its associations, and so on all the way to Lechlade in the Cotswolds where there lived a certain lady I had not seen for some years and thought I might surprise.

Besides, the breeze was blowing steadily from the south and like all those enviable heroes in every adventure story you've ever read, my time was my own – I was in no hurry to get to London. The decision was easy. I would go and chart the length of the Thames before turning around and making the final run down to the capital.

It was glorious to be out on a wide river again. I had barely been able to sail at all over the last eighty miles and my progress had been a fitful series of stops and starts. But here on the Thames it was different. With a southerly breeze I was able to ripple along upstream at a good pace, past the islands and outskirts of Reading, past the riverside houses with their velvety lawns, their elaborate Tudor boathouses and their monkey-puzzle trees, and so onward to the Goring Gap. This was a very different river from the Severn. Here was wealth, here was prime real estate, here along the waterside fringes of each stripy-mown lawn was a coil of brand-new razor-wire – a picturesque detail that somehow got left out of *The Wind in the Willows.* On the Severn, meandering down that wild Welsh border, people rely on the indefatigable brambles – or vicious swans or mad bulls or the Severn Bore – to secure their property from passing boaters, but here in the broker belt trespassers are warned off by movement-sensor spotlights, Securicor personnel and the absolute certainty that one will be sued for damages by the family lawyer if so much as a croquet hoop is displaced.

Above Reading long hills rear on either side. These are the Chiltern Downs flanked with beech forests turning to red gold, and topped with grassy ridges seamed with bridleways and footpaths through the springy turf. At their feet nestles the mellow-stoned manor house of Mapledurham, the model for Ernest Shepard's illustration of Toad Hall. Then comes Pangbourne crouching by its wide white weir. Here I stopped for the first afternoon and totally failed to appreciate its prettiness and charm due to the rain that had suddenly blown up from the south and settled into a steady soaking downpour.

I had, up until then, been extraordinarily lucky with the weather. Now, however, the rain seemed set to stay, so I moored up at the Swan Inn above the weir and trudged off to find my favourite of all places when in a strange town: a laundromat. You can keep your tea shops and coffee houses and pubs, where one is never far enough away from one of those cappuccino machines that sound like mating fire-extinguishers. On cold rainy days there is nothing quite so cosy, quite so warm and womb-like as the local laundromat. Outside the big plate-glass windows, shoppers hurry past in the downpour, heads down, coat collars up, dancing along the kerbs between dirty puddles and ducking in front of steamy-windscreened buses. But here is the blast of warm air and the comforting hum and rumble of tumble-dryers, the clean smell of soap powder and endlessly fascinating articles in eight-month-old women's magazines about Forgiving His Nasal Hair Problem or Attractive Christmas Wreaths You Can Knit Yourself.

Laundromats are also the best place, the *only* place in fact, to write letters, which is how I planned to spend my rainy afternoon in Pangbourne. A long, important letter to write and hours to do it in. But first, a quick phone call from the booth across the road ...

Here's a good trick you can play if ever you're bored. Take a cigarette, half-smoke it, and then, without stubbing it out, leave it smouldering in the Coin Return flap of a public telephone seconds before someone arrives to use it. Then watch from a distance as said person finishes his call and sticks a probing, change-searching finger straight into the flap and onto the still-burning cigarette butt. Wait for the yelp, appreciate the faint smell of scorching flesh and the loss of temper, and then run like blazes. This stunt is provided courtesy of the Pangbourne High School student body and is guaranteed to prevent the victim from holding a pen comfortably for the next three days. So, while my washing went round and round, instead of writing letters I sat and read how to avoid unsightly earwax build-up instead.

*

The next few days saw the weather alternate between solid rain and bright skies, but all the while a blustering knockabout wind drove me up the river in a succession of squalling blows that patted the steely brightness of the water to slate-dark catspaws. It was so swift and exhilarating that I remember very little of the countryside and landmarks that I passed. All my concentration was on where the next gust was coming from, and watching for a sudden gybe that could easily capsize me.

I came to Oxford late one afternoon just as the purple skies opened once more. Before I could moor up, I was drenched to the skin and shivering with cold, flexing my cramped hands after long hours of holding the mainsheet hauled in. Abandoning *Jack de Crow* I hurried up Headington Hill to find warmth, dryness and a large drink at the house of an old friend, Jo.

Jo, an energetic woman in her late forties, has the zip and crackle you get when you throw a bicycle into an electrical substation. Over the last few decades I had enjoyed the hospitality of her family in Yorkshire farmhouses, villas on Ithaca, cottages on the Cornish coast or in deep Devon woods, the Dordogne, the Highlands and by quiet Surrey golf courses – that easy brand of hospitality that points out where the coffee is kept, throws you the *Times*' crossword and makes it quite clear that sofas are for curling up on.

For the next four days the rain continued to blow in gusty waves, and Jo insisted that I stay until the weather cleared up. This I was only too happy to do; four days of sleeping under a quilt the size and softness of a cloud, of writing letters (my scorched finger had healed), reading books and cooking all the exciting things to be found in Jo's kitchen cupboards that had not yet made it to the

"And No Birds Sing ..."

Ellesmere Supasave: sun-dried tomatoes and tzatziki, pesto, ciab-
atta, Mocha coffee and Malaysian starfruit-flavoured yoghurt –
things like that. Four days also of dashing out between the showers
to cycle on Jo's bike around Oxford: the Radcliffe Camera; the
Eagle and Child pub where the Inklings met to read aloud their
works in progress; the grounds of Magdalen College and its deer
park; the wild, beautiful graveyard of the Church of the Holy
Cross where Kenneth Grahame's tomb lies amid a tangle of briar
and seeding grasses; four days of renewed admiration for the
group of Oxford dons and their friends who in the 1940s spun

enchantment out of their scholarship like gold from dust and straw.

After four days of ease and Jo's good company and artichoke pesto on pumpkin-seed toast, the weather brightened and I had no longer an excuse to linger. After bailing several bathtubs of rainwater from poor abandoned *Jack*, I set off once more to row upstream, through Oxford and beyond. I had always imagined the Thames (or River Isis as it is mysteriously called in these parts) to flow past all the Colleges, the dreaming spires, the lawns with their wallflowers and ancient groundsmen, the honey-warm stonework and mullioned windows, and black-gowned academics cycling absent-mindedly to lectures cancelled in 1945. But it doesn't. Instead, it rather half-heartedly dives for one edge of the town, slips under a few bridges, skirts cautiously around the Head-of-the-River pub where rah-rah-ing Oxford Rowing Club types sit on sunny afternoons and drink themselves silly, and then makes a dash for the countryside again without so much as a glimpse of a College Quadrangle or a Porter's Lodge.

Above Oxford the character of the river changes again. It narrows to a meandering lane of green, wandering like a lost child between flat meadows and reedy banks – sailing around these wiggly curves had the old excitement of playing at follow-my-leader. Then in a more serious mood the stream straightens out between row upon row of iron electricity pylons and thin plantation trees whose paper-dry leaves whisper and rustle in the dying breeze.

As I rowed into the featureless dusk, songs and stories and snatches of poetry ran through my mind in a steady litany to keep the weariness at bay: Father Brown and Flambeau rowing up a winding creek beneath a goblin moon to find Prince Saradine in his house of reeds and mirrors; Tolkien's errant mariner who '*wandered then through meadow lands to shadow-lands that dreary lay*'; Saki stories where a walk among English hedgerows and flat fields reveals wild beasts and casual death – a child taken by a hyena, a girl gored by a stag; and from *La Belle Dame Sans Merci* the mournful words:

> *O what can ail thee, knight-at-arms,*
> *Alone and palely loitering?*
> *The sedge has withered from the Lake*
> *And no birds sing.*

What can ail thee, knight-at-arms? Lack of food, lack of beer and an over-vivid imagination, that's all. The twinkling yellow lights of the lonely Maybush Inn shining out through the darkness at last cured all three. An hour later the gentle rocking of *Jack de Crow*, a cosy sleeping bag and deep dreamless sleep drove all the dark phantoms far, far away.

*

I had visited Lechlade many years ago when I first arrived in England. Before I had left Australia one of my students, a gentle girl called Emily, had said to me, 'Oh, when you get to England, you must go and visit my aunt. She's just lovely. AND single,' she had added pointedly. 'Her name is Daisy May and she lives at The Meadows, Lechlade. You'll get on so well.'

Daisy May of The Meadows! With a name like that, how could I not get on well with her? In my year's travelling to England overland, especially on hot tropic nights, I had held a picture in my mind, a picture of a muslin-smocked Daisy May gathering forget-me-nots in her Cotswold cottage garden and waiting for me to turn up. Oh yes, and singing madrigals. She was bound to sing madrigals, from merry morn to moonrise, Daisy May of The Meadows ...

When I arrived in England, I found my footsteps meandering towards Lechlade and soon enough, just to be sociable you understand, I found myself standing on the doorstep of a cottage whose name-plate had half vanished under a cloud of honeysuckle and yellow roses, and knocking on the old green door.

Silence, while I went through various explanatory opening lines.

'Hello, you don't know me but I was told by your niece Emily whom I taught in Australia which is where I'm from to come ...'

No, too convoluted.

'Hi, Sandy's the name, you must be Aunt Daisy.'

No, too familiar.

'Do you sing madrigals?'

Possibly, possibly ...

My reverie was broken by the door being flung open and a voice snarling out of the gloom: 'Yes? Well?'

The figure before me was not quite what I had conjured up in my mind on those sleepless tropic nights. She stood before me, a gaunt, iron-grey woman with short-cropped hair, a hatchet face and aggressive eyes, swathed in a crumpled dressing-gown. Visions of forget-me-nots and muslin smocks dissolved. She had something of the wolfhound about her, and if she sang madrigals at all, she would probably be taking the bass line.

'Oh … er … um,' I stammered.

'Oh, er, um?' she echoed. 'Hardly helpful. What do you want? Speech therapy?'

'Ah … I … oh,' I continued.

'Oh, for God's sake!' she snapped. 'Stop doing vocal warm-up exercises and tell me what the devil you want! Well?'

I decided flight was a better option than explanation. She had begun to bare her teeth.

'Look, I'm terribly sorry to have disturbed you. You don't know me, I was just calling on the off-chance but I see it's not a good time to call and I'll be off now,' I babbled as I backed down the cottage path.

'Oh no you don't. You've woken me up. You've dragged me to the door. You'll explain to me right here and now who the blazes you are and what you want or I'm calling the police. You have thirty seconds. One. Two. Three …'

Somehow an explanation, involving hot tropical nights, Miss Daisy May, my single status and forget-me-nots, tumbled out in a rush.

From the doorway came a snort of grim amusement.

'Daisy? You want Daisy? She lives next door at The Meadows. This is actually Number Three, Meadowgate Cottage. People of low intellect like the postman are always muddling the two. Bell's the name, Frances Bell. Come and have a drink.'

Relief and embarrassment swept over me in equal measure.

'Oh, look … no … I … '

'Oh for God's sake, don't start that again,' she growled. 'You'll come in and have a drink now that you've disturbed me, or I *will* call the police. Daisy's out but will be back in an hour. And if you stutter again, I'll have you shot.'

And that is how I met Mrs Frances Bell. Within minutes I was seated on a large shabby sofa with a gin and tonic in hand and deep into a conversation about T.H. White, C.S. Lewis, William Morris, the Pre-Raphaelite painters, The Anglo-Saxon Chronicle, the deplorable state of Eng. Lit. among Oxford graduates these days and terminal cancer – the last of which, by the way, she had. Hence the mid-afternoon nap, the dressing-gown, the cropped hair and wolf-like expression.

Her reaction to the condition was to give it extremely short shrift, along with anybody presumptuous enough to express sympathy. Bouquets of flowers left by well-wishers, I later learnt, were put immediately through the compost shredder, wrapper and all. Repeat offenders had the resulting mulch returned to them in small paper bags. 'Get Well' cards were cut up into individual letters and rearranged in the manner of a hostage note to spell rude anagrams.

When I questioned her about this, she replied very firmly, 'Look, Sandy, to the whole village, goodwilled or not, I have suddenly become an object of interest, of tattle, of gossiping sympathy – a potential invalid with a dramatic disease that can handily become the focus for all their latent mothering instincts, all their charitable Sunday impulses and a boost for the bloody florist. Once I accept that role, the role of dying mother of two boys, the brave-but-cheerful-to-the-end victim, then I'm done for.'

But aren't you anyway? I thought but could not of course say out loud. She read my mind.

'Of course I'm not done for. This is my body and my mind where I live, and I will not have things going on uninvited inside it. And I will certainly not pander to it by smiling wanly and building a tomb for myself out of flowers and bloody cellophane. No buts, Sandy. If it's a choice between playing the tragic but gracious invalid or staying alive until my boys are grown up, then I think I know which is the more important, don't you? I'm not fighting it, because there's nothing to fight. Unlike the local council – now there's a battle worth fighting!'

And her grey eyes sparkled as she lay on the sofa and told me about her ongoing campaign against the idiocy and greed of various council members who were planning to build a housing estate on the quiet brook-bordered meadow that lay beyond her window. Frances was conducting a one-woman war against the proposals and had so far, it seemed, been successful. All over the Cotswolds, members of the Lechlade Council were known for their nervous twitches and haggard eyes, and sales of hard liquor had soared at the local bottle-shop.

Before I departed that first afternoon, she invited me back to dinner to meet the family the following Wednesday. When I explained that I would be in London then, she curtly handed me a train timetable and said, 'There *are* trains, you know. Big choofy things that get you from A to B. London is A, Lechlade B. Work it out, chum.' I reckoned the local council didn't stand a chance.

In years following I was invited over once or twice and continued to come away exhausted, exhilarated and more admiring than ever. (I think on one of these occasions I did actually meet Daisy May, but she rather paled in comparison.) But the last I had heard from Lechlade was that the cancer had gone into remission – panicky retreat from Moscow more likely – as had the local council, whose members had finally given up the unequal struggle and left the meadows to the larks and dragonflies and forget-me-nots.

It was four years since I had seen Frances and the family, and I pulled in eventually under the Ha'penny Bridge on an afternoon of blustery rain. For the last few miles the tall Cotswold-grey spire of St John's church had dominated the horizon ahead, wavering to and fro like a swinging compass needle as the river meandered and wound through gentle meads.

I left the boat moored under a willow by the old woolpack bridge and made my way through the wet streets. Even under grey skies the Cotswold stone glowed with characteristic warmth, and the shops and houses on either side of the broad High Street looked prosperous and well proportioned. Antiques and old prints sat comfortably alongside genteel fabrics; second-hand books and William Morris tapestry cushions tempted me from shop windows but in vain. I found the little lane between stone walls that led to Meadowgate and walked along it, startling a blackbird bathing in a puddle. It flew off in a glitter of scattered raindrops and sat scolding from a nearby pear tree whose golden fruit hung over the wall as perfect as one of those Morris cushions.

But when I reached the gate of Frances' cottage, I knew that there would be no gruff bark or caustic quip after all. There was an air of dereliction about the place; a row of untended shrubs in terra-cotta pots, now greening over with mould, a drab curtain that hung half shut and askew in the sitting-room window, and the honey-suckle, a massed tangle of dead brown twigs and curled fading leaves which hung too heavily over windows and doors. There was silence, of course, when I knocked damply on the door. I didn't wait very long, but turned back up the little lane and made my way back to town. There on the High Street was the little art shop run by

Daisy May, but when I pushed my way through the bell-tinkling door I saw a lady that I did not know standing behind the counter. Daisy, it seemed, had gone to Australia for a month to visit her relatives out there ... and yes, I was told with a rueful shaking of the head, poor Mrs Bell had died three months before. The cancer had returned, and the end had been really quite quick. Such a loss, she murmured. Such a very ... *spirited* lady, she added, and I wondered briefly if this was one of the kind souls who would be picking shredded cellophane out of their garden beds for years to come. The family were away at the moment, but was there a message?

I stepped back out into the dull afternoon, despondent and suddenly very tired. I stood for a while indecisively and then made up my mind – my main reason for coming to Lechlade had been chopped from under me, so I would follow my original idea. I returned to *Jack de Crow*, donned my pith helmet (how Frances would have cut me to shreds over that) and set out to row upstream as far as I possibly could while the afternoon light lasted. The physical action of rowing soon cheered me a little – Kipling's cure for the camelious hump seems to work just as well for despondency – and I resigned myself to the fact that she had had her wish after all; the two boys must be grown now, through school and out of the nest. And she had fought long and hard and with grim humour to save what she believed in ... though I fully expected her to break through from the other side the moment I mouthed to myself those mawkish words ... and besides, one cannot be soulful for long when there is a boat to row, and the light green and dark green of willows and water are melting and merging on the river's glassy palette and a golden wagtail has just flitted, chipping fitfully under the white span of the foot-bridge ahead. It was only when I rounded a bend half a mile above Lechlade and saw the big new board in a field on the bank that comfort deserted me.

THAMESMEAD ESTATE, it read. *50 ACRES OF PRIME RIVERSIDE PROPERTY TO BE DEVELOPED FOR HOUSING AND RECREATION.*

For details, contact Town Clerk, Lechlade Council, High Street.

Had there been an observer on the footbridge or by the curved walls of the curious Roundhouse there that afternoon, he may have wondered why the boatman in the little yellow dinghy was propelling his craft along with oar strokes of such needless and sudden savagery.

Frances Bell had died in July. By mid-August, after a seven-year stand off, the bulldozers had moved in and work had begun.

My journey upstream was nasty, brutish and short. A few miles beyond the Roundhouse on its willowed island, the Thames had become little more than a brook between high banks. Ash and osier and willow closed in overhead, thick sedge and reeds clogged the river's course, and where they did so the current trebled in strength, making it all but impossible to work my way upstream. Some sour remnants of anger and adrenalin drove me onwards, my oars catching in clumps of vegetation every few strokes and the low branches raking across my hair. Visions of the Morda Brook closed in around me. Finally, I came to Hannington Bridge, a lonely stone bridge half-hidden in trees. Here the stream tumbled swiftly down over a shallow rocky bed beneath the arch, chattering between fallen lumps of rubble and masonry, and five attempts to propel *Jack* up and into the quieter pool beyond proved fruitless. As I rested on my oars after the fifth time, a kingfisher, dragonfly-blue, came skimming upstream, flashed past me and vanished through the darkened arch. An omen? A sign to struggle on through?

Possibly. But *Jack* and I were weary, and besides, it had begun to rain again. 'Out oars for Narnia,' I cried, turned *Jack*'s nose and started the long haul downstream.

Return to Reading

I chatter, chatter as I flow
To join the brimming river,
For men may come and men may go,
But I go on forever.
　　　　　—TENNYSON, *The Brook*

I rowed and sailed down the long empty miles to Oxford aware only
of a heron beating slowly downstream ahead of me or the quick rustle and clop of a diving water vole on the bank. It is here in these
infant waters of the Upper Thames that one can most easily set *The
Wind in the Willows*. There is the great meadow where Mole came
running on that first morning; here is the bank where Ratty lives,
his eyes twinkling like twin stars in the darkness of his hole. Over
yonder is the Wild Wood, the menacing mass of Wytham Great
Wood as mortals call it, where Oxford University scientists do eco-
logical experiments on carol-singing dormice and foot-shuffling
hedgehog urchins, and where you are not allowed to go unless you
are a biologist or a personal friend of Mr Badger's. And somewhere
here surely in a reedy backwater by a foaming weir is that island,
Pan's Island, the setting for the most beautiful chapter in English
prose ever written: 'The Piper at the Gates of Dawn.'

Rowing back through Oxford I turned up the Cherwell River to
see if I could find a scholastic mooring place as befitted the bookish
Jack de Crow. The Cherwell is a dark, quiet, tree-shadowed river that
winds its dank and mossy way between the Botanic Gardens and
various secluded College grounds up to the Magdalen Bridge. Here
every year after the celebrated May Ball, a hundred or so honking
students ruin an equal number of dinner suits by leaping from the
ancient stone parapet into the slick-dark waters below, under the
mistaken impression that being drunk, plastered with duck-slime
and removing water-snails from their crannies for weeks to come
will render them irresistible to the opposite sex.

Just below the bridge I pulled *Jack de Crow* up onto a fine lawn of green-striped velvet beneath yellowing horse chestnut trees in a secluded arm of the Cherwell and set off with my rucksack to spend another night at Jo's place up the hill. Finding a way out onto the public streets was trickier than I thought, involving as it did crossing over several white wooden bridges, traversing a couple of willowy islands, ducking through tunnels, edging along wall tops, and finally climbing over a low gate onto the Magdalen Bridge itself. I felt rather like a participant in the Konigsberg Bridges conundrum or some Lewis Carroll problem in topology. It was not far from this very spot, in fact, that *Alice in Wonderland* was written, with its wealth of logical and mathematical problems disguised as hallucinatory fantasy. (How do you reassemble a chessboard to lose one square? Why does a mirror's reflection reverse from side to side but not top to bottom? Can one behead a Cheshire Cat if it is all head and no body?)

The next morning I sauntered down to the Magdalen Bridge and threaded my way through the gates-bridge-tunnel-island maze once more to where *Jack* lay deep in horse-chestnut leaves on the hidden lawn. Rowing hard and fast down the inky Cherwell, I made my way out into the broad glitter and sunshine of the Thames once more.

Thence to the Iffley Lock and Abingdon. The latter is the oldest inhabited town in Britain, claims the museum there, which celebrates that fact somewhat surprisingly by displaying nothing more than a collection of paper doilies through the ages, watched over by a hawk-eyed lady hovering in case anyone is overcome by the sheer excitement of it all. I managed to stay upright and calm, and kept on downstream.

It was early evening when I turned into the narrow entrance of the River Thame and rowed up between high rushy banks, snaking my way to the ancient Roman town of Dorchester-upon-Thame. This quiet village lying amid flat meadows and high earth dykes was once the cathedral capital of ancient Wessex and Mercia; the abbey was built in the seventh century and boasts a unique window whose branching stonework imitates living trees. The rector, I had been told, was a certain John Crow – perhaps a cousin of our own beloved *Jack*. It seemed a perfect place to stop for the night.

Yet as I moored in a little meadow under the shadow of the abbey where the little Thame had dwindled to a mere brook I felt terribly lonely and tired and dispirited. The sun had set like a frozen red blood-orange behind thorn trees ragged and bare. For the first time since leaving, the air was icy cold and already it seemed that a blue frost was crystallising on the bleached grass of the field. As I struggled with the awning and the decking to prepare *Jack* for the night, I noticed with dismay how wet with dew everything had become. I toyed feebly with the idea of treating myself to a bed and breakfast room that night, but told myself firmly that such extravagance was unwarranted. What was the point, I scolded, of making a beautiful awning and a lovely decking and setting off to have exciting adventures if I just kept bolting for hot baths and warm duvets every time it got a little dewy round the ears?

'Oh, shut up, shut up, leave me alone,' I whimpered. Then I violently jerked the awning into place with a frozen hand and fell backwards into a clump of nettles.

'See!' said that other voice. *'That's what happens when you get all grumpy. Now stop making a fuss. Besides, the stings will keep you warm.'* I was on the point of mentally clubbing my inner school-marm with a metaphorical brick when a real voice intruded into the conversation. It sounded remarkably like the one I'd been about to silence.

'You! What is that boat doing there?!'

An iron-haired lady was looking over a gate above me, two black labradors panting frostily at her side. Green wellies, padded jacket, leather dog leads held like some mediaeval weapon; I recognised the formidable archetype of the English countrywoman. A little wearily I replied, 'Sorry, is this private property? I'd thought the river banks would be common land.'

'I've no idea,' she trumpeted back. 'I'm simply curious why a Mirror dinghy – it is a Mirror, isn't it? – should be tying up in the middle of nowhere. And what on earth's that blue thing?'

I explained the purpose of the awning.

'Lord! You're not going to sleep on the thing, are you? It's freezing.'

'I – '

'Nonsense!' she rapped. 'I've got a spare room and half a chicken that needs eating up. Now come along!' she called briskly.

'Um ... I – '

'Hurry up! The dogs are getting cold and need their supper. Chop chop!'

In ten seconds flat I had grabbed my hat and rucksack and without a backward glance at poor *Jack* was trotting to heel along the icy

Farewell to Oxford

road. After fifty yards she turned to me and said, 'Now, I'm a widow, mind you, and alone in the house, so I'm taking a risk. Still, I'm trusting you. I don't think you're a madman.'

A pause.

She stopped, glanced at me, her eyes lingering on the pith helmet. Then she added, 'Well actually, I do think you're mad, but I don't think you're dangerous,' and strode onward into the dusk.

People are extraordinary. I set out on this voyage with no very clear aim in mind, no Northwest Passage to discover, no treasure to find. But one treasure I did find on the way was a wealth of kind hearts and courageous spirits; I discovered a strange world where, despite the daily assault on our fears by the media, people are full of goodwill and take a positive delight in trusting each other. It seems the best way to get there is by Mirror dinghy.

On the following morning, after sincere and hearty thanks – it had been a delightful evening: she had lived and sailed in New Zealand as I had, was a gardener with a special interest in medicinal herbs, and her chicken in leek and white wine sauce was divine – I walked back to my abandoned *Jack* via the ancient abbey and rowed off to the Thames to continue south.

The day was yet again glorious, and it seemed that even in the fortnight since I had rowed up this stretch of river, the bright banners of autumn had unfurled on every tree and bush. However, although the sun was shining in a bright sky, there was a chill breeze over the water – when I rowed from sunshine to shadow, the air breathed icily on my bare neck.

As I rowed down past the Palladian water-steps of Rush Hall, past the busy, vulgar cheeriness of Benson's Boat Yard and round the river bend onto the long empty stretch down to Goring, I turned over in my mind an idea that had been growing ever since Bath. Somewhere, somebody had told me of a man who had planned to take his narrowboat from the Black Country to the Black Sea, crossing the Channel to Calais and entering the French canal system. From there, I had heard, it was possible to navigate on inland waters all the way across Europe to the Danube Delta on the Black Sea. The story sounded highly dubious to me. Weren't there some mountains called the Alps in the way? Wasn't the Rhine River full of rocks and rapids and Lorelei sirens luring sailors to their deaths? Wouldn't this man have been shot by Slovakian Secret Police or brainwashed by Bulgarian Communists – if he ever made it beyond the Anglophobic, onion-hurling French, that is? And as for crossing the Channel in a narrowboat ... well, that was plain suicide. Narrowboats are roly-poly, unwieldy vessels made of solid cast-iron and about as seaworthy as a tin pig. Ridiculous to even consider it.

But a Mirror dinghy? Now there was an idea. The more I thought about it, the more the idea appealed. I had tentatively mentioned it to one or two people along the way and met with various reactions. The main difficulty would be the other traffic; the Channel is the busiest shipping lane in the world. Jo in Oxford had explained that to cross the Channel in a Mirror would be like trying to cross the M25 at peak hour on hands and knees. John and Di on *Diana* had been cautiously polite, reluctant on so short an acquaintance to throw me to the ground, bind me hand and foot and slap me till I came to my senses. Several times Captain Eggersley had appeared in feverish dreams holding up shipping statistics and tide charts and threatening to shoot me with an emergency flare. Most worrying of all was the phantom appearance of Terry in those same dreams, standing on the bridge of *King Arthur* and giving me a cheery thumbs up and his *No worries, easy-peasy* grin while skeletal figures danced a grim hornpipe on the decks behind.

But as I hoisted sail after Benson Lock to catch the fresh northerly breeze and felt the rippling rush of water under *Jack*'s keel, noted her sturdy buoyant frame and valiant scarlet sail, and the way she dipped and heeled under the following wind, the landscape melted in my mind's eye and became quite, quite different. The silvery osiers solidified, calcified to white and shot skywards. The cold blue waters softened to salt-green and swelled in gentle rolling waves. A pair of nearby swallows transformed into a couple of great gliding gulls, suspended on a mild sea breeze that sent me skimming along under the White Cliffs of Dover on my way to France.

Yes, I thought. You have to try these things.

I had such a steady breeze that day and so full were my thoughts of P&O ferries out of Dover Harbour, Calais cockles and the salt tang of sea air on my lips that I swept past the undoubted delights of Wallingford and Moulsford all unseeing, rippled gaily beneath several fine Brunel railway bridges, whose curving brickwork beneath the arches does odd Escher-ish things to one's sense of perspective, kept up a shouted conversation with an elderly jogger on the river path for a mile or so (he thought a Channel crossing was a stupid idea as well) and found myself just downstream of the Whitchurch Bridge at Pangbourne, an elegant span of white iron and woodwork where herons roost, as the sun set in an apple-green sky.

With dusk, the wind died to nothing and a consultation of the map showed that I had two choices. I could either row back upstream the mile or so to Pangbourne or row the six miles down to Reading. Heaven knows why, but I chose the latter option. In fact, I found on my whole trip a deep, irrational reluctance ever to retrace my route, even by so much as half a mile and even when the benefits of doing so were clear. It stemmed, I think, from the feeling that this trip was in some sense a peregrinatio, the mediaeval practice whereby a monk or pilgrim would climb into a small coracle without oars or sail, push out to sea and go where the winds and waves took him. In this way, so the theory went, the holy traveller could be sure that he was going where God intended, undirected by fallible human agency. It was a way of putting oneself fairly and squarely into Divine hands and relinquishing that flawed desire to control one's destiny. St Brendan on one such trip even discovered America, Divine Providence working on a particularly grand scale on that occasion, though the canny saint had actually equipped himself with oars for the trip, contrary to the rules.

I, too, had oars, and a sail, but I felt that whenever the river current, the winds or my own lack of timekeeping skills took me further than was wise or swept me one way rather than another, I should take that as a cue. To ever go back, retrace my course, unwind the past was, I thought, to deny the designs of Providence, even if it did mean rowing six miles down a dark river to Reading of all places.

I had only rowed half a mile when Divine Providence manifested itself in the shape of three thirteen-year-old boys in a dilapidated motor launch. When a young tousled head popped out of the cabin and asked if I'd like a tow, I was delighted and flung him a line, saying, 'Gosh, thanks, yes if you don't think Mum or Dad will mind,' assuming the presence of adults below – a family on a boating holiday in a hired cruiser, perhaps.

The lad calmly tied my line on to his stern, replying over his shoulder, 'Mum or Dad? They won't know nuffink about it. They're at 'ome. Hang on to yer 'at.' Then he called below into the cabin, 'Righto, Eric. Let 'er rip!'

'Okay, Rodney!' came the reply and the launch shot off on a spurt of foam into the darkness. A second later the towline went taut with a resounding drip-flinging '*twangngng!!!,*' *Jack* shot forward like an excited puppy and I went over backwards from my standing position to a crumpled heap in the stern. Icy water welled up around my buttocks and for a heart-stopping minute I thought *Jack*'s bow had been pulled clear away from the rest of the dinghy by that mighty yank, leaving me to sink swiftly into the night-time Thames in the remaining half of the boat. And the life jacket was in the bows, of course, keeping safely out of the action as usual.

On recovering myself I found that the dinghy was intact – the impression of sinking was due to the flood of water bubbling up through the centreboard case with the spurt of speed. This water continued to fountain into the dinghy in excited sloshes while I lay there floundering. I struggled into a sitting position, jammed the centreboard down to quench the flow, edged nervously forward in the boat now skidding and surfing over the motor launch's wake, and called out, 'Excuse me … thanks for the tow and all that, but … um … could we take her a little slower, please?'

'Wot? Can't 'ear yer!' came back the reply.

'Um … could we slow down? SLOW DOWN PLEASE!'

'Wot?! 'Ang on. I'll cut the motor – '

'No, no!' I screamed. 'If you DO THAT, you'll – '

Too late. The young skipper gave me a smiley thumbs up and shouted below 'ERIC! Cut the motor!'

A half-second later, the roar of the engine died, the motor launch wallowed to a sudden stop, and *Jack de Crow* surged forward on a great rolling wave of glimmering foam. She nose-butted the launch's stern with a resounding crack and sent me once more reeling, face-down this time, into the watery bilges.

'So, wot was it you was saying?'

Soon, however, I found myself gliding down the river under star-light at a steady pace in the more capable hands of the skipper of the boat. This was Martin, another thirteen-year old boy, who had taken control of the launch out of the enthusiastic hands of Eric and Rodney.

'Sorry 'bout that,' he confided to me. 'They're me mates, but they're a bit thick sometimes. I'm tryin' to get 'em trained.'

Actually Eric and Rodney, when not in pivotal roles aboard ship, were thoroughly delightful, as was Martin. He had, he explained, inherited the boat from his grandfather. Most evenings he was on the river with or without his crew, exploring the backwaters, getting to know correct procedures in locks and marinas and equipping himself with the experience to run a boating business as soon as he could leave school. He had an air of purpose and quiet confidence rarely seen in one so young, and practical skills enough to negotiate Mapledurham Lock by moonlight unaided – no easy task when one is towing a small frail dinghy.

Eventually the lights of Reading came into sight around a bend and just above Caversham Bridge Martin expertly cast me loose and turned his motor launch upstream. Just before he chugged away he called out, "Ere! Wotcha gonna do when yer get to London?"

'I'm not sure yet,' I replied. 'Finish there, I suppose.'

'Nah!' came back the reply in triple chorus. 'Yer wanna keep goin'. Take 'er to France. Take 'er to the Med. Yer could go anywhere in that!' And off they went back up the river to their mums and dads and 'omework to be done before tomorrer. So that was it. My Channel-crossing idea endorsed by experts. It was good to know there were other right-minded folk in the world.

Capsize and Colleges

Then rose from sea to sky the wild farewell –
Then shriek'd the timid, and stood still the brave, –
Then some leap'd overboard with fearful yell,
As eager to anticipate their grave.

> —BYRON, *Don Juan*

That night it was bitterly cold. A peep out from under the awning at midnight showed stars flashing like crystals of ice against a blazing black sky. But the next morning was the loveliest yet. A thick white mist lay over the river and my awning and decks were furred with frost. Swans ghosted in and out of sight, heraldic birds in a silver world, and the early sun spun the mist from the river in skeins of palest gold. Before it had fully lifted, there came from somewhere down the river a sweet whiffling chuff-chuff-chuff-chuff – not the harsh snarl of a petrol motor but the unmistakable sound of a steam-launch.

Soon it came into sight, a little affair of polished teak and gleaming brass, chugging upstream with a snowy plume of steam billowing from its shiny funnel. The waters furled cleanly away from its bow in a V that set the river mist swirling and *Jack* rocking gently against the pontoon, and the day had begun.

Part of the point of a peregrinatio is that you do NOT say, 'I must get to Windsor Castle by tonight, come Hell or high water.' This annoys the Deity and He is likely to produce both of the above elements in copious quantities to make a point. Nevertheless, I had a commission to carry out. In a letter received some days before, my mother had set out in the clearest possible terms why it was imperative that I reach Windsor Castle by Saturday night: namely, so that I could attend the choral Eucharist there the next morning at St George's Chapel in the Castle. Why? Well for one, the service and setting were exceptionally beautiful. Secondly, every one of my numerous uncles had sung there as choirboys in their youth and would expect their nephew to visit as a mark of respect. Thirdly, the Queen might just be there and if it wasn't too much bother, Mother had a message to pass on to Her Majesty about tapestry wool or some such thing. I really can't remember. All in all, I was given the impression that it would be a serious dereliction of filial duty if I were to fail to make it on time. Thus I set out that Saturday morning with a good will to row the seventeen miles down to the royal seat of Windsor.

From the start things conspired to slow me up. A rowlock had begun to weaken around the woodwork and at mid-morning I had to pull in to a waterside boatyard to see if I could fix it – a messy and time-consuming job. By the time this was over, I found myself rowing into a boat race, a rather serious one, with motor-boats chugging up and down full of bossy men with megaphones telling me to creep slowly along the banks while the slim gulls-wing eights sped by, race after race.

It being a fine Saturday of sunshine and clear skies, the locks were busy and often there was a queue. This meant balancing on one's oars in the wake of much larger vessels charging in and out of the lock-cuts, ready to scramble for safety out from beneath a cruiser's bows or row like fury to make it through the lock gates before some happy holidaymaker slammed them shut under my very nose.

Thus it was that by five o'clock in the afternoon I had only just descended Boulter's Lock and still had seven long miles and several more locks to go before I would reach my destination. Divine Providence all day had been throwing large hints at me not to continue this headlong rush downstream to Windsor, and in ignoring them I missed the rich literary heritage of gracious Marlow – *Frankenstein* was written here, *The Wind in the Willows* just nearby – and missed also the opportunity to call in at Cookham and speak sternly to a certain Mr Barber who lives there. He holds the unique appointment of Her Majesty's Swan Keeper and I'd been keeping a running list of complaints about his charges and whiling away the lonely hours by thinking up some amusing swan-culling ideas I felt he should consider.

By the time I had crammed my way in and out of Boulter's Lock, I was shaky and sweaty with the effort. I was also aware that it had been three days since I had had a wash. My shirt was clinging stickily to my back, my skin was gritty with sawdust from my rowlock-mending efforts, and I was thoroughly fed up.

Then as I plunged crossly downriver below the lock, a narrow-boat chugged up behind me. Sensing my urgency the skipper called out, 'Want a tow? Where are you hurrying to?'

'Windsor!' I called.

'Windsor? We're going down beyond Windsor. Throw us a line.'

Two minutes later I was sitting back in the dinghy, relaxing for the first time that day and apologising to the sky, the water and the trees for my bad temper. Life is good, I told myself. People are kind, the world is beautiful, and another night without a bath would do me no harm at all.

After another couple of minutes, life got even better.

'Like a beer?' called the skipper, waving a brown bottle at me from the narrowboat's stern.

His mate started hauling the twenty feet of towline in closer and closer to the narrowboat and soon I was riding the wash, *Jack*'s nose just half a foot from the stern, swaying and surfing playfully like a dolphin trailing a liner's wash.

'Here we are,' said the mate, leaning over the stern rail as far as he could go. I strained forward to reach the bottle … nearer … nearer … one knee on the foredeck … shift of weight a little more and … and …

And life suddenly got a lot worse. *Jack*, creaming along at an unaccustomed speed, swerved under the weight on her foredeck and slowly, gracefully, inexorably turned turtle.

I disappeared under the icy green water in a tangle of stays and ropes, and into the Netherworld.

The River is a person. I did not know that until now. Up there in the sun and air the river is a highway, a playground, an artist's landscape, pretty-as-a-picture in white and blue. But here, down below the surface, I make the acquaintance of the Lady. She is cold-limbed and amber-haired and her teeth are the colour of gravel. Her skin is stippled all with rose-moles and glassy shadows play upon it. She arrays herself in fresh and flowing weed; silver fish-scales hang in her ears. Her voice is too low for human ear, but as she sucks and nudges she tells me her woes. I am seeking a new husband, says she, and if you stay another year down here, you shall be King, King of the River, blind as an eel.

Where is the sky?

Somehow, eleven months later, I kicked free of rope and stays in the waterish gloom and surfaced spluttering and wide-eyed, still, to my astonishment, with beer bottle firmly in hand. The skipper hauled me dripping out of the river onto the boat where I placed the bottle carefully on the deck. Then, spreading my arms in an extravagant gesture of thanks, I knocked the rescued bottle straight overboard again. Without thinking, numbly and automatically, I cried 'Whoops!' and dived straight back into the water to rescue it. Only on this second immersion did the icy shock of the water clear my head and I realise that perhaps I did not have my priorities straight. The bottle had, in any case, sunk like a stone – a sacrifice to the river-queen, and rather it than me. As the skipper hauled me out for the second time onto the barge, he said, 'Please, *please*, forget about the beer-bottle. We have others.' Then, with rueful eyes, together we surveyed the scene.

Jack de Crow lay completely upside down in the water, her yellow hull wallowing half submerged like a strange luminous turtle. On the broad bosom of the river floated various bits of debris – my parrot cushion, my pith helmet, my small rucksack that contained my writing equipment, wallet and so forth. The oars were making a spirited bid for freedom some way down the river, and only the Lord knows what had happened to the main baggage stowed in the dinghy – my rucksack, awning, mattress and sleeping bag. Gone to join the beer bottle no doubt, and live it up with the Maidenhead mermaids at the bottom of the deep green Thames.

A little motor launch was coming up behind us and it spent a busy ten minutes circling with a boathook, hauling the flotsam from the river and returning it to the narrowboat. Meanwhile, I had stripped to my underwear ready to dive back in to see if I could right the dinghy. As I stood there shivering in the evening breeze, I thought about it. The usual method of getting a capsized dinghy upright again is to stand on the lip of the hull and, putting all one's weight on the end of the protruding centreboard, lever the whole boat over rather as one might roll a small portly whale onto its back by hauling on its dorsal fin.

The problem here was that there was no fin – the centreboard had not been in place when she tipped. If it had sunk, as was likely, I too was sunk. Turning *Jack* over would be almost impossible. However, there was a chance that the centreboard might be jammed somewhere under the upturned hull in a tangle of lines. There was only one way to find out. Taking a deep breath, I dived deep into the icy green water and swam beneath the hull, soon finding to my relief the centreboard jammed against the submerged gunwale. So

Capsize!

far, so good. I surfaced again for air, dived once more and went through a slow-motion blurry-visioned struggle to poke the board back up through the centreboard case. Drifting lines snatched at my limbs, a coil of the mainsheet snaked softly around my head and I felt the sharp twang of one of the wire stays slice into my toes at one point, but at last it was done. The centreboard was poking up and out through the exposed hull. I surfaced, gasping for air. It was almost a surprise to see the late sunlight still there and the reassuring bulk of the narrowboat floating nearby, the anxious skipper watching on. Finally I went through the routine of righting the boat – a slippery clamber up onto the yellow woodwork; toes jammed against the gunwale lip; a steady haul on the fin; and the slow rolling of the boat onto its side as I fell backwards into the river's icy green bosom once more.

An agile sailor will clamber onto the centreboard itself as the boat comes half over and continue the rolling motion by hauling on the upper gunwale, even nipping over this and into the dinghy as she fully rights herself in one continuous move – a little like an acrobat staying atop a rolling barrel. This graceful manoeuvre I signally failed to execute; it was another twenty minutes of floundering and flopping before *Jack de Crow* was wallowing upright and I was sitting in her flooded bilges surveying the damage. Remarkably, there was hardly any loss. My rucksack had jammed tightly under the thwart and the various other items had been secured by straps, which seemed all to have held. Indeed the only thing irretrievably gone was my tin-whistle, which had been lying loose on the decking. And at least, I thought, as I began to shiver uncontrollably, I had had that much-needed and long wished-for bath.

While I had been performing clumsy aquatic stunts in my underwear, those aboard the narrowboat had made their own preparations. As soon as *Jack* was upright again and bailed out, I was taken aboard, wrapped in a warm, dry dressing-gown and handed a large hot whisky and lemon. It all goes rather hazy after that. I remember protesting and the skipper's wife pushing me firmly into a bunk-seat and assuring me that I would be delivered to Windsor that evening. When I tried explaining through chattering teeth and whisky fumes that it didn't really matter, it was just Mum and the Queen and St George's Chapel and the choir and Sunday mass and something-or-other, it all came out rather garbled – I think they got the impression that I was due to attend my royal mother's funeral service or something equally momentous. Whatever it was, the skipper's wife held a hurried consultation with her husband up on deck and they both came down with a new steely look in their eyes, saying: 'Don't worry, son. You'll not miss that service, even if we have to burn every stick of furniture aboard.'

*

The next three hours passed in a golden fog of warmth and vague contentment. Hot coffee followed the whisky, a light supper of cheese toast and poached eggs came somewhere along the line, and then more whisky again. Meanwhile, all my clothes and half the contents of my sodden rucksack were drying in the engine room, draped over hot pipes and valves and grills. To this day I regret that I cannot remember these people's names, though I do know that the skipper's wife was marvellously beautiful; also that when I asked the skipper what his profession was, he rather shamefacedly admitted that he was a North Sea rescue officer, more accustomed to pulling people *out* of sub-zero waters than tipping them in.

Several hours after dark, when my clothes were merely damp, my head had stopped swimming and I had finally persuaded them that they would not be receiving a letter from my solicitor concerning damages due, we reached Romney Lock just below Windsor. They were planning to get down to Weybridge that night and I had delayed them enough, but they still took some convincing that I would be alright – this stretch of the river was after all dark and empty, and they really didn't like to abandon me. In the end, to reassure them I told them that I had a friend living here, right here, not five minutes walk from the river, a very old friend who would be delighted to see me and yes, I was fine, honestly. They could sense, I think, that I was being cagey but perhaps assumed, from earlier rantings, that this 'friend' about whom I was being so vague was in fact the Queen, or at least some member of the Royal Household, and that I was not at liberty to divulge too many details. In any case they allowed me to reload my dinghy, made a final offer of a bottle of whisky to take with me (declined) and waved me goodbye with the faintest of curtsies and a royal bow as I rowed off to the bank, allowing them to chug away downstream into the night.

Once their lights had disappeared, I climbed out onto the shelving bank beneath an ornamental willow and considered my position. I didn't, of course, have a friend near here – in fact, I wasn't sure where 'here' was. It was unthinkable that I should sleep aboard the dinghy that night, with my sleeping bag soaked through and *Jack* still awash with water. It would have to be a bed and breakfast – it was to be hoped that they would accept soggy five-pound notes. If I could find one, that is. I appeared to be on the fringes of some large, dark, empty park. The night was clear and starry but bitterly cold, and I was beginning to shiver. Grabbing my wet rucksack and hat I strode off across smooth grass beneath stately trees towards a distant solitary light. This turned out to be a lamp post by a pair of high elaborate wrought-iron gates flanked by pillars. On one of the pillars was a name carved into the stone and gilded with a crest above it, dimly lit by the lamp. At last I knew where I had washed ashore: the hallowed grounds of possibly the world's most famous school, Eton College.

The security at Ellesmere had been fairly ferocious. What it would be like in the school where Prince William was no doubt sleeping in some nearby dormitory, not to mention the various young Honourables, Viscounts and Marquises dotted about the boarding-houses? Any minute now I would be arrested and shot as a deranged stalker of adolescent boys; or, more likely, a paparazzo attempting a few sneak shots. My dishevelled appearance was unlikely to reassure anyone.

Eton ...?

Slowly my mind clicked to a halt. By golly, I thought. I *did* know someone here after all. Not the Queen, but a Housemaster. He had taught at Ellesmere long before my time but remained good friends with some of my colleagues there, and I had dined with him once or twice.

I thought that in my present soggy plight, this slim acquaintance might justifiably be taken up. It was even possible that my House-master might welcome me with open arms; I seemed to remember that he had an interest in sailing – might in fact acknowledge a fel-low mariner in distress.

I knew his name but not which House he ran; a ring on the first doorbell I came to elicited a hollow reply from a speaker-phone set in the wall, which sent me off to an imposing Georgian porch down the road. Here I stood, composed myself and considered how best to initiate proceedings. I rang the bell there and waited until the door opened.

'Johnny-boy! Hi! Remember me? That night at Ellesmere three, no, four, years ago? Sure you do! We had some laughs, eh? Well here I am, so let the party roll.'

Or perhaps,

'Hello, I'm hypothermic, in desperate need of food and warmth and a bed for the night. We HAVE met but I wasn't blue then, I'll explain over breakfast in the morning. All right?'

Or maybe I should ...

'Yes, hello. Can I help you?'

I blinked. This wasn't the figure I remembered. John had been taller surely, with a moustache and brownish hair. This person before me was quite, quite different: short, silvery hair and wearing a skirt and blouse. It was, in fact, Mrs Doubtfire.

'Is Mr Clarke here by any chance?'

'No, he's out this evening, I'm afraid.'

Inwardly, I sighed. My newborn visions of hot baths and soft sofas were fading even in their bright infancy.

'Oh ... Oh, thank you. No, no message. Goodbye.'

'Goodbye then,' the lady replied and started to shut the door.

But just before she closed it, she glanced at me, poked her out-stretched palm through the doorway and asked, 'Is it raining? I thought it was fine.'

'No, it's not raining,' I replied. 'It's quite clear.'

'But you, you're soaking wet! How on Earth …?'

'I fell in the Thames at Maidenhead, you see, and I came ashore here and – '

'You SWAM seven miles from Maidenhead?!' she exclaimed, door wide open now and eyes wide with alarm.

'Oh no, no, no,' I stuttered.

'I think you'd better come in, dear, and warm up. Are you a friend of Mr Clarke's?'

'Yes … well, no … well, sort of.'

'Dear me, I don't think you're well. Let's leave that and sort it out later. Now come in and tell me all about it.'

And that is how I came to be sitting in the cosy parlour of Dame Jenny Jennings, Eton Housekeeper and surrogate mother and nanny figure to the sixty-odd boys of John's house. Before half-an-hour had passed, she had indeed sorted things out. There was no question of sleeping on a sofa; there was a bed made up in the spare room. John was out late with a friend who was also returning to stay the night, so one more down for breakfast would hardly matter. Meanwhile, a hot bath was running and if I dug out my pyjamas from the sodden rucksack she'd have them dried and toasty warm in a jiffy, and after that a light supper of boiled egg and buttery toast soldiers.

When it came to bedtime, I was fully expecting to be tucked up by the good Dame, say our bedtime prayers together and kiss Teddy goodnight, but she contented herself with letting me know that she would leave a note for John to advise him of my presence and would see me in the morning about getting the rest of my stuff dry. Mean-while, if there was anything I required, anything at all, she was just down the hallway.

I awoke early next morning. The large House was very quiet – all the boys were off on Half-Term – and soon I would have to saunter downstairs in Mr Clarke's second-best dressing-gown (my clothes were still damp), wander into the dining room and nod hello to the other stranger there and attempt to explain to Mr Clarke why I had presumed on our somewhat slim acquaintance.

So I lay staring at the high white ceiling as a lozenge of sunlight crept slowly across it and birdsong filtered in from the garden trees outside, my thoughts churning like butter, wondering what on earth I was going to say.

A tap came on the door, a jovial voice called out, 'Are you decent? Your morning tea, sir,' and into the bedroom bearing a tray of tea things bustled, of all people, Keith – Keith of the Ellesmere Common Room, Keith of the Morda Brook, dear and familiar Keith whose presence suddenly made everything alright.

An hour later we were sitting down to that breakfast, and Keith, hooting with delight, was exclaiming about the coincidence that had washed me ashore here on the one weekend in the year when he was down visiting his old friend. And yes, of course John remembered me; in fact Keith had been telling him only last night how I had sailed away down the Vyrnwy and was last heard of somewhere near Bristol, and that he'd not expected to see me alive again – and now here I was devouring bacon before his very eyes. John, though a little bemused by the coincidence, was kindness itself – in fact, Keith was staying on another night so I must too. The gods were keeping their promise; I'd had Hell and high water, but now the rewards were dropping into place one by one as neatly as alphabet blocks clocking into a box to spell a word – three words, in fact; a phrase: something along the lines of MACKINNON: LUCKY SOD.

*

Oh, to be in Windsor on a bright October Sunday! The massive grey walls of the Castle rose above the town and the guards in their scarlet uniforms had marched straight off the lid of a Quality Street chocolate tin. From the battlements the town below looked as a royal capital should look, a toy town of red roofs and cobbled streets, of golden weathercocks and starlings in swift squadrons, and the river glimmering away in a silvery ribbon towards the south-east.

And I had no excuse to linger. I bade farewell to Keith and John and Dame Jennings and made my way through the grounds to where *Jack* was waiting. To my surprise she had been neither stolen nor confiscated, not even by some titled under-gardener, and apart from several trees' worth of yellow willow leaves lying in her, she was fine and ready to go. I loaded her up, untied her and soon we were rowing steadily down the river watching Windsor Castle dwindle behind us into blue haze. We were heading once more for London.

London and the Law

A mighty mass of brick, and smoke, and shipping,
Dirty and dusty, but as wide as eye
Could reach, with here and there a sail just skipping
In sight ...

—BYRON, *Don Juan*

The Home Park, Old Windsor; Runnymede and the island where
the Magna Carta was signed in AD 1215; a fleet of Harlequin ducks
looking as ducks would look if they went in for Samurai dress code;
the M25 motorway bridge in its grey pall of exhaust: these are dimly
noted stages in the journey into London's outer suburbs. I remember
coming across a sailing vessel even smaller than my own just above
Staines, a three-foot model yacht whose rudder and sheets were
controlled by a tiny remote-control motor. It was being operated
from the bank by a young man absorbed in the task of sending it
tacking to and fro across the river, a ship from Lilliput manned by a
phantom crew racing me down the Thames.

I remember also watching an exotic flash flying off into some
treetops, a rainbow-coloured bird with a long tail and a piercing
screech. It looked for all the world like a parakeet in vivid green,
lemon yellow and azure, with a red splash visible on its back as it
flew. I was thrilled to think that I had spotted a rarity, obviously a
naturalised escapee, and was busy composing a letter to the *Times*
and the RSPB about it when several miles downstream I came
round a bend to see an extraordinary sight. In the middle of the river
was a tiny island bearing nothing but three maple trees. The ragged
leaves had almost finished now, and they were lying in crumpled
brown swathes at the trees' roots, but every branch was full of a rustling and squawking and fluttering – two hundred parakeets as
bright and glossy as tropical fruit, looking like one of Jenny's painted
silk designs back in Shropshire.

Down through Staines and Chertsey the river bungalows crowd

along the shore and fill the islands that punctuate the map with their intriguing names: Pharaoh's Island, D'Oyly Carte Island, Dumsey Eyot and Penton Hook. There was an awful lot of hard tacking against biting wind under a cold clear sky, zigzagging to and fro past the waterworks of Sunbury and Hampton where my grandfather had been Chief Engineer during the War, and my mother and her brothers had spent their childhood playing among the filterbeds and gooseberry bushes and boating on the Thames. I moored that night opposite Hampton Court, with its famous maze, at a charming pub called Fox-on-the-River.

I woke the next morning to find the early sun combing the vapour off the river in phantom strands. The grounds of Hampton Court lay ice-blue and white on the opposite bank behind their high iron railings. I expected that night to have reached journey's end: Surrey Docks just above Greenwich. Here, living aboard a narrow-boat, was a friend of mine, Tim, the brother of Rupert the vet who had brought me the original Jack de Crow. The idea was to sail up alongside, tap on a porthole and, when Tim appeared and asked with mild surprise why I was in a dinghy, casually mention that oh, I'd just rowed from Shropshire, thought I'd pop in. I was also rather hoping that he and his girlfriend Babette would not mind boat-sitting for a few months while I wintered in Australia, ready to return in spring to attempt the crossing of the Channel.

For this I had now decided to do, definitely. Why not? *Jack de Crow* had proven herself buoyant and stable and manoeuvrable in all weathers and conditions, tough enough to withstand the bumps and batterings sustained in locks and weirs, and it seemed that judging from the fine weather that had shone almost continuously about me, I was in fact a sun god upon whom it could rarely if ever rain.

With these happy thoughts revolving in my mind, I set off down the river on the last leg of the journey into the heart of London. The frosty morning was still as glass so I glided along with the oars paddling out their soothing rhythm on the silken surface, a steady *ONE and two-three, ONE and two-three* composed of soft creaks, splashes and clunks; it is exactly the same rhythm as the introduction to one of the famous arias from *Carmen* but lends itself equally well to any number of Latin dances, so I hummed my way through Sambas and Salsas, Rumbas and Tangos down those gentle suburban reaches towards Teddington and the tidal Thames.

At Teddington is an enormous weir and the means to measure

precisely how much water flows down the river each day: in times of flood up to fifteen billion gallons. There are three locks, including the tiniest lock in Britain, designed to hold just one little punt or rowing skiff; and down this I went. It was a peculiar experience; I relived old nursery fears of going down the plug-hole when the bathwater is let out. But when the lower gate opened, I looked out onto a dazzling window of river and was once more seeing tidal waters, the first since Bristol.

I had arrived just before high tide, so the current was running upstream but sluggishly, hardly perceptible in its movement, and I had little difficulty in rowing on down the river against it. Down through Twickenham I went and moored for a while to explore Eel Pie Island, finding it to be a jungly little eyot with damp and fading bungalows crouched under thick foliage but with names redolent of a braver age, an age of exploration upon the world's high seas: Coromandel House, Mandalay, Admiral's Rest, Cape Cottage. There is something about all islands everywhere that is utterly enchanting, something wrapped up with weatherboard and whale-bone, with seashells in dusty rows and thick pale-green glass in the windows, with telescopes and hibiscus and haphazard footpaths: Madeira, Nantucket, Iona, Norfolk Island, Inish Mor ... these by their geographical isolation are linked by invisible isthmuses each with another, and here too with Eel Pie Island on a sunny Wednesday morning in late October.

Richmond Bridge, glowing honey gold above the green river, I passed by, and then rounded the broad bend to Kew. Just above Kew Bridge, however, the gentle monotony was broken abruptly by a noisy motor launch driven by three youths who roared up the river on a tidal wave of wash, steered straight for me and ducked aside with three feet to spare, sending *Jack* and myself heaving madly on the wake and scarlet with fury. The mast swung wildly to and fro, the bundled sail, gaff and boom thumped savagely from side to side, and a curling wave of filthy water bearing with it a debris of plastic bottles, polystyrene foam and frothy scum sloshed over the gunwale in a stinking tide. No sooner had I recovered my balance and picked the worst of the debris out of the bilges than I saw with dismay the launch returning. These youths were not in the same league as my three Reading lads; they were out for laughs and thrills. As they drew near, I could see a crate of shiny brown beer bottles in the cockpit and four or five empties lolling on the deck. Even as I watched, one of the crew picked up a pair of bottles, held one in each hand over the side and smashed them together, laughing at the sudden vicious tinkle of broken glass.

I tried rowing steadily on, ignoring the blare of the ghetto blaster propped in the cockpit and the shouted comments ricocheting over the water. The river seemed suddenly very wide and lonely and *Jack* horribly exposed. I steered in towards the Kew bank, but this too was empty of people as far as I could see in either direction. Before I could get close in, the launch shot between me and the bank on a snarling wave and started to describe a tight circle around me, a ring of savage foam and choppy water encircling the dinghy. Briefly half a dozen literary parallels ran through my mind – pirates, of course; the sea serpent that drew its deadly coils around the *Dawn Treader*; the tactics of killer whales in some half-remembered and highly inaccurate adventure story; the Hullabaloos in *Coot Club* menacing the peaceful Norfolk Broads with their wash and radio blare and reckless disregard for others. But literary examples, so enhancing in times of peace, are sadly inadequate when faced with genuine thuggishness. Stripped of all romance, of plumes and pistols and parakeets, I was horribly at a loss and floundering mentally as much as *Jack* was by now floundering in reality on the motor launch's wash.

These reams of philosophical musings only occupied a couple of seconds of real time before my body took charge of things. Tired of waiting for my confused brain to sort out sea serpents, Arthur Ransome and eighteenth-century perceptions, it stood up in the violently rocking dinghy, held up my folded map case like an identity pass and to the amazement of my disbelieving ears shouted, 'River Police! I have noted your vessel's name and registration number, and you are exceeding the speed limit!'

Before my horrified brain could catch up with what it had just heard my body say and correct it ('*Er … no, sorry. Not true, actually. I'm just a helpless citizen and this is just a map case*'), the three thugs had blanched, straightened up and cut their speed to a demure four knots before heading off up the river arguing in furious whispers: '*Whose stupid idea was it in the first place? … Yer Dad' ll KILL yer when the police get through to 'im … Nah, 'COURSE 'e was river police like 'e said, cos 'oo else'd wear a silly hat like that, it must be part of the uniform …*'

As I waited for the waves to subside, I bailed the boat, set the oars back in place and wondered what the penalty was for impersonating a police officer – what's more, for bringing the Royal Thames River Constabulary into disrepute by carrying out the deception in a ridiculous hat. Ten years at least, I reckoned, as I took to the oars once more and rowed on somewhat shakily down the river.

On I slogged through Fulham and Wandsworth, alternately drifting and rowing past the extraordinary Wagnerian fantasy of the Harrods Depository in red terracotta, past the smart modern flats of Chelsea Harbour and under the splendid iron tracery of the Albert Bridge, where a thousand starlings rustled and cheeped and roosted in a cheerful, squabbling swarm. Soon the sun was westering and the sky was turning pink and gold beneath the clear cool blue. Night was coming on, and I decided to check the map. One glance confirmed what I had suspected: Southwark Docks were another eight miles downstream and quite unreachable that night. But where else could I go? As I rowed, the sky deepened to crimson and scarlet, a blazing furnace of a sunset the like of which I have rarely seen. The black silhouettes of the Battersea Power Station stood like cut-out cardboard shapes against the vivid sky. I could feel also that the water beneath my keel was behaving in an uneasy manner. This was no longer the placid silk-cool Thames I had been used to; the outgoing tide had turned the river into a broad, wrangling churn of grey water that poured under the arches of the Grosvenor Bridge and on towards Vauxhall. Before I had reached Vauxhall Bridge, a new hazard was apparent. Huge ferries swept by, and their wake, rolling against the current, set the river waters sloshing and slapping in a racing chop. Between the sheer embankments of concrete, these waves rebounded magnified and sent *Jack de Crow* crashing and reeling from side to side in the deepening dusk.

Before I had reached Lambeth Bridge, it was completely dark and the waves were high enough to be sloshing over the gunwales. I was terrified. So choppy was the water that I could barely use the oars. Somehow I managed to steer myself inwards to the north bank, cursing the ferries as they churned up the river, lit up like Elijah's fiery chariot and all unseeing of the little lightless dinghy bobbing down on the racing tide. Ferries were not the only peril. A smaller motor launch went zooming upstream along the further bank, red and blue disco lights flashing and some incomprehensible garble issuing from speakers, a jet of spray flung up behind from its rocket-like speed.

In the midst of all the fear there came one moment of sheer magic, as I realised that I had reached the heart of London. There I was, bobbing down beneath the Houses of Parliament and the land-mark tower of Big Ben, just as it was striking seven. From my din-ghy I could see into the lit windows of the Palace above me: a brief glimpse of some fan-vaulted ceiling, high panelled shelves lined with books in green and maroon leather with the gilt glinting on their spines. Some sort of drinks party was in progress: an assembly of figures in dark suits and silver hair, each with a cut glass of amber sherry in hand. As I passed, one youngish-looking man came to the window and stood staring out beyond the glass into the darkness over the Thames. He rested his forehead for a moment against the cool glass. He looked tired and a little glum, I thought, as though he longed to be away from that lit room, its secrets and its linenfold panelling. Perhaps he longed to be in a small sailing dinghy off to foreign parts on an outgoing tide under the stars.

For my part, I would have been quite happy to swap places right then. I had had enough. This was quite definitely the most danger-ous and stupid thing I had ever done and was also quite likely to be the last thing I'd ever do. I was being swept along at eight knots in a roaring world of darkness and glaring sodium-lights, which daz-zled the inky black water with liquid orange slashes that baffled the eye. The pylons of Westminster Bridge surged by in a welter of ech-oing current not three feet from my left gunwale, and as I shot out from under the black arches I pulled sharply in towards the floating pontoon of Westminster Pier. Just before I was swept past the end, a wave slammed me against the pontoon's steel rim and I grabbed a railing with both hands, determined to stop here before I was sunk by a passing ferry.

I myself might have been determined to stop. *Jack*, however, was equally set on keeping going. The tidal current swept the faithless dinghy from under my feet, my arms were nearly wrenched from their sockets, and half a second later I found myself with my hands still clinging to the railing but with my feet hooked over the tran-som of *Jack* who was trying to race away downstream. The rest of my intervening body acted as a badly designed bridge between the two, hanging horizontally over the dark racing Thames and sagging slowly drinkwards.

An agonising period followed in which I attempted to drag *Jack* back upstream to a position under me, an exercise involving more stomach muscles than I customarily use and during which my mind absented itself and wandered away humming hymn tunes to itself until the crisis was over. Eventually, helped by a rogue wave that swept *Jack* towards me for a moment, I had got her beneath me and was sitting once more in my proper place on the thwarts. Then I grabbed the painter and tied it firmly – very firmly – onto the pontoon railing. 'That certainly won't be coming undone again in a hurry,' I told myself. 'Here we are and here we stay,' I said curtly to *Jack* as I started to climb onto the pontoon looking around for someone official to let them know they had a guest mooring for the night.

Just then a resounding BOOOHHHM! shook the night, the sort of sound one associates with supertankers in foggy Atlantic sea lanes rather than inland river traffic. I turned to see an enormous ferry crowded with passengers just swinging in to dock at the pontoon. In twenty seconds, *Jack* would be crushed like a matchbox between ferry and pontoon. I took a flying leap back into the dinghy, fumbled furiously with the extra-secure clove hitches and bowlines I had spent a careful ten minutes tying and prayed to all the gods in Heaven to stop doing this sort of thing to me. Somehow I managed to cast loose three seconds before the giant stern of the ferry swung in with a grinding thud against the railings where I had been moored. Even so, the swirling kick of the propeller-wash sent me bucketing and spinning downstream into the darkness, and before I'd recovered myself I was a hundred yards down the river, helplessly adrift once more.

Beneath Waterloo Bridge, the echoing swell of oily black waves decided me. If I survived this night, I would not be going to Europe. How could I have ever been so presumptuous? It was sheer folly to dream of crossing the Channel in a rotten little tub like this. If the choppiness was this bad so far inland up the Thames, how would it be further down the estuary and out into the Channel? It was unthinkable. No, I had clearly been indulging in a fool's daydream, lulled by the exceptional conditions of the Bristol Channel that long-distant day and carried away by unrealistic – and all too typical – conceptions of my own abilities. If I got the blasted boat to Southwark Docks tonight, or indeed anywhere safe, that's where she would stay until she could be shipped back to Ellesmere to lie among the dandelions for another thirty years. As for me, well, I wasn't sure quite what I would do – possibly dedicate

Night Tide

my life to God, join a monastery in a desert somewhere; anything so long as this heaving, bucking, swooping, blind nightmare stopped right now.

As Waterloo Bridge spat me out from under its booming arches, another pontoon on the left bank swept into sight. A little more carefully this time, I somehow oared alongside, grabbed at the huge black tyres that lined its edge and let *Jack* thump to a halt against the giant rings. I tied on, climbed shakily aboard and called out a cautious 'Hello?'

The pontoon was about fifty feet long and consisted of a long decking facing the river backed by a row of four rooms, each one with its door opening onto the deck. Keeping an eye out for approaching ferries that might suddenly want to dock, I ventured to call out a little louder: 'Hello? Anyone there?'

No answer. Funny. Each room had its lights on, and all the doors stood wide open. I went to investigate. The first room seemed to be a sort of mini-gym, with weights and training equipment and lockers along the walls. The second was a small television lounge; an old sofa and a few armchairs lined the walls and the television was on, the seven o'clock news quacking and flickering its bluish light over the shabby carpet. The next room was a small brightly lit kitchen: a toaster, a small hot plate and a kettle, and on the bench-top two mugs of steaming coffee. Visions of the *Marie Celeste*, of abandoned ghost ships riding the ocean waves, of ancient brigs manned by phantom crews, fluttered through my mind before I reminded myself that this was central London and not the still-vexed Bermoothes, and the existence of a haunted pontoon was unlikely to have gone unnoticed within fifty yards of Somerset House. The last room explained the nature of the place, if not the mystery of its abandonment. It contained a large VHF radio, a computer, a desk and filing-cabinets, and over the back of two chairs hung a couple of uniforms; river-police uniforms, standard issue, not including pith helmet. I had better scarper sharpish.

As I stepped outside onto the decking again, a fast motor launch zoomed up alongside the pontoon nearly swamping *Jack de Crow*, and I recognised it as the reckless vessel with the disco lights I had seen blaring up the river in the dark earlier. On closer inspection I also recognised it for what it was: a river-police boat, with two irate-looking river-policemen just hopping onto the pontoon. One of them was speaking into a walkie-talkie, and I heard him say, 'It's alright. We've found him. He's on *our* pontoon. Over.'

There was something very *Who's-been-eating–MY-porridge-ish* in the way he said it. The other man stepped up to me, stabbed a finger at my chest and said with some asperity, 'We've been looking for you!'

Oh dear. I hadn't thought the crime of impersonating a police officer would come to light so soon.

'Hello, officers. Can I help you?'

'We've been looking,' he repeated, 'and I quote,' – here he consulted his notebook – 'for a lunatic in a pith helmet out of control in a small dinghy without navigation lights, as reported to us by no less than three ferry captains. Can we assume that you are said lunatic?'

'Well, this is, in fact *a* pith helmet, officer, but – '

'Right, yes, lunatic would seem to be an apt description then. Are you aware of the Rules of Navigation that demand adequate navigation lights on any vessel sailing between the hours of darkness on public shipping lanes?'

'Ah, yes. Well, no. Well, I could make a stab at them … er …'

'Are you aware of the dangers to yourself and to others of proceeding in such a fashion on this waterway at a time of maximum tide-flow?'

'Um …'

'And during our coffee-break?' interrupted the other policeman in an aggrieved tone.

'Oh. Sorry.'

'Nescafé Gold Blend it was. That new stuff. I'd just poured it.'

His senior colleague shot him a warning look and resumed his interrogation.

'And the penalties for distracting us from our more serious duties?'

'Penalties? No, I wasn't aware …'

'Where, may I ask, have you come from in that vessel?'

'Er … Shropshire.'

There was a pause. A glance between the two.

'Blimey. Need a cup of Nescafé Gold Blend then? We'll make some fresh.'

Ten minutes later I was steadying my nerves with a hot mug of much-needed coffee while the two police officers quizzed me about the whole voyage so far – Ellesmere, the Morda Brook, the Shropshire Weir, the Ironbridge Gorge and the passage through the Bristol Channel. Both had been all over the waterways of Britain and were flatteringly interested in the trip, and though neither revised their first opinion of me when it came to lunacy, they seemed to forget the penalties and charges of dangerous navigational practices on the night-time Thames as I took them along the Kennet & Avon Canal and up to Lechlade and back.

They in their turn explained how, having received a call from a concerned ferry captain, they had flung themselves into their launch and sped upstream along the south bank to look for me, not wasting a second to lock up, turn the television off or grab their jackets. Meanwhile, I must have just crossed to the north bank and watched them speed by, mistaking them for another boatload of hooligans such as my tormentors up by Kew.

Finally it came to the crunch – and Goldilocks had an idea. Could I leave the dinghy here tonight, and fetch her away tomorrow? Wilf, the sergeant, fixed me with a stony eye.

'Are you a member of the IRA?' he asked.

'No!' I replied in some surprise.

'Is your vessel packed with Semtex or explosives of any kind?'

'No.'

'Right, you can leave her here tonight. Where are you going to sleep then?'

I poked my head outside. With every wave *Jack* was slamming up and down against the pontoon tyres with a vicious jerk, rising five feet and then plunging into a dark trough of racing water each time. Sleeping aboard was out of the question.

'I don't suppose you know a cheapish hotel or hostel nearby, do you?' I hazarded.

'You are, my son, about two hundred yards from the West End of London. Hotel prices start at about ninety pounds per night. How much have you got?'

'Um … forty pounds?'

'You ARE a lunatic, aren't you? Hold on, I'll see what I can do.'

He turned to a telephone, stabbed the buttons and leaned back in his chair.

'Royal Adelphi Hotel? Good. Wilf here, Wilf of the River Police. Yes, yes. Look, got a room for tonight, have you? … Uh huh, yes, it's for one of our boys …' Here he looked me up and down; pith helmet, faded shirt, khaki shorts. 'Plain-clothes division,' he added, winking enormously. 'Good, excellent' (thumbs up). 'Now what are your rates?' (pause) 'Now surely you can go lower than that … lower … lower. Okay, hang on.' He covered the mouth-piece and whispered, 'Is thirty pounds alright for you, sonny? It's as low as they'll go for the boys in blue.'

I gave a delighted thumbs-up in return, Wilf confirmed the booking and hung up.

'Good little place, the Adelphi – just off Trafalgar Square. Should suit you nicely. And now, what are your plans from hereon?'

I sat and told him how ever since the Bristol Channel I had half thought of attempting to sail across to Europe, but that he would no doubt be relieved to hear that the last two hours had cured me of any such ambitions. I was going to go on and tell him that in the short space of time since passing under Lambeth Bridge, I had already mapped out several cosy options for a boat-less year ahead – settling down to produce an illustrated herbal of plants growing in arid regions of the world; taking up archaeology in the waterless wadis of Northern Africa; auditioning for a remake of *Lawrence of Arabia* – joining that desert brotherhood even – anything as far removed from the soggy pursuits of nauticalia as possible. But to my surprise, Wilf hadn't responded with the same eyebrow-raised grimace as my previous confidants in this scheme. Instead he pursed his lips, looked at me thoughtfully and said: 'Now why not, I wonder? Dover to Calais? I reckon you could do it if you had a mind to. Not now, of course. Go home to Australia for Christmas, but next March, say, when the weather's getting warmer, there's no reason why you shouldn't.'

I must have been gaping at him, because he continued: 'You'd need to pick your day, of course, and you'd want someone to accompany you in a larger boat, but no, I don't see any real objection.'

'Ah yes,' said I, thinking of the dark and swirling waters beyond the pontoon lights, the looming bulk of the ferries, the swamping waves and the fear I had felt so recently. 'Yes,' I repeated, clutching for once at straws of prudence, of caution, of excuses not to go, 'but where on Earth would I find someone prepared to accompany me across? I don't exactly know anyone with a large boat, and – '

'Yes you do,' interrupted Wilf. 'Me. I have a trawler which I take across four or five times a year.' (*My arid herbs crumbled to fragrant dust.*) 'I'll be going round about March.' (*Archaeology died a sudden death.*) 'Here's my number. Give me a ring early next year and we'll arrange an escort for you.' (*Lawrence galloped off and turned into the mirage he had always been.*) 'Don't worry,' he added cheerfully, seeing my face fall. 'The voyage need not end here after all. There's nothing to stop you and little *Jack* sailing all the way to the Black Sea! Have another coffee ...'

That night, although the bed in the Royal Adelphi was soft and comfortable, I may as well have been aboard *Jack*, bucking wildly on the Thames. All night the mattress seemed to sway and jolt on a tide of darkness; phantom ferries loomed out of the fogs of sleep, manned by politicians sipping sherry; and the giant figure of Wilf kept handing me a sheaf of secret documents and a toy boat and ordering me to sail to France in it, saying, 'Don't worry, my lad. You're our man in Europe. Plain-clothes division.' And when I found the toy boat sinking beneath me, someone kept saying in a rich avuncular voice, 'That's right ... you can go lower than that ... lower ... lower ... lower ...' until I drowned in the soft, thundering billows of slumber.

*

And so I come to the last day of this long and winding tale of reeds and rivers, weirs and willow trees, swans and sails and sunlit days and the secret ways of Britain.

I did not hurry that morning. Wilf had told me that the tide would not begin running out until one o'clock in the afternoon. Besides, Surrey Docks was only five miles down the river and there was no point in arriving at Tim and Babette's barge until they were both home from work. I spent the morning exploring the National Gallery, trotting around Covent Garden and then visiting Kelvin Hughes, one of the best suppliers of maritime goods and charts. Here I found what I was looking for: a large map of all Europe and a good deal of Russia showing every navigable waterway, river and canal from Ireland to the Caspian Sea, from Norway to Turkey. And there in plain blue was a route through, from the tangle of canals clustered like varicose veins around Calais to the long single thread of the Danube running out into the Black Sea. It was, after all, possible.

The last stretch down to Surrey Docks was straightforward. The day was dullish but warm, with no wind to speak of. Wilf had advised me to get straight across to the south bank and stay well over, thereby avoiding the faster shipping traffic that kept to the centre. In broad daylight and as the river widened I had more leisure to look about me and enjoy the novelty of being a spectacle on the river – and a spectator. Here was the newly rebuilt Globe Theatre, remodelled exactly as Shakespeare would have known it, and the only building in the City of London to be allowed a thatched roof since the Great Fire of 1666. Over there was the dome of St Paul's Cathedral rising above the more modern bankside buildings.

Tower Bridge passed by in its lofty blue and gilded splendour, and the Tower of London on the far bank, much cleaner and whiter than I remembered from a visit twenty-five years earlier. Old songs from a production of *The Yeomen of the Guard* flooded back and I went rowing down the river singing *Tower Warders, Under Orders* with its fierce brisk rhythm, and my favourite of all Gilbert and Sullivan songs, *I Have a Song to Sing, O!*, the sweet, simple rolling tune sung by the melancholy jester Jack Point.

And so too, my own *Jack* was singing his own lap-lapping melody as we crept down the last dull-eyed miles between the warehouses of Wapping and Bermondsey to Greenland Pier and the lock entrance to Surrey Docks. There a young lock-keeper took me up the lock, opened a swing bridge between one compound and another, and I rowed through into the placid waters of the Surrey Docks marina. There was *Ilanga Umfula*, Tim and Babette's smartly painted narrowboat in royal blue and yellow, and there was a warm yellow light pouring out into the greyness of late afternoon on this, the last day of October. I had arrived.

The journey had covered something approaching 481 miles, I had traversed 160 locks and had been travelling for 59 days, statistics that to my mind seem meaningless. It had often struck me on the journey, whenever I reached for a map to show 'where I really was' on some stretch of the river or canal, in what odd a sense we use the word *real*. There I would be, tucked in a reedy corner of the river, an alder tree scattering its golden coinage on the black waters, a farmhouse drowning its warm red-brick reflections in the river's stillness, and I would be reaching for a piece of printed paper to tell me something more real than the wet grasses and the rustle of reeds in an evening breeze. 'Ah,' I'd say, putting my finger on a squiggle of blue ink and red dots, 'here we are!' And I'd read out a name – Crowmarsh, Bampton, Oakhill Down – an airy nothing of syllables and spit – and then, only then, would I confidently plant my banner of recognition and turn away satisfied, no longer needing the cool bright air and the reedy curve and the red bricks fading into dusk.

So I give the figures and statistics above merely to pay a nodding homage to our map-god, and then turn to better things: to the colours seen as September flamed into October and rivers merged with the sea; to the aerated minty smells of rushing water in deep locks and woodsmoke in country pubs; to kingfishers and coots and cloud-palaces in the sky; and to the goodness of people met along the way whose numbers defy arithmetic. Not because there were so many (though there were), but because each one held in the mind fills it entirely, floods every cell, admitting no others to jostle into a merely countable rank. There are no queues here, not in the Courts of Heaven.

The last of these were, of course, Tim and Babette, who reacted with all the pleased astonishment I had been rehearsing for them in my mind. We sat that evening under a dusky sky, chatting of this and that – their own forthcoming wedding; my plans for the coming year, poring over the map I had bought that morning and tracing out possible routes to the Black Sea. Across the Thames, the great glass tower of Canary Wharf raised its gleaming pyramid high into steamy clouds of its own making and flashed its brilliant white light to flicker on the dim night sky.

It was Hallowe'en. The sprites and boggles of the English country-side would be out in force tonight – the Peg Powlers and the Urisks and the Water Kelpies, the sea-sirens and the marsh-folk, the wil-low-men and alder-witches, and Ellesmere's own Jenny Greenteeth whom I'd left so very far away – all would be abroad. But *Jack de Crow* had eluded them each and every one and was safe at last in the soulless heart of the great city.

But even here there was perhaps a little magic. For with the talk of Hallowe'en, I had remembered something. Hopping down into *Jack* where she lay snugly moored against *Ilanga Umfula*'s side, I rummaged deep into her front locker. Ah yes, here it was: that curi-ous brown bottle of Hobgoblin Ale given to me in Bristol by my old student Alex. I had been keeping it for this moment.

Three glasses and a bottle-opener were fetched out onto the stern decking of the narrowboat where we sat watching the night sky. Then, as Tim lifted his glass for a toast, a burst of pink fireworks flowered in the southern sky over the water. Again and again they came with a volley of distant thunder, giant chrysanthemums of rosy light blooming the city skyscape and dissolving into showers of fire – a display, Tim explained, put on by a nearby Tesco store. But the prosaic nature of the event could not spoil the beauty, the aptness, the sheerly perfect timing of the spectacle, and perhaps I may be for-given for mentally claiming them as my reward. I almost ... almost ... expected them to spell out *Well done, Sandy!* in letters of pink fire against the broad sky. I said as much to Tim.

'Yes, Sandy,' he replied, but knowing me fairly well, was kind enough to add, 'clearly just a technical hitch. They'll have ironed out the problems by the time you reach the Black Sea, you just wait and see. Cheers! To adventure!'

Jack shifted comfortably beside us in the darkness, dreaming of foreign parts. She seemed happy enough with the idea and so, I realised, was I. 'To adventure!' I replied, and drank up. 'To adventure!'

End of Part One

Part Two

My Purpose Holds

Dooms and Delays

Come, my friends,
'Tis not too late to seek a newer world.
Push off, and sitting well in order smite
The sounding furrows; for my purpose holds
To sail beyond the sunset, and the baths
Of all the Western stars ...

—TENNYSON, Ulysses

Let me tell you briefly about Fermat's last theorem, a clairvoyant and my bottom.

Many years ago my mother took my sister and myself off to see a clairvoyant. We didn't tell my father that, of course, because he would have worried that we were getting enmeshed in a New Age cult. No, we told him that we were going off to buy some herbs and shrubs for the new border and that was all. Which was true enough, because this particular clairvoyant owned a nursery and played the Delphic Oracle only as a sideline.

He was a giant of a man, sporting a jutting beard, frizzy eyebrows and a huge pair of boots, and his name was equally impressive: Mr A.J. Mackenzie-Clay. He had – or so he claimed – been struck by lightning no less than three times, and it was after the third strike that he had woken up to find that he now had clairvoyant powers. These manifested themselves through the medium of numerology, he explained. By adding up the numbers corresponding to your birthday, your age and the letters in your name, he could predict your future, diagnose likely health problems and reveal the inner secrets of your soul. All this was accomplished while striding around his vast nursery and loading you up with another three pots of tradescantia, a tub of lemon verbena and a sack of organic compost to take home.

To my sister Margaret, his predictions were detailed, fascinating and unlikely – and mostly set so far in the future that by the time

they came true – or failed to eventuate – he would be long underground and taking a more active role in the production of organic
compost than ever before. Only one prediction was worth storing
away: namely, that after the next four years of considerable hardship
my sister would find that the beginning of the fifth year would bring
a long-deserved reversal of fortunes. The long night would be over,
and she would emerge victorious.

Meanwhile, what about *my* future? While Maggie and my
mother went off to inspect some Iceland poppies, I awaited my turn,
half cynical, half curious. Mr A.J. Mackenzie-Clay jotted down my
name, birth date and other details on the back of an old seed
packet.

'Hmmm,' he intoned. 'Interesting, very ...'

I looked at the scribbled grid of numbers he was rapidly producing. He added up a column of numbers here, dashed down a total
there, and drew a swift arrow to an earlier grid. Then he jotted down
a hasty question mark, grabbed another seed packet and started
again.

'Yes, odd, one doesn't often get such a ... Ah, but wait a minute.
Here's a double eight. Yes, that *is* interesting. With a preponderance
of fives too. How very ... sad.' He finished on a sigh and shook his
head.

My mother returned. 'Well,' she inquired, 'and what about this
one?'

'Ah, yes,' said the prophet, gazing into the middle distance over
the glass cloches to the eucalypt-blue hills beyond. Then he
announced my doom: 'He will always have trouble with his bottom.'
And with that he strode away between the salvia beds and not
another word would he utter.

In the long history of prophetic utterances, among the whole
smoking, writhing, pale-mouthed league of Pythonesses, Cassan-
dras, Weird Sisters, Sybils and Norns, has there ever been a forecast
so undignified, so banal, so downright embarrassing as that particular piece of oracular lore? We drove home, me sitting in an outraged
silence among the verbena, Maggie smiling quietly to herself and
my mother pondering aloud the meaning of that last cryptic remark,
saying, 'Well, yes, you *have* always had a problem in that area,
haven't you? Don't you remember that time ...?' until I was forced
to silence her musings with a fierce and heartfelt denial of *any* problem in that area *whatsoever* since the age of two. I did not give Mr

A.J. Mackenzie-Clay's numerological prognosis another thought until five years later when I was preparing to set sail in *Jack de Crow* down the Thames to the open sea.

*

That is the tale of the clairvoyant. Now let me tell you a little about Fermat's Last Theorem. Fermat was a renowned mathematician of the eighteenth century who is famous for his last theorem; he proposed that no matter how far you looked, you could never find two cubes that would add up to make a third cube. What is more, he scribbled an airy comment in the margin of his notebook to the effect that he had found an elegant little proof of this fact which he *would* jot down here but there wasn't quite enough space, so another time perhaps.

Then he went and died.

For the last three hundred years that breezy assertion has been driving the world of mathematics to the brink of despair. It seemed such a trivially easy thing to prove, especially as Fermat was so offhand about it, but it has proved anything but simple, and has taxed the greatest brains of the last three centuries to no avail. Few students of mathematics since then, professional or amateur, have not idly tried to be the first to recapture whatever flash of insight led Fermat to make his claim.

For therein lies its fascination for the amateur: the idea that the proof, if it exists, does not rely on any complex supermaths but in a simple quirk in the way of seeing the problem, accessible to any curious puzzler. There are certain conundrums involving the cutting up of chess-boards, or the movement of a knight around the board to visit all the squares once and once only, that are almost impossible to solve by traditional mathematical means. However, take a child's set of crayons, colour in the squares in a certain pattern and the solution comes leaping out at you. The nature of the problem has not been altered by the colouring-in, but the filters through which we see the problem have rendered the answer obvious. It is just such a twist of perception that most likely lies at the root of Fermat's Last Theorem, and it is tempting to seek to be the first in three hundred years to see just what it was that Fermat saw.

Or so, at least, thought I. Thus it was that as I whiled away my days preparing *Jack de Crow* for the rigours of the journey ahead, my evenings were spent covering sheets of paper with formulae, diagrams of cubes, Pascal's triangle, Fibonacci's series and a whole set of things that I dubbed '*Incompatible Numbers*.' (Don't ask.) And the fact is that I was onto something. I really was. I was working along lines that had just the right sort of quirkiness and amateur knowledge that was called for, and I had seen all sorts of odd and beautiful things about cubes that I had never heard anyone else mention. Yes, there were some really very promising insights emerging. By the time I had fully developed my theory I was writing in a mathematical shorthand of my own invention, mysterious hiero-glyphs as meaningless to the casual observer as Mr A.J. Mackenzie-Clay's jottings all those years ago.

All terribly exciting, as you can imagine.

Or possibly not, if you have been looking forward to the continu-ation of the roving adventures of *Jack de Crow* upon the high seas and are now a little bewildered by the absence of waves, dinghies and seagulls, and justifiably puzzled at the intrusion of clairvoyants, mathematical formulae and the author's bottom. There is a point to all this, I assure you, but before we get to it, let me turn swiftly to the details of *Jack* and the one or two preparations that had to be made before I set off on the second leg of my odyssey.

There was much to be done. The first thing on the list was to ring Wilf, the River Police Sergeant who last October had offered to accompany me across the Channel in his trawler on my return from my Christmas break in Australia. As this was the only conceivable condition under which I could attempt the crossing to France, I had to phone to find out if the jovial Wilf had been quite well when he had made that extraordinary offer, or if, with the leisure to reflect, he had since decided to declare temporary insanity and retract the offer.

When I got through to him, he was as blithe and cheery as ever, and said that if I could get myself round to Dover, then all I had to do was to give him a ring in mid-March and he would take a few days off to escort me across to Calais.

The next thing to do was to make sure that *Jack de Crow* was fit to make the journey. Her adventures had left her in a sorry state. Most of the bright buttercup-yellow paint had been scraped off her keel, her topsides were a leprous rash of peeling varnish, her prow and gunwales were battered by the walls of a hundred-and-thirty-two locks, and she still had a slow but irritating leak in her hull that allowed a couple of inches of water to slosh about in her bilges.

I managed to sand off the worst patches of flaking paint from her hull and sides before heading off to a purveyor of marine paints and varnishes in Lincoln's Inn, there to discover that an edict had recently been passed by an environmental board banning the sale and use of buttercup-yellow paint. It apparently has a toxin in it, not present in paints of duller hue, that poisons all the aquatic wildlife with which it comes in contact. I thought back to how much of the stuff I had left in smears and scrapes along the docksides and lock-sides of England's waterways and was surprised that so much as a tadpole still survived between London and the Irish Sea.

In lieu of yellow paint I bought several large tins of bright blue and a smaller can of gloss black and spent a merry morning slather-ing it on, covering with blue all that part of *Jack*'s hull that would be below the waterline, and then, because I had already scraped away large patches around her prow, re-painting those bare parts with blue as well, trying my best to make the patches look deliberate and well designed. I repainted the name, *Jack de Crow*, in gloss black, and as a flourish painted a set of coiling black spirals on her pram-nose that trailed backward along each flank to turn into black-feathered wings. When I had finished, she looked as cheerfully eccentric a vessel as ever sailed. Her colour scheme was perfect and the jackdaw wings along either side lent her a brave air, rather like a jaunty Viking. She also, miraculously, stopped leaking. She was ready to fly once more.

Which is where Fermat's Last Theorem and my bottom come back into the story. As the grey March days progressed, two things started to develop rapidly. One was my work on the Theorem, and the other was a degree of discomfort in what the gentry of the eight-eenth century so charmingly called 'the fundament.' I thought at first that I had merely bruised my coccyx when sitting down too rapidly on a London bus-stop seat, but as the days went by, instead of the tenderness subsiding, it grew worse and worse and was accompanied by a feeling of nausea and lassitude.

The crisis came on the last and worst day of a blustery March, a foul day of heavy rain and strong winds, ushering a thunderstorm up the Thames and releasing it upon the city like a sullen buffalo. I dashed around the streets of Southwark dodging the rain showers and trying to accomplish a dozen last-minute errands: maps, charts of the Thames Estuary and the Channel, waterproof bags, a pot of varnish, and not least, a telephone call to my sister Maggie in

Edinburgh to find out how she was coping with the latest in a long line of battles at her university laboratory. As the day progressed and errand after errand failed (the chart shop closed, the waterproof bags too flimsy, the varnish tin leaking all through my bag), the pain in my tail increased to an angry throbbing.

Eventually, on the off-chance, I wandered into a doctor's clinic and dropped my trousers for a quick inspection of the trouble spot. An hour later I was being admitted to the Kingston Hospital for emergency surgery. It transpired that I had a serious pilonidal abscess on my lower back ... well, the very base of my spine really ... well, alright, let's be honest, on my bottom. This had been merrily pumping poison into my bloodstream for a fortnight and needed to be operated on without delay. It was the last straw in a particularly frustrating day, not least because while I had been busy getting soaked for no good reason, I had suddenly seen a way of getting those Incompatible Numbers to work for me, a neat little twist that could very possibly be what I had been looking for. All my notes and equations were back in the docks covered in varnish, however, and in all the rush I had had no time to try out my new idea. Now here I was lying in a hospital bed waiting to go under the general anaesthetic, and my chance to solve the greatest mathematical mystery of all time would have to wait until after the operation. That is, if I still remembered my new idea after the drowsy limbo of anaesthesia. Didn't funny things happen sometimes? Memory loss? A wiping clean of the mental slate? The situation struck me as grimly humorous: the fact that the last person to make this breakthrough, namely Fermat himself, had died before he could share it with the world, and now the only other person in three hundred years to do so was likely to lose his memory on the very brink of triumph.

Or die, even, I jested to myself bleakly.

Outside the hospital window a blink of white lightning flared out in the late afternoon darkness and all the lights dimmed for an instant as the bolt struck home somewhere nearby. A second later the thunderclap shook the air, but a minute later it came as a re-echo from further off. Of course. The storm was moving swiftly westwards. Lightning never strikes twice in the same place, I mused.

Suddenly I sat upright.

Mr A.J. Mackenzie-Clay, thrice-stricken ...

His bearded face swam before me, his sad eyes on the distant hills. What was that ridiculous thing he had said all those years ago? My bottom? That my fate would come to me through my bottom?! Was this then the dread unravelling of Fate, the ignominious end?

No, I told myself firmly. This was nonsense. This was as nonsensical as I had thought it all those years ago, and nothing had changed since then. I would stop feeling morbid, stop worrying about Fermat until after the operation and start thinking of something or somebody else – such as Maggie, whom I had still not managed to telephone. The time for the operation was not until after midnight, so I had plenty of time to ring and hear about the latest act of petty sabotage perpetrated by her senior colleague, the man who had been systematically destroying her confidence at work over the last three years.

So I did. A phone was brought to my bedside by a nurse, and I listened as Maggie told me the latest news. Good news, it seemed: the tide had turned. He had gone, the persecutor, last Monday, and gone for good, his dark schemes brought into the light. From now on, things would be better … had already improved beyond measure in that last week, in fact, with an exciting breakthrough in one area of Maggie's malarial research and a new grant slotting into place. It was all just peachy, just marvellous … and just, I slowly realised as I hung up, precisely as Mr A.J. Mackenzie-Clay had predicted it five years ago. The fortunes of my sister had indeed suddenly turned. So what did that say about my fatal bottom and the sad look in the prophet's eye? I'll tell you what it said. I clearly had mere hours to live, and what's more, Fermat's Theorem still to solve. I gave the phone back to the nurse, requested pen and paper and set to work to make sure that mathematical posterity was not cheated a second time.

Well, I did it. At three minutes past midnight, just into the new month, I scribbled on a hospital notepad the equation that proved beyond doubt that two perfect cubes could not be added to make a third perfect cube. It was simple, really, and depended on a certain insight into the fact that all cubes are actually composed of Incompatible Numbers in factors of six, and that these – well, never mind, there isn't quite the room here, but I'll get back to it later if you like.

I wrote across the top of the paper '*Fermat's Last Theorem* … *SOLVED!!*' Then I added in big letters '*PLEASE DO NOT THROW AWAY*' and wrote in the date for posterity: *1/4/1998*. There!

Very important, that date. It made the whole thing official. Finally I flopped back exhausted, but very, very smug indeed – surprisingly smug for someone who was certain that he was not going to survive the impending operation.

It was only as I was groggily melting under the anaesthetic in the operating theatre and the two young doctors were assuring me that yes, of course they knew which leg to amputate, ha, ha, only kidding, chum, it's that time of the year again, that I realised what I had failed to take into account. Oh yes, the proof was fine, and yes, I had remembered to add in a translation of all those home-made hieroglyphics and explanations of how to generate Incompatible Numbers. But I knew for a certainty that the proof of Fermat's Theorem had yet again been whisked away by the tricksy hand of Fate. For, of course, no one finding the paper after my untimely demise would look twice at the document or at least not beyond the carefully dated title. It was, after all, April Fool's Day.

*

I survived, of course. And on the bright morrow, realising with satisfaction that I was still alive, I realised another thing. Not only had I cheated my bottom-based doom, but I had in the meantime found the Holy Grail of mathematics. I'd be in all the journals. English Teacher Cracks Fermat. In fact, wasn't there a million-pound prize? I reached excitedly for the papers by my bedside. I scanned my proof eagerly … and two minutes later, put the papers down again. Now that my blood was no longer sloshing with septic substances and my brain had cooled from its high fever, it was easy to see just how febrile my racing mind had been. My hieroglyphics, when translated, seemed to be particularly insistent that pi was NOT divisible by the Archangel Gabriel and that the Fifth Euclidian Solid was, in fact, a stoat. Moreover, I seem to have based the entire proof on the starting axiom that I was a small white duck and proceeded from there. Fermat's Riddle was safe. I laughed at myself, a little wanly it must be admitted, and turned my mind back to the practical matters of life with a sigh. The operation had left a gaping wound which needed daily dressing by a qualified nurse for the next month, a fact that made any thoughts of rowing away to France an impossibility. The first thing to do was to ring Wilf and let him know that the proposed crossing would be delayed. When he answered the phone and heard my voice, he immediately started talking.

'Sandy? Thank goodness you rang, I didn't know where to contact you. Bad news, I'm afraid.'

'Oh yes?'

'Yes, I'm afraid that yesterday I broke my foot, duffer that I am. I'm out of action for at least a month. Sorry, old boy, but the crossing's off, or at least as far as my involvement goes. Unless you'd like to leave it till late April, of course. But I expect you're anxious to be off, aren't you?'

A pause.

'Ah, funny you should say that actually. Let me tell you about my bottom ...'

*

And that long hiatus brings me at last to the dark and early hour when I stowed the last of my belongings, untied Jack's painter, whispered a quiet farewell to Tim who had got out of his bunk to see me off, and set off down the Thames before dawn to see if I could find my way to Europe and beyond.

Tide on the Thames

This City now doth, like a garment, wear
The beauty of the morning; silent, bare,
Ships, towers, domes, theatres and temples lie
Open unto the fields, and to the sky;
All bright and glittering in the smokeless air ...
The river glideth at his own sweet will:
Dear God! the very houses seem asleep;
And all that mighty heart is lying still!
—WILLIAM WORDSWORTH,
Composed upon Westminster Bridge

On the night in London before I resumed my voyage, it poured with rain, lit in dazzling curtains by the camera-shutter flashes of lightning. Over the river from the Thai restaurant where we sat enjoying a farewell meal, the dome of St Paul's and the wedding-cake steeple of St Mary-le-Bow were momentarily etched against black like an old-fashioned silverpoint engraving of the City. As the rain came down in leaden sheets outside the huge plate-glass windows, my resolve to leave on the morrow waned steadily until it was as limp as the coriander-leaf salad on my side plate. But no, it had to be done. I had lingered long enough, seeking excuses to put off going, and I was feeling fat and discontented after too much idling around. Besides, with every extra day I waited, the hour of high tide became earlier and earlier; another few days and I would be forced to leave at midnight, sailing five hours in darkness. As it was, I would be leaving at half-past four in the morning.

Another flash stamped the nearby antennae and radar masts of *HMS Belfast* onto my retina, and thunder rolled like a tympanum over the river's ringed flood. I uttered a silent prayer that the elements would settle at least to a damp drizzle for my pre-dawn start, and turned to tackle the green Thai curry with fragrant black rice that had appeared before me. Tomorrow was another day.

Another day and, as it turned out, another weather pattern altogether. I woke to a sky watery with stars, big and soft and pale from recent washing. The air, too, was cool and fresh, and in the east there was the faintest hint of grey seeping into the sky downriver. My first miles of rowing filled me with joy, strong and fluid as the dark banks sluiced smoothly by: the dismal docks of Limehouse, the Canary Wharf Tower still steaming like a sci-fi diamond volcano, then Greenwich Palace fast asleep, the Royal Observatory, more warehouses and docklands, and somewhere far off but very loud and sweet, the melodious song of a solitary blackbird. It seemed such an incongruous sound for the dark hour and drab urban landscape, but, with my new sense of freedom and adventure beginning, I found myself singing the old Paul McCartney song:

> *Blackbird singing in the dead of night,*
> *Take these broken wings and learn to fly*

And hard on the heels of that, with the grey suffusing to a pale primrose beyond the giant tracery of the Millennium Dome, there came to me that older song sung by David at the court of Saul:

> *Yea, though I take the wings of the morning*
> *And fly to the uttermost parts of the sea,*
> *Even there shall Thy hand guide me,*
> *Thy right hand shall hold me firm.*

I had my wings again and was off to the east at last, sailing into a new sunrise. I was extraordinarily happy again, and could not think why I had delayed my departure so long.

There is a thing called the Thames Barrier which everybody had been warning me about. 'How are you going to get through the Thames Barrier then, eh?' they'd ask. 'Didn't think of that one, did you?' they'd add, smiling knowingly. When I endeavoured to find out exactly what the Thames Barrier was, people would go all vague and say, 'Well, it's a barrier, innit, on the Thames, see. Huge great thing. Major obstacle if you're in a dinghy, mate, I can tell you!'

So I was relieved to discover that the mighty Thames Barrier, which I had imagined as something like a titanic version of the Shrewsbury Weir, looked instead like seven miniature Sydney Opera Houses all in tin, their shiny silver nautilus shells set on seven concrete blocks strung out across the river, but with enough room between each block to allow two aircraft carriers to pass abreast.

Or one Mirror dinghy with slightly wobbly steering.

I aimed for the centre gap, found myself swept by a mysterious submarine force towards the left bank, decided to compromise by rowing hard towards the *second* gap to the left, quickly decided that the tugboat currently chugging upstream through that one deserved the right of way, and squeaked through the gap nearest the bank under the very nose of the man in the control tower who was shouting what I like to think were words of lively encouragement. They were indistinct, but certainly energetic in their delivery.

Below the Barrier I found myself among the industrial docks where huge tankers and freighters were just coming to life, bossed and fussed into place by the little tugs like huge battle-grey cuckoos chivvied by mother wrens. The river was broad enough, though, and I was able to steer well away from the ponderous monsters as the channel swept on southwards to the flat sewage works of Gravesend. The landscape here should have been dreary with its loam fields and vast waterworks and empty wharves, but there was something clean and fresh about the air that early morning, a watercolour landscape still wet on the page, with pale yellow light and a clear sky and a blue breeze beginning to ripple out across the wide grey waters. This is what I had been waiting for, and as soon as I could I stowed the oars, loosened off the sail tyers and hauled the scarlet sail skywards.

By ten o'clock London lay behind me with a thick smudge of soot-dark cloud over it, and the river had widened into a broad estuary, the land receding on either side to melt into blue smears along each horizon. Here for the first time I encountered the intriguing world of marine buoys and navigational markers. Every mile or so, I would skim by a channel marker, regular green bell-shaped buoys on the northern side of the channel and red box-shaped buoys occasionally coming up on the southern bank. These, I knew, marked the starboard and port edges of the deepwater channel, which sounds straightforward enough, but is that going downstream or coming upstream? I guessed the latter, and this proved to be correct. My brand-new chart showed all the buoys and hazards, but I was soon bewildered by the discrepancy between the number of markers printed on the map and the number of markers scattered about the channel. One by one I tried ticking them off as I passed – the

Tilbury South Cone, Ovens Bell, Mucking No. 7, Mucking No. 5 and so on – but what was that red box over yonder? Surely not the Lower Hope port buoy already? And if so, where was Mucking No. 3? And what was the West Blyth marker doing over yonder? Having grown familiar with the large scale and meticulous detail of the Ordnance Survey maps through the waterways of England, I was finding the broad scope and blank spaces of nautical charts misleading. The estuary was far wider than it seemed from the chart. A steeple was indicated on the north shore, but instead of a clear needle of stone thrusting up from the low horizon, there was only a tiny speck floating above a distant glimmer, which may or may not have been the Monkswick spire telling me I was off the Holehaven Sands. Strange monstrous towers and chimneys sprouted in the middle of perfectly blank swathes of the chart, and where it indicated the entrance to some great tidal creek carving its way through the Essex flatlands, the blue line of land on the horizon seemed to spread thin and unbroken as far as the eye could see.

As I ventured down the estuary, clouds came flying up from the east in extraordinary clumps and billows. When a boy, I had spent many a happy hour drawing treasure maps of exotic islands, richly bedecked with volcanoes, waterfalls, palm-fringed beaches and skull-shaped hills, and of course each and every map had sported a beaming golden sun in one top corner and a ferocious, puff-cheeked storm cloud in the other. Here, my childish drawing fantasies became fact. Each cloud that swept up the river to greet me was a perfect Pauline Baynes cloud-god, its lips pursed, its eyebrows curling and snowy, its chins and double chins indigo with shadow. They trailed cloaks of whipping rain and with pudgy fists they struck the water to slaty bruises. *Jack* would heel sharply beneath those swatting blows, the sails would crack and beat, and the tiller would hum and wrench beneath my tired hand until I could barely hold on another second. And then, suddenly, it would be over. The cloud would pass overhead, a giant cherub boy racing up the river to catch his playmates, and the decks would be steaming in the hot sunshine once more.

By mid-afternoon I was on the long stretch between Blyth Sand and Yantlet Flats, and the day had settled into fine weather once more. The estuary was so wide that the northern shore had reduced to a faint thread of silver and grey along the horizon, intermittent and sketchy. Along the nearer southern shore, wide empty fields and pastures crept by beyond the mud-flats, where nothing moved but the occasional crazy flight of lapwings rolling above the vacant green. Far, far to the south-east, a huge gradual hill of bright chrome yellow reared, unnaturally bright against the dim blue of distance, and for a long time I could not guess what it was. A vast heap of Kentish swedes covered over with several acres of yellow tarpaulin? An experimental station of some sort, its hectares of tin or glass roofing painted this luminous primrose? Only much later did I realise that it was a distant crop of oilseed rape, its acid-bright blooms surely the most disturbing colour in nature. Meanwhile, I was puzzled about a more pressing problem. All day the heady pace I had been setting had astonished me. Since dawn I had rowed and sailed an extraordinary fifty miles or so, and had been congratulating myself on the swiftness of my oar strokes and the skill and balance of my sail setting. In fact, a few quick calculations at midday had me confidently expecting to pull into Dover Harbour by suppertime. So it was with some frustration that I spent the long hours of the afternoon wondering why I seemed to have slowed to a snail's pace. The Tower of St Mary's way over beyond the marshes inched to the stern by slow degrees and the long-awaited Yantlet Creek mouth refused to crawl into view ahead. By four o'clock I had barely made another few miles and realised that at present progress I would be lucky to make it to Sheerness, which had just begun to emerge from the general flat silver as a solid line of houses above a long bar of tan shingle and a seawall. What is more, the afternoon breeze was dropping and I had to take to the oars again.

Now I'm not stupid. I know about tides. I've read the cautionary tales about rips and treacherous currents, small vessels being swept out to sea and the deceptive nature of coastal tides. But of all the writers who have dealt with the subject of tides and small boats, no one has seen fit to point out a crucial aspect of the phenomenon: its undetectable nature. You see, implied in the very phrase *'swept out to sea'* or *'in the grip of a fierce current'* is a sort of inbuilt image of swirling waters, racing buoys, receding jetties, helplessly spinning cockleboats and frantically waving pocket handkerchiefs. Given any one of these cues or clichés, I will be the first to nod and say, *'Ah, yes, tides, old boy'* and *'Got to expect 'em in these waters, of course,'* and *'Remember the Swallows, eh?'* and *'You should read Erskine Childers, old chap!'* But the fact is that these telltale hints and clues simply don't exist in the real world.

Imagine that you are sitting on a lawn one warm May day in the middle of ... oh, I don't know ... Worcestershire. It is the lawn belonging to a gracious old manor, and is sprinkled with summer daisies. About you, but a little way off, are the borders and the flowerbeds and old, established trees that mark the boundaries of this thoroughly delightful garden. The sky is above, the grass is cool beneath your shoulderblades, and very soon someone will come out of the house with a tray of afternoon tea and a bowl of strawberries and cream.

Are you going anywhere? Certainly not. It is far too comfortable here beneath the chestnut tree, and besides, a certain pleasant drowsiness is stealing softly upon our senses.

Are you going anywhere? No, we've already been through this, please leave us in peace. Somewhere a couple of wood pigeons are cooing high in an elm.

Are you going anywhere? Look, just what *is* your point, you irritating little man? Have a strawberry or go away.

The point is ... the point IS ... that yes, you *are* going somewhere actually, you and your strawberries and your daisies and your wood pigeons with you. You are drifting out into a new region of space with every second that passes – imperceptibly, inconceivably, but – and this is the frightening bit – horribly, horribly fast.

That is what it is like in a dinghy, a mile off Sheerness on a golden late afternoon, rowing placidly through the glassy water to the welcoming row of whitewashed houses built atop the old sea wall. It is a beautiful afternoon, and twenty more minutes – surely no more – of rowing will bring us to the beach of orange shingle where the figures of two small boys are playing and an older gentleman is walking a cocker spaniel. It is pleasing to see the way that with every oar stroke, the gentle waters furl cleanly away from the prow, and a row of bubbles streams out in a tidy wake behind. I stop and rest on my oars for a minute, the dinghy gliding to a halt and hanging motionless on the broad mirror of the waters. The sun is warm on my shoulders, and the faintest of breezes cools the damp fringe of hair on my brow. Ten more minutes and I will be sitting down to order a well-deserved pint in the Sheerness Arms. Better start rowing again, I suppose, and bring this long and lovely day to an end.

There is a swirling, chuckling noise off to one side. A boat approaching quickly but quietly? No, not a boat chugging past, just

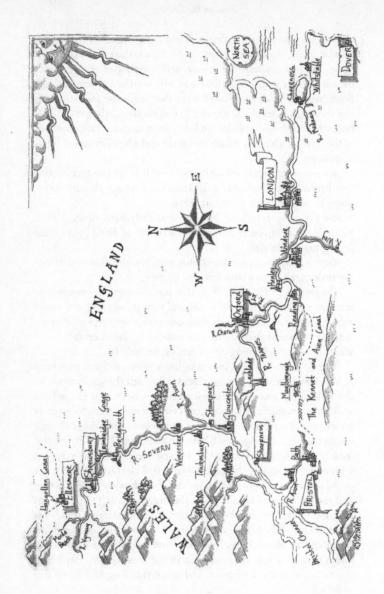

Ellesmere to Dover

an old upright beacon post, black with barnacles, steaming along up the estuary like the periscope on an antique wooden submarine. Its movement through the water is creating quite a bow wave – a good thing it didn't hit me on its way to wherever it's heading. I wonder where it *is* going, by the way? I turn back to my oars and continue rowing in to the shore.

Wait a minute?

I pause ... think ...

What do I mean '*Where is it going?*'? It's not going anywhere, you fool, despite the fact that it has just steamed past me at a good four knots. It's attached to the seabed, as are the three large blackened posts with the red signboards on them that even now are hurrying up behind to overtake me at a similar rate. So if they are not going anywhere, then that means ... then that means that I *am!*

Good grief, I'm drifting out to sea and I'm caught in a tide and I'm going to make the headlines because I'm going to get run down by a liner and what is the *point* in reading *Swallows and Amazons* if you're going to make the same classic idiotic mistakes yourself and I really do *not* believe this is happening and my! isn't it getting late all of a sudden?

And yes, sure enough, looking over my shoulder, Sheerness is now not a mile away, but two miles away and further west than it had been. The two boys on the beach are mere dots of brightness. Before I was able to see the colour of their hair. I set to the oars with a will, straining and heaving and driving myself mightily through the still-glassy water, but those three gaunt posts, the rotting masts of some sunken ship I guess, saunter up behind and overtake me in an idle but inexorable glide. A pair of green buoys steam upstream, and all my efforts to catch them up are to no avail. Sheerness is fading into a gold blaze of westering light as I drift helplessly out into the North Sea. And still, that overwhelming feeling of calm stillness persists, the impression of being at rest upon a summer lawn awaiting the arrival of strawberries and tea.

There occur very rarely in the life of Man times and situations where he is utterly powerless to decide his fate. In almost any situation, no matter how desperate, there is something he can do, some last card to play – whether to make that one phone call to his solicitor, or try one last plea to his captors, or make one desperate attempt to trap an animal using a bootlace and an old safety-pin and so survive another day in the wilderness. But when a situation comes along where there is *nothing* to be done, no final trick, no last resource, no eleventh-hour plea, then a great calm comes over him – in my experience, even a sort of glee. '*Crikey, I'm in for it now!*' goes a very tiny way towards expressing that mixture of exhilaration and curiosity and total abdication that I have felt on the three such occasions in my life. It is partly to do with the fact that whatever happens now, it is quite certainly out of our own hands, and this brings with it a weird certainty that therefore the hands in which the matter now resides are there, as they have always been, ready and sure and infinitely more capable than ours. The Mind that keeps the sun spinning and the cells dividing and the green grass growing is ready to take the reins that we have at last been forced to drop. It is a sense of relief, really, like being a child on piggyback again.

Well, the sun spun in its ordained course, and the land cooled and the seas stayed warm as they were designed to do, and because of that discrepancy in temperatures there sprang up a breeze in the last hour of that long day. It blew straight from the open sea to the little town of Sheerness, and I rode with it on my scarlet wings. Even now, the effect of the tide created a bizarre surrealism, for whereas before I had seemed to sit on a glassy mirror at peace and in reality had hurtled seawards, now with the wind in my sails and the foam curling at my prow and the rip-rip-ripple of water racing beneath the keel, I seemed to be flying across the sea as swiftly as a boy on a bike, and yet the beacon post twenty yards away stayed resolutely in its spot, refusing to draw an inch nearer despite my headlong approach.

But eventually as the tide slackened, that stand-off-ish beacon post deigned to draw near at last, allowed me to overtake it, and once more Sheerness assembled itself out of the gold and blue of the western horizon. Two hours after my first decision to row the half-mile to shore, I pulled in to that long strand just as the sun dipped below the sea wall. My chart showed a proper harbour another mile back up the coast and round into the mouth of the Medway, but I was deeply weary of all things nautical. I had been aboard for fourteen hours and had had neither a bite to eat nor a drop to drink in that time. I had come sixty miles, and refused to row a stroke further.

Jutting out from the sea wall was a tall pier of solid concrete, which offered me the only chance to tether my dinghy along the whole length of ochre shingle. The seaward end of this pier was currently ten yards or so from the sea's edge, so I had to drag or lift *Jack de Crow* up over the shingle to place it at the pier's foot. This I did by recruiting the two urchins whom I had spotted earlier. On closer acquaintance these turned out to be two eight-year-old boys called Matt and Luke, tow-haired, ruddy-cheeked and wellie-booted who said things like 'Coo!' and 'Cor!' and "Ere, Mister, are youse a pirate then?' and generally seemed straight out of *Oliver*. They helped me bail the boat out and drag her up beyond what I fondly imagined to be the high-tide limit, and after I had climbed up onto the pier they threw the long painter up to me so that I could tie it onto a ring bolt. All the while they asked a million questions and, when they ground to a halt, offered to keep guard on the boat the *whole* night against 'feeves 'n' robbers' of which, they earnestly assured me, Sheerness was full. *'And* pirates,' they added solemnly. I declined their kind offer, but playing the amiable Captain Flint to their Death and Glories, tipped them a gold sovereign apiece for their help in stowing *Jack* so well. (Well, a pound, but you know what I mean.) Seeing me as a possible source of further wealth, they insisted on taking a bag apiece and accompanied me along the promenade to the Seaview Hotel, squabbling cheerfully over who got to wear my pith helmet. It was only once I'd checked in at the front bar, and suffered the baleful glare of a few old sea-salts who clearly regarded the front bar as a resolutely child-free domain, that I managed to recover my hat and send them away with another fifty pence each and many earnest promises on their behalf to keep an eye on the boat.

The Seaview Hotel was a grand edifice built, I suspect, in the port's palmiest days. One lounge was called the Montgomery Room and had a plaque explaining that the Montgomery was a ship that had run aground and sunk during the Second World War. Its derelict masts protrude from the treacherous waters just off Sheerness (*Ah, that's what they were …*) but, as its hold still contains sufficient explosives to take the whole Island of Sheppey with it, all craft are expressly forbidden to go anywhere near it. The only exception to this rule is small Mirror dinghies drifting uncontrollably on the tide, I believe.

I found a room on the second floor with a view along the beach to where *Jack* lay in the distance, so that I could keep half an eye out for the 'feeves 'n' robbers' I had been warned of. Much good this did me, because in less than ten minutes I was sprawled on my bed fully dressed and fast asleep. It had been a long day, I had come a long way, and even the promise of a hot bath and a cold beer could not prop my eyes open a moment longer. But I had made a start at last. The long journey had begun.

Of Shallows and Shipwreck

They hadna sailed a league, a league,
A league but barely three,
When the lift grew dark, and the wind blew loud,
And gurly grew the sea.

The ankers brak, and the topmasts lap,
It was sic a deadly storm;
And the waves cam o'er the broken ship,
Till a' her sides were torn.
—Anonymous, *The Ballad of Sir Patrick Spens*

There is a thief in Sheerness Town on Sheppey Isle. He wears a grey cloak sewn with stars, he steals about in the darkness on silent feet and he sighs all night at his work. He shows no respect for the property or life of any man, and the only voice or law he heeds is that of his mistress, the Moon. And when I awoke the next morning, still in my rumpled clothes, and looked down the shingle shore, I saw at once that he had been at work on *Jack de Crow*.

This kelp-handed robber had more than burgled her. He had taken her and trounced her and set her on her stern against the pier wall before rifling her pockets and leaving her petticoats and stays all in a dreadful tangle, seemingly broken and bent. To put it plainly, the first thing I saw from my bedroom window when I awoke at five that morning was that the tide had come in during the night and left *Jack* in a horribly precarious state.

When I hurried along the promenade to assess the damage, I found that things were not as bad as they had first looked, but it had been a narrow escape. The painter had caught around a protruding iron bolt set in the concrete, probably when the tide was at its fullest, and when the tide had dropped away again it had left the poor dinghy hanging from her bow on the now-shortened tether. Only her stern rested against the shingle. With the angle she lay at and the battering she must have received half the night, one of the mast-stays had come loose so that her mast now leaned drunkenly to one side, the bundled gaff and sail unravelling in a tangle of ropes and tyers onto the sharp shingle. The front lockers, too, being doorless, had been scoured out by the swill of the sea and their contents stolen away, leaving only a scrape of gritty sand and a few crabs scuttling in their recesses.

The greatest loss was the jib. This is the smaller triangular sail that runs from the prow up to the masthead, which allows a boat to sail much closer to the wind and assists in bringing it around onto a new course every time you tack. On the narrow rivers I had found that I was usually running downwind, a course where the jib is not useful enough to be worth the bother of setting in place, but here on the open waters I had been planning to use it regularly. To that end I had bought in London a set of brand-new ropes to use with it, and these too were missing.

There followed an hour or so of re-rigging and scrubbing and emptying while the residents of Sheerness slowly woke to the new day and peered out their windows to see the foreigner at his task. At the end of that time I straightened up, stretched widely and realised that I was ravenous. I had neither eaten nor drunk a thing for thirty-four hours; the last food to pass my lips had been the Thai green curry on my last night in London. I stowed the last of my stuff, marched straight back to the Seaview Hotel and ordered the full cooked breakfast and a gallon of coffee. I wolfed it down, and then ordered exactly the same again.

I had been studying the chart carefully. Two possible routes lay open to me from Sheerness. I was at the westernmost point of the Isle of Sheppey, which lies like a great green pancake off the north coast of Kent, separated from the mainland only by the thin muddy trickle that is the West Swale and the broader but shallower East Swale. I could either choose to continue along the northern coast of the Isle, remaining in the Thames Estuary proper, or I could duck back round up into the Medway and thread my way through the two Swales to emerge further along the coast at Whitstable. The outer route would be shorter but more exposed to the wind and waves that even now were getting stronger; the inner route would be longer but provide a more sheltered route – and a more interesting one, I antici-pated, as I navigated my way through the tidal creeks and secret ways of the Swale. So before the wind grew any stronger, I made my

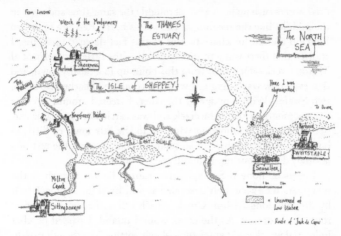

Map of the Isle of Sheppey

choice. Pushing the dinghy out from the shingle, I hoisted the sail and ran down the strengthening nor'easter to the mouth of the Medway and into the calmer waters behind the Isle.

*

It was a pleasant run up the Medway to the narrow entrance of West Swale Creek, with mirror-grey waters and a following wind, and the bliss continued up the Swale as it snaked its way through the low grass pastures and mud-flats of this deserted landscape. Herons flapped slowly away across the waters, the odd knot of waders dibbled and pattered on the shore, and the only cause for mild alarm was the sight of the Kingsferry swing bridge ahead, its red warning light telling all ships to stop and wait for the bridge to be lifted. All ships, that is, except the redoubtable *Jack de Crow* who pleases herself when it comes to these obstacles, who dips her tall gaff in stately salute to the goggle-eyed bridge-keeper and goes on her way unhindered.

I had been thinking that I would make it at least to Whitstable at the further end of the East Swale by that afternoon, but when I reached the point where the two Swales meet, I found that the incoming tide which had carried me so smoothly up the West Swale would now be against me if I tried to sail down the East Swale. The tidal waters rush up both arms at roughly the same time and meet in the middle, like the meeting of the waters in the Red Sea to drown Pharaoh and all his chariots. But as this fact dawned upon me, I realised that there was a third way to take – the little grey serpent of Milton Creek which runs from this point up to a nearby town, and that even now was filling fast with the combined floodwaters of the two Swales. With a nudge of the tiller, I steered around into the narrow mouth of this baby creek and was carried by my magic carpet of tide and a following wind up to the fair town of Sittingbourne. I would be there in an hour, and could spend the rest of a leisurely day devouring more full cooked breakfasts.

Let us be honest. Sittingbourne cannot by any stretch of the imagination be accurately described as fair. Even the approach to it by dinghy along Milton Creek, which offers the most romantic route in, is dreary. As the creek wound inland, I passed derelict industrial wreckage at every turn, slowly rotting into the salt marsh. Here an abandoned factory, there an old rusting goods depot; now a snarl of cyclone-wire fencing protecting a compound of oil-drums, and then a ruined farmhouse with boarded-up windows and graffitied walls. Occasionally my heart would lift at the sight of a fellow vessel ahead, until I drew nearer and found that it was the rotting skeleton of an ancient hulk decaying into the mud. Despite the essentially modern character of this industrial graveyard, there was also something strangely Dickensian about it. I half expected to see Magwitch come stumbling over the salt marshes or Pip escaping from murder in the ruined lime kilns.

I eventually moored behind a sheet-metal factory, manoeuvred my way past barbed-wire compounds where Alsatian guard dogs snarled frenziedly, and made my way into the town. I suppose the residents of Sittingbourne must feel a loyal fondness for the home of their forefathers, but honesty compels me to admit that I found it a dismal place that afternoon. The B&Bs in town were fully booked (Lord knows why), and I had to search further afield before I obtained accommodation in a large hotel that had prices inversely proportional to its charm.

I knew that the next morning I would have to time my departure to the minute. I must leave at the very top of the tide; any earlier and I would be fighting the in-sweeping current, any later and I would find that there was not enough water beneath even *Jack*'s shallow keel to float her. The upper reaches of Milton Creek would reduce to a filmy rivulet within minutes of the tide turning. My tables informed me that high tide was at 4.30 the next morning – another pre-dawn start – so I would have to leave the hotel at 3.30 to walk down to the creek. As I was paying for that night's accommodation, I was asked if I'd be taking breakfast before I left.

'Breakfast? At that hour?'

'Certainly, sir, and we can bring it up to your room if you wish.'

Determined to get my money's worth, I agreed, put in my order for a 3.15 wake-up call and a 3.30 room-service breakfast, and went upstairs for an early night feeling that perhaps I had been too harsh on the good folk of Sittingbourne. Room service? Gosh!

At precisely 3.30 the next morning I came wide awake in that mysterious instinctive way that humans have despite the absence of alarm clocks, sunrise cues or, indeed, pre-arranged wake-up calls. I rang Reception.

'Hello, Hotel Reception, Jason speaking, can I help you?'

'Yes, I'm in Room 450, my name's Mackinnon, and I was expecting a wake-up call fifteen minutes ago.'

'Certainly, sir, would you like me to make that call for you, sir?'

A pause.

'No,' I said, speaking very slowly, 'I'm awake now. That is how we are conversing at present.'

'Yes, sir, what is your room number please? I'll just check that for you, sir, and we'll soon have the problem sorted.'

Another longer pause. This boy has clearly been ingesting mercury out of a nearby creek for most of his life.

'Look, don't worry about that now, my room is 450 and I ordered breakfast to be sent to this room at 3.30. I'm on a bit of a tight schedule, you see, so I was wondering if it's on its way.'

'Certainly, sir, I have the order written here and it should be on the way up. Room number 330, yes?'

'Four-fifty.'

'Yes, sir, I'll just change that breakfast to 4.50, sir. You enjoy your lie-in, sir.'

There followed some very clear, very crisp instructions from my end, and we finally established the correct room number and the fact that I needed the breakfast immediately. The crispness of my tone went no way towards driving out the sing-song chirpiness of the youthful Jason's response.

'Yes, sir, enjoy your breakfast, sir.'

At 3.45, I had washed, shaved and was ready and packed, awaiting my reviving hot brekker.

At 3.55, I rang downstairs to Reception again.

'Hello, Hotel Reception, Jason speaking, can I hel …?'

'Yes, it is *Mackinnon* in Room 450, anxious to eat that breakfast that hasn't yet arrived. Any hope of it arriving soon-ish? I should have left ten minutes ago.'

'Certainly, sir, I'll just have it sent up, sir. Room number please?'

(A long sigh through flared nostrils) '*FOUR-FIFTY*. It is on the fourth floor.'

'Certainly, sir. Glad to be of service, sir.'

At 4.00, the phone rang.

'Wake-up call for Mr Mackinnon, wake-up call. Jason from Reception, sir, just calling to wake you up, sir.'

'I'm *awake* already, and I am *waiting* for my *breakfast!!*'

'Very good, sir, happy to be of service, sir. I'll send it up. Room number please …'

At 4.15, breakfast arrived. It consisted of two triangles of leathery toast, a polystyrene cup of tepid coffee and an assortment of those little plastic tubs of apricot jam that are completely impossible to open once your fingers have been made greasy by struggling with the foil-wrapped tiles of frozen butter. Somehow I managed to get a smear of conserve onto each triangle and wolf it down, and then I pelted downstairs to settle the bill, and, if possible, the receptionist.

While the acned Jason struggled to jam my Visa card into the machine the wrong way round, I realised that it was now too late to walk the distance and get to the boat in time for the tide, so I called an all-night taxi. When it arrived, I bundled into it and gave the order to the driver: 'The derelict warehouse down on the old industrial estate, please.' Considering the ungodly hour, I may as well have added 'just some unfinished business with Vinnie the Grass and a sack of quick-setting concrete.' At any rate, the driver showed the whites of his eyes, paused on a question, thought better of it and drove straight there, depositing me amid rusting barbed wire and burnt-out cars. Then he drove off rapidly, mentally erasing all memory of the trip.

There was still water in the creek, but not nearly as much as there was in the boat. She was yet again up to her gunwales in mud, crabs, stinking weed and salt-ooze. Perhaps she had caught under some projecting ledge as she lifted higher and higher on the incoming tide, or had snagged on something similar as she dropped again, or a dozen other playful possibilities. Whatever the facts, the result was as though she had spent several centuries under the sea and had just now been brought to the surface like some miniature latter-day *Mary Rose*. There was so much water in her that as I climbed out of my long trousers and into some swimming trunks in order to bail, I thought she may even have managed to hole herself, settling onto some underwater spike during the night. Only time would tell.

When the boat was clean and dry again, there was only a faintly glimmering eel of water winding down the creek. I would have to hurry if I didn't want to spend another twenty-four hours in Sitting-bourne. I set to the oars with a will, launching myself into the day's journey. With the last of the tide carrying me down the creek to the East Swale and thence to Whitstable, I reckoned, I would be well on my way by the time the morning was half done. Then perhaps an easy run down the coast to Margate, where I could stop for lunch, and then a jolly slosh round the coast to Dover in time for a six o'clock pint and a bash at the cryptic crossword before supper. Super.

So it was that, despite the darkness of the hour and the distressing odour of rotting crab still clinging to me, I set off in a jaunty frame of mind for what was to be, without a doubt, the worst day of my life.

*

5 a.m. – 9 a.m. I row down the rapidly emptying creek, shaving mudbanks as I go, the dismal waste on either bank still mercifully hidden in the grey murk of a dark dawning. Soon a breeze springs up. It rapidly increases to a stiff wind, blowing directly on the nose from the north-east and countering any effect the outgoing current might be having. A moment's respite to play with the idea of hoisting the sail has me two hundred yards back upstream grounded on a rapidly drying mudbank. A few Olympian heaves with an oar haul me off into the stream, but it takes me half-an-hour to regain my former position. By nine o'clock I have only just reached the confluence of the Swales and can turn eastwards down the broad stretch of water lying behind the Isle of Sheppey. At last I can hoist the sail and tack into the wind.

9 a.m. – 12 noon. After the four-hour strain of rowing into the wind, it is delightful to be sailing. I must be careful, though. Although the water stretches broadly away to either side, the navigable channel is narrow, and even I in my shallow little craft must not venture too far from it. Once or twice, in an attempt to lengthen a tack, I feel the centreboard drag stickily in the soft mud and must pull it up before I ground completely. Navigation buoys mark the way, my old friends the green bells and red boxes, but I am also introduced to a new type of buoy, the cardinal markers, and these cause me some small confusion.

After several interesting encounters with mid-channel mudbanks, I have formulated a working theory on how to treat these cardinal buoys and am pleased to see that I am making good progress. The landscape is exactly as I imagine the setting for Ransome's *Secret Water*: a huge sheet of water between low, featureless land, the tallest thing the old black beacon post rising out of the glass-grey mirror. To the left, the Isle of Sheppey rises gently in one vast green expanse, sloping up to a solitary farmhouse in a clump of trees and a windpump. To the right, the distant rises are painted in swathes of that artificial chrome yellow that I have seen from afar two days ago; the remote fields of oilseed rape beginning to glow radioactively under a darkening sky.

12 noon. I have reached the end of the Isle, and the Swale has bent north-east and widened out into a great triangle to join the sea. The town of Whitstable lies visible across a wide expanse of lumpy grey and white water directly to the east, but now, at low tide, this is barred and broken by the oyster beds of Whitstable Flats. I must continue in the main channel as it runs straight into the nor'easter for several miles until I can bear away to starboard and head directly to the shelter of the harbour. The wind, now that I have emerged from the shelter of the Isle, has become stronger. It is an iron bar ruled straight across the sea from Holland, thrashing the waves to a savage chop of white horses, and already I am beginning to feel the strain of these heavy seas.

12.30 p.m. This is dreadful. The waves are too big – distinctly 'gurly' in fact, as Sir Patrick Spens would have it. Without a jib I am having a hard time tacking into the wind, and the main problem is trying to go about each time. With a jib, one needs only put the tiller across and the wind catches behind this little sail and pulls her nose around, readying her to shoot off on the next zigzag. But each time that I try to change tack I lose way, am slapped sideways by the next grey fist of water and find myself blown back down the channel a hundred yards before I can regain control.

Another problem is that the vast triangular acres of Whitstable Flats are too shallow to allow me to sail directly across them to shore, but not yet so dry that they prevent the vicious combers from sweeping across, driven before the wind like grey Furies. I am suffering the double disadvantage of being out on an exposed body of sea and yet hemmed in a narrow channel – and I am not coping.

After half-an-hour of weeping frustration battling with the wind and waves, I learn a trick when going about. At the very moment of changing course, I release the tiller for a perilous few seconds, grab an oar and haul *Jack* bodily around onto the next tack. There are a few seconds of jolting and sloshing and the frenzied flogging of the mainsheet, and then the wind fills the sail and the brave little dinghy kicks off towards the further bank of the channel. I then have a minute or two to bail the boat like a madman with my plastic half-milk-bottle, before repeating the process. Even this bailing is a precarious task. To balance the force of the wind in the sail, I must sit out as far as I dare go, my bottom right on the windward gunwale, my torso leaning out backwards over the sea and clinging onto the mainsheet for dear life. To bail, however, I must lean right in, stooping to scoop the water from the bilges, and then the dinghy, no longer balanced, threatens to tip right over. There are two occasions when the lee gunwale sluices right under and *Jack* is suddenly awash with the briny flood, and I decide that bailing is perhaps something that can wait a little.

Having said all this, I am, incredibly, enjoying myself. I am wet through, I am bone-cold and my tiller hand is cramped painfully to its task. I am also making a bare mile in the hour. But I am filled with adrenalin, I am singing *When the Foeman Bares his Steel* defiantly to the storm winds, and I am enjoying establishing a balance to counter the worst of the gusts. And besides, I am nearly to the open stretch and will soon be able to turn and reach smoothly down to Whitstable. Tee-hee and Taran-taraaa!

1.23 p.m. I stop singing Gilbert and Sullivan and start singing *For Those in Peril on the Sea*. My boom has just broken.

Well, no, not my entire boom, just the vital bit. The mainsheet to control the mainsail is attached to the end of the boom by a large pulley. It is this pulley that suddenly decides that our chances of survival are actually not that high and decides to make a break for it. One moment it is there, the next it has vanished with a splash overboard. The sail flogs uncontrollably. The loose mainsheet convulses into knots. I coolly re-attach sheet to boom with a special knot invented on the spot and continue to sail. We have just blown back half a mile in the interval.

1.27 p.m. I discover that my new knot is a rather clever sort of self-jamming knot. Although I can still haul the sail *in*, I cannot let it out again, it seems. This means that when gusts come, I can no longer spill the wind to balance the blow, but must instead lean out even further. This is only made possible by actually *standing* on the gunwale, a stunt for which Mirrors were not really designed. I am now riding *Jack* like a windsurfer, and the rigging is emitting strange moanings and hummings. I am astonished at just how fast a Mirror can go. I am going to die.

1.52 p.m. Bailer blows overboard.

1.53 p.m. I turn the dinghy sharply to retrieve it. This is a feat of utter stupidity, for in doing so I run straight onto the eastern mudbank that here lurks a foot below the water. There is an almighty *CRRA-A-A-C-CK* from beneath the keel. Centreboard? Possibly …

1.59 p.m. Bailer is back in Sittingbourne by now. Boat still sailing into the wind, oddly enough, so it can't have been the centreboard after all. Boat horribly full of water, so I use the pith helmet to bail. Marvellous! Much better than the old bailer, can't think why I didn't think of it before. Am beginning to get really rather cold and tired. Make slow but steady progress towards the corner spit just five hundred yards ahead, sloosh, slap, wallop, splash, thud, plosh, clunk. Thank God I don't get seasick.

Ever.

I think …

2.35 p.m. Getting there. I am going to make it. I am actually going to make it. Decide to experiment tentatively with the centreboard. Gingerly try pulling it up a little. Stuck.

Tug harder.

Still stuck.

Another pull and … whoosh! Up she comes like a cork from a bottle – or rather half a cork from a bottle. I am left clutching just the top half of the bloody thing, broken off in a jagged line halfway down, while the lower half drops smoothly out of the bottom and reappears as a distant and useless bit of flotsam a hundred yards away. I'm sorry, but bugger, bugger, bugger, bugger, bugger. I *am* going to die.

2.40 p.m. I have allowed myself to drift onto a nearby mudbank. I am two miles out to sea. Consider myself lucky that I am in a flat-bottomed dinghy and not in some deep-keeled yacht. I take my anchor, newly bought in London, wade ankle-deep to the end of its warp and proudly stamp it home in the mud. I shall have to sit out here and wait for the tide to come in and cover the flats, and then drift or sail straight to the nearest bit of dry land when I'm ready. All shall be well and all shall be well and all manner of thing shall be well ...

2.47 p.m. No, it won't. I am quickly freezing to death. Being soaked to the skin and sitting fully exposed to the North Sea gale is rendering me inexpressibly miserable. I need to be cool and resourceful yet again. I decide to rig my blue awning up over the boom, which is immediately and surprisingly effective in keeping the wind out. Then I change out of my wringing wet clothes into some merely damp-through ones I find at the bottom of my bag. And then – and I think this is really the bit of my entire year's trav-elling that I am most proud of – I – listen to this – I make myself *a brand new centreboard* out of some matchsticks, a safety-pin and an old gull's wing. Well, no, sorry, carried away there a little, not out of those materials, but, almost as ingeniously, out of one of the duckboards that I use for sleeping on at night. This is the right thickness, but needs trimming to size with my Leatherman Multi-Purpose Handy Saw Attachment. Then it needs a hole drilled through the top so that I can jam a stout bit of rope through to make a handle. I also rig up a much better arrangement to allow the mainsheet to run freely to ease off the mainsail. By the time the tide comes in, my little ship will be equipped to sail to shore with dignity.

Those tasks done, I have nothing to do but wait. The tide is beginning to race in again, but it will be another hour or more before the stretch of flats downwind of me will be fully covered. As the waters race over the sands, they slap and jolt the sides of *Jack de Crow* and she crunches uneasily in the two inches of grey-tawny water. The wind is stronger than ever now, and I fear for *Jack*'s poor bottom. I am also, for the first time in my life, feeling distinctly nauseous, with the *crinch, slap, judder* of the boat beneath me. An hour or more to wait.

There is nothing for it. The usual solution. Hauling out my mattress and my sleeping bag, I think of another storm long ago over Galilee and fall fast asleep.

4.30 p.m. I awake. *Jack* is fully afloat and there seems to be a clear run to the shore about two miles away to the south. In that direction I can just make out what seems to be a long line of cottages above a strip of shingle, but after my experience in Sheerness I am reluctant to trust the dinghy to the vagaries of an exposed beach again. Besides, there will be no pubs or B&Bs so far out of Whitstable, which lies further off to the east. I stow my sleeping bag (damp), my mattress (damp), put on heavy-duty clothes (soaking), pack away the awning (sodden) and take in the anchor (damp but it doesn't matter). I then hoist the sail and begin the four-mile skim to Whitstable Harbour, which I decide is a much better choice than the row of rather snooty cottages on the beach. All will be well, and all …

4.33 p.m. Bugger Whitstable Harbour. In three minutes I have hit five oysterbeds and my Admiralty chart says quite distinctly that vessels grounding are liable to pay damages. Snooty cottages it is. I can get there without having to lower the centreboard, and, more importantly, before I die of hypothermia. It has begun to rain.

5.07 p.m. I have made it. I ground on the shingle with a rushing crunch, carried the last few yards by a sudden swoop of scum-topped wave. I am numb, exhausted and wetter than an incontinent walrus, and want nothing more than to find a hot bath, a mug of Bovril and a warm dry bed.

But I can't, not yet.

The sea has dumped me on the steeply sloping beach only half-way up the tidal reach. I cannot leave the dinghy here, but nor can I lift it any further up the shingle unaided. There is nothing for it but to spend another weary hour crouched shivering by *Jack*'s side and, with every wave that comes swirling in higher than the rest, to float her another foot or two uphill. An hour later, and it is nearly dark. The last and highest sea-wave takes her up with an almighty rush as though spitting her contemptuously from its mocking jaws, and she settles with a weary creak and scrape onto the dry shingle above the tide. She is safe now.

6.15 p.m. I climb, bone-weary, out of my sodden clothes and find some relatively dry ones to wear. In doing so, I receive the final blow of the day. Somewhere between the early departure of the morning and this late staggering ashore, I have lost my wallet. Credit cards, bank cards and seventy pounds in cash. This has happened almost certainly while I was thrashing my way in and out of dry-ish clothes while sitting out in mid-ocean. Therefore, the wallet is now in all probability at the bottom of the sea. Well, thank you very much, God. That is positively the last time I sing hymns to *you*, mate. I may as well just lie here and let the herring gulls finish me off.

6.20 p.m. An angel appears. It is not in the form I have become accustomed to, that of an elderly but sprightly lady bearing brandy, dog leads and good advice, but rather an anthropology student called Arif. He is a Moslem, and I am changing my religious allegiance forthwith. He takes me to his flat nearby, gives me two mugs of hot Bovril, lets me ring the Sittingbourne hotel to see if by chance I have left the wallet there ... no, I haven't ... and then loads up my sodden luggage into his car and drives me into Whitstable to a bed and breakfast, pointing out the laundromat and bank on the way. The B&B is, under normal circumstances, utterly charming. Tonight I bitterly resent the fact that it is located right on the seafront, as I never want to see salt water again in my life. Nor gulls, nor ships nor frilly shells, nor lighthouses nor lampreys, nor oilskins, oysters or compass-roses. In fact, for the next three hours the pavement beneath my feet is going up and down, side to side, to and fro, and I cannot walk a straight line. I am dying for a drink to compensate for the wobbling, but my new-found religious beliefs will not allow it, let alone my penniless state.

7.20 p.m. – 11.30 p.m.

1. A visit to the laundromat to put my clothes through the wash with a handful of borrowed change from Arif, blessed be he and his sons and his sons' sons forever;

2. A train ride back to Sittingbourne and a dreary walk to the derelict warehouse to see if I dropped my wallet on the wharf-side when I changed into boat-bailing gear in the early hours of the morning, but to no avail;

3. A visit to the taxi office to see if the driver has found my wallet dropped anywhere in his cab as I paid him that morning, only to be told that that particular driver has gone home and cannot be contacted;

4. A return by train to Whitstable to find that the laundromat has closed for the night with all my washing still safely inside but me outside and condemned to walk the streets shedding small crustaceans with every step and smelling like a fishing net;

5. A return to the B&B to find that the taxi company *has* managed to contact its driver and that, yes (praise be to Allah), my wallet has been handed in;

6. Another train journey back to Sittingbourne, a joyful reunion with my credit cards, and then the last train back to Whitstable, there to find that every bloody pub in town has just closed – except one: the Turk's Head, appropriately enough to my new faith, which serves possibly the nicest bowl of red-hot Hungarian goulash the world has ever known;

7. Bed.

The day has undeniably been a disaster. I am more tired than I knew it was possible to be. My left wrist, from thirteen hours of gripping the mainsheet in icy conditions, is hurting abominably; my little ship is lying on a distant stretch of inhospitable shingle with a faulty main-pulley, a jury-rigged centreboard and no bailer. I have spent an entire day suffering the strain of battling against wind and tide, the elements at their foulest, and have travelled all of seven miles. I have abandoned the faith of my childhood and grown to loathe the sea. And as I lie here between white linen sheets, and the rain drums on the windowpane and the old sea slap-slaps the wall beyond the darkness, I realise the oddest thing of all. I am happier than anybody else in the entire world.

Good night.

Cake and Carpentry

> Gae, fetch a web o' the silken claith,
> Another o' the twine,
> And wap them into our good ship's side,
> And let na the sea come in.
> —ANONYMOUS, *The Ballad of Sir Patrick Spens*

Whitstable is a seaside town that got left behind in the 1930s, the sort of place where Enid Blyton children still go to buy ginger pop and paper kites for a shilling before cycling back to their secret camp on the downs to foil all those spies and ruffian smugglers. It is the sort of place where fishing boats come into harbour trailing the coconut flakes of sea-birds, and the huge orange crates of dead fish on the wharves are picked over by squabbling, sardonic herring gulls. There are weatherboard houses in salty-white or tarry-black, converted net-drying lofts or kipper-smoking rooms, with names like '*Hove-To House*' or '*Sou'wester Cottage*' or '*The Oysterbed B&B*.' Each one has a large ginger cat and a brass telescope in the window. Along the sea-front there is a continual parade of headscarfed housewives with shopping bags off to buy a bit o' fresh 'addock for 'is Lordship's tea, or retired Colonels walking their tartan-jacketed Scotty dogs, or young mothers wheeling pushchairs with toddlers in them and their hair blown all over their faces, and everyone says, "Allo, luv!' as you pass, except the Colonels who say, 'Bit fresh, what?' as they march by into the gale. It is a peaceful, safe sort of place to spend five or so days, the only danger being from the Famous Five if they think you look suspiciously foreign and spy-like.

The reason I was forced to stay in Whitstable for the next five days will soon become apparent. For now that we have wandered on this sunny breezy morning along the seafront, past the gaily striped beach huts (whose proud owners enjoy a day at the seaside by huddling together around a kettle and a transistor radio out of the sleet and drizzle of an English summer's day), we have come at last to the outlying village of Seasalter, the long strip of shingle backed by the cottages and strewn with driftwood, including the rather sorry sight of a small and sea-battered Mirror lying high up on the tideline of kelp.

With a spring in my step and hope in my heart, I have come armed with a new pulley, a packet of screws and a couple of bits of timber to fix all that went wrong yesterday. What I have *not* come prepared to do is fix the gaping hole in her keel. That last mocking wave of the night which deposited *Jack de Crow* above the tideline had dumped her fair and square on a wicked iron spike hidden in the black kelp, and this had punched a raw hole right through her hull. It is still there, in fact, stabbing through the timbers from below. She is mortally wounded and I possess neither the tools nor the skill to mend her. Nor, to be honest, the heart. The journey, it seems, ends here.

'Yoo-hoo!'

A lady has emerged from a nearby cottage. If she has come to ask me to remove my dinghy and myself from her property, I will drown her here and now. She is certainly walking towards me with a sense of busy purpose, and has the air of one who has come to be polite but firm to vagabonds.

'Yoo-hoo! Young man?! Is that your dinghy?' I resign myself to the lecture about trespassing.

'Look – ' begin I, but am cut off by the torrent.

'If I'm being terribly nosy, do send me packing, but I couldn't help wondering if I could be of any use. And I'm simply dying to know who you are and where you've come from and what on earth you think you're doing. And whether you'd like a coffee? I'm Daphne, Daphne Dunster, by the way. What a dear little boat! *Can* I help? Or shall I just tiptoe away again?'

Daphne, says her husband Peter, is of the Mongoose Tribe – her motto is '*Go and find out.*' On further acquaintance, I found this to be indubitably true, but it would also appear to be backed by various other mottos such as '*Offer Assistance to Possible Lunatics,*' '*Ruthlessly Organise Those Less Capable Than Oneself*' and '*Try my Date-and-Walnut Slice and Die.*' I experienced all these philosophies over the next five days in a giddy whirl of kindness and competence and good fortune unparalleled in the history of seafaring. From the moment when I first allowed myself to be chivvied inside by the ever-so-slightly bossy Daphne for a coffee and a good cry, she and her husband ... and later her entire family ... went into action to make sure that *Jack* and myself had no excuse for abandoning the voyage there and then.

Blast them.

The first thing she told me over morning coffee was that her husband was a keen yachtsman, and consequently his shed was full of equipment: power-tools, drills, varnish, marine ply, screws, fittings, paint; anything I might need, in fact, to rebuild a centreboard, fix the boom and generally sort out the problems that had arisen at sea in the storm. Meanwhile, although she couldn't put me up here in the house because the entire Dunster tribe was arriving for the May Day holiday weekend, nevertheless she expected me to join the family for lunch the following day and to start work on the boat. I mournfully pointed out that though I had at last acquired *some* sort of competence at carpentry, the gaping gash in the hull was quite beyond me; she countered by playing her trump card. One of her numerous sons-in-law due to visit was a boat-builder, and of course he would be delighted to help and advise me in the mending of the dinghy. And now, if I had no more objections, the poor little thing couldn't stay there on the shingle any longer, so would have to be moved up onto their lawn at once ... and look, there's a couple of joggers, such nice-looking young men, who will be happy to help haul the boat up.

And off she trotted with a plate of date-and-walnut slice to bully the passing joggers into manhandling *Jack de Crow* up onto the grass outside the French windows to await the ministrations, expert and otherwise, that would fit her out for the crossing to France and beyond.

The next five days were utterly wonderful, and so make poor telling, alas. It would be nice to linger here over the carpentry and the coffee and the cake, the long, leisurely lunches with the Dunster tribe, and the bright May days spent passing screws and pliers to Paul the carpenter son-in-law lying on his back under the propped-up dinghy while he did clever and mysterious things to the hull and got varnish dripped in his eyes. It would be nice to be back there, in fact, forever in the limbo of that sunny pause, Odysseus entertained by the gracious Phaecians, able for a while to turn my back on the grey sea with plausible excuse.

Meanwhile, *Jack de Crow* was knocked into shape by the inestimable Paul. I must add that I didn't entirely leave him to it; I did at least see what was going on, and for those who are interested, I will explain briefly the process of fixing a hole in the keel. First we had to cut out the damaged section, leaving a neat rectangular hole in the bottom of the boat. The edges of the hole had to be bevelled slightly, like the sides of a plug hole in your bathtub. Then a plug had to be made to fit, a rectangular piece of wood with similarly bevelled edges, and this we made out of a stack of old marine ply from the shed, part of an older vessel. Then a larger piece of ply had to be made as a sturdy plate. This plate would sit in the bottom of the bilges over the plug, screwed to the hull and with the plug screwed to it from below. Finally, once everything was in place, the whole had to be slathered in a noxious red syrup whose name I now cannot recall, but the fumes of which stung the skin and eyes at fifty yards and, when inhaled too heavily, had me thinking that I had cracked Fermat's Last Theorem once more. There was the odd purple flying lobster to swat away as well.

After five days, it was time to be off. As I wandered down the long shore to the Dunsters that morning, I pondered the good fortune that had driven me ashore at just this spot at just such a time. Are there many cottages along that stretch of the North Kent coast where boat-building is provided at the drop of a hat, accompanied, what is more, by five days of warmth and hospitality and good humour? I am fortunate enough to be accustomed to kindness in others, but this latest display had left even me bewildered. Was I suffering from amnesia? Was I actually a member of the Dunster family who had suffered a blow on the head and forgotten who he was? Would I suddenly come round, triggered by the fortieth slice of date-and-walnut loaf in five days, look about me and cry, '*Mother? Father? What has happened? Where have I been? And whose is that ridiculous dinghy?*' and then trot upstairs to my old bedroom and start to piece together my old life as a native of Whitstable? There seemed no other likely solution as I humped my bags along the shingle to Seasalter for the last time.

The wind was perfect. It was setting due west, just right to take me along the coast to Margate, and beyond that to the North Foreland Light and the heel of England. There the coast turned sharply southwards towards Ramsgate and Dover, and I could happily reach down that section, sailing across the wind which would in all likelihood be diminished by the bulk of high land blocking it from the west. Such was the theory.

I had said my farewells to Peter and the rest of the family the evening before, so it was just Daphne and me who carried *Jack de Crow* down to the sea's edge. There Daphne presented me with a new bailer, something I had forgotten to obtain, gave me a last big hug and a stern admonition to be careful and to write when I reached France, and then steadied the dinghy in the waves while I climbed aboard.

Those first few seconds of launching are always a flurry and a fury, especially when there are waves attempting to spew you back onto the shore like a cat rejecting worm tablets. There is the sail to hoist, the rudder-string to release and the centreboard to jam down when one is confident of being out in deep enough water. Then there is the first alarming slop of a wave over the bows, and the sudden awful fear that one is being driven back onto shore again, followed by the hand-over-hand hurry to haul in the mainsheet, already wringing wet and salty. But with that action, the wind takes hold, the little boat spurts forward, meets a wave, rides up and over it, and the tiller thrums once more beneath the hand. Only then do we have the leisure to turn and wave to Daphne on the shore, and we are surprised to see how far we have come already. She is two hundred yards away and diminishing further with every second, her hand upheld in a last heartening wave. Another wave threatens us, and we must turn our attention forwards again, so that is the last we see of her. Five minutes later she has gone inside and the shore is empty.

But we are on our way again, and the *Crow* in her new and precious plumage is flying well. With our trap firmly closed, we sail on to Dover and the Channel crossing.

Dashing to Dover

'What matters it how far we go?' his scaly friend replied.
'There is another shore, you know, upon the other side.
The further off from England, the nearer is to France –
Then turn not pale, beloved snail, but come and join the
    dance.
Will you, won't you, will you, won't you, will you join the
    dance?
Will you, won't you, will you, won't you, won't you join the
    dance?'
    —Lewis Carroll, *Alice's Adventures in Wonderland*

I have described at some length the discomfort and weariness of beating headlong into a brisk wind at sea – the strain of hauling on sodden ropes, the six-times-a-minute dousing with a pailful of cold salt water, the difficulties in hauling the boat about at each tack. But give me a choice between all that and the sailor's dream of a following wind and I will take the beating every time. Running downwind that day was utterly terrifying.

For most of the time I was surfing down each wave into a green-grey valley of water, the blunt bow, never designed for these speeds, sending two great fans of spray up on either side like egret's wings. So highly powered was the boat with the sail out wide that the dinghy constantly threatened to nosedive into the waves and send the whole contraption somersaulting forward like a cyclist who has incautiously applied the front brakes too savagely on a steep descent. At times the prow did dip under, and the sea would sluice over the foredeck in a shining torrent, filling the dinghy with another few gallons of Channel water. What is more, with the wind off to one side, one can always balance the boat by leaning out into the wind on the opposite side of the sail. But here, with the wind directly aft, the whole boat rocked and swayed alarmingly with every swell and I was forced to sit crouched on my haunches in the middle of the dinghy, leaning from side to side to counteract each new wallow. An added danger was that of gybing, when the wind catches behind the sail and slams it across to the other side with murderous force. Had this happened, I could not have escaped capsizing and breaking the mast at the very least.

Lastly, there is the sheer speed of travel. I was planing most of the time, a phenomenon usually associated with more hydrodynamic boats than a Mirror, skidding wildly down the face of each tremendous wave and setting every fibre of the old wooden hull straining and humming and vibrating until I thought she would disintegrate beneath me. All in all, the experience was rather like surfing on an elderly cello.

One thing can be said for that leg of the voyage. I covered the miles with a rapidity I had not yet experienced. Whitstable vanished astern, Herne Bay came and went, and then the North Foreland Cliffs. This is the Heel of England, the point beyond which you cannot even pretend that you are still in the Thames Estuary. You are now in the Channel. You are now officially at sea.

*

All morning I had been praying hard for a chance to stop that precarious, headlong rush downwind, sometimes as many as three prayers a second, and as I rounded the Foreland, my prayers were answered. The wind changed in several ways: firstly, it doubled in speed and strength, and secondly, it now blew straight from the south, straight on the nose, and I was back to tacking. Two minutes later I was thinking back with tearful nostalgia to all that glorious surfing downwind and wondering how I could ever have thought that tacking was preferable.

But I have written enough about the discomforts of marine sailing in a boat built for the quiet inland waters of lake and mere. Let me record here that through all the drenchings, the haulings, the salt-slap-batterings of wave on bow, there was a great exhilaration, almost a lunatic hilarity, in my progress. There was an almost parental pride in the way that the rigging, as old-fashioned and Heath Robinson-ish as those little model boats I once made out of corks and matchsticks, was standing up to the strain and buffet of the winds: not least those bits of rigging I had had to glue and screw and bind myself with whatever had been handy at the time. For a thing of shreds and patches, she was doing well.

The Heel of England

So down that coast I tacked, at times drawing in close under the red cliffs where the wind lessened, and I glided between mats of slippery kelp before being forced by the black seething reefs to tack and turn out to sea once more. Then the wind would strengthen again, and the waves roll higher, and I would find myself in the dreadful quandary of fearing to tack, but knowing that as we drew further from the shore, the seas would grow fiercer and the winds gustier with every minute that passed. Then there would come the moment of courage, the thin cry of 'Ready to go about?' to my phantom crew, their white-faced nod of approval, and the pushing of the tiller to send us around. 'Ready about!' I would cry. The waves would heave, the sail clap like thunder, the poor dinghy would pitch and toss like a rearing pony, and then we'd be round once more, running for the shore and wondering if it was worth-while bailing the boat yet again.

At about six in the evening I tacked in behind the huge pier of

Ramsgate Harbour, right under the bows of a beautiful old Dutch sailing-schooner called the *Noordenlicht* – timber, two-masted and with tan sails – which had kindly stopped to let me go first. Small wonder that havens and harbours are used so often in hymns and religious imagery: the still beauty of calm and windless waters behind a breakwater, the reassuring elegance and symbolism of a lighthouse, the security of tying up to a pontoon with shaking fingers and knowing that soon they will be shaking no more, that somewhere beyond the final stripping off of sodden clothes a hot bath is waiting – these are surely foretastes of Heaven.

The local branch of Heaven in Ramsgate is known as the Royal Temple Yacht Club. It sits perched halfway up the cliffs above the harbour, a huge redbrick Victorian edifice. Behind its doors I found an enormous and elegant saloon with deep leather armchairs, old marine oil-paintings of ships and seascapes, a gigantic trophy cabinet blazing with silver cups and pewter platters and mahogany shields, newspapers to read at one's elbow – and a bar. This bar was attended by a young man who had spent most of a very quiet afternoon watching in fascinated horror from his lofty vantage point my slow zigzag progress down the coast, his hand hovering over the phone for the Emergency Services every time a larger-than-usual wave obscured me from sight. He admitted to me later that when he finally saw me slip in behind the harbour wall he had poured himself a large vodka and downed it in sheer vicarious relief. This barman then proceeded to introduce me to the members of the club who were now drifting in for a sundowner, and they in turn kept buying me drinks, impressed by what they saw as my intrepid courage, rather than recognising it for what it was: the inability to read a weather forecast properly. I saw no need to disillusion them.

Later that night in Ramsgate I met the sixteen crew members from the Dutch schooner, which, it transpired, had just arrived from the Azores. I thanked them warmly for their courtesy in having stopped earlier that afternoon at the harbour mouth to let me in first. They informed me a little curtly that they hadn't stopped to let me through out of courtesy, they had steered to avoid my erratic course and run onto a sandbank, thank you very much. Still, by the end of the evening the skipper was sufficiently thawed to offer to put *Jack de Crow* and myself aboard the next day and take me across safely to Ostend – he possibly saw this as one way to remove a shipping hazard from the Channel, the major ports of Europe and from beneath the bows of his fellow skippers.

Here was a quandary. The offer was certainly a good one, and seemed to be a gift on a plate, the hand of the gods again. The offer, though fuelled by an evening of beer and good company, appeared genuine – and what an opportunity to see the graceful *Noordenlicht* up close! To be sure, I would find myself in Ostend rather than Calais, but my map showed that here too there were canal entrances whereby I might enter the waterways system of Europe. How about it? The Channel crossing made easy? Nay, the Channel crossing made *possible*?

I declined. I do not to this day know why. This was just the sort of serendipitous opportunity I revel in, but something stubborn in me won that evening, something wilful and daring, something that whispered that if I really *could* cross the Channel unaided in a Mirror, then that would be a story worth telling. In fact, it urged, why even bother Wilf with his broken foot?

I could do it alone.

*

The wind had died right away by next morning, and the day was fair and warm with just a ghost of a breeze to carry me southwards. The misery of the last section had dissolved into a dew, as shimmering and insubstantial as the mirage over there on the horizon, the glassy slurring of the sea that showed where the fabled Goodwin Sands were drying out under the hot sun. To my right, the sweeping shoreline of Pegwell Bay receded into the distance, faded greens and sand-whites and ochre smudges. Beneath the bow, the water was clear blue-green, rippling happily as we footed forward at a gentle two miles an hour. So still and calm it was that I spent much of the day basking belly down on the foredeck, having rigged up the tiller in such a way that I could steer with a length of rope attached to an idle foot.

It was bliss. It was boring. Beyond the Sands a yacht ghosted by, barely moving. To while away the long hours, I took compass bearings off distant landmarks and drew lines on my chart to pinpoint my exact position. I wrote a couple of postcards. I sunbathed again until, at my head, a large fish jumped from the water, startling me awake, and I realised that I had, in fact, been snoozing.

By about four in the afternoon I had reached the White Cliffs themselves, and the little breeze had died to nothing, so I took to my oars and set myself rowing the last stretch to Dover. The Cliffs themselves were beautiful, more so than I had supposed. Most of the White Cliffs are topped by green pasture, vivid now in the late afternoon sun against the white chalk, but what architecture there is to be seen from below is varied and charming: a windmill, a row of fine gabled houses, a lighthouse, an obelisk and finally the grey ramparts and bastions of Dover Castle. They are the story-book structures from some giant-child's toy box, all set out with loving hands among the folds of green counterpane and white fall of linen sheets at the edge of the nursery bed that is England.

But before your ever-ascending eye reaches this homely array, there are the cliffs themselves, which still contrive to be as wild and giddying as Edgar describes them to poor blind Gloucester in *King Lear*:

> *Stand still. How fearful*
> *And dizzy 'tis to cast one's eyes so high!*
> *The crows and choughs that wing the midway air*
> *Show scarce so gross as beetles. Half way up*
> *Hangs one that gathers samphire – dreadful trade!*
> *Methinks he seems no bigger than his head …*
> *Look up a height; the shrill-gorged lark so far*
> *Cannot be seen or heard. Do but look up …*

Finally, on the upward flight, one's gaze floats up beyond the chalk, beyond the green turf, beyond the last lofty cupola of tower or windmill and up into the sweet empyrean blue, the lark-singing English sky of a late afternoon, and the tune has changed to Vera Lynn and her bluebirds over … and the long day's journey is nearly done.

*

Nearly, but not quite. Dover Harbour has two entrances, and I am approaching the northern one, rowing sluggishly against a turning tide. I am trying to creep in at the very foot of the strong-based promontory and do not see the emerging ferry until it rounds the harbour wall with a throbbing roar and a mighty surge of wash – far bigger and more beetling, it seems, than all the White Cliffs stacked on top of one another. At least the Cliffs stay still, give or take the odd tectonic shift every few million years. The ferry captain quite certainly does not see me far, far below his lofty bridge, so throwing overboard the time-honoured dictum of *Steam Gives Way to Sail*, I plunge wildly to one side and sit out the swell that threatens to swamp me.

Ten minutes later when the maelstrom has subsided, I try again, this time checking carefully for the least sign of an out-bound ferry. That is how I am caught completely unawares by the *in-bound* ferry that chooses that precise minute to steam up behind me, missing me by mere yards. This time, the tsunami-like wake flings me right up the harbour wall like a rejected lobster and very nearly over it. A pity it didn't, as it would have saved the patrol boat the bother of coming out to tow me in, as I'm sure they were very busy men and really didn't want to be bothered with a nuisance like me and all that tedious paperwork to fill in when they charged me *fifty pounds* for the privilege of their piloting skills.

Fifty bloody pounds, eh? Odysseus, Doctor Dolittle, Tom Bombadil – in their entire histories the words *chequebook*, *credit card* and *piloting fee* never get a single mention. As I rowed the last stretch to the wharf, I muttered to the departing patrol men, 'Where were you on the Morda Brook, eh? Where were you in the Jackfield Rapids? The Caen Hill Flight? Under Waterloo Bridge, eh, and on the Whitstable Oysterbeds when I really needed you?'

I didn't like Dover. Like a doormat, there is something gritty and utilitarian about the place. Useful, breezy, it is somewhere to wipe one's feet on entry to the country, but not a place to linger, to luxuriate. I considered the tourist options, came across one called, thrillingly, The White Cliffs Experience, and at that point decided it was time to get out of Dover as quickly as might be.

And there was the rub. I was at the end of the springboard. No longer could I put off the decision – the call to Wilf or the choice to go solo. I had now to speak to the local people, the coastguard, the yacht club, the Harbourmaster, everybody and anybody who could advise me about the Crossing. And it was now that I found an odd thing. Ever since I had first considered the idea, while I was still deep in the heart of Oxfordshire, people had been advising me in the strongest possible terms against such a course of action. Elderly couples cruising on the placid upper Thames in narrowboats called *Meadowlark* or *Buttercup* had warned me of the speed and size of oil tankers that ploughed the Channel day and night. Kindly landlords whose sole nautical experience had been regular weekly viewing of *The Onedin Line* twenty years previously seemed fully up-to-date on the casualty statistics pertaining to the North Sea. Whenever I had tried to introduce the idea of the gallant little ships of Dunkirk, *The Snowgoose* and all that, I had firmly been given more modern analogies, such as the one about attempting to cross the M25 at peak hour on your hands and knees. But strangely, as I approached the sea, people had become less dire in their outlook. The Dunsters had thought it was possible – with an escort, of course – and the Royal Temple Yacht Club members, at their most tanked-up, had been positively enthusiastic.

And here, now, in Dover itself, as I did the rounds, the attitude could best be described as blasé. When I said, 'Call it mad if you will, but I'm thinking of taking my Mirror dinghy across the Channel, ha, ha, I know, crazy, eh? Any advice?' the response ranged from boredom to indifference. The President of the Yacht Club said, 'Yes, and ...?' The Harbourmaster said something along the lines of, 'Really, yes, my seven-year old daughter sailed her Optimist across last July, got a pen-friend across there, you know what young girls are like.' Various seasoned sailors I met, picking up on the fact that I was after reassuring advice, merely mumbled, 'Lovely weather for it. Wouldn't leave it too long if I were you.'

Disturbed rather than comforted by all this half-hearted shoulder-shrugging, I decided to go to the experts. I took myself off to a phone-booth armed with a pad of paper and pen and rang the Coastguard. When I outlined my plan, I was relieved to hear a note of stern warning creep into the official's voice. 'Across to Calais, you say? In a Mirror dinghy? Right, now look here, son, I feel that I must most strongly advise you – '

'Yes, yes?' I asked, pencil in hand to take down some vital bit of marine wisdom.

'Are you writing this down? Good. Well, when you get into Calais Harbour – '

'C-a-l-a-i-s H-a-r-b-o-u-r,' I wrote.

'Past the green entrance buoys – conical things – '

'G-r-e-e-n / c-o-n-i-c-a-l'

'And you turn to starboard – '

'S-t-a-r-b-o-a-r-d'

'There's a huge white building ahead that acts as a landmark, have you got that?'

'Yes, huge white building.'

'Good. Well, it's a restaurant, see, and whatever you do, don't have the *moules au vin* there. I did last bank holiday and was as sick as a dog for a week – overpriced too, mark my words. Apart from that, have a good crossing. Cheerio!'

And that was it, the sole piece of advice from the marine authorities about the crossing of the busiest shipping lane in the world in an unpowered Mirror dinghy. I went to bed that night singing to myself a jingle half-remembered from many years ago:

Will I, won't I, will I, won't I, will I join the Dance?
The further 'tis from England, the closer 'tis to France!

Interminably it revolved in my head as I tried to place it. Wasn't it something from Lewis Carroll, and something to do with a melancholy Mock Turtle? And wasn't it a whiting or a Dover Sole making the invitation to the dance? Was I being invited by all the fishy, finny folk of the North Sea to join them under the briny blue, my bleached bones to dance to the tune of the tides in the salt and oozy depths?

Full fathom five thy father lies;
Of his bones are coral made;
Those are pearls that were his eyes …

As I drifted off to sleep, I reflected that I'd have to check the weather forecast for the next week or so, find a 'window' as they say in nautical circles. I'd have a chance to visit the Castle tomorrow perhaps, brush up my knowledge about thirty-million-year-old chalk at that other place maybe …

*

It seems I was to be given no excuse. The next morning was fine, so I went.

Crossing to Calais

Wherefore my heart leaps within me,
my mind roams with the waves
over the whale's domain, it wanders far and wide
across the face of the earth, returns again to me
eager and unsatisfied; the solitary bird screams,
irresistible, urges the heart to the whale's way
over the stretch of the seas.
—ANONYMOUS ANGLO-SAXON FRAGMENT,
The Seafarer

It was on the tenth day of May that I made the crossing, a day in which the elements so combined that all the world could stand up and say, 'This is the day to cross.' I needed a wind strong and steady enough to allow me to move swiftly through the water and cover the twenty-two miles before nightfall, and yet not so strong that I would be in danger of capsizing. The day also needed to be warm and clear, to enable me to stay comfortably in the open and to see where I was going – poor visibility would spell disaster – and yet a blissful calm such as I had from Ramsgate to Dover would be equally disastrous, leaving me idly adrift in mid-Channel with only my oars to propel me out of the way of the tankers and ferries that ply the waves with ferocious speed. This day was it.

Just before I leave, I pay a last visit to the Harbourmaster's office and they allow me to ring the local Coastguard. Despite their casual attitude of the day before, they give me a special number to ring and ask me to let them know when I reach Calais that evening, just so that they are not up all night worrying. With a final warning to watch out for the *moules au vin*, they ring off and I have no more excuse to linger.

At about ten o'clock that morning I untie from the sheltered pontoon beneath the harbour wall and row towards the harbour mouth. Before I am even halfway there, there is a breeze sufficient to warrant hauling up the sail and I glide smoothly across the gentle swell of water towards the entrance between its concrete moles. Even as I do so, I note that there is a swirling current around the northern mole, sweeping me towards it almost as fast as I am sailing forward, but I clear it with a good fifty yards to spare and am then out on the open sea. I have my compass lying on the central thwart, held in place by an elastic bungy-strap. The compass dial is set to the exact degree I must follow, 125 degrees, so all I have to do is steer in such a way that the quivering red needle is kept pointing to the large red N on the dial and I know that *Jack* will be pointing her nose at Calais somewhere over there beyond the horizon. Of course, it is not quite as simple as that, because with every wave *Jack* veers about as she mounts the oblique slope of one comber and races down the further slope in a skidding sideways glide, but as long as the average of all her gyrations keeps the needle wavering about the red N, then nothing can be too amiss.

I am excited and elated and yet feel secure. I have learnt all my lessons over the past fortnight, so have started this leg properly prepared. I am clad snugly in my large green cagoule, my fleece and my waterproof trousers. I have gardening gloves on my hands – not exactly *de rigeur* for the Cowes yachting set, but adequate for the prevention of blisters and cramp, though with a tendency to leak indelible navy-blue dye all over one's hands. Ship's provisions consist of two Mars bars and an apple. My trusty and beloved pith helmet is on my head: warm, broad of brim to prevent sunstroke, and sturdy enough to ward off any sudden blows from the boom should they occur.

Not that such mishaps are likely today. The wind is what every sailor prays for, coming straight on the beam from the north-east, balancing the boat beautifully and sending her along with the optimum speed and security. Yes, there is the occasional gust that sends a fine arrow-flight of spray into my eyes and face, to be wiped laughingly away. Yes, there is the odd rogue wave that catches us unawares and dollops into the bilges a lump of sea water, there to slosh and swish about my shoes until I can bail it out again. But these are no more than the spice on the adventure, reassuring, friendly knocks to remind me that this is intrepid stuff, this is real, this is remarkable.

It is difficult to keep watching behind me for the White Cliffs dwindling astern. One minute they are there, faded blue and hazy white. The next time I turn around, I am out of sight of all land, ringed by the wide horizon, and there is nothing to show where England has vanished to – nor that before me lies the vast Continent. I am at the very centre of a huge green-grey plate about five miles wide, and licked clean and empty of every living morsel but myself.

My moment's reverie is broken by a particularly wet slap in the face by a passing wave and a threatening shake of the irritable sail. What can the matter be? A glance at the compass shows me that the needle is pointing wide of its mark, that I have allowed the boat to swing too far north and into the wind. I hastily correct her course and settle down to concentrate on the frail red needle in its clear perspex case. Soon, however, I discover that the direction of waves and wind is so regular that I can steer on the whole by ensuring that I am angled into each new wave correctly. To get the maximum speed out of the sail, I have eased it off to a point where, let out any further, it would lose its taut curve and start to flap. Thus if I start heading too far north and into the wind, the leading edge of the sail will start bellying fretfully and I will know to ease away a little. Less and less must I keep glancing at the compass; more and more I feel like some seafarer of the ancient world, steering by wind and water and the flight of birds overhead. This is the whale's way, the haunt of scaly Fastitocalon, the wine-dark sea of Odysseus.

It soon occurs to me that the sea really *is* rather empty, especially as this particular stretch is supposed to be the busiest shipping lane in the world. Not only should there be all the traffic steaming up and down the Channel, but surely there should also have been a few cross-Channel craft by now. But no. Far, far off to the south is a tiny dot on the horizon that might just be a ship and there is a vaguer smudge ahead that might even be land, but of all else the sea is empty. There is just me, my compass and the thrumming rigging.

Actually, this thrumming has begun to baffle me a little. It has grown distinctly louder in the last few minutes. I can see where the bottom edge of the sail is vibrating tautly in the wind, making a sharp buzzing rattle, but it would also appear that the whole ship is emitting a deep throbbing roar. Can wind and water on tightly stretched stays and hollow timber produce such a sound? A sound that one could now almost call a snarl? I glance around again, scanning the horizon and the skies for any sign of another craft that could be responsible, but there is nothing, nothing at all.

The snarl has begun to crescendo, and every rope and stay seems to be vibrating like a manic set of harp strings, with the whining roar echoing from all about, sea and sky and wooden hull. I am beginning to wonder if this is what victims of the Bermuda Triangle witness before being carried to their doom, when a panicky glance over my shoulder reveals its source. There, just a mile from my dinghy where there had been a blank horizon merely a minute before, is a Sea Cat. In two minutes flat, it has hurtled past in a snarling cloud of spray just one hundred metres to the south of me and disappeared over the horizon, leaving the sea as empty as it was before but still with that noise reverberating from the sky on every side. It leaves me in a state of wide-eyed, stiff-backed sobriety, realising for the first time that day just what a precarious position I am in. The speed of these Sea Cats is deadly, and had I been directly in its course there would have been no chance of it spotting me in time to avoid a collision. I doubt whether the captain of such a demonically fast vessel would even be aware of hitting anything. As I recall, there are another four or five such craft due to make the crossing today, quite apart from the ones returning to Dover or leaving out of Ramsgate, and suddenly I feel keenly the aptness of the M25 analogy.

There is nothing to be done but to keep sailing onward – the sooner I get to the other side, the better. Meanwhile, that faintest of specks on the southern horizon has materialised into a large orange tanker churning its way up-Channel, and I am able to see at first-hand how fast these ships move as well. When I first identify it as a ship, it seems to be virtually straight off my starboard bow and about four miles away. It will quite clearly pass behind me. Ten minutes later and I am not quite so sure; it now appears to be very much closer and heading straight for me. After another five minutes of willing *Jack* to skip along faster and cross its path well ahead of it, it becomes apparent that far from slipping under its bow, I will be crossing its wake only when it is halfway to Rotterdam.

Meanwhile, the wind is growing brisker and the waves bigger, but it is nothing that *Jack* and I cannot handle. An hour ago we passed a large green buoy and I guessed that it might be one of the ones I had seen earlier on a chart marking the shipping channel. I estimate that soon we should be passing a buoy marking the further side of the three-mile-wide highway and then we can start reasonably looking for signs of Calais.

An hour later and I am puzzled by the failure of any buoy to appear. I have just had to dodge yet another tanker, a large rusty freighter with Cyrillic lettering on its hull, close enough to feel the temper of its wash, so am probably still in the main channel. I do not know exactly how fast *Jack de Crow* travels, but I would estimate about three or four miles per hour in this wind. I have been travelling for five hours now, and I really am expecting to see signs of Europe. It is quite a large place, I believe.

I see a mile ahead a large buoy and breathe a sigh of relief. I am more than halfway across. Beyond and to the right of it, I can also see yet another large ship moving northwards. Something strikes me as odd about the ship's motion – it would almost appear to be sailing backwards, blunt end first as it drifts along the far horizon past the buoy in the foreground. And then, like Tweety-Bird in the cartoon, I find myself exclaiming out loud, 'It *is*! It *is*! It *is* moving stern-first, naughty puddy-tat!' and wonder at the sheer irresponsibility of these Russian freighters that not only steer outside the main shipping channel, but also try clever stunts like sailing backwards, all tanked up on vodka, no doubt, tut, tut.

It is only when I have left the buoy behind me and am approaching the backwards freighter that I discover another anomaly. It has a large anchor chain sloping at an angle into the sea. It is, in fact, at rest. As was the buoy, presumably. Urr …? Brain cogs whirr slowly. Synapses feebly kick-start into life. Dimly remembered trigonometry lessons float out of the past to prompt me. *If a sailing boat passes a buoy at three knots and the angle between the buoy, the boat and an anchored vessel has increased by ten degrees in four minutes, how fast is the tide carrying the boat?*

Tide? Again? Not out here, surely. But a few minutes later I have worked it out. There is indeed a tide, a current carrying me northward almost as fast as I can sail east-south-eastward. Already the buoy that I have left a mile behind me is in fact nearly a mile south of me as well. Despite all my care with the compass and keeping angled consistently into the wind and the waves, nothing that I have done has compensated for the strong current carrying me all this time *up* the Channel. That is why it has taken me so long to cross the main channel, why ships have sailed backwards against buoys in the foreground, and why – mercifully, I now realise – I have not been mown down by every Sea Cat and Cross-Channel Ferry out of Dover that day. They have been plying their direct route straight across between Dover and Calais, unhindered by this petty piece of matchwood that has pursued its own diagonal course out of harm's way.

For this unwitting mercy, I am grateful ... and alive today ... but it still leaves me with the problem of being adrift I know not where in the English Channel and with the hours of daylight shortening. That I have drifted north, I am now sure – but how far? What course must I take to reach Calais? If I turn south, will I be battling with a current too strong to make any headway against? Would it be better, perhaps, to keep struggling eastward in the hope that I will come at least to some land, any land? I try picturing the map in my head, trying to remember what lies north of Calais. Dunkirk? Ostend? Den Haag?

Norway?

Resolutely I turn south and hope for the best.

After only half-an-hour of sailing, steering an uneasy course between due south and south-east, I am in luck. There ahead of me and off to the left is a long dark smudge on the horizon. It is indistinct, but there seem to be several tall chimneys and blocks that could well be factories or the skyscrapers of Calais. (Does Calais have skyscrapers?) I steer towards the long, low mass with a feeling of relief. That could have been a disaster, I tell myself firmly, and it's only due to your usual good luck that ...

... that ...

'Calais' is near enough for me to see it clearly and has revealed itself as not the gateway to a continent but as yet another tanker, anchored in mid-Channel. It is *enormous*, about the size of Luxembourg in fact, but it is not land. My heart sinks. How far have I come off course to discover this phantasm? Where now is Europe? Apart from the vast bulk of the ship, the horizon is utterly empty. I might as well be in the middle of the Atlantic Ocean.

With grim resolution I turn southward once more. The light has begun to take on that faint golden tint of late afternoon, flushing each wave with a gilded crest and making my scarlet sail glow warmly in the levelling rays of strong sunlight. It is a classic light, the sort of light used by Edward Hopper in his Cape Cod seascapes, side-lighting solitary lighthouses and seaside houses of whitewashed weatherboard, or throwing the long violet shadows of abandoned sandcastles across emptying beaches where each breaking comber glows emerald and aquamarine in a caught curl of colour. It is a light that heralds an end-of-the-day happiness, plod-home tiredness, supper-on-the-table contentment, and the coming of the night. Of this last aspect I am acutely conscious.

Another ten minutes ushers in a new and promising streak of towered grey on the horizon, this time off to the east. Half-an-hour later, this too has resolved itself into the shape of a vast tanker, and I am beginning to despair. The sun is really quite definitely westering, and I am zigzagging around the open sea in a ten-foot dinghy like a blowfly on a windowpane. I have by now lost any real sense of where Europe should be, and I realise that very soon I am going to have to do something absurd. I am going to have to approach one of these tankers – there are now two or three anchored around me – sail my tiny vessel up to the beetling iron cliff of its hull (somehow avoiding being dashed to pieces by the swell of waves on steel) and knock on the side to try to attract the attention of someone aboard. I will probably have to knock quite hard. What I will do once I have their attention, I am not quite sure. They will, after all, be some sixty feet above me and possibly Russian. Will they understand me when I call up in a tremulous voice, '*Er … excuse me. Sorry to bother you, but could you tell me the way to Calais?*'

*

I have just made up my mind that this, unlikely though it seems, is my best option, and am carefully choosing the friendliest-looking tanker, when I change my plan. For at this moment a flock of seagulls comes flying by. They are the first birds I have seen all day, and even in my present circumstances I am carried away by how lovely they are, crisp and clean-lined and keen-eyed. And more to the point, these gulls look purposeful. They are flying in a neat flock and heading due south, even a little westward, and have about them the air of gulls who, after a hard day's fishing, are heading home for a quiet beer and a night in front of the telly. They also look distinctly French to me – something about the beaks, perhaps, or the careless tilt of their wings. In fact, I am sure of it. They are Calais gulls, and they are going home right now. Without a single sensible thought in my head, I turn my back on the tankers and follow the seagulls across the empty waves.

And ten minutes later, Calais, unmistakable Calais, heaves into view on the southern horizon.

That last run is splendid. The wind is now behind me, but not so much as to be precarious. The Edward Hopper light I can now enjoy to the full, knowing that within the hour I will be safely in harbour. Off to my left are what seem to be long dunes and empty stretches of shore, and for a moment I am tempted to abandon the idea of Calais Harbour and run ashore on the wide sandy beaches re-enacting my own private Dunkirk, but common sense and a keen appetite for beer and omelette prevail, and I keep my course.

Just as I round the great northern wall of the harbour, precisely the same thing happens to me as happened when I tried to enter Dover. A monstrous Cross-Channel Ferry is emerging at full speed from the harbour just as another ferry is arriving. For one awful moment I am caught like a tiny cork between the two steel chasm-walls of either ship. There is barely twenty feet on either side, and one or the other must have seen me, because there comes a booming foghorn blast from on high that threatens to overwhelm me with its sheer volume. But the moment passes and, once the wake has stopped throwing me carelessly about, I lower sail and row hard for the far pier. A few minutes later, I have slipped into a smaller inner harbour and tied up to the foot of a black and barnacle-covered ladder. The tide is ebbing, so I make sure that *Jack* is tethered on a long painter and then climb wearily up to the pier top. It is six o'clock, I have been sailing for eight hours, and I have made it. I am in France.

*

Despite my overwhelming sense of relief and achievement, many things remained to be done. I went first to find some accommodation, carrying only my small day sack and leaving the rest of my gear in the dinghy, but when I returned an hour later to fetch it all – fresh clothes, toiletries, dry shoes and so on – I found that the ebbing tide had deposited *Jack* onto the harbour bed, and worse, onto two sharp lumps of rubble lying at the foot of the wall. There didn't appear to be any damage yet – she had settled gently enough – but I also found when I clambered down the slimy ladder that this ended four feet or so above where *Jack* now lay. Ordinarily this was no great distance to jump, but lying as she was, I knew that any attempt to climb aboard would surely impale the dinghy's keel on those pointy rocks. My dreams of a hot shower followed by climbing into clean, dry clothes were on hold until the tide floated *Jack* off the harbour bottom again. A quick calculation told me that this would not be until about midnight.

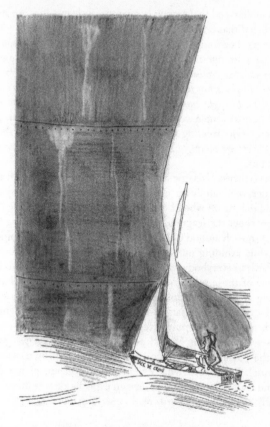

"Er ... Is This the Way to Calais?"

The other problem was that the number I had been given with which to ring the Coastguard was also in the dinghy, and equally unattainable. I had promised to let them know of my safe arrival, and if I were to leave it until midnight, they would no doubt already have had the rescue helicopters out looking for me – or at least had sent out that seven-year-old in her Optimist for a quick look around. In lieu of a better plan, when I rang my long-suffering sister Maggie to let her know of my safe arrival, I asked if she wouldn't mind doing me a small favour and phoning the Dover Coastguard to pass on the news. For those of you not fortunate enough to know my sister, you must understand that among her many saintly qualities is a strongly held belief that one should not bother complete strangers with odd messages. For someone of my sister's shy and retiring disposition, ringing a strange man out of the blue and saying, *'I'm so sorry to bother you, my brother asked me to tell you that he managed to sail his Mirror dinghy across to Calais safely today, does that make any sense to you, this is the right number, isn't it?'* is as awesomely embarrassing as most normal people would find a request to walk in on a stranger's funeral service wearing nothing but a pink feather boa and shouting *'The Piglets are coming!! The Piglets are coming!!'* during one of the quiet bits.

Nevertheless, Maggie agreed to do this, as well as ringing various concerned family members around the world. Then she gave me a good ticking off when I told her about the ferries, chuckled gratifyingly about the seagulls, and rang off. I then had nothing else to do but squelch around Calais in soggy shoes, find myself some supper while avoiding mussel-poisoning, and write thirty promised postcards to everybody who had helped me along the way so far.

One of those postcards would be to the Master-in-Charge of Sailing at Ellesmere College. Readers with long memories may recall a certain conversation on the sunny banks of Whitemere in North Shropshire almost a year before, something involving the phrases *'borrow a dinghy'* and *'pick it up from wherever you get it to'* and the possibility of Gloucester, say. I felt that by crossing the Channel, I had somewhat extended the concept of borrowing beyond its normal limits, and now an explanation was due. Consequently, one of the postcards read something like this:

Dear Phil,

Note the postmark and the picture on reverse! Arrived safely, both I and *Jack de Crow* cheerful and intact. Eight hours crossing in good NE wind, clear skies, but rotten navigation. Failure to take northerly current into account nearly had me landing in Denmark. Lost Europe for a while there, but saved by passing gulls.

Er ... about the dinghy? Can we now regard that loan as more like, say ... um ... a theft? Or will a £200 bribe do it? Please advise.

Best wishes,
Sandy & *Jack de Crow*

With a cheque dispatched along with the postcard, I knew that my request was more in the nature of a *fait accompli*, but trusted that Phil would understand and buy the sailing club a new Laser or something else more up-to-date. Meanwhile, the fugitive *Jack* and I were at liberty to make our way across Europe, our debts settled and our hearts footloose and fancy-free. But for tonight there were another twenty-nine postcards to be getting on with, and that was a lot of writing. It was time to find an all-night laundromat, somewhere to sit and wait for the tide to come back in.

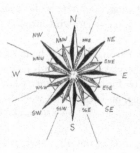

Dead Dogs and Englishmen

Spring, the sweet Spring, is the year's pleasant king;
Then blooms each thing, then maids dance in a ring,
Cold doth not sting, the pretty birds do sing,
Cuckoo, jug-jug, pu-we, to-witta-woo!

The palm and may make country houses gay,
Lambs frisk and play, the shepherds pipe all day,
And we hear aye birds tune this merry lay,
Cuckoo, jug-jug, pu-we, to-witta-woo!
—Thomas Nash, *Spring*

Now there starts a period of travelling that, as I look back upon it, seems out of some enchanted story, some eighteenth-century Arcadian idyll, a heady mixture of Nymphs 'n' Shepherds and Hey-Nonny-No, so much so that I fear to strain the reader's credulity. For it was May, the pleasant King of the Year, and I was in Picardy, whose very name conjures up for me – who can say why? – troubadours in patched coats, antique roses and dusty white roads, and the Queen of Flanders' daughter. And I was in a little boat, rowing by day and sleeping by night under warm stars, and living the life of a Scholar Gypsy.

It was not entirely a picnic, I must add. There were moments – whole days sometimes – of raw ugliness and back-straining frustration, but transforming memory has leached these things away and left only a sun-gilt tale with the clarity and oddly tilted perspective of a mediaeval illuminated manuscript. How much is it now my duty to record the truth of those next few months, the routes taken, the mileage of the days, the locks ascended, the sights seen? Am I Baedeker or Thomas Cook? What is the reality of that strange voyage, gliding like a gilded barge through the woods and poppied fields of France? That the distance from Cambrai to Douai is twenty-six kilometres? Or that the banks are lined with walnut trees and each one holds an echoing cuckoo among its broad and spicy leaves? I feel I must add to these notes the old maritime warning: *Not to be relied upon for navigational purposes.*

*

The first day out of Calais had me rowing through countryside in a surprisingly short time, out between banks frothing with cowparsley in the hot May sunshine. Once I was clear of the last houses, a gentle breeze sprang up from behind and I was able to hoist my sail and ripple along sweetly, passing French fishermen, young and old, sitting on the banks dangling their lines in the green waters. French anglers seem to be more genial and complacent than their English counterparts; even when a momentary lapse in concentration sent me straight through a fishing line and had me dragging rod, stand and all into the canal, the owner merely grunted good-humouredly, muttered *'De rien'* and set about retrieving his tackle. This went a long way to reassuring me of the friendliness of the natives – I had been assured at regular intervals from Shropshire to Kent that it was all very well relying on the goodwill of the English, but that anywhere beyond the Channel I was likely to meet with unabated hostility, surliness and unhealthy amounts of garlic. I was to find over the next few months that this was a pernicious lie, except about the garlic, and that I didn't mind at all.

As afternoon drew on to evening I found myself rowing along an empty stretch of pastureland where long rows of Monet poplars, mauve and smudgy and thin-stemmed, marched away in spindly avenues across the flat fields. I came at dusk to a small hamlet, tied up in a clump of nettles and climbed ashore to find that the nearest café was back in Calais. Just as I was standing there feeling a little cross with France for being so unhelpful, a man pulled up on his motorbike – middle-aged, pleasant-seeming and curious about the presence of *Jack*. In halting schoolboy French I managed to explain what I was doing and two minutes later found myself sitting on the back of his motorbike, arms wrapped around his chest, tearing along a dirt track beside the canal. Soon we turned off into the courtyard of an airy modern villa, the bike spluttered to a halt, an ear-splitting scream rent the air and a magnificent peacock flapped to perch on a white railing. Alain, for that was the farmer's name, showed me inside and introduced me to Benedicte, his pretty wife,

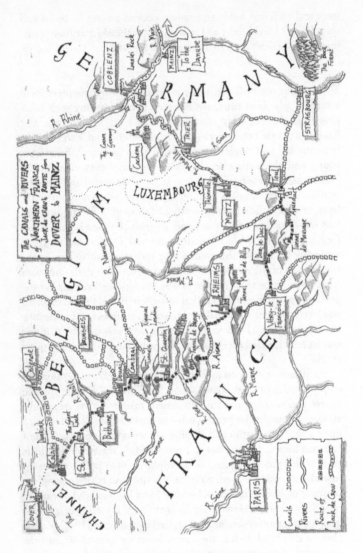

The following labels appear on the map:

GERMANY
BELGIUM
LUXEMBOURG
FRANCE
THE CHANNEL

COBLENZ
R. Main
Lorelei Rock
MAINZ
To the Danube
R. Rhine
STRASBOURG
The Black Forest
TRIER
R. Saar
The Canal of Germany
Cochem
The CANALS and RIVERS of NORTHERN FRANCE
Jack de Crow's Route from DOVER to MAINZ
Thionville
TOUL
METZ
Toul Aqueduct
R. Meuse
Bar-le-Duc
Tunnel de Mauvage
R. Marne
R. Meuse
RHEIMS
Tunnel Mont de Billy
Vitry-le-François
BRUSSELS
R. Meuse
Tunnel de Tupigny
R. Scheldt
Cambrai
Tunnels de Riqueval
St. Quentin
Tunnel de Braye
R. Aisne
Douai
R. Marne
Ostende
R. Lille
Dunkirk
Calais
The Great Lock
Béthune
St. Omer
R. Somme
R. Seine
PARIS
R. Seine
DOVER

Canals
Rivers
Route of Jack de Crow

The Canals and Rivers of Northern France

and their golden-haired three-year-old son, Aurelian. Is it just me, or is that the most beautiful name in the world?

It had not yet been made clear to me why I was there. My poor level of French comprehension had led me to believe that Alain was taking me to a café where I could get supper. Now he explained that he had brought me home for supper and to stay the night if I wished. Which I did, yes, very much and *merci, monsieur et madame.* In discussion with Benedicte, I was able to say nothing that involved any more extensive vocabulary than *j'aime* and *beaucoup* and *bon* and a list of simple household goods remembered from Third Form French. At one stage she asked me if I liked ears, which had me floundering until I remembered that *oeufs* means eggs, not ears. In my relief at comprehension I enthusiastically nodded and gesticulated, admitting that, yes, I adored eggs, I loved eggs, I had *une grande passion* for eggs – or at least compared to ears, to which I am largely indifferent. This resulted in a supper consisting of no less than five poached eggs for me alone, swimming in butter, lightly peppered and quite the best eggs I have ever tasted. They were all of different shapes and hues, ranging from bright sunny yellow to a bloody orange, and one of them had an alarmingly greenish tinge about the albumen. Hazarding a guess as to the origin of these wonderfully varied eggs, I dredged up some more vocabulary from *Parlez Français! Lesson Three: À la Campagne* and asked if these were eggs *de canard* and eggs *d'oie.*

'*Oui,*' Alain and Benedicte responded, pleased with my progress. From outside in the dusk came that ear-splitting scream, the scream of the foolish, jealous peacock in all his finery, angry that the Crow was here in the house being so well entertained.

Ah! I remembered something. I might muddle eggs and ears, but I was hot on French birds. '*Et cet oeuf?*' I burbled happily in my newfound tongue, pointing at the last one on my plate. '*Cet oeuf, est-ce que c'est un oeuf du paon?*' I asked, remembering with some pride the word for peacock.

Alain and Benedicte glanced at each other with amused pity. '*Non, monsieur, ce n'est pas possible,*' Alain gently explained, and then mimed an instructive biology lesson to the effect that peacocks, being male, are not generally relied upon for their egg-laying qualities. Outside, the cry of *le paon* had in it a note of derision. We changed the subject.

In the morning I was awakened from deep slumber by the smell and sizzle of breakfast being cooked, which turned out to be another three eggs, fried this time. What is the French word for cholesterol? After breakfast Alain offered to take me back on his bike to where I had left *Jack de Crow*, but just as I was leaving Benedicte became terribly formal and presented me with a small red-leather notebook. It was, she explained, for me to keep a journal of the voyage so that one day I might write a book, and it is this very notebook, much battered and travel-stained, that sits beside me now as I write.

*

The next four days were four days of blistering slog along canals made hideous by the hand of industry. For the most part the Canal du Nord that I found myself joining ran between straight high banks of sloping concrete, often too high for me to see any of the surrounding countryside. What little view I did glimpse was of flat featureless fields baking in the scorching sun and, hazy in the distance, what at first I took to be the spires of a remote cathedral, but which turned out to be yet another pylon or factory chimney, the only lofty landmarks in all that wasteland.

Another disagreeable feature of this region's canals was the number of drowned creatures bobbing in the murky waters. Many of these were small, anonymous creatures, unidentifiable in their distended forms – hairy, slimy balloons, bloated and swollen with gas – but there also seemed to be an inordinate number of drowned dogs among the flotsam. I rowed gingerly through an ever-increasing flotilla of these ghastly buoys – dachshunds, poodles, Alsatians, Rhodesian Ridgebacks – terrified that an incautious oar stroke might burst one of the carcasses and send it spurting and wheeeeing foetidly about my head like a released balloon at some ghoulish party. At one stage my oar briefly scooped up what, to this day, I would swear was the corpse of a long-dead platypus, though I do not pretend to guess how such a creature came to be in the Canal du Nord.

Another menace was the *péniches*, the large industrial barges that I here encountered for the first time, but which were to become all too familiar on the way to Romania. These are long grim barges of black iron, the freight-trains of the waterways, and ten times bigger than the little narrowboats of the English canals. Their speed was frightening and there was no question of them slackening their pace for the likes of a little rowing boat. While on the major canals,

I was as out of place as a donkey cart on a motorway and had to accept that here the *péniches* had right of way at all times. As they steamed past, their wake, echoing and ricocheting from the steep concrete walls of the canal, would send my little dinghy pitching and tossing in a dredged-up stew of scummy water and dead spaniel, leaving me unable to row on for another ten minutes until the wash had subsided.

It was slow progress I made in those four days, hot and frustrating and gritty for the most part. Nevertheless, I also remember passing a hot dusty field in which grazed, unmistakably, a zebra, calmly feeding amid a ragged herd of brown horses. (How very French, I mused. Even the horses here wear black-and-white stripy tops.) A little while later I pulled down a side arm into the sleepy town of Aire to find some lunch and discovered that the town fountain runs a bright Curaçao blue, quite the least tasteful thing I had seen in a long time. I siesta'd there beneath a shady willow tree in a park, setting the pattern for the next few months – it was simply too hot to row in the middle of the day.

Occasionally the concrete walls would give way to a pleasanter stretch of bank. One day I rowed past an endless avenue of magnificent horse-chestnut trees, each one laden with candles in pink and creamy-white that threw welcome shadow over the waters. Here a man was exercising his German Shepherd by the novel method of pushing it into the canal and, whenever it tried to clamber out again, pushing it back in with a stout stick. This continued unabated, although after ten minutes the dog was clearly exhausted and beginning to founder. At one point the poor creature sensibly gave up on its master and swam after *Jack de Crow*, attempting to clamber aboard. I was on the point of hauling it into the dinghy and not releasing it until we had found it a new owner when the man whistled from beneath the chestnut trees and the dog launched itself loyally back into the water to swim to the bank. The last I saw of it, it was yet again being laughingly fended off from the bank by its master. Here perhaps was an explanation for the number of drowned dogs I had been bumping my way through, if this was standard French dog-exercising practice.

At St Omer I encountered my first major lock. It was what is known as an *ascenseur* and was vast, unlike anything I had encountered in England. I thought for a minute that the canal had come to a dead end. Before me rose a giant wall of solid iron, black, riveted in plates and set between two great concrete pillars. Above this wall, three or four storeys up, was perched a little control-tower office with green glass. I was beginning to turn my dinghy around, thinking that perhaps I had missed the main turn-off some miles back, when the black water beneath me started welling and bubbling in alarming swirls, and I saw that the iron wall was beginning to rise. It was like the moment in a James Bond movie when a large section of a volcano glides smoothly aside to reveal the arch-villain's hideout. Once the gate had ascended fully, I found myself looking into a chasm between black walls, about three hundred metres long and sixty metres high. There was no sign of human life, nobody waving me in or shoo-ing me away, so I rowed gingerly into the canyon, my oar-clops setting up sinister echoes across the dark, slapping waters. Once I had rowed about fifty yards, there was a low, loud humming and I glanced back to see the massive iron gate sliding down in its grooves until the way was closed behind me. And before me. And on either side. This is the point where in all the best films an Eastern European voice booms out over some hidden speaker: *'Welcome, Mr Bond! You have rowed into my little trap with less than your customary prudence. I am, I must confess, a little disappointed. Still, it will be all the more amusing to watch you die. Farewell, Mr Bond.'* Then water starts pouring in on all sides and the walls start closing in and James has to do something awfully clever with his watch, his belt and a shoe-lace to escape.

At this point water *did* start pouring in on all sides, or at least began to well up from unseen depths with frightening rapidity. After a moment of panic I was able to steady the boat and keep her balanced in the middle of the *ascenseur* and note that the massive bollards set in the walls at intervals were actually rising with the water: they were attached to floating drums that rose or fell in long hollow vertical grooves. Thus a ship could tie up to a bollard and not fear being pulled under when the water rises, or being left hanging when the water drops. I was extremely grateful for the existence of these things; they made my experience in the biggest locks a safe and easy one for, despite the vast quantities of water involved and the extraordinary rate of filling, there was very little turbulence and *Jack* rode up as sweetly as a gull on the tide. And each time the unseen evil mastermind apparently changed his mind and let me row out the other end unscathed.

Now for the first time since leaving London I started sleeping aboard *Jack*. Each evening I would take the planks from under the thwarts and lay them across the boat to form a temporary decking. If the night was fine, that would be the full extent of my preparations. If, however, I wished to protect myself from dews and chills, I would pull the tarpaulin tautly into place. A strip of Velcro at the mast end of the tarpaulin closed that end off completely. The stern end remained open to the night air, a triangle of starry darkness and river reflections beyond my muffled feet.

When the weather was fine, I took the much simpler option of finding a level stretch of grass on the bank, spreading the tarpaulin out and making my bed there, leaving *Jack* to her own devices. And the weather *was* fine. Each day was hot and sunny, and the nights were cool, clear and starry. St Omer one night, Bethune the next, and thence to Lens where I slept in a leafy park beneath an ash tree where a grey cuckoo chimed late into the starry evening and recommenced at dawn. Then on to Douai after which I turned with relief off the main Canal du Nord onto a quieter waterway that wriggled its way southwards to Cambrai and St Quentin.

Now there were pastures and woods and banks frothing over with cow-parsley and hawthorn and elder trees all in bloom, their umbels like heads of clotted cream on every bough. I pulled into the little town of Cambrai and found to my surprise another English boat there, a smart little narrowboat called *Oyster*, whose owners, Mike and Judy, kindly lent me a power drill to mend the pintel which yet again had begun to wobble loose. Then, somewhere south of Cambrai, I came across the first lock on this stretch of the canal so far. All the locks on the Canal du Nord had been fully manned giants but here, on this smaller pastoral waterway, the locks were homely – willow-framed, fern-sprouting, sunny. I approached the gates with steady oar strokes, wondering as usual how long I would have to wait before the lock-keeper would spot me and start emptying the lock in order to permit my entry. The lights here, however, stayed resolutely red. I waited about fifteen minutes, idling on my oars, and then lost patience. I rowed up to the bank, tied up and strode along to the lock to see what was happening. There was nobody there. Really! Typical French, I thought to myself without a shred of fairness. A small office stood on the sunny lock quay, but its door was locked and a glance through the windows showed me a dusty room empty of all but an ancient swivel-chair, a stack of empty bottles and five or so dead flies on the sill.

Puzzled, I explored the lock itself. It was empty, but the lower gates were fast shut and there seemed to be no winches or beams with which to open them. I found two iron rods that dangled down the sides of the lock, one blue, the other red, and obviously important. I tried to make out the signs painted in flaking paint on battered tin plates above them, but apart from strongly suspecting that the red rod was there strictly for emergency purposes, I could not understand their function. Tentatively I jiggled the blue rod. Nothing happened. There was also nearby a large steel box with perforated holes in it and a few buttons which seemed to serve no obvious function apart from humming gently.

I stood and pondered in the warm sunny stillness, wondering where the absent lock-keeper was. Suddenly a mechanical whirring broke the silence, and I watched as the lower gates started to open of their own accord. And there downstream was my friendly *Oyster* chugging up the canal, approaching the lock in a steady glide. Hardly stopping to wonder where the phantom lock-keeper was who had spotted it coming, I raced back to my dinghy, cast off and rowed like a maddened windmill to follow *Oyster* into the cool moss-smelling depths of the lock. I was, I confess, a little hurt by the fact that Mike and Judy chose to start closing the massive gates while I was still ten feet from them – it was not cool common sense but a spurt of indignation that sent me driving forward between those black crushing jaws and allowed me to squeak through with mere inches to spare.

Once in the lock Mike and Judy were cordial enough, seeming to ignore the fact that the doors they had just slammed had come within a whisker of killing me; they seemed more anxious to talk about eyes and electronics and something else – to be honest, it was hard to hear as the water boomed and rushed in the echoing chasm of the filling lock.

By the time the water level had risen to the top, there was a splendid breeze blowing from astern and I was in a forgiving mood. In fact, I was in a mood for showing off. As we waited for the gates to open (where *was* that lock-keeper hidden?), I unbundled the sail and made ready to hoist it so that I could glide out of the lock under full sail, a resplendent sight in anyone's book. The gates swung wide. *Oyster* churned out in a flurry of wake, and I hauled the sail to the masthead. The breeze caught the sail, swung it wide and *Jack de Crow* began to glide along the lock, heading for the open gates.

Mike and Judy, glancing back, applauded the fine sight and then turned their attention forward again to the bend ahead – and so missed the next stage. The mainsheet, dragging along the quayside, neatly looped itself around a bollard and pulled the dinghy up with a jerk. She bumped heavily nose first into the concrete and was held fast for a minute while I tried to free her. By no means a disaster, but the gates ahead started swinging shut again. I was trapped in the lock, and yet again it seemed that a phantom lock-keeper was doing all he could to thwart my progress. By the time I had freed the straying loop of mainsheet from the bollard, the gates were firmly shut and I was locked in. *Oyster* had vanished around the bend ahead, and I was left alone cursing the momentary showing-off and the trap it had left me in.

Fortunately, just above the lock was a family of picnickers enjoying the warmth and the waterside, spread out on the grassy bank with bottles of wine and baguettes and lumps of white brie. After a little while I worked out in my head enough French to ask for their aid, and they were kindness itself in helping me unload *Jack*, de-rig her and drag her bodily over the gates and into the canal beyond – even feeling that all that effort warranted a glass of wine and a brie sandwich. I rowed away from that lock feeling cheerily replete but still without the faintest clue about the strange behaviour of the haunted lock mechanism.

It took me four more such experiences that day and the next before I understood. Let me explain.

The French locks are, as narrowboat owners throughout Europe will tell you, the best, the safest, the most convenient to be found anywhere between the North Sea and the Mediterranean. They operate on a rather nifty electronic-eye system. Any boat approaching a lock automatically activates an electronic eye set in the bank some fifty metres from the lock itself. Thus activated, the lock fills or empties (as appropriate), the gates open and the barge can glide in, activating a second eye set near the gates as it does so. This second eye will, after a short time-delay to allow safe entry, close the gates, and it is at this point that the skipper of the boat must put down his morning paper and do something to assist the process. This involves strolling along the deck to where the long iron rods run up the side of the lock wall. A quick tug on the blue rod activates the next part of the process – the filling (or emptying) of the lock, the opening of the gates, and the stately glide out of the lock and into the next section of the canal. The departure of the barge activates the eye at the open gates once more, which closes both gates for safety and re-sets the whole system for the next boat to come along.

It is a system of the utmost simplicity, and should win several major design awards. It was not, however, designed with *Jack de Crow* in mind. Being small and wooden, she was utterly unable to set off any of the electronic eyes so vital to the process. It had been the steel bulk of *Oyster* that had activated the gate-opening-and-shutting of the last lock and not some secret spite on their part – nor the work of a hidden lock-keeper lurking in the loosestrife. Though I felt a little better when I realised this, it didn't make my progress through the locks any easier. I did find over the next few days that if I was very observant, I could detect the position of the electronic eye on the bank and by rowing right up and waggling an oar in front of it for some minutes I was sometimes able to trigger it to open the gates for me and show a green come-along light. Then I would have to ensure that as I rowed into the lock itself, I triggered the second eye at the lock gates. Unfortunately, the only way of knowing whether I had triggered it was by seeing if the lights had changed back to red. As the traffic lights were usually set ten feet or so back down the canal, I would have to row back to glance at the lights. If sure enough they *had* gone red, there would be only fifteen seconds before the gates started closing, and I would have to make a dash for the narrowly closing gap like some nautical version of Indiana Jones diving under the traditional descending tomb door.

More often all the oar waggling in the world would not trigger the eye and I would be forced to land, climb up to the lock quay and make use of the large steel box with perforated holes that I had noticed earlier. This turned out to be a sort of phone. Into it I would speak in very slow and painstaking French and be countered by a babble of static-ridden, crackly French spoken extremely quickly of which I understood not one word. However, after a while I learnt that such an exercise would invariably result in the appearance some fifteen minutes later of a small white Fiat hurtling along the narrow dusty track that bordered the canal. Out of it would climb possibly the most patient man in the solar system. This was the *éclusier*, the lock-keeper, whom over the next three days I disturbed some twenty-seven times in the same manner, and who seemed utterly unconcerned about having yet again to drive to yet another remote lock to operate manually for the thirteenth time that day the supposedly automated lock for the increasingly apologetic and grovelling Englishman in *le chapeau drôle*. He waved aside my attempts to abase myself, smiled serenely into the middle distance, ushered me in and out of the lock at the appropriate moments and struck me altogether as an enormously contented soul.

None of this prepared me for the French canal tunnels, the first of which I encountered at Riqueval, lying halfway between Cambrai and St Quentin. I had been told, for reasons that I did not fully understand at the time, that one could only go through at midday, so I spent the morning driving the dinghy along with oar strokes that made her skip across the water like a demented frog. To keep time, I sang '*Green Grow the Rushes, O!*' (*I'll sing you one, O!*) at full volume for five miles straight without stopping and arrived at the tunnel mouth ten minutes too late. The fact is that the tunnel, at seven kilometres, is so long that boats must be towed by a special electric tug, which is itself hauled along a submerged chain. As there is no ventilation in the tunnel, no combustion engines can be used. No, nor unpowered dinghies, so don't even ask. Or at least that was the implication of the look that the guard gave me as I rowed up streaming with sweat and hoarse from singing. The next tow through? *À six heures et demi, m'sieur, ce soir.*

For the next six hours I sat in the shade of an old garden wall above the canal, dozing, writing letters and consuming a large hunk of strong salami and a bottle of beer. As the hot sun cooled to a fragrant afternoon, full of the smells of grass and horses and warm old brick, the electric tug hummed into sight and I joined three other vessels. We were to be towed through together. There had been much headshaking and Gallic muttering about the dangers of allowing such a small and frail boat to attempt the perils of the Riqueval Tunnel, but in the end I had merrily flung my painter around the stern-post of the last boat and feigned smiling incomprehension at the serious talk going on above me. After a few even more Gallic shrugs, we were off.

There is a scene in *The Voyage of the Dawn Treader* where C.S. Lewis describes the children sailing into a mysterious island of darkness, which turns out to be the terrible land where dreams come true. Not daydreams, but dreams – and nightmares included. His description of the swift fading of the sunlit world, the draining away of colour and warmth and light, of sea-blues and sun-golds, to be replaced with chilly, black silence, haunted me as a child for many years. This was like that. Very soon the arched end of the tunnel had dwindled to a tiny spot of greeny-white far behind, and then vanished altogether. Above me was the high curved roof of the tunnel, soot-black but smudged here and there with the dead white of some fungus or mould and the odd glimmer of filmy water seeping through the brickwork. The passage of the boats through the tunnel was almost entirely silent, with only the swirl of water beneath the bows magnified and echoing into the darkness, and the steady hum of the electric boat some twenty yards ahead. After ten minutes of this chill and lonely voyage, strung on the end of a long line being towed through the darkness, I dug out my tin-whistle and started playing. Sweet and pure the notes sounded as I played Crimond and *Abide With Me*, and all the hymns of sorrow and comfort that have ever been written. They echoed away on each quivering cadence and came ghostly back again from the curving walls in a mournful descant. I understood why Orpheus took his lyre into the Underworld. In the darkness, music is the only light.

Two hours later we emerged into the waning light of day. The other vessels detached themselves and hurried off down the canal, hoping, no doubt, to make St Quentin before nightfall. The electric tug vanished back into the tunnel and I was left alone. I found that we had emerged into a steep defile where beech woods marched up either bank in ominous ranks of grey pillars and interlacing boughs. Such beautiful trees, usually, but here they closed in, crowding over the water, tangled blackberry brambles at their feet, and the sky a remote strip of primrose far above. So steep was that unnatural valley that no lingering light of day touched anything but the highest treetops on the further ridge; all was shadowed and chilly and beginning to grow damp with evening dew. My feelings of unease were confirmed when, mooring by the only bramble-free patch of canal side for the night, I discovered a large dead crow lying tumbled in the weeds. Its plumage was glossy still, shot with purple and green, but already there were white maggots in its empty eyes; both *Jack* and I slept ill that night under the satirical stars. It was the Valley of the Shadow of Death and I did not allow my thin piping to disturb the shadows that night.

*

Next morning the steep beechwood defile continued unbroken for another five kilometres. There was a hint of thunder in the air and the sullen leaves hung lifeless on the beeches' coppery tracery. Then I came to the entrance of the next tunnel, the Tunnel de Lesdins. Here there was no sign of a tug, no guards, no notices – just a single set of lights showing green, and the small familiar grey box housing the electronic eye at the tunnel's mouth.

I stopped, pondering. What was meant to happen now? There was no evidence of a tug, so it seemed that one could not expect a tow. But how long was the tunnel? And what happened if I met another boat coming the other way? But no – surely if there was a green light at this end, there would be a red one at the other end? Of course it would be safe.

Two crows dropped heavily out of a nearby beech tree and flapped away down the gorge croaking. The water steamed in the hot morning sun. Flies danced.

Unless …

Unless that green light was simply left over from the last boat to go through from this end … and … think now … the system was now set equally biased to either end. It would wait for the first boat to enter in either direction and only *then* trigger a red light at the other end to stop oncoming traffic. In which case … er? … I was still alright. I should stop shilly-shallying about and just go.

A large fish turned lazily in the scummy water, breaking the oppressive silence with a soft flop. The ripples spread sluggishly and died.

Yes …

Unless … hmmm. Unless, as was most likely from the experience of the past few days, my little wooden craft failed to trigger the electronic eye and so register my presence in the tunnel, in which case I was fair game to be turned to pâté by anything that came along in the next hour or so.

Hmmm. There was nothing for it. I would just have to take a deep breath, trust to luck and row like blazes.

Cranking up Crimond, I entered the tunnel.

The Lord's my-y Shep-he-erd, I'll not want;
He ma-akes me down to lie,
In pa-a-stures green, He lea-ea-deth me,
The qui-i-et wa-ters by

Black walls, white mould, seeping damp again, but this time,

Into the Darkness

every hundred feet or so, a yellowing light bulb dimly illuminating the tunnel and, disconcertingly, the alarming state of the ceiling and rotting walls. I had preferred complete darkness. Every now and then there would sound above the hollow clop and creak of the oars the distant spatter of falling water. It would grow nearer and louder, and then I would be right under it, freezing water clattering in a chilly rope from a crack high above in the curved ceiling and drenching me for a second or two. Then the strong notes of Crimond or the Passion Chorale would go oddly squeaky for a moment and the lyrics would switch from the profound to the profane.

It was hard to estimate how long the tunnel was, or how fast I was moving through it. One of the major disadvantages of rowing as a means of propulsion is that one travels through life backwards, and I was forever craning my neck around to see if in the darkness ahead there was that which I feared most: the steady light of an approaching barge. On the other hand, one of the major disadvantages of always craning one's neck around to look *ahead* in a rowing boat is that you never spot the barge rapidly approaching from *behind*.

Or at least I never spotted it until I heard it, and that was very nearly too late. There it was, a yellow light coming up behind me and growing rapidly and steadily bigger. I glanced around. The exit was in sight but only just, a tiny half-moon of daylight seemingly three hundred miles away. To my right was a concrete ledge that acted as a sort of rough towpath through the tunnel, but it had along it an ancient, rusted railing, and besides, was hardly wide enough to pull *Jack* onto even if I could have got her over the waist-high rail on my own. There was nothing for it but to row, and row like buggery.

Sacred music of a lyrical kind gave way to tunes considerably more robust. *Onward, Christian Soldiers!* was galloped through *accelerando*, *Judas Maccabeus* swelled its trumpet cadences in adrenalin-charged defiance of Death, but it was, I think, *Tell out, my Soul!* that sent me winging out of the darkness fifteen minutes later and into the welcome arms of the day. I shot out of the tunnel mouth a mere ninety seconds ahead of the fifty-foot barge that emerged at full, pâté-making speed behind me. A blast on its siren as it passed indicated that this was the first it had seen of me.

It did not look happy.

I, on the other hand, despite the shaking limbs, the sobbing breath and the sweat-stinging eyes, was just about ready for another verse of Crimond.

Et in Arcadia Ego

'Tis not through envy of thy happy lot,
But being too happy in thine happiness, –
That thou, light-wingèd Dryad of the trees,
In some melodious plot
Of beechen green and shadows numberless,
Singest of Summer in full-throated ease.
—JOHN KEATS, *Ode to a Nightingale*

In St Quentin I visited a bookshop and the only two titles I could find were *The Tempest* and a book of Keats' poetry. These I bought, determined to defeat the boredom of rowing by learning some verse off by heart. As I rowed out of the town the next day, I had the Keats propped on the back thwart and started with *Ode to a Nightingale*. My heart aches, and a drowsy numbness pains my sense …

From St Quentin onwards, the countryside became utterly lovely. I rowed through a Pre-Raphaelite landscape where the dog roses dropped blushing petals on the water, where flag-irises stood in yellow fleur-de-lis along the banks, where elderflowers frothed like heads of sparkling champagne on every bough and each new bend of the tranquil waterway cried out for a drowned Millais Ophelia or a Lady of Shalott swathed in tapestries aboard her tragic barge.

That night I pulled into a little village in a clearing in a forest and moored up next to a tiny white cruiser. As I was preparing my awning for the night, the owner of the cruiser came down from his house across the grass, introduced himself as Jean-Philippe and, almost inevitably it seemed, invited me to dinner with his wife, Valérie, and Lucat, their eleven-year-old son. Lucat, a keen naturalist, was fascinated by my little flag depicting *Jack de Crow*, so in the course of the meal we discussed in halting French the differences between jackdaws and crows, ravens and rooks, with the aid of a large and colourful bird-book. The flag in question had been

sewn for me by my mother and showed a heraldic crow on a yellow
background holding in its bill a golden ruby ring; it flew proudly
from my stays to show the wind direction. The design was based on
the Ellesmere College crest, depicting the Raven of St Oswald
holding his royal ring, but of course also representing the original
Jack de Crow, my tame and thieving jackdaw of many years ago. So
crow or raven or jackdaw, all these possibilities were earnestly
explored over the steaming cassoulet and good red wine at Valérie's
table.

Once my halting French caused some confusion. When asked by
Jean-Philippe where or how I slept at night, I tried explaining about
my sleeping arrangements and my mattress by replying, 'Ah, c'est
bon! Ce n'est pas un problème. La nuit, je suis très confortable parce
que ... um ... j'ai une ...what's the word! ... une petite maîtresse.'

Amid Valérie's stifled mirth, Jean-Philippe explained to me gently that the word I was looking for was '*matelat*.' My choice of
'*maîtresse*' could well lead to some interesting questions. Where, for
example, would she live during the day?

And some weeks later, when I was asked the same question, I got
it wrong again. This time I remembered not to confuse *mattress* with
mistress, but in casting around for that final word I hit triumphantly
upon '*matelot*.' The admission that what kept me happy and comfortable at night was the presence of my own little sailor boy left most
people hurrying away determined not to enquire any further into my
sleeping arrangements.

*

Two days later I sailed into the city of Rheims, arriving by chance in
the middle of a waterways festival celebrating one hundred and fifty
years of the French canals. There were boats and barges of every
description ploughing up and down the canal, banners hung out to
welcome visitors from all over Europe, and large marquees set up
along the banks. I was pleasantly surprised by the reaction to my little boat: cheers and waves from people drinking champagne aboard
a VIP ship, and blasts on the hooters and horns of each vessel that
sailed past. When I tied up at the marina, I was greeted by a chain-
bedecked official resembling Hercule Poirot, who earnestly shook
my hand, kissed me on both cheeks and handed me a glass of champagne, waving aside my questions about mooring fees. Proudly he
called some colleagues over and pointed excitedly at my two flags,

the Union Jack and, oddly enough, the Jack de Crow pennant, and I explained that yes, I had come from England.

'Oui, oui, d'accord!' he cried, embracing me once more. 'From England, oui, c'est vrai! And especially for our fête des canals, non? C'est magnifique!'

'Well, I didn't actually know about this festival but – '

'Non? Mais oui, monsieur, you play ze little jest on us, I zink. How can you not know about ze great festival of Rheims, and you wiz ze little flag of our great city flying oh so proud 'ere on ze brave little boat, non? Quel honneur, m'sieur, quel honneur!'

Only then did I look more carefully around me at the banners and pennants and flags that fluttered and cracked in the rising breeze. Every one of them bore a strangely familiar design: a heraldic black crow bearing in its bill a ruby ring. This, I found, was the ancient crest of the city, immortalised in Southey's poem *The Jackdaw of Rheims*, telling the tale of the theft of the Cardinal's ruby ring by one of Jack de Crow's ancestors. It was clear that *Jack* and I were meant to be here.

*

After Rheims I travelled south-east on the Canal de l'Aisne à la Marne, passed through the Tunnel de Mont Billy and onwards to Châlon-sur-Marne, and thence rowed up the Marne system to Vitry-le-Françoise. There I turned eastwards onto the narrow Saulx and rowed on through Sermaize, Bar-le-Duc and Ligny, climbing steeply to cross the last watershed before the long descent to the Rhine Valley. Here, at the top of the range, I plunged through the last tunnel, that of Mauvage, and descended swiftly to Toul and – oh, sweet relief! – the head of the Moselle River. Those twelve days were spent almost entirely in rowing, entirely in fine weather, and entirely in a daze of beauty, Keats and birdsong. What else is there to say?

Well, the windmill I saw for starters, just outside Rheims, perched on a gentle rise striped with the green and golden rows of vines and cut through with the zigzag line of a white and dusty road. Then there were the midday stops when the sun had grown too hot for rowing and I skinny-dipped in lonely bends of the River Saulx that ran alongside, just down the canal bank. Here the water was fast flowing and greeny-jade over amber gravel, and cool on the skin. I clambered out of the river naked and watchful, up banks of comfrey coarse as sandpaper, there to lie in deep beds of tickling vetch and loosestrife and dry out in the May sunshine. Sometimes on the outskirts of a village where I had just lunched on a metre-long sandwich and a bottle of beer, I pulled my mattress out and spread it beneath a shady walnut tree and dozed for an hour or so while the noonday sun declined to a tamer heat. There were tall poplars along the bank now, and every one of them was shedding a gentle snow-gale of drifting white down, making breathing a hazardous occupation. Soon the dinghy was full of fuzzy fluff and I was in danger of choking if I breathed incautiously.

There were days when I stopped rowing and rested, especially as in this part of the country the canals close on Sunday. Sunday also happened to be market-day in many of the little towns and villages, so I would spend a mildly irritable day moving from café to café in search of a quiet corner to sit and write letters while outside in the market squares there would burst a profusion of colour and noise and smells: roast chickens, flaky buttery pastries, barrows of peaches and nectarines and deep bloomy plums, racks of cheap gaudy clothes and everywhere the relentlessly cheery drone of accordion music over loudspeakers. ABBA was also very popular in that corner of France, played day and night, and any form of creative thought in the form of letter writing was effectively quashed. Add to this the presence of loud French youths in combination with those rattling, thumping table soccer games, and Sunday was the noisiest day of the week. I had become so accustomed to the silence and sweet bird-song of woods and meadows that my temper frayed readily at the clatter of radio-tuned humanity enjoying itself. I had become a cantankerous hermit.

On the fourth day of June I came at last to the little town of Demanges, the last before the Tunnel de Mauvage. This would take me through the last great watershed before the land slopes gently away to the Moselle valley and thence to the Rhine. Here I was told, however, that 'le Directeur' would not permit me to row through the tunnel, or be towed. Reluctantly it was agreed that I might *walk* through the five-kilometre tunnel hauling *Jack* behind me. How I would do this, though, I was not sure.

I went to sleep that night on the grass of a secluded bank by the canal and watched a spider perfectly silhouetted shuttling to and fro between the mast-top and hoisted gaff. She was spinning an invisible web against the deepening blue sky, entrapping only the faint stars, diamonds in new constellations. Seeding grass stems nodded above my head, likewise silhouetted, as delicate and finely drawn as a Chinese print. They stirred and bended in the faintest of river breezes. In an ash tree nearby, there was a sudden rush and trill of song and with a jolt I realised that it was a nightingale. I had never heard one before, but my mind had been full of the very thought of them for years – not only the famed Keats but all the other niches in myth and literature that this beloved bird has held. For a few minutes I listened in rapture, carried away by the perfect poetry of the moment.

I must be honest, though. I doubt very much whether Mr Keats and company ever actually heard a specimen of the bird in full song, because if they had they would have searched around for a more suitable subject for their rapturous verses. True, the song starts off promisingly enough with a few very sweet, piercingly loud whistling notes, so loud in fact that it sounds as though the bird has been miked up. But having got one's attention, so to speak, it then burbles into a hotchpotch of shrieks and shrilling, mixed with hisses, rusty creaks and catlike yowls, for all the world as though engaged in some life-and-death struggle with a tomcat and a couple of angry kettles. It is certainly not the lyrical outpouring, a singing *'of Summer in full-throated ease,'* that Keats would have you believe – more like the Emperor's clockwork nightingale in the last stages of mechanical seizure.

And while we are in a mood for honesty, let us dispel once and for all any fanciful notions on the subject of dew. It is all very well bedecking with fairy jewels the morning cobwebs, glistening on cowslip leaves or lying in a pearly blanket over the back lawn, but no one ever seems to mention its chief quality, which is that it is simply damp. It is especially damp when you turn over at four in the morning and find that the other half of the pillow is sodden and clammy against your ear, that the foot of your sleeping bag is squelching with condensation, and that the wretched nightingale is still hacking and wheezing away above you at full volume like an elderly squeeze box falling into a cement mixer.

Note, too, that dew comes accompanied by slugs. There was hardly a morning that I did not arise to find myself heavily encrusted with glistening black slugs sitting stickily on my lower belly or insinuating themselves gently into my left ear. On one occasion I woke and was puzzled to find that despite all my attempts to open my eyes and greet the dawn they appeared to be gummed shut. A groping hand soon discovered the cause: a fat slug lying across each eyelid. Worse still were the snails which would crack with a soft and dreadful splitting noise if I inadvertently rolled onto them in my sleep. The joys of outdoor sleeping, the stars, the night breezes, the smells of grass and water and cool air, were somewhat offset by these natural details that rarely make it into the odes and sonnets of the Romantic Movement.

My morning routine falls into a steady pattern during this period of fine nights and hot days. I roll my mattress and sleeping bag – they are damp now but will be dried later in the midday sun – I climb out of pyjamas and I slip into a comfortable old pair of bather shorts. I don't bother with a shirt or vest, as already by seven o'clock it is warming up and I tend to row bare-chested to show off my new tanned, demigod-like torso. I also make a point of shaving daily, sitting on an old stump by the canal. Then, to wake me up properly, a bailer of river water over head and shoulders (bronzed, demigod-like shoulders, did I mention?), a last quick stow of odds and ends and I'm off, gardening gloves on hands, stroking steadily through a light polleny mist rising off the canal as the sun strengthens. All that is left to show that someone has spent the night is a flattened patch of grass on the bank where even now the crushed stems are slowly stretching and unbending and breathing again and half-a-dozen bewildered slugs are heading slowly back to bed.

*

The Tunnel of Mauvage, through which I had been forbidden to row, proved to be only a minor challenge. The problem was to work out how to prevent *Jack* from bumping into the concrete tunnel wall as I hauled her on a rope along the walkway. I solved this after a short period of trial and error by attaching two lines to her, one to the bow and another to her stern. I then shipped her rudder, holding it at an angle with an elastic strap on the tiller, so that she was constantly steering away from the towpath. Thus, though the bow rope was pulling her *into* the bank, the rudder and the stern rope were urging her out again, and between the two she kept a straight course about three feet out from the wall.

The other end of the tunnel led out into the green, warm, moist, grass-smelling world of daylight again and I found myself at the

In Full Flight

head of a gentle valley, winding away into a blue distance. Beech and ash woods rose steeply on either side, but the valley floor was flat, consisting of sunny meadows and pastures, seeded with grasses and a thousand wildflowers – poppies, buttercups, scabious, lady's bedstraw, crosswort and valerian. Overhead two crows flapped out of the wooded hillside and began mobbing a large bird of prey soaring and tilting just above the treetops. Whatever was it? Too big for a kestrel, but not the heavy blunt build of a buzzard. Then I saw the forked tail, the tapered scimitar wings, the glint of red bronze on its back – a red kite, no less. For the next four hours I would have one or two of these princely birds above me, sometimes stooping to pluck something from the canal, sometimes circling effortlessly high over the valley; on one occasion staging an aerial battle with a rival kite for some morsel held in its talons.

I was falling in love with the dragonflies as well, miniature sun-fuelled helicopters. The females were bronze-green-gold with black stripes; the males were iridescent blue – kingfisher, sapphire, turquoise refracted in a glass splinter. There was a third type, though these might have been damselflies; they were deep, deep satiny midnight-green and their wings were of fine inky gauze. They looked like rich jewelled assassins in mourning veils, and they were everywhere.

In the mid-afternoon a steady following wind sprung up that polished all the canal to clean hard blue and silver. It was the first breeze in eight days, and the kite above me was making the most of it, angling and tilting on the wind's plane. Mile after mile I sailed as the valley widened out and flattened, past a small, ugly town, past a huge industrial quarry where no fewer than eight red kites wheeled and squabbled, and so at last to a three-mile run along the curving flank of a hill high above a valley.

Here there was an aqueduct of grey stone and steel, carrying the canal in one graceful span across the valley floor far below. I really should have stopped to take down my sail, but throwing caution to the gods I ploughed on regardless. A second later I was regretting my rashness. For as I sailed onto the aqueduct, the wind speed increased dramatically and I shot across that dizzy height like a pea through a pea-shooter. Each side of the channel was nothing but a stone kerb, six inches high and less than a foot wide. This was all that separated me from a ninety-foot drop to the river far below and I was ricocheting along this watery tightrope at a speed sufficient to send my wake slopping over the rim in a great running wave. No sooner was I onto the aqueduct than I realised the folly of this sailing in the sky but could do nothing about it; I hung on and held my breath. Two minutes later I was over, and was relieved to find myself in another wood, windless and still and safe. I could not help wondering what a strange and splendid sight I must have made to a distant watcher on the hillside: an aerial ship with scarlet sails, like *Skillibladir* in the old stories, sailing on the rainbow's bright arch to bring Frey home again from distant lands.

And so to the end of a long day, the last hour spent rowing to the little *halte fluviale* at Pagny. I fell asleep under an apple tree, and at three in the morning it began to rain, a thin wetting drizzle, the first for almost three weeks now. It was my last night in the Arcadia of the French canal system. Farewell to ferny locks, to walnut trees, to midday snoozes on grassy banks. Farewell to cuckoo-echoing woods and elder-froth, to pleasant, sleepy *éclusiers*, to slugs and dew and the strange enchantment of Philomel beneath the stars.

Adieu! Adieu! Thy plaintive anthem fades
Past the near meadows, over the still stream,
Up the hill-side; and now 'tis buried deep
In the next valley-glades:
Was it a vision, or a waking dream?
Fled is that music: – Do I wake or sleep?

I slept. And the next day I reached the start of the River Moselle.

A Jollyboat in Germany

Oh, sweet is thy current by town and by tower,
The green sunny vale and the dark linden bower;
Thy waves as they dimple smile back on the plain,
And Rhine, ancient river, thou'rt German again!
                    —HORACE WALLACE,
        Ode on the Rhine's Returning into Germany from France

From the town of Trier, the Moselle loops along its steep-sided valley all the way down to Coblenz on the Rhine, and this stretch of
river was perhaps the most beautiful part of the entire voyage from
Wales to Romania. The gorge was so winding and sinuous that
often I found myself travelling twenty kilometres and ending up one
or two kilometres from where I had started, just across some high
ridge or saddle. The valley walls were clothed on either side with
terrace upon terrace of vineyards, all stripes of greeny-gold like
young gooseberries, draped over the curves of each hill, and here
and there in their midst a tiny shrine or chapel or crucifix, or a
statue of the Virgin to bless the harvest. As the miles passed, the
hills became steeper and craggier with great cliffs and buttresses of
reddish sandstone breaking the terraces and looming over the water,
but even here the vine rows straggled along the narrowest ledges,
stringing along inaccessible ledges and filling gullies and ravines so
that it became impossible to guess at how the grapes could be har-
vested without the aid of mountain-climbing equipment. At one
point, in fact, I saw flimsy ladders swarming up the cliff faces, seemingly as frail as willow sticks, and on some cliffs were painted giant
sundials, presided over by yet another plaster Mary, watching the
slow shadow tick around through the long summer days.

The very steepest crags were forested with pines and beechwoods
and invariably topped by a grim castle: sometimes complete and
restored like a great gingerbread cuckoo clock, but more often just a

ruinous tower like the stump of some black and rotting tooth. In the crook of each bend, a little fairytale town glided into sight – beamed houses, a tall onion-domed steeple, a gilded and painted Rathaus, a little pier for boats and a huddle of shops and high-gabled houses, bright with window boxes of petunias and geraniums. Best of all were the roses. Every house and café and gasthaus seemed to cultivate these, great rambling trails and trellises of roses, usually deep carmine and smelling of heavenly wine, nodding over doorways, bending over cool stone archways, drooping down to kiss café tables, swarming up sunny walls. I kept stopping to smell them and thinking of all those Germanic fairy tales: Beauty and the Beast, Snow White and Rose Red, Rapunzel or a dozen other stories where to pluck the enchanted rose was to court disaster.

I didn't actually pick any, and disaster seemed to be steering clear on the whole. Unless you count the hailstorm that blew out of nowhere one afternoon and in five seconds flat filled the world with a seething, icy, blinding roar. It stung my bare arms and legs, filled my boat with hailstones and sent me careering out of control down a river that had become a hissing white blistered maelstrom. Fortunately I had just come out of a lock so had not yet raised my sail; had I done so, I have no doubt that the suddenness and force of the wind would have snapped the mast like a matchstick. Even as it was, with the sail tightly furled, the wind was enough to drive me downstream for a few minutes as fast as though I were sailing in a good breeze under full sail. Then, as quickly as this vicious fist of hail and ice had struck, out came the sun and I spent an hour gently steaming and drying out as I sailed along in the warm afternoon.

Despite such moments of drama, an astonishing question kept insisting: why wasn't everyone else doing exactly as I was? For there was no doubt about it: this was the most perfect occupation known to humankind. When the sail was out full and I was propped up in the stern on cushions, feet up on the thwart, idly nudging the tiller with my elbow, I was the envy of the valley! Workers high up on the terraced hillsides tying up vine tendrils pointed and laughed and sighed. They were mere dots of bright colour on the green slopes, but I could tell that they resumed their hot work dreaming of sails and pith helmets and lands downstream. On gleaming cruise ships, wealthy tourists from Detroit paused, a glass of overpriced Moselle to their lips; they loosened their collars a little as they contemplated diving in and joining me, to send later perhaps a brief postcard to their bosses back home, saying, '*Gone to Black Sea. I'll explain later.*' Or perhaps no note at all …

I spent one night in a village purple with columbines and famous for an ancient stone carving of Romans rowing a ship full of wine barrels, and another in a *Weinkeller* overhung by lime trees where nested a redstart, and so arrived at the jewel of the Moselle Valley: the fairytale town of Cochem. Here, Germanic fairytale architecture comes into full flower. It is a mediaeval town of wood-carved gingerbread houses and steep alleyways o'ertopped by a castle from Disneyland. At certain hours twenty bells in one of the carved gables chime out music-box tunes. The carvings on the gable ends of the Mayor's house are caricatures of the Mayor's chief rivals and tell an amusing story which I have now forgotten – as indeed I have forgotten the reason why there is a nearby statue of a goat being crushed in a wine-press.

Cochem was so delightful that I decided to spend a few days there and replenish my funds with a spot of busking. I got out my tin-whistle, propped my pith helmet in the main square by the fountain, and started to play. I half expected, as the fluting notes echoed through the gabled streets, to hear the patter and chatter, the squeaking and rustling and rumbling, of half a million rats come pouring out on every side on their way down to the rolling river to perish. However, the only result was the occasional clink of a handful of deutschmarks being thrown hatward, and with that I was more than happy. There were many tourists in the town and at one stage a group of Americans came panting into the square following the strident voice and raised brolly of a lady tour guide. Oddly, with the whole square to choose from, she strode over to within three feet of me and my tin-whistle and mustered her flock in ringing tones.

'Gazzer round, ladies und gentlemen, qvickly if you pleez. Here ve see ze marketplatz of Cochem viz ze byootiful fountain und all ze liddle carvings, *ja?*' By this time I was pressed up to the fountain-coping by the woman's gesturing brolly and she was enunciating with consonants that would chop wood, so I brought my rendition of 'Danny Boy' to an end and waited for her to finish and move away. After some minutes, in which I heard the amusing story of the mayor and the gable ends, and an explanation of the bibulous goat, the woman pointed at a far corner of the square and shooed her brood in that direction, urging them to 'climb ze schteps und ve all meet at ze schloss, *ja*, *gut*!' As they were moving off, I sent them on their way with a medley of 'Yankee Doodle Dandy' and the 'Dixie March.' There were a few smiles and some of the tourists threw some money my way, happy to hear something other than accordions and Oom-Pah-Pah music, played by someone who wasn't wearing *lederhosen* with a shaving brush stuck in his hat. But just as I was breaking into 'The Yellow Rose of Texas,' back came the tour guide, her brolly stabbing at the cobbles. Over the top of my playing she rapped out a question of which I only understood one word: 'deutschmarks.' Assuming that it was something like, 'Oh, what beautiful playing, and how you enhance our little town with such sweet melodies, I'd like to reward you with some good German deutschmarks,' I nodded towards my pith helmet to indicate where she could throw a token of her appreciation. At that she strode over to the hat, rummaged around in its depths, *extracted* three deutschmark coins and held them up to my nose before pocketing them.

'Zat,' she explained sternly, 'is for listening to my tour.' And with a click of her heels and a curt nod she strode off. Pipers still get short shrift in fairytale German towns, it would seem. Bring back the rats, I muttered, and couldn't refrain from a quick burst of the *Dambusters* theme and a bit of Vera Lynn to send her on her way.

Later that day I too climbed up the steep steps to the castle. I remember a lot of roses, balconies, carved wood and a lamp fashioned like a mermaid with a lucky red breastbone to rub and make a wish. I did so, wishing for a cooling breeze on the morrow to take me onward on the next stage of the voyage.

The following morning I woke to find that my wish had been granted. The sun was still bright but a cool breeze had sprung up from the south to bear me swiftly downstream to Coblenz and the mighty Rhine.

The scenery now, though still pretty by any normal standards, began to fade a little in enchantment. Swifts screamed in the sky, redstarts were common, and the riverside had become painted with the mauve of scabious and vetch, yellow St John's Wort and the sinister greater celandine with its livid orange juice bleeding from snapped stems. These are the plants of high summer, of dusty dry highways, and the river itself was feeling like a country road as it drew nearer and nearer to the big city of Coblenz and the highway of the Rhine.

Approaching Cochem

In the last twenty miles or so, the wind gave out and my rowlock began to present a serious problem. With almost every stroke of the oars, the timber of the gunwale was creaking and cracking, slowly working loose around the rowlock pin, and indeed as I looked around, I realised how shabby poor *Jack de Crow* had become. Her foredeck was a mass of peeling blisters, and the prow had been battered into a crunch of splinters by some careless handling in a lock.

I limped around the last bend, through a great grimy lock and beneath a blackened bridge thunderous with traffic. There, a short way ahead, lay the Rhine River. At this point I panicked. Here on the right bank of the Moselle mouth was a sheer wall of concrete where huge white river cruisers were docking and departing with a flurry of propellers and hooters. On the left bank was a waste of black boulders and weeds fringing a wild sort of park. The chances of mooring a small dinghy safely seemed very small. Furthermore, to carry on down and into the Rhine itself was out of the question. Not only was it impossibly busy with traffic, but it was flowing in quite the wrong direction for me. I suspected that if I so much as ventured out into its main stream I would find myself in Holland by suppertime.

The decision was taken out of my hands. A blast of a hooter sent me scuttling across the Moselle to avoid the gleaming iceberg prow of a cruiser looming up behind. A churning whirl of a reversing barge sent me zigzagging back to the left-hand bank of the river all too close to those black and bulky rocks. As I scooted along that inhospitable bank, I hauled desperately at the oars to avoid being washed onto the rocks by the wake of yet another passing leviathan, and the flimsy rowlock gave way at last with a splintery crunch. One heedless haul on the remaining oar sent me lurching towards the bank – just in time to see a narrow channel that led through to a dank lagoon off the main river. I paddled in and looked about me.

I was in a basin surrounded by steep banks topped by serious-looking buildings. A solitary and rather rusty dredger was moored at a pontoon on the northern bank. The place was quite clearly not a public marina, but for now it was the only place where I could moor in safety. Tying up alongside the dredger, I climbed the steep flight of steps to the complex of buildings above. When I was halfway up, my heart quailed. At the top had appeared six or seven young men who were now staring at me with grim and unfriendly expressions on their faces. Crew-cuts. Tattoos. Short-cut black T-shirts with packets of fags tucked under the sleeves. This was not the local Oom-Pah-Pah band come to give me a hearty traditional welcome. They seemed to my eyes to be crew members of a local stevedore gang, or possibly inmates of a local borstal. To a man they seemed singularly unimpressed by the pith helmet and the jaunty little dinghy bobbing on their private pontoon.

Just as they were preparing, I am sure, to charge down the steps and beat me senseless, a quiet voice floated down, and immediately the youths stopped, turned and skulked back up the steps like a pack of hyenas denied their carrion treat. As they vanished into a doorway, a figure approached me down the steps, a quiet neat figure in a trim beard and grey eyes behind big glasses. Five minutes later I knew that yet again that strange brand of serendipity had come into play. His name was Peter Pohl, and I was in the grounds of the Coblenz Waterways Management Training College. Here trainees fresh from school were taught all the rudiments of commercial waterways maintenance, maritime law, river navigation, lock engineering and, happily for me, boat repairs. Happier still was the fact that Peter was the lecturer in boat-building and himself a master carpenter. In fact, I had moored at the very brink of his workshop.

And yes, of course, he would be more than happy to help me fix that broken rowlock, and while he was about it, tidy up the varnish work and the prow and one or two other jobs that his practised eye immediately picked out as necessary. Meanwhile, I could moor here as long as I needed and use the staff shower at the top of the stairs if I so wished. And now, he had a class, so if I would excuse him …?

I was not terribly surprised actually. Since I had bumped into Alan Snell at the very start of my voyage just in time to share a bottle of chardonnay and have my rowlock fixed, I had grown accustomed to this sort of thing. The friendly boat shed in Bristol, the shipwreck at Whitstable and the wonderful Dunster family – it seemed that no sooner had *Jack* snapped off a vital part of her works than a friendly hand was reaching out of the sky with the offer of a drill, a bunch of screws and a load of expertise. My only concern was how to write this home in letters to friends and family without stretching credulity to breaking point.

Peter not only fixed one rowlock but also reinforced them both with metal strips. Then between us we sanded off all the peeling varnish, applied several new coats to the decking, and did the same job for the rudder and centreboard. Finally he replaced the little flat prow section that had been smashed with a cut-out sheet of perspex, screwing it tightly to the gunwales where they met to make the bow. By the time we had finished, *Jack de Crow* was looking as neat and shipshape as she had when we had sailed away from Whitstable. These repairs were to carry her all the way to the Black Sea without a hitch. In the meantime I explored Coblenz and, more importantly, investigated the possibility of getting up the Rhine to Mainz and the confluence of the Main River.

I soon realised that I had made a serious navigational error some weeks before. I should have continued along the French canals after Rheims and headed south-westward towards Strasbourg, hitting the Rhine further upstream. I had, however, been told that the prettiest section of the Rhine was the ninety or so kilometres *upstream* from Coblenz, so I had decided to come this way. What nobody had seen fit to add was that those scenic ninety kilometres of river were picturesque for a reason: the waters poured between precipices and gorge walls with a ferocity against which even fully powered barges struggled to make headway.

On seeing the rolling brown surge of the Rhine, I realised that I had to abandon any notion of making it under my own steam and seek the aid of local shipping. Peter advised me that my best bet was to speak to Mick, the owner of the local *Bunkerboot*, a sort of floating petrol and supply station for the industrial barges. He knew all the bargees and was in constant radio contact with them. The problem was finding him, as he moved around a lot, sometimes mooring in the Moselle mouth, sometimes in the main Rhine River. Once *Jack* was fixed, I said my farewells and heartfelt thanks to Peter and rowed off to find Mick on his *Bunkerboot*. After some hot and fruitless oaring, I heard from a passing barge that he had moved over to the eastern bank of the Rhine and would be there for the next few days. There was nothing for it – I would have to risk crossing the Rhine.

As soon as I hit the current, I knew that my fears were warranted. Facing diagonally upstream, I pulled valiantly to haul myself across the five hundred yards or so to the opposite bank. Despite my cracking limbs and straining shoulders, I moved crabwise across the river to eventually end up on the eastern bank but some two hundred metres downstream from where I had started. Mercifully I was not bothered by any major traffic. I think that every barge on the river was slewing wildly to avoid the idiot in midstream, but the effort and sweat in my eyes made me oblivious to all about me. Having reached the opposite bank, the real challenge began. I was now some seven hundred metres downstream from where the *Bunkerboot* was moored, seven hundred metres of sheer bank fringed with large black breakwater rocks, with no place to tie up for a breather. Seven hundred metres does not sound very far ... it didn't *look* very far ... but I was now rowing full into the current of the largest river in Western Europe. Those seven hundred metres took me two hours. For much of the time I seemed to be sitting perfectly still, yards from the bank, gazing at the same park bench or litter bin for what seemed an eternity. Then some extra effort on my part, or some mysterious slackening of the current, would allow me to crawl forward a couple of yards, barely enough to be gazing at the upstream end of the same bench.

The only thing that kept me going through all this fruitless, neck-straining, heart-pounding exertion was the reaction of three old German men leaning on the riverside railing watching my agonies. I was, as ever, clad in my pith helmet, and, along with the utter futility and lack of progress, was fully and happily conscious of the eccentric picture I was presenting. To this end I kept grinning foolishly at the trio and calling out things like '*Englische, ja!*' and '*Ich bin ein dumkopf, nein?*' and other pidgin-German inanities, if only to let them know that I was aware of my own folly and didn't mind if they wanted to break into howls of derisive laughter. They didn't. They didn't even flicker, not once in the whole hour I sat opposite them going nowhere. Their faces were set in a grim expression of stolid disapproval at the whole stupid enterprise. *Buy a motor, you stupid little foreigner*, they seemed to be saying. *Don't come here with your so-called charming English eccentricity and expect us to be impressed.* A sour glance at the hat. *Go home, in fact.*

I think it was as much a determination to see whether I could raise a smile in these three old cormorants as a desire not to be swept down to Rotterdam by nightfall that kept me straining away until I finally reached the *Bunkerboot*. There I introduced myself shakily to Mick, who immediately called the police. This rather threw me until he explained that he wanted them to tow me the remaining one hundred yards upstream to a little pontoon where I could moor for the night. For that I was grateful, as indeed for the fact that he then got onto the radio to start organising a tow for me right up to Mainz. Before long he had contacted the owner of an industrial barge called *Barbara*, who agreed to pick me up on Sunday morning.

Meanwhile, the police had arrived and towed me upstream and handed me over to Wilhelm, the Hafenmeister. He, they assured me, would look after my every need. This I somewhat doubted. The grim unsmiling set of his jaw, the contemptuous iron in his eye and the baleful sighs and tuts with which he greeted every word of explanation by the police made my three aged friends from downstream look positively frisky and lambkin-like by comparison. I don't know what the police were telling this sour old buzzard, but from his look of exasperated distaste I suspected that my Rhine crossing had been the cause of a major collision and the facts were even now being reported to Herr Wilhelm, chief shareholder. After the third baleful glance in my direction, I decided that I was not going to sleep aboard *Jack* tonight and asked about nearby accommodation. At this the Hafenmeister rapped out '*Kom!*' and strode off down the road without a glance behind him. Fearing to disobey, I grabbed my pack and followed.

Soon my grim guide was charging up some steps cut into the cliff, and on reaching the top he plunged into a tunnel carved into the rock. This looked nothing like a public thoroughfare – it seemed more like an abandoned mine, lit by a string of bare bulbs. Trying to catch my breath as I jogged after him, I attempted to re-phrase in my mind the request for accommodation: *Nein, nein, mein Herr. Not the buried Nazi war treasures, please. Ein gasthaus, bitte.*

But by the time I had worked this out, he was a distant silhouette and I had perforce to hurry on after him. At times this tunnel branched off in various directions and the Hafenmeister unerringly plunged down one or the other, calling back over his shoulder '*Kom! Raus! Raus!*' while I stumbled on through the darkness after him, wondering where in Hades we were headed. Then it was up some more steps, round a few bends and we emerged into a little wooded glade caught in the cleft of a hidden gorge. Here, half hidden in hazel trees, was the wheelhouse of an ancient chairlift – the cables soared up and out of sight overhead. My morose guide was engaged in a bad-tempered altercation with the man in the wheelhouse.

'There seems to be some confusion, *mein Herr*,' I started. 'I was hoping to – ' but he cut me off in mid-sentence.

'My English, it is not good. But here, my friend, are tickets for this gondola, and this will take you where it is you want. You will see, yes. Now, on the Sunday this gondola it does not work so early, *ja*, so I come to pick you up in my car at six at the hour of the morning. This way, you will meet *Barbara* and be on your way.'

When I started protesting at this unexpected display of helpfulness, he cut me short.

'No, my friend. For me it is a great privilege. You, I think, are someone special, no? I have been telling my friend here all about your travels. We are all very proud, *ja*?' At this the chairlift operator nodded vigorously. A faint tear gleamed in the corner of Wilhelm's eye. 'Very proud! So, I see you again on Sunday.'

And at that he strode off into the tunnel and out of sight. As I took my seat on the chairlift, I reflected on how badly I was doing at reading the Germanic manner.

As the chair soared up and out of the little gorge, I saw that I was heading for the top of a very steep cliff surmounted by a vast wall of orangey-sandy stone. In this there was a great gate and it was at this gate that the chairlift gently deposited me. This was, it seemed, the local Youth Hostel. When I wandered in through the great arched gateway, I found myself on a huge terrace of reddish stone whose further edge was some fifty yards away. Here was a low balustrade and beyond that, nothing could be seen but sky. On reaching the balustrade I found myself looking straight down to the Rhine far, far below and beyond it to the great equestrian statue that sits at the confluence of the Moselle and the Rhine, known as the Corner of Germany. From that vantage point, too, I could see the Moselle directly opposite and could even fancy it winding away in my mind's eye into its enchanted valley to Cochem and beyond. Almost directly below me, tiny as a buttercup petal, *Jack* bobbed at her mooring and I could see the tiny figure of Hafenmeister Wilhelm tidying her lines and securing her for the night.

The next day I tried busking once more. It was going splendidly due to the response of a seven-year-old girl and her three younger brothers who had gathered to hear me play. They were, I thought, delightful in their waif-like way, and I was rather touched when they danced to one of my jigs and people stopped to look on and smile. I thought of the Pied Piper again, but not the rats this time. No:

> *All the little boys and girls,*
> *With rosy cheeks and flaxen curls,*
> *And sparkling eyes and teeth like pearls,*
> *Tripping and skipping, ran merrily after*
> *The wonderful music with shouting and laughter.*

When fifteen minutes later, however, they took it upon themselves to pass the hat around, my delight turned to uneasy embarrassment: '*Nein*, er, *kinder*, please leave the hat alone. Where is *papa und mama, ja?*'

In response to my atrocious German, the youngest pointed a grubby finger at me and giggled 'Papa!' and they all simultaneously started playing at being puppy dogs and sitting up to beg. 'Yap! Yap!' they went, putting their tongues out and panting, and the good folk of Coblenz shot me a collective dirty look and turned away. To them it was evident that I had my own children out, forcing them to perform on the street, and the fact that the urchins looked none too clean or well shod served only to outrage the populace further. In vain did I try to shoo the children away. This merely excited their histrionic talents, and the oldest came and hugged my knees and burst into tears, begging me, I think, not to send her back to the mill. Eventually, spotting a police officer who was strolling nearer with questions in his eyes, I fled.

*

On the day of my departure I was up early to meet *Barbara* and her crew at the *Bunkerboot*. After various trials we de-rigged *Jack* and hoisted her up on such a short towline that her nose was resting right up against *Barbara*'s stern rail and only *Jack*'s transom was in the water. In other words, she was nearly vertical. Then, after heartfelt thanks to Wilhelm and Mick, we were off. The crew of *Barbara* consisted of the Belgian skipper, his ox-like but amiable son, and a wretched black dog called Wulf that kept trying to bite me. After it defecated in a mustard-coloured smear all over my bundled mast and sail, I took it by the collar and threw it overboard. Well, no, I didn't, but I would very much have liked to. The Captain and his son were kind enough, but as there is a limit to what you can get across with a fixed grin and a nod, I soon retired to the bow of the barge and played my tin-whistle. As the bow was several miles from the wheelhouse at the stern, I didn't think I was in any danger of disturbing their concentration.

For this I was grateful. The current was so strong along this stretch of the river that steersmen had to be extremely skilled. Barges approaching from upstream seemed to hurtle towards you, slewing their way across the water, sometimes seeming to turn almost broadside on as they swept downstream around a tight bend. On the other hand, barges like ours churning their way upstream hardly seemed to move against the current, although it raced by in torrents and frequently poured over the low gunwales. The scenery was itself distracting. Here the river raced through a broad gorge for mile after mile sprinkled with the usual Christmas decoration clutter of gilded castles and cuckoo-clock towers. Soon we passed beneath the fabled Lorelei Rock; not, as I had imagined, a siren-topped rock in midstream, but a tall promontory of cliffs around which the Rhine swept in a fierce bend. As we passed it, I thought at first I was dreaming, or transported back into the Wagnerian legends, for it seemed that I could hear the low sexy song of the Lorelei herself. Then a further golden cadence fell from the high cliffs above me and glancing up I saw the flash of sun on brass. It was a French horn player who, I gathered later, went there every Sunday to play on the pinnacle, busking, no doubt, far from the reach of urchin children intent on adoption.

This stretch of the Rhine is a sight that retired couples from all over the world pay a fortune to come and see, safely aboard one of the many gleaming river cruisers that ply their trade there. It is one of the great scenic trips of Europe. Unforgivably, once past the Lorelei Rock I slept through most of it. The ox-like son had shown me the forecabin right in the bows and indicated that I could make myself at home. There is nothing quite so cosy as the forecabin of a Rhine barge. It is dim, it is warm, it is slightly stuffy and smelling of blankets and rope. The whole thing vibrates and hums soporifically and the only other noise is the endlessly comforting swirl and chuckle of water sluicing by an inch from your ear on the other side of the steel hull. I kicked off my shoes, lay down for a few minutes and woke up seven hours later some ten miles up the River Main.

We were still progressing slowly into the dusk, and the skipper and his son calmly suggested I stay aboard for the night. It was too late to unhitch *Jack*, and, besides, there would be nowhere to stay on the banks, the skipper explained in mime and gestures. Meanwhile, Young Albert, as the son was called, was cooking supper for us – a first, I was told – and he, Old Albert as he was known, would carry on steering. Perhaps I would like a beer?

And so it was settled. Supper was an extraordinary affair, consisting as it did of burnt fried potato, burnt fried egg, burnt fried bread and what I think was burnt fried liver, which I usually hate but which had been rendered edible by the simple expedient of reducing it to carbon.

And then to bed and another eight hours of warm, humming sleep while the Alberts took it in turn to steer the *Barbara* all through the summer night up the River Main and into the heartland of Old Germany.

In the morning I found that we had passed Frankfurt and were now some fifty-three kilometres up the Main approaching Mulheim Lock. Here Albert and Albert bade me farewell, wished me luck, refused to take any payment and set me adrift. It was an overcast morning but there was a gentle breeze blowing from astern, so I re-rigged the mast, set sail and was soon on my way upstream to Hanau. It was here that I intended to stop voyaging for a while. My sister Maggie had just completed her Ph.D. in Edinburgh and the graduation ceremony was coming up soon. To this end my parents had flown all the way from Australia to Scotland, and it seemed too good an opportunity to miss. Besides, I was tired. Tired of rowing, tired of Keats, tired of feeling foreign, and most of all, tired of my own company.

At Hanau there was a waterways maintenance yard. It was without the slightest feeling of surprise that I found there three cheerful workmen who had apparently been waiting for me to turn up so that they could have the pleasure of hauling my boat out of the water on a little crane, emptying her, storing the rigging in a dry shed, turning her upside down under a tarpaulin and promising to keep her safely for whenever – if ever – I returned.

I did what Odysseus could never do, what no great traveller ever permits himself. I caught a bus to Frankfurt, a train to Holland, a plane to Birmingham and I hitched to Ellesmere. Within thirty hours I was back to where the whole voyage had begun ten months before. I was ready for a break.

End of Part Two

Part Three

Into the East

Contrary Currents and Kindness

Does the road wind up-hill all the way?
Yes, to the very end.
Will the day's journey take the whole long day?
From morn to night, my friend.
—CHRISTINA ROSSETTI, *Up-Hill*

Over the three weeks away I made some firm decisions. I had been appalled to note how much money I was getting through as I travelled, but when I stopped to consider, it was hardly surprising. Too many nights I had tied up, looked at the awning and the planks lying ready to be put into place, then said to myself, 'Not tonight, Josephine,' and gone off guiltily to find a *Gasthaus* or *auberge* for the night.

All that, I said to myself, was about to change. I vowed that from now on I would sleep aboard *Jack* every night, no matter what the weather or how much the thought of hot showers and clean sheets appealed. Likewise, I would shun cafés and restaurants and discover the delights of a bread roll and a hunk of cheese eaten in the open air, with a bottle of beer as an occasional treat. As for money, the use of my Visa card would be strictly rationed. From now, I was on a budget.

It was a pity, therefore, that I arrived at the start of a stretch of grey rainy days and cold dripping nights. For three days I slogged up a river whose contrary current was far stronger than I had anticipated, sluggishly hauling between endless banks of silver-grey osiers and dreary willows that hemmed me in and blocked the view on either side. It rained most of the time, a thin wetting rain that soaked through my cagoule and trickled down my face. When the rain cleared, it did so only to make way for strong contrary winds that had me hauling the sail up in hope, but taking it down again ten minutes later as I realised the impossibility of tacking into the wind against the current and without a jib. I was hard pressed to travel more than fifteen kilometres a day, as compared to the fifty or so I had been making on the Moselle.

Still, I kept doggedly to my new regime and my new budget, forcing myself to sleep aboard each night, although the rain seeped in under the awning and dampened my sleeping bag and pillow. I stuck to one meal a day, usually a bread roll and some salami that I bought from villages along the way. In a perverse way I enjoyed my Spartan life. I didn't sing as I rowed, I didn't recite poetry, I didn't think thoughts or talk to myself, or do anything. I became grim and morose and silent and dour, like an elderly badger with toothache. I went to bed, woke up, rowed, ate a bread roll, rowed some more and went to bed again. I don't think I spoke or exchanged glances with anyone for three or four days – a bit of a record for me.

And then, just as I was settling into my role as curmudgeonly hermit, the world glanced around, noticed me and said, 'Oh, stop moping, Sandy!' and handed me about three hundred nice things on a plate to snap me out of it. Things like a red squirrel scampering along the bank, a spiral maze painted outside a village church, an elder hedge to dry my clothes on, a skinny-dip from a little secluded beach of red sand, a daffy girl called Meg with broken teeth who proposed marriage to me as she pursued me along the bank (unconnected, I think with the skinny-dipping), an ice cream bought as a special reward to myself for persevering with the stoicism and a whole host of other things. Those days ... and in particular that ice cream ... did teach me just how often we indulge ourselves purely out of habit before any real need or desire has arisen. We do this so often that, like the citizens of Huxley's *Brave New World*, we forget what it is even to feel a need, let alone the pleasure of satisfying it. We eat before we are hungry, we drink before we are thirsty, we amuse ourselves before we ever feel boredom ... and slowly go numb inside. Our insides turn into the spiritual equivalent of pâté de foie gras.

The world also clearly decided that I was no longer to be left on my own. I found myself adopted by a German family aboard a cruiser called *Carpe Diem* whose two boys, Mario and Florian, persuaded their parents that I might add some interest to their river cruise, if only for the alarmed expression on my face as I coped once more with being towed at high speeds in an unstable dinghy. I also found myself mooring up one night next to *Barbara* and I was able to buy a bottle of wine to take to Big Albert and Little Albert as an overdue thank-you present for the tow up the Rhine. They offered me supper – the smell of blackening fat was already in the air – but I beat a hasty retreat to the company of my new friends on *Carpe Diem* and joined them for their nightly custom. This was to drink one kirsch liqueur for every lock they had been through that day, calling out *'schleuse!'* ('lock!') each time they downed a drink. After my self-imposed abstinence from both drink and talk, my tongue was loosened as never before, and before long we were old friends ... or so I assumed as they all politely listened in to a fascinating, if somewhat slurry, explanation about Fermat's Theorem and my bottom.

As I went further and further up the Main, this kindness of strangers reached almost bizarre proportions. Take the village of Himmelstadt. After watching me moor for the night at the lock, the fat lock-keeper came down from his concrete tower to urge me to take myself along to a nearby bistro, the ancient and renowned Himmelkeller. I had finished the last of my somewhat dry bread, so off I trotted, thinking that perhaps I might treat myself to a bowl of soup. The place was quite crowded, but no sooner was I in the door than the *Kellermeister* welcomed me warmly and started to introduce me to the guests sitting at the long oak tables, proudly proclaiming me a 'famous globetrotter.' It appeared that the fat lock-keeper had rung ahead to warn the host of my arrival. As I sat and ate my humble bread and soup, I was bombarded with questions, which I tried to answer as best I could. The soup finished, I was rising to go when the host appeared with a huge plate of sausages swimming in leeks, carrots and white wine. Alarmed, I tried to explain that I did not order this and that there must be some mistake. 'No, no,' piped up a quiet couple sitting at a corner table a little distance away. 'We did. We ordered it for you, and of course we will pay for it. It is a speciality of this region. Do you like it?'

Well, yes, I did, thank you very much, how kind. And much later, when I went to pay the bill for the soup and the several beers I had drunk, the host said, 'No, no. This is paid for.'

'The sausages, yes, but surely not ...'

'Yes, all of it,' explained the couple in the corner. 'You are our guest tonight. Perhaps if you reach the Black Sea, you will write us a letter.' His name was Engelbert, which means 'bright angel,' and as the village of Himmelstadt means 'heavenly place,' I suppose I should have expected no less.

To top the evening off, the host presented me with a complimentary bottle of the local wine to take with me, a pale greeny-gold wine to remind me, as he said, of the good folk of Himmelstadt. I staggered back to the lock reeling with bemusement at all this unsolicited kindness.

The following day, several locks up the river, I was told firmly by the keeper there that I must stop and wait. For what? But the keeper's English was not up to explaining the reason for my enforced wait. As I sat in my dinghy, a cold host of thoughts crept over me. Could it be that I had misunderstood the business with the bill last night? Had I walked away from the *Weinkeller* wrongly assuming that the bottle of wine was a gift and now half of Himmelstadt was after me as a thieving opportunist? Had the German Waterways Authorities finally caught up with the fact that I was traversing their country without a licence? Did I actually need one?

At last the mystery was solved. A very sweet young woman with clear grey eyes turned up with a microphone and a tape recorder, explained that she was from Radio Bavaria and asked if I would mind giving an interview. She had been pursuing me all morning up the river but had kept missing me, until she had managed to get hold of the lock-keeper and arrange for me to be stopped. And how did she know of my existence? My jolly fat lock-keeper of the night before had been busy on the telephone proclaiming my exploits to the world.

That evening I found myself tying up at the pontoon of the Wurzburg Marina. There is a beautiful old bridge here with fourteen statues of various warrior bishops and florid princes perched along each balustrade as though about to leap off the bridge and end it all in the deep green waters below. *Carpe Diem* was moored just up the river and I joined them for a last 'schleusen-schnapps' session. As we had each been through a different number of locks that day, we resolved the question of how many shots to down by the simple method of adding together the number of locks we'd *both* been through that day – and so finished off the bottle. The local marina staff had heard the Radio Bavaria interview that afternoon and given me free run of the clubhouse, so I slept on the floor there on my mattress after a welcome hot shower. The good fortune was holding, it seemed.

On the following day I set off as the hot afternoon was dimming off to a cooler gold, and five or six miles up the river came to a backwater set in the left-hand bank. The sun was setting and *Jack* and I were nowhere near a town or village. This suited my mood; despite revelling in the good company and generosity of the last few days, I felt that I wanted to re-capture the illusion at least of the wandering solitary life.

The place where I stopped was pleasant enough, a sandy bay backed by a lonely field and a little promontory with a scattering of ash trees between the backwater and the main river. For an hour I had the place to myself, but after that a family arrived to camp. I was not sorry. My need for solitude had evaporated about ten minutes after landing. Helmut, the skinny, dark-haired father, lit a campfire on the promontory while his three or four children played in and out of the firelit shadows. There were three boys and a girl, a little pale thing quite unlike the sturdy boys. Helmut invited me to join them around the fire and I did so gladly, sharing between us some sausages and cheese on toasted bread, chatting about hang-gliding and mountain-climbing. While we spoke, some small creature, a water rat or vole, crept right in about our boots and stole crumbs from the very edges of the embers. At some point I asked the name of the children and Helmut told me the three boys' names.

'And the girl?' I asked.

'The girl?' replied Helmut in some surprise. 'But she is not mine. I thought she was your little girl.'

When we called the children over out of the shadows, the girl had vanished. The boys have been playing with her but no, they do not know where she has come from or where she has gone to. Perhaps she is a wood-child or a river-daughter …

Later that night, after the others had gone off to their tents, I sat for a while by the glowing embers of the fire looking out over the river. The moon was full and made little bright stabs of silver on the satin-black water with every fish-rise. The night was warm and the air full of white moths, and the dark night-river world seemed full of enchantment.

I went out to the hazel wood,
Because a fire was in my head,
And cut and peeled a hazel wand,
And hooked a berry to a thread;

And when white moths were on the wing,
And moth-like stars were flickering out,
I dropped the berry in a stream
And caught a little silver trout.

When I had laid it on the floor
I went to blow the fire a-flame,
But something rustled on the floor,
And someone called me by my name:

It had become a glimmering girl
With apple blossom in her hair
Who called me by my name and ran
And faded in the brightening air.

The stars, the white moths, the fading fire, the waif girl who belonged to nobody; all these were the elements of Yeats' poem. Despite the warmth of the summer night, the hair on the back of my neck stood up and my heart pounded as I waited for the magic to manifest itself.

But no. The moon rose and set, the water vole rustled once or twice more in his foraging, and the embers faded to nothing. I slept.

*

I woke early to clamorous birdsong to find that my boat had vanished. Perhaps the glimmering girl had set it adrift in the night. It did not take long to find; it had drifted across the backwater and caught in a tangle of black hazels beneath a steep bank. I had to swim for it, and when I hauled myself in, dripping wet and naked, I found it full of white moths' wings, thick as apple-blossom.

I set off early before Helmut and his family were up, and rowed on through the morning, stopping briefly in Ochsenfurt to stock up on groceries and write postcards. My diet had settled down to the following: a couple of bread rolls, one with salami and mayonnaise, one with tomato and mayonnaise. The tomato roll was always sprinkled liberally with black pepper and salt from a little cruet set. After the main course I usually finished up with an apple and downed the whole lot with a glass of wine or a small bottle of beer. All this was prepared by placing the broad centreboard across my knees as a table, digging out the tupperware box and my knife from the fore-locker, chopping and cutting and spreading as necessary, and then – ah! this was the best bit! – simply scraping the crumbs and scraps over the side and wiping the centreboard down with the big sponge that lived in the bilges. In the next few months, this was to be almost my exclusive diet and I never tired of it. Even today the making of a tomato sandwich can conjure up the lap-lap of water, the hot sunshine and the sheer happiness of that period of my life.

Later that afternoon I had cause to be grateful to an unsmiling grandfather and his two grandchildren who chugged by in a rubber Zodiac dinghy and offered me a tow. With their aid I reached the outskirts of the village of Schwarzach. Here there was a wide field flowering with yarrow and tansy and I found a corner to lay out my tarpaulin and sleeping bag for the night. After a cooling swim in the river I made myself a salami roll, devoured it hungrily and prepared to go to sleep in the last fading light of the hot day.

But I could not. I sat up five minutes later with an overwhelming craving for milk. Not nicotine, not gin, not sex – just milk, but I must have some. I tried water from my water bottle but this had nothing to do with thirst and the craving persisted. It was ridiculous. I had never had a craving in my life. I tried to turn over and go to sleep again, but my thoughts were filled entirely with the smooth creaminess of cold milk in a tall glass. I got up, got dressed and wandered off into the blue dusk in search of milk. I found that the village of Schwarzach was a more interesting place than I had first supposed. A mile down the road there was a huge Benedictine monastery with grand gates and a gatehouse, but all was silent and barred. I wandered on. Opposite the gatehouse was a restaurant, all heavy stone and coach lamps and vine leaves and diamond-paned windows. I waltzed in, trying to ignore the fact that I was the only person not dressed in evening wear. I breezily ordered a glass of milk. I was told firmly that they did not serve drinks only; I must purchase an entrée at the very least. My funds and my patience would not tolerate this, so I wandered out again and found my way round to the kitchen door. In vain I tried to appeal to the sweating chef on the other side of a fly screen door; he made it quite clear with a wave of his cleaver that milk-begging mendicants would find no satisfaction here.

The craving had now reached fever pitch. I remembered with a fierce yearning long, hot days spent up Brownhill Creek as a boy and coming home in the evening smelling of sweat and grass and mint and downing a long, cool glass of milk in the kitchen. I remembered further back to when I was very little, guzzling milk out of half-pint bottles amid the crayons and plasticine of primary school. I couldn't remember the last time I had drunk a glass of milk, but I knew I needed one now. Wandering back disconsolately to my flowery meadow and resigning myself to a night of cold turkey, I passed a house where a middle-aged man was digging onions in his front garden at twilight. I was so desperate that I found myself blurting out some incoherent pseudo-German in which the words '*milch*' and '*tod*' were predominant. Whether or not he thought he was being threatened with death, I didn't care. The important thing was that he retreated to the house and emerged with two pints of blessed milk, cold from the fridge, and I downed the lot. Politely he asked whether he could fetch me a third pint, but no, the craving was gone and I was sane again. After a short chat about onions, I walked back contentedly to my field and fell asleep watching a weave of gnats above me against the deep blue sky.

*

I woke the next morning to a curious swish-swishing noise and something flashing regularly past my slumbering head. I sat up blurrily rubbing sleep and slug-dew from my eyes to make out an alarming figure looming over me. It was tall, dark and wielded the unmistakable silhouette of a scythe. For a few seconds I wondered if the odd craving of the night before for the things of infancy had presaged my death and here was the Reaper himself to gather me in. Then my eyes cleared and I saw that it was simply an old German farmer in dark overalls cutting the meadow. He had clearly been up since dawn. The whole meadow was mown and the old fellow had courteously and carefully mown all around me. In another five minutes' time perhaps he would have had to prod me awake to finish off this last little square, but as it was I packed and dressed and beat a hasty retreat to the dinghy before I lost an ear.

That was not the only surprise of the morning. The couple of horses that had been at the far end of the field the night before seemed to have become curiously distended in the night. And spotted. And now surely there were more of them, though these newcomers had shrunk to the size of Great Danes. And the whole menagerie was being tended by the ugliest red-faced dwarf that could be imagined; even now he was shaking a fist at me and shouting across the field in some unearthly language of hoots and shrieks. It was only when I saw the striped red and yellow canvas of the Big Top that had sprouted overnight in the field like a giant gaudy mushroom did I realise that I was looking at the trappings of the

celebrated Circus Trumf. Two llamas, five palominos, three Shet-
land ponies and a furious baboon – my enraged dwarf – were now
tethered in the field. After such a bizarre and delightful start, I had
high hopes that the day could only continue to enchant.

It didn't. A mile upstream I came to a large lock that refused to
open. On climbing ashore and making my way up to the concrete
tower where sat the lock-keeper, I found out the lie of the land.
Here, it seemed, the waterway split into two. The River Main above
this point curved around in a great seven-mile bend like a capital C,
and a new stretch of canal had been constructed to short-circuit this
bend in a straight cut of about four miles. It was this that I could see
from the control tower where we stood: sheer-sided concrete walls
dwindling away into the heat-hazy north. The problem was that
only powered vessels were permitted to use the cut; all other craft
had to go around by the old natural river route. The young lock-
keeper explained this to me very nicely and rather apologetically but
assured me that the river route was terribly pretty and here, have
these chocolate-coated energy muesli bars that his wife had packed
for his lunch but he didn't want. Buoyed up by his enthusiasm for
the delights ahead of me, I accepted the snack bars, returned to the
dinghy and set off into Hell.

I suppose it is not fair to expect that your average German lock-
keeper will be completely *au fait* with the subtleties of English
usage, especially the semantic difference between the two verbs *may*
and *can*. Were this particular young man ever to ask for assistance
on this matter, I would perhaps give him the following example:

1. Unpowered boats *may* not use the canal-cut
but
2. Unpowered boats *can*not use the river loop.
See? Simple.

Yet again, as on the Rhine, the lock-keeper's insistence on the
scenic nature of the river loop failed to explain the very essence of
that scenery: namely, rapids. Possibly the gift of the energy muesli
bars was a gesture from the wiser subconscious part of the man's
brain, which knew full well that I would need every ounce of extra
energy I could muster for the hours ahead.

For the first few miles the river slipped away beneath me smooth
and beer-brown as I hauled myself along, singing *Poor Wandering
One* with gusto and tucking into one of the muesli bars. But by the
fourth mile the current had become seriously strong and it was all I

could do to make any headway. Then the nature of the river changed. Along the right-hand bank, tapering groins of loose stone projected about twenty feet into the river at right angles to the bank. These spits were set at intervals of about one hundred yards and had created calm stretches of water lying along the right-hand half of the river. Consequently, the left half of the river flowed all the more fiercely. Nevertheless, by sticking closely to the right bank I could row in relative stillness for a hundred yards at a time. But then problems arose. To get around the tip of each groin into the next backwater required a combination of hydrodynamics, trajectory motion and sheer brawn that would tax a twenty-pound salmon with a degree in higher physics. The trick was to get a good run up to each spit, emerge at the last minute into the current that ran fiercely around it, and row like blazes. A moment's hesitation and the current would take the bow and swing me round to the left and broadside to the flow, waltzing me fifty yards downstream again. If I was very quick and very clever, I could so manoeuvre the boat that the current caught the stern instead and turned me neatly into the next backwater, there to sit shaking and sweaty and panting before setting out up the still stretch to try the whole thing again. (Remember in addition, dear Reader, that all this fine calculation of distances and angles of approach had to be made while facing backwards in the boat. At least salmon get to face the way they are going.)

After several hours of this erratic progress, during which time I don't think I noticed the pretty scenery once, the current grew so strong that I simply couldn't get past one of the stony points. After three attempts, and three subsequent swirls downstream, I noticed an opening in the right-hand bank that I had been too sweat-blind to notice before. This led through into what appeared to be a large shallow lagoon enclosed by high banks, and it curved away out of sight to the north, the direction I was heading. And sure enough, I could see further up the river beyond the worst of the current what appeared to be another opening in the bank. The other end of this secret lagoon, perhaps? A serene bypass of this impassable rapid? This could well be my Northwest Passage. I abandoned any further attempt at rounding the rocky spit that had so mocked me and struck out for the gap into the lagoon.

I found myself in what had possibly been an old clay pit. The broad and sluggish water shimmered with dragonflies and water boatmen and smelt of mud and weed and rotting vegetation. But there was still possibly a way through, although the water looked shallow in places. It was. Three strokes later I had grounded on mud. I floundered for a little with the oars, but this served only to settle us further onto the sticky grey bottom. There was nothing for it but to get out and haul *Jack* off by hand. With a resigned hey-ho I climbed out into ankle-deep water and promptly disappeared up to my waist in mud.

After the initial shock I laughed heartily at the comic-book predicament I was in and set about extricating myself. Ten minutes later I was seriously panicking. The mud had a grip on me, a slow, slurping, porridge-like grip, and nothing I could do seemed to make the slightest difference. To make matters worse, *Jack*, lightened by my disembarkation, had bobbed free, come off the bottom and drifted to sit a little way away, clearly not wanting to get involved. Without her gunwale to support me, I had no way of hauling myself out of that sucking grip. After another twenty minutes I was convinced that the early-morning apparition of the reaper had been exactly as I thought: a presage of Death. It was such an ignominious way to go, I thought. I wasn't sinking further, but I was certainly not going anywhere. The sun was increasingly hot, the dragonflies had come to regard me as a fixture and were using me as a bridal suite, and being out of sight of the main river I had serious doubts that I would be spotted by a passer-by. I rather thought that in a fortnight's time some stray picnicker would find a bloated, blackened corpse sticking stiffly out of the swamp, infested only with the swarming life of dragonfly larvae.

At last I stopped writhing, and as soon as I did a gentle breeze, the very faintest of zephyrs ghosted up and sent a shimmer over the stagnant water. The relief it brought from the fierce heat was welcome, but it brought me something better, much better. *Jack*, having sat motionless on the glassy water above her painted reflection, drifted closer, closer ... closer still, nudged by the ghost-breeze ... until finally she was in reach. Two minutes later I had hauled myself out and flopped shaking into her arms, smearing grey mud over everything and kissing her all over in sheer idiotic gladness. Then carefully, ever so carefully, I poled her out of that dreadful lagoon and back into the main river.

My troubles were not yet over. I still had the rapids to face, and this I decided would require me to throw myself overboard again (after checking carefully that the riverbed was solid pebbles this time) and stride up the stream chest-deep hauling *Jack* behind me. Before doing this I dug in the very front of the forelocker for a pair of old sandshoes that I had last seen in Dover; these would protect my feet from the sharp, rocky bottom. They emerged from the darkness covered in something bright red and highly sticky which could only be blood. Appalled, I rooted around further, fully expecting to find a severed head that someone had stowed while my back was turned. Instead, I found only that a can of toxic red syrup used all those months ago in Whitstable to mend the hole in *Jack*'s hull had burst and was oozing through my possessions. Putting this firmly in the category of Things To Be Dealt With Later, I ate the second energy bar, climbed into the noxious sandshoes and once again jumped overboard.

I can say this for the next few hours: they were wonderfully cooling. The day had become scorching and the chance to stand up to my chest in cold running water was one that I was thankful for. The next two hours were spent slipping and sliding over submerged rocks, bodily hauling *Jack* up against an increasing current. Sometimes the stretches were shallow enough to allow a gentle wade upstream, with *Jack* tugging behind me on her leash like a fretful labrador that has sniffed an interesting lamp post two hundred yards back. At other times the going underfoot became treacherous and I would find myself plunging chin-deep into some hole between the boulders while the racing water threatened to rip the painter from my hands and send *Jack* spinning downstream. At one particularly tricky point the banks closed in steeply on either side and the river was too deep to wade except where the left-hand bank was overhung with low hazels. Here the current was steady and strong, a smooth amber muscle of water pouring down, and progress required a painful wade chest-deep among the spiky hindering branches of hazel. Then my foot slipped and I found myself borne away under the black water to end up in a submerged beaver's nest of roots and rotting boughs, held down for a few horrid seconds by the tangling net of vegetation before breaking through to the surface and the bright air.

In time I reached an impasse. The river ran in a fierce rapid over a shallow bed of pebbles in midstream. It was only waist–deep, but the current was so strong that I couldn't budge *Jack*. Every now and then I would try to shift my footing to gain a better purchase, at which point the river would flip my feet from underneath me and *Jack* and I would end up fifty yards downstream before I could resurface. This happened four times. Each time I would spend another twenty minutes hauling *Jack* back up to the same rapid, and the whole thing would happen again. I didn't know what to do. There was nothing I could do.

At last, above the rush and swirl of water about my knees, I heard the faint drone of an outboard engine and glory be! around the downstream bend came the little rubber Zodiac of yesterday with the unsmiling grandpapa and the two boys. I had learnt by now not to judge a German by the expression he chooses to wear on his face, and this man was no exception. Before very long he had thrown out a line, instructed me to tie my painter to his and then to swim over and hop in with him. With the engine revving madly and a blue cloud of fumes ascending to the afternoon sky, the Zodiac inched forward and *Jack* slowly rode clear of the rapids into a broad pool upstream.

There were, it appeared, only a couple more kilometres before the weir and lock that would take me onto the main navigable river again just above the new cut, so Papa Grim towed me the rest of the way, keeping a sensible silence above the buzz of the motor. Occasionally the propeller blades would clatter on some submerged rock as we negotiated our way up another rapid, but we finally emerged into the wide and sandy pool below the weir and the struggle was over. I was bruised, battered and cut from a hundred collisions with underwater boulders, my hands were raw with straining on the thin painter, and my sandshoes appeared to have bonded onto my feet with an irreversible epoxy resin. But it was over. I had traversed the scenic section of the River Main and shown that not only *may* unpowered boats take the route but that they *can* as well. And very pretty it was too.

The last hour of that strange day was spent rowing in windless heat up a few more broad bends of the Main and stopping at a little sandy bay to give *Jack* a thorough spring-clean. Epoxy resin, slimy mud, hazel leaves, bilge water and the sodden remains of my bread and salami were all slooshed out with the bailer and wiped away with the big sponge. At some point in this procedure a naked man trotted out of a nearby copse, waved in a friendly fashion and vanished across a field. Perhaps the Germans did this sort of thing. Then, with the boat as clean as I could make it, I rounded one last bend, tied up in a little side-arm hidden deep under an overhanging willow and marched off to find a beer and a meal, feeling it had been a good day after all.

When I came back two hours later, some bastard had stolen my pith helmet.

That night I really couldn't care. I watched a nightjar hawking over the starlit meadow and then slept the sleep of the truly exhausted.

*

The next morning I cared alright. My pith helmet! Gone! It had been given to me by that same Rupert who had brought me the original Jack de Crow, so the hat and the boat had, as it were, a common godparent. I had worn it poling a dugout canoe through the Okavango Swamp, rafting on the Zambesi, hitching across the Mogdagadi Desert and climbing in the Cuillin. I know that it has been, throughout this account, an affectation, an eccentricity deliberately adopted. But nevertheless it had become an important item for me in more ways than one. Every hero has his hat: Indiana Jones rolling back beneath the sliding stone door of the tomb to retrieve his old leather headpiece; Doctor Dolittle returning to the unpleasant Throgmorton Manor for his beloved topper; Sherlock Holmes striding around in his deerstalker. But the pith helmet had also played a more practical part in the voyage. It had collected blackberries and deutschmarks in good measure; it had kept off the Picardy sun and the Oxfordshire rain; it had mollified suspicious lock-keepers and been admired by Eton boys; it had done service as a splendid bailer during my shipwreck in the North Sea; and when on countless occasions an unexpected gybe had sent the boom swinging murderously at my head, it had saved me from concussion and possible death.

And now it was gone, pinched I'm sure by some village urchin who had no idea of what a treasure he had purloined. Or perhaps by Lurking Naked Man for reasons unknown. May he get good use out of it, wherever he is now.

I found myself missing it sorely the next day. Temperatures had soared to forty degrees in parts of Germany: Europe was experiencing the severest heatwave in a century of records. And it was through this that I was rowing hatless and sun-struck up the wide, windless highway of the Main. Perhaps 'drag strip' would be a better phrase. It seemed that every speedboat, every jet ski, every water-skier in Germany was out in force that Sunday on the Main. They zoomed and snarled up and down, throwing great wakes behind them that sent the trees swaying in panic along the river banks and the coots

Stuck Fast

scuttling from their nests. Each time one passed, the wake was enough to rock me wildly to and fro, my oars slapping the water helplessly and disturbing the strong rhythm that is so vital to oarsmen in their craft. I hated the boats with a passion as they arrogantly churned by: their virile tanned crew in reflective sunglasses, their bathing beauties draped over the sleek prows. It seemed that without my hat, my wonderful hat, I was no longer a figure of mystery and adventure hailing from foreign lands, deserving a little awed respect from the locals, but merely a hot and bothered middle-aged man who couldn't afford a speedboat and was turning a rather amusing shade of beetroot.

As the scent of the lime trees was growing sweet and drowsy with the coming evening and the glare had gone off the molten river along with the powerboats, I came at late dusk to a village whose name I did not record. After tethering my boat I wandered through the lanes of this place and found them utterly deserted. There were two inns, large dilapidated buildings; one of them was closed, the other boarded up. The whole place smelt of straw and manure and was strangely quiet. The only living things I saw were three magnificent horses, dark chestnut, who cantered nervously and endlessly around a small field sloping to the river. They seemed terrified of something and their fear unnerved me. I sat somewhat uneasily in the next field and ate my supper, and then found growing in a thick bramble hedge around a lightless witch's cottage a single huge blackberry, almost as big as a small orange. That was my dessert, and exquisite it was. That night I woke to find a silent man standing over me with a torch. He didn't say anything. As I came awake, he snapped off the torch and strode off. In the gibbous moonlight I could see that under his arm he held something long that gleamed with a rod of reflected light – a gun. In the next field the three stallions were still circling restlessly. I could hear them in the night. An odd place altogether.

The next day took me without event to the little village of Eltmann, and there, through a series of bizarre events too tedious to relate, a succession of complete strangers managed to turn my expected supper of half a stale bread roll and a lonely evening into … wait, I have a list here somewhere … four eggs, seven tomatoes, three bottles of beer, a large carton of chocolate milk, a bag of cookies, a further bag of iced pastries, five apples, a bottle of white wine, a corkscrew as a present and a bank-side rendition of 'Lili Marlene' by an elderly grandmother, herself called Lili, who thought I was a good, good man.

Why if I am such a good man did I ultimately come to feel stifled, resentful of this outpouring of generosity and interest? Why was I now anxious to get onto the canal and away from this enchanted river where a vagrant stranger could do no wrong, could come to no harm? Why, when I finally sailed away from Eltmann on a morning breeze with one of the many benefactors from the night before still there snapping photos of my departure, did it feel so like some sort of escape?

The Kaiser's Canal

The Bear went over the Mountain,
The Bear went over the Mountain,
The Bear went over the Mountain,
To see what he could see.

—NURSERY RHYME

The rose garden terrace of the New Bishop's residence in Bamberg is the loveliest place to sit and write letters between Calais and the Black Sea. A thousand blooms cense the air with perfume; petals of every shade, scarlet, crimson, white and yellow, pink and apricot, carmine, garnet, soft as velvet, cool as wine, fill the wide terrace with colour and fragrance. Fountains tinkle into round basins where fat goldfish nibble and dip, and here and there from the sea of flowers rises a marble cherub or a draped Venus. The terrace overlooks the red roofs and copper-green spires of old Bamberg, where the River Regnitz plaits its way in a number of channels, mill-races and long, still reaches through the heart of the finest town in Germany. It is also a nice place to have a cup of really excellent tea and pat oneself firmly on the back for having reached another milestone.

Bamberg marks the end of the interminable River Main and the beginning of the Main-Rhine-Donau Canal, a long-sought-after goal. I had heaved a sigh of relief when the previous day I had rowed up the last thirty kilometres of the Main in stifling, thundery weather and come at last to the 384-kilometre mark – 384 kilometres! I had stopped for lunch and a swim on the green spit between the two watercourses and discovered that my tuck-box still had an egg in it from the night before. Being raw, it was no use to me unless … ah, the very thing. A nearby children's playground had a slippery-dip in it, the shiny silver metal burning hot in the sun. An experimental dob of butter on the flattened end of the slide sizzled, and a few minutes later I was scraping off a fried egg onto the bottom half of a buttered roll. True, it was a little runnier than I liked, but I enjoyed the intrepid nature of such bush cuisine. I also enjoyed turning my back on the meandering Main after fourteen days of upstream rowing and looked forward to the still waters of the canal ahead.

After fourteen days of sleeping on my boat or under the stars, I decided to treat myself to a hotel room in Bamberg. My timing was perfect. That night saw a thunderstorm of Wagnerian proportions, the lightning striking the spires of the town all about me. Brilliant white flashes crackled in the window frame, and at one stage illumined a terrified cat pawing at the glass like Gallico's Thomasina back from the dead. The poor ginger puss spent the rest of the night curled up damply on my chest and clutched ever more tightly with each new crack of thunder overhead.

How accustomed I had grown to the outdoors life! I found the walls of the hotel room that night unbearably claustrophobic, the windows and doors and taps unnecessarily fiddly. The water running from the taps seemed to me a thin and etiolated trickle compared with emptying a bailerful of cold water over the neck and shoulders each morning under a clearing sky. The hot bath for which I had so longed was a tepid, steamy, hip-pinching affair after skinny-dipping at noon in a wide, lonely bend of the river with cool mud squishing between the toes and the smell of green river-weed in one's nose and mouth. How clinging and marshmallow-like seemed my quilt that night; how yellow and feeble glowed the light-bulb for shaving with the next morning. And the big plate of *putenschnitzel mit butterknudeln unt grunesalat* I ordered for dinner was four times the amount I could comfortably eat and took ten times longer in the preparation than my beloved daily tomato-and-mayonnaise roll. I rolled groaning from the table feeling as if I had just consumed a vat of porpoise blubber. I longed to be out of the city and on my way again.

The Rhine-Main-Donau Canal links the top of the Main River with the Danube and so serves as the passageway between the two great river systems of Europe. Its existence allows ships to travel all the way from the North Sea to the Black Sea without ever touching the Mediterranean. I had first learnt about its existence from my mother, who had informed me with a great deal of enthusiasm and a total disregard for accuracy that there is a wonderful canal that crosses the Alps, just think of it, built by none other than King Ludwig, Mad Ludwig they called him, and anyway, this canal is one of

The Author Dreams of Gingerbread

the great feats of engineering, terribly old, you realise, and it follows the Crusaders' route to the Holy Land, or perhaps that's something else, but yes, there is, a canal that is, I read all about it in a book.

With this introduction in mind I pictured an extraordinary engineering marvel, a waterway that wound its dizzy way through the heart of the Alps, edging along precipices, scaling in flights of locks, a hundred at a time, the knife-edge ridges of glacial peaks, spanning the vast abyss of blue valleys via aqueducts of spidery slenderness a thousand feet above the swollen rivers below. I also imagined that being built by the infamous Mad Ludwig, each lock-house would be constructed in a cluster of turrets and needle-spires, dove-grey and icing-sugar-white, each possibly equipped with its own troop of red-jacketed soldiers in cock hats. The style would certainly be ginger-bread, but – a cold thought struck me – if Ludwig was as mad as they said, would the construction materials be gingerbread also? The main danger, I surmised, would be getting entangled in the belay-line of a mountaineering party climbing up over the ice on their way to the Jungfrau; or avalanches possibly, set off by the high bleat of a passing chamois or the distant thunder of an alpenhorn quartet.

As it turned out, my impressions were wholly fanciful: the Rhine-Main-Donau Canal has as much eccentric charm and baroque splen-dour as a major motorway. It does not, for one, pass remotely near the Alps, though it does of course cross a major watershed. This water-shed consists of a vast flat plateau of farmland interspersed by pine plantations, small patches of heathland and medium-sized towns of little character. Secondly, it was not built by Mad Ludwig but by quite a different Ludwig who was by all accounts a man of great industry, practicality and efficiency and had no time for gingerbread at all, tending more to the sauerkraut school of architecture. It was he, presumably, who chose to drive the canal across the practicable emptiness of the Bavarian Plateau rather than swing southwards through the ski-resorts of Switzerland. In fact, there wasn't a ginger-bread aqueduct or a yodeller in sight.

The locks on this canal were to prove increasingly troublesome as I progressed. These were not the mossy beamed devices of the English waterways with geraniums spilling gaily along the lock sides. These resembled your average-sized Soviet hydroelectric plant, with vast walls of white concrete and towers six storeys high topped with control rooms paned in green-tinted glass. Each of these offices held in its high and remote fastness a *schleusemeister* of a severity and efficiency to match the mighty complex under his care. It was his job as a modern-day Moses to send the waters hither and thither through his titanic pondage at the push of a but-ton and the flick of a switch. It was *not* his job, as was soon made clear to me, to swill thousands of tons of water about for the sake of every passing boatman who happened to be out for a Sunday jaunt on the waterways. Such frivolous creatures were pointed in the direction of a distant noticeboard and expected to get on with fol-lowing instructions. I soon worked out that near each board was a device like a bicycle rack, and locked to this by a coin-release sys-tem was an aluminium trolley or *bootwagen*. The idea was that skippers of unpowered pleasurecraft could release such a trolley, roll it down a ramp into the canal and haul their little craft out of the water. Then it could be wheeled with relative ease along the lock and lowered again into the next section of the canal; on returning the trolley to its frame and clicking the lock shut, the coin would be recovered and the merry mariner could continue on his way – all without disturbing the Patriarch in his Sinaian height.

Such was the theory. In practice I found that a little feigned ignorance and whimsical pleading with the *schleusemeister* would usually get me through at the tail-end of an industrial barge that happened to be passing through.

*

The canal is travelling along its own high causeway above the landscape, rather as a railway travels along the top of an embankment. It feels unnatural but exhilarating to be travelling thus so high across the fields and woods. One evening I come to a lonely stretch of heathland and scattered pine forests. Here there is a strange monument on the right-hand bank, a thin upright wedge of white cement oddly curved and pointed. It marks the highest point of the canal – that is, the watershed of the whole of Europe. Behind me the land falls invisibly away into the Black Forest, the valleys of the Main, the Rhine, the Rhone, the Moselle all the way down to the grey shores of the North Sea and the old Atlantic. Ahead of me a mass of land falls away to the Danube, which tumbles endlessly down through Austria, through Hungary, across the vast Magyar Plain, cuts beyond the Carpathian mountains and peters out into the wide wetlands of the Danube Delta. That night I check my maps and figures. I am not only at the highest point of my travels but I am almost exactly halfway between North Wales and the Black Sea. It is all downhill from here.

The usual routine: a swim in the green waters of the canal, applying a bar of soap to hair and skin with great vigour, then clambering out onto the sweet grass to dry off. The towel is hung to dry on the boom; it will still be wet first thing tomorrow from the dew, but an hour later it will be stiff and dry with sunlight. Then as the light fades I pull out my tupperware box and make a sandwich.

Behind me, as I sit facing out over the canal, a steep bank drops away to a pine forest. The bank is covered in mullein, their tall spires of sulphur flowers luminescing faintly in the dusk against the British

Racing Green of the forest. There is a high shriek from somewhere in the trees and a quick rustle: some small animal meeting its death at the claws of an owl, perhaps? The stars are coming out, wavering in white S's and ?'s in the deep blue of the canal. I am suddenly desperately, hungrily, cravingly in need of company. It is as fierce and persistent a desire as my thirst for milk a few weeks ago. I remember that I have a bottle of white wine in the hold, a present from one of my benefactors in Eltmann. I open it with the new corkscrew and fill a glass. Then I very solemnly raise the glass to the night and say out loud a toast of thanks to all the people of Wales and England, of France and Germany, that have sped *Jack* and myself on our slow ascent to this height. I make a small, foolish speech and drink the wine. It is excellent. Whatever it is in the wood kills again, and I think for a fraction of a second about such things as the Surrey Puma and the Dartmoor Panther. Is there a ... *check map* ... a Hilpoltstein Tiger, perhaps?

After a third glass of wine I am about to climb into my sleeping bag which I have spread on the soft grass of the bank when in the gloom of the opposite bank I see the shadow of someone moving. He is directly across the canal from me. After a little while there is the flare of a match and a fire is lit. The shadow is a man, about my age I guess, and he settles down to make himself some supper. He too has a bottle ... beer, I think ... and I make out a rucksack by his side. He is setting up camp for the night. I doubt if he can see me in the darkness across the width of the canal, though perhaps he has seen the pale yellow lines and mast of *Jack*. I am tempted to call out to him, but what would be the use? The canal is too wide for easy conversing and there is nowhere to cross for miles. Besides, he is almost certainly German and what if he doesn't speak English or understand why someone is calling out of the darkness to him? I am snug in my sleeping bag now, and the craving for company has been drowned in the wine. I let it go and sleep, and when I wake the next morning he is gone. I like to think that he was a fellow traveller, someone walking from the Black Sea to North Wales, that we passed unawares in the darkness and shall never know the truth of it.

*

Now that I was going downhill, the lock-keepers refused to succumb to foreign eccentricity and utterly forbade me to enter the locks as I had been doing. They pointed sternly to the *bootwagens* and insisted

I use them. In vain did I plead that *Jack* was a seasoned traveller, well accustomed to the perils of every variety of lock between here and the North Sea. *Not zis vun*, they would crackle through their intercoms. *Use ze bootwagen. Iss fur ze kleine booten.* Click.

This was all very well, but *Jack* was no kayak. At one lock the keeper was particularly abrupt down the intercom and I had to return three times to explain that the coin-release mechanism on the trolley was jammed. He did not believe me and on my third attempt hung up and refused to answer. Hot and bothered, I managed to clear the dust and grit out of the slot with my knife and hauled the trolley all the way up to the top pound where *Jack* was waiting. There I lowered the trolley on the end of a rope down the ramp into the water. Then, waist deep in the canal, I manoeuvred *Jack* over the top of the trolley frame and tied her bow rope onto the upright 'prow' that made the handle. Gripping the rope tightly, I started to walk slowly up the ramp, hauling *Jack* behind me. The effort needed was tremendous. The boat, heavy with rigging and luggage, was nearly impossible to pull up the slope, and I strained and strained with all my might to inch *Jack* up out of the water. Then my feet slipped from beneath me on the green slime of the concrete ramp. This was not just a stumble or a skid – it was a perfectly executed Buster Keaton stunt: both feet shot from under me in synchronisation, ending up perfectly level with my head. My horizontal body hung there for a good three seconds, three artistic seconds that allowed my head to turn to face the camera, and a brief glance over my shoulder to see where the ground had got to. Then my eyes closed in resignation and there followed the swift plummet onto the concrete slab below, accompanied by a comic whistling noise and a loud splat as I landed in the green slime. And the routine was not yet over. Somehow in the course of my aerial acrobatics the towrope had become tangled around my neck, and as the laden trolley rolled gracefully back into the canal I went with it, drawn headfirst down the ramp on the end of the rope like a trussed walrus. So stunned was I that I disappeared completely under the water, my position marked only by a line of bubbles breaking the surface.

Who could resist such slapstick? Not I. Although I was covered in green slime and had a ringing head, my bad mood was dispelled. That day ended with the canal descending into the valley of the Altmuhl, and my grateful entry onto that beautiful and little-known river. The Rhine-Main-Donau Canal was behind me and I was launched on a current that would take me two and a half thousand miles to the Black Sea.

When I emerged onto the Danube, though, the water was sluggish and black and the banks were industrial and bare. I had expected a swift and sweeping current in a wooded gorge similar to the Altmuhl, and my first sight in the fading light was sorely disappointing.

Pulling through the oily waters in the dusk, *Jack*'s bow went *clunk* on something and I saw that I had hit a floating bottle. A second glance showed that it had in it a piece of orange paper, and on an impulse I dragged it out of the water. It was as I had thought: that classic mariner's find, a message in a bottle. I struggled to remove the cork and extract the piece of paper, and found that it was scrawled in a childish hand in coloured crayon. It was in German and read: *Good luck on your adventure, dear Captain. I hope I will meet you one day when I too have a ship.*

It could not have been more clearly intended for me. I was no scavenger picking through debris on the shore. I was no boatman out for the afternoon. Of all the people on the river, surely I was that dear Captain on an adventure that the child had seen in his or her mind's eye? The childish writing, the aptness of the find, and above all the tremendous optimism implicit in the act of consigning such a message to the currents, conspired to send me singing on my way through the darkening dusk. I had been wished good fortune and fair sailing by an anonymous child yet to learn the sneering laws of chance, and I looked forward to the day when I should shake hands with the young author of that fortunate note. Meanwhile, here was a marina, here was light and company and food, and here was rest for the night. I had reached the Danube and it was surely easy going from here.

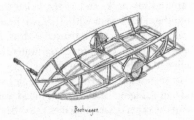

Bootwagen

Pigeons and Palaces

Much have I travell'd in the realms of gold,
And many goodly states and kingdoms seen ...
—KEATS, *On First Looking into Chapman's Homer*

I needed to make a phone call. The marina didn't have a phone, so I found myself wandering along a country road at night heading for the town of Kelheim two miles away. After half a mile I came across a building, cheerful and lamplit, standing by itself with bare fields on either side. Along with the warm light that poured from its windows into the night there came the homely buzz of voices and the clink of glasses that betokened a pub. In fact, as I peered at the building's frontage, there did seem to be a sign of sorts, and a name in German. This was clearly the German equivalent of the Red Lion or the Fox and Hounds, though here it would be the Two-Headed Eagle or the King of Prussia. At any rate it would have a phone and I could follow up with a pint or two of good German beer to celebrate my arrival on the Danube.

I pushed my way through the doors into a congenial smoky atmosphere and there were the customers sitting around several long tables drinking and chatting animatedly. The look of surprise they gave me as I entered was soon explained; they were apparently in the middle of a pub quiz, with paper and pencils scattered among the beer mugs and coasters. I was a late arrival, perhaps, having misread the starting time. Did I want to join in? I assume that was the question, because at my first halting words of greeting one of the men said, 'Ah, English, *ja?*' and the question of my joining the quiz seemed to be dropped. I asked if there was a phone I could use, and after some head-shaking a large man pulled out his mobile phone and handed it to me. I protested, but he was insistent so after I had made my call – a brief but important one to a friend in Stuttgart – I handed the phone back and offered to pay. At this there was much discussion among the jovial group and an older man was dispatched to fetch an item from behind the bar.

This, to my mild surprise, was a large plastic pigeon.

It was shaken vigorously under my nose, but only when the man grew tired of my dim-wittedness and stopped agitating it did I notice that there was a slit in the top of the bird's head. It was a piggy-bank, or rather a pidgy-bank. I dropped a couple of deutschmark into the pigeon's head, and now that the business of the phone call was concluded, turned my attention to the bar.

'Um ... *ein bier, bitte,*' I said, 'if that's okay.'

The barman looked taken aback (even I flinched at my attempt to speak German), but soon the beer was produced and I dug into my pocket to pay. To my surprise, out came the plastic pigeon and I was invited once more to insert my deutschmarks in the creature's head. As I took the first welcome swig, I pondered the eccentric cash-till procedures of these otherwise efficient Germans. Soon I was invited to sit down at a table with the others – they seemed happy enough to suspend the quiz for a while out of courtesy to a stranger – and my life story was dragged out of me. There were the usual exclamations of admiration and disbelief, and for the next half-hour we conversed in a mixture of broken English and German. After my second drink, once more paid for by a donation to the pigeon, I relaxed enough to take stock of my surroundings. It began to strike me as a rather odd pub. There was very little coming and going – in fact, nobody had arrived or left since I'd been there – and everyone seemed to be taking turns behind the bar, helping themselves as they pleased, with the sole proviso that each time the pigeon appeared like the Holy Spirit to claim its due. And as I looked around, I noticed that there was a definite theme to the décor. A series of shining silver trophies along one wall were topped by little winged hats. Various pennants hanging from the rafters each displayed, as a symbol of peace, the winged dove fluttering upwards. Lastly I focused on a large faded poster on the far wall, which showed the breeds of pigeons, wild and domestic, from around the world: fantails, pouters, wood-pigeons, rock-doves, bronzewings, turtles and, of course, racing pigeons. A horrid doubt crept into my mind as I sipped my second beer. The quiz still hadn't recommenced. A long pause had opened in the conversation and there was now the indefinable air of well-bred patience wondering how to be frank.

When the silence had extended long enough, filled only with the nervous shuffle of papers and the clatter of a dropped pencil, I took the bull by the horns.

'Excuse me, this *is* a pub, isn't it?' I asked.

Shuffles of embarrassed feet. Then one of my hosts spoke up. He spoke very kindly.

' Well, now zat you ask, *nein*, zis isn't a pub actually. This is ze Kelheim Racing Pigeon Club, and' – here he glanced around his fellow members – 'vell, zis is our Annual General Meeting. But please,' he added hastily as I rose to my feet and started backing out the room, 'it has been a pleasure to have you here' (hasty nods all round). 'But now' (as he picked up paper and pen) 'if you haf had enough beer, perhaps ve get on with ze meeting, *ja?*'

*

After Kelheim, the Danube – or Donau, as we must now call it – flowed across a wide plain between green fields and low dykes. Here and there were solitary steep hills, as abrupt as loaves of bread, and each of these was the seat of some *Schloss* or *Kloster* with red roofs, perched high above the flat expanse and looking over a watery vista of silver and blue and flooded green stretching to the horizon.

I had continued my learning of Keats' poetry all this while. I was only four verses off knowing the whole tedious length of *The Eve of St Agnes* by heart but had also been concentrating on *Ode to Psyche* as a break from Madeline and her vague regardless eyes. As I was revelling in the last stanza of *Psyche*, I rounded a broad bend of the river and saw a sight that made me gasp. There ahead of me was one of these great isolated hills, and it looked as though it had fallen there from the gilded frames of a neo-classical painting, a Gainsborough perhaps. Flanking its steep slopes were groves of pine trees, luxurious in their sable fur, and great cedar trees soaring like scented green thunderclouds supported on redwood pillars.

Sitting on its crest against black pines and blue sky was the Parthenon. Not, you understand, that flaking ruin baked in the blinding glare and taxi fumes of Athens, crawled over by hot tourists picking their way through fallen columns and construction-site debris; no, this was the real Parthenon, a gleaming temple in white marble, every pillar and cornice intact, and looking as though it had been completed last week. A great flight of stairs swept up the hill beneath the cedars to the portico with its familiar colonnade of pillars and shallow-pitched roof, displaying the perfect proportions of the Golden Ratio. The background of dark pines and verdant grass, and the vista it commanded of meandering river and wide, wide skies, made it the very embodiment of Arcadia.

At the foot of the hill there was a wooden jetty awaiting my magic barge. Feeling like Parsifal in a dream, I moored up and climbed the three hundred steps, from terrace to terrace to terrace, with a sense of awe:

> *Who are these coming to the sacrifice? …*
> *What little town by river or sea-shore*
> *Or mountain built with peaceful citadel*
> *Is emptied of its folk, this pious morn?*
> *And, little town, thy streets for evermore*
> *Will silent be …*

As I approached the top, the sheer size of the place struck me. I was to find out that it was an exact full-scale copy of the original Parthenon, but it seemed three times bigger than the dusty Athenian ruin I remembered. Inside I found a spacious hall, a splendour of gilding and mosaic and carved capitols, and on pedestals ranged around the four walls countless busts and statues. But here at last there was a difference. For where the ancient statues would have been of gods and goddesses, divine youths and mighty Olympians, smooth-limbed and lissom, or thunder-browed and haughty, the statues here were of famous German statesmen of the last few centuries: chancellors, generals, philosophers, writers and economists. Full of the German virtues of thrift and efficiency these good men might have been, but as models of physical beauty they could barely muster a divine feature among them. Balding heads, stout tums, ridiculous whiskers, bulging eyes, double chins, full-fed faces – they looked as commonplace as any modern-day meeting of town-planners. The temple was clearly devoted to celebrating the inner qualities of German greatness rather than the external aesthetics, and the sculptor had gone for realism rather than flattery.

I discovered that this marvellous fantasy was commissioned by none other than King Ludwig the Sane, the same man who had built the Rhine-Main-Donau Canal. I was pleased to find that he seemed to have inherited some small streak of madness from his namesake after all. Nevertheless, as I stood there in the portico,

Valhalla

gazing out across the wide and sunlit plain under an afternoon sky borrowed from Canaletto, I couldn't help thinking that this was the finest building between here and North Wales. Had Ludwig turned aside briefly from his economists and his engineers to read a young English poet and then made the dreamer's vow a reality?

> *And in the midst of that wide quietness,*
> *A rosy sanctuary will I dress …*
> *With buds and bells and stars without a name …*
> *And there shall be for thee all soft delight*
> *That shadowy thought can win,*
> *A bright torch, and a casement ope at night,*
> *To let the warm Love in!*

Ah yes. Love. Even the double chins and gooseberry eyes could not diminish the love that had so evidently gone into the temple's making.

*

The river quickened its pace once more, sluicing down between banks of osier and willow, occasionally passing through a town or village, but I had caught the river's mood and I too was hurrying, reluctant to stop until fifty miles a day was under my belt. The rowing was easy – I could slot into an automatic rhythm which took me for hours, sometimes so dreamily that I would wake with a start to wonder where the miles had gone. A feature of the river now was the presence of channel-marker buoys, red for port and green for starboard. These were large hollow cylinders of tin with conical noses, surmounted by a fin-like flag rising out of their rounded backs. With the current racing past them, they gave the appearance of forging through the water upstream, the water spurting from beneath their tin noses and their bodies skidding and swaying with apparent velocity. They looked for all the world like squat antique torpedoes. I was musing on this when there was an almighty clang and I was propelled out of my seat into the bilges. I clambered up in time to see that one of these missiles had struck me a glancing blow on the bows: even from here I could see the smear of yellow paint against the green. I checked *Jack*'s woodwork: apart from a crunching dent in the prow there seemed to be no damage done, but I woke up after that. It would be a pity to sink, torpedoed by these tin sharks.

One of the nicer things about travelling downstream in a dinghy rather than zooming about on well-signed motorways was that one was never fully aware of where one was about to get to. Quite often I found myself in the unusual position of arriving in some picturesque fortified town and, like some ancient traveller in a fairy-tale, asking, 'What fair town is this, pray?' The startled look on the faces of those I questioned seemed to ask, 'Well, how did *you* arrive? Out of the sky? From beneath the cobblestones?' No one ever seemed to think of the river as a means of ingress. To the townsfolk, it was as static and permanent a feature as the town park or the castle gates. It would be like a stranger standing at the foot of the Pyramids and idly commenting, 'Hmmm. Interesting structure. So what do you call these then?'

In this way I came to Passau, another of the great medieval cities of Germany, surpassing all that I had seen so far. It sits on the junction of three rivers, as here the River Inn and the minor River Ilz flow into the Donau from either side. This fact was much lauded in the tourist brochures of the town. 'Passau! Witness the Natural Miracle of Three Rivers Conjoining!' they cried in a passion of exclamation marks, apparently unaware of other features that have a better claim to be called natural miracles: Angel Falls, the Great Barrier Reef, the Grand Canyon, to name but a few. It was odd, too, because Passau was not short of sights worth seeing. The Stephansdom with its twin bronze-green onion-domes had inside a giant gilded pulpit, every inch of which was carved with figures of the four Evangelists and their fabulous menagerie: lions and bulls, eagles and winged spirits, rioting in a baroque tangle of allegory and allusion. The location of the town, perched on a narrow spit between the deep green of the Donau and the milky turbulence of the Inn, gave it the charm of an island fortress. Quiet walkways ambled between the river and gracious waterside residences, where weeping ornamental trees uncoiled their foliage down walls of warm buff stone. Twisting wisteria hung from trellises, dropping its purple confetti into the stream, and small archways ducked up into some courtyard where a bronze fountain played to an empty house.

Rowing away from Passau the next day, I passed the point off the southern end of the town's spit where the Inn flowed in from the west. Here the milky waters of that fierce river, laden with chalk sediment from the far-off Alps, mix with the bottle-deep Donau, and from that point on the river beneath me was never clear again. It remained a murky hue, like paintwater at the end of the art lesson, sometimes a delicate grey-blue, sometimes a choppy fawn, but never again the limpid clarity of old glass. And a few miles downstream, the river in its new khaki marched briskly out of Germany and into the fair land of Austria.

*

There is an elfin piper who haunts the steep woods below Schoning. '*Tweet-toot*!' I would pipe on my tin-whistle, and a perfect two beats later, back would come from the cliffy woods, '*tweet-toot*!'

'*Tiddle–iddle-tweet-toot*'

and

'*Tiddle-iddle-tweet-toot*' would come the reply.

The hidden faun and I played this game of echoing melodies for a full blissful hour as I swanned along in morning sunshine through the gorge. Here, a day's sailing from Passau, the Donau curves around in a series of sharp hair-pin bends between U-shaped valley walls clothed with thick forest. Like everything else in Austria, this looked neatly brushed; dark pine and fir mostly, with the odd swathe of silvery-green ash streaked up the hillside or the lime-gold splash of maple. The forest came down to the river's edge, but every now and then I sailed past a flat open meadow where stood perhaps a single inn, primrose yellow or lily white, with carved window-boxes of scarlet geraniums and a white cat. Between the house and the steep forest there might be a tiny orchard of apple trees rosy with fruit, or a huge neatly stacked pile of wood, a few timber outbuildings, three caramel horses grazing and sometimes a church with square white tower and bronze-green onion dome. The inn or farmhouse looked newly painted, the horses freshly groomed, the grass new-cut and the cat just fed on thick cream. The innkeeper's wife had been out that morning polishing the apples to a gloss on each old tree. This was Austria.

And oh, so silent, so peaceful, so tranquil in the bright morning sun. No noise … no noise that is, except for the pure high notes of a tin-whistle echoing down from upriver where a man in a little red-sailed dinghy is rippling downstream before a light wind, steering with an idle elbow as he plays. And somewhere high up in the sylvan darkness, in a sweet Purcellian contrapunto, the teasing echo of the faun.

This enchanted valley lasted only till noon. The lock-keeper at Aschach explained that I would have to wait three hours before he could let me through and pointed helpfully in the direction of the boat trolley, an inadequate device designed more for a child's kayak than the portly timbers of *Jack de Crow*. A passing family out on a day's cycling were quickly dragooned into helping me haul and heave *Jack* onto the pram. Their early enthusiasm for the task, spurred on by father, had waned long before the task was completed and a threatened mutiny on the part of the teenage daughters nearly left *Jack* stranded in the wayside blackberry bush into which the runaway pram had tilted her for the third time. We eventually carted her the remaining distance and launched her once more, the poor father trying to apologise simultaneously to both me for his family's impatience and his family for having got them involved with the bossy Englishman in the first place. Once launched, I struck out to see if I could make it to Linz by nightfall. This was, in hindsight, a stupid thing to do.

Determination sent me oaring steadily through the afternoon, past banks of sheltering willows, past pretty hamlets where horses grazed, past the lovely *Schloss*-dominated village of Ottensheim at sunset where cheerful café lights begged me to tie up for the night and halt my headlong slog – and so eventually at ten o'clock, arms aching, shivering with cold and exhaustion, illegally rowing through the darkness, to arrive at the much-lauded Winterhafn of Linz. Here I looked around me in dismay. Where was the brightly lit clubhouse winking gold and copper out into the frosty night? The lively bar breathing warm gusts of beer and tobacco and chatter from its welcoming doorway? I searched in vain for the spotless bathrooms and hot showers I had been striving towards all day, the Swedish sauna perhaps, the yachties waiting to offer a fellow skipper hot toddies, free life membership and the hands of their daughters in marriage.

I found myself rowing instead into a dank industrial arm of the river, empty and desolate except for the silent hulks of gravel-dredgers and scrap-metal barges. The sole amenities consisted of a small portacabin of toilets (locked) and lots of cyclone-wire fencing. The nearest lights, orange sodium lights with their ugly glare, were a mile away along a windswept road between warehouses and wasteland. Thinking of the cosy villages I had spurned all that afternoon, I wept.

Starving and cranky, I trudged off down the road towards the distant lights and found, surprisingly, a huge hotel just as the cyclone wire ended. It was a vast and soulless affair, rather like an airport hotel, and there was absolutely no way I was going to allow myself to be tempted to book in to one of its overpriced, over-amenitied rooms, not an intrepid adventurer like me. But they did allow me to buy a bowl of warming soup … and a beer … and another beer … and a warming whisky … and before I knew it, I had succumbed. A hot power shower, sachets of complimentary shampoo, soft white towels, a hair-dryer, a remote control TV, a digital alarm clock-radio, a mini-bar with salted peanuts and cans of Heineken, and crackly sheets and stiff pillows. I was, for one night at least, back in the late twentieth century, an anonymous businessman on a routine trip to sound out possibilities in the expanding European market.

As for the owner of that ridiculous little dinghy abandoned down in the deserted Winterhafn, he had stepped off the world for a little while and could not be contacted.

I found it hard to warm to Linz. It was grandiose in a wedding-cake way, with monumental public buildings and white marble everywhere, but lacking the cobbled-together charm of German towns. The weather matched the city; a bright but chilly sky, and a brisk policeman of a breeze keeping the blood tingling and the shoppers from loitering in the streets. Busking, I was told, was out of the question, so I decided to spend my time there more profitably. I sorted all my dirty laundry and hauled it into town but could find no laundromat anywhere. Eventually I was informed by the official in the Tourist Office that most Austrians possessed their own washing machines so that public laundromats were hardly necessary, and probably – like buskers – a danger to public health and safety and just one more reason why Austria was a superior country to all others. But welcome! Welcome to our warm and beautiful country, not in any way to be confused with that of our cold and humourless neighbours, the Germans.

*

As the river widened, I seemed to become less and less fortunate at finding places to moor up at night. One night I ended up in a deserted industrial boatyard, so crowded with rusting gravel-boats, half-sunken hulks and abandoned barges that I could not tie up anywhere near the bank but had to moor up alongside an old tug. From there, my only route to the shore was a labyrinthine route. I clambered over railings, along gang-planks, up onto iron decks – no, a dead-end – back down this hatchway and over onto the next boat, along the deck – blocked by a pile of crates so back onto the original tug, and so on. Under gantries, down ladders and across pontoons I swarmed, negotiating at least seven different craft along the way, and involving several giddy leaps across gulfs of rust-stained water until I finally reached the sodden bank. A light drizzle had started and the nearest village was a mile away. I trudged there. Everything was closed. I trudged back. Was it a weekend? A holiday? Or had my luck changed for good? How long had I been doing this daft journey and when could I legitimately call it a day? When I got back to the dinghy, having threaded the rusty maze once more, I crouched under my tarpaulin hating the whole world and got out my diary to record that fact. It was the second day of the month, the 2nd of September – a familiar date? I realised that it was exactly a year ago that I had set out from Colemere Woods on that fine evening, waving goodbye to my friends standing on the canal bridge in the twilight. Thinking of this, my crankiness gave way to tears and I became horribly maudlin. I was sick of rowing, sick of being alone, sick of travelling, sick of never getting any mail via Poste Restante – all my friends had seemingly forgotten about me – and I was sick of the drizzle and the damp and the whole damn dinghy. I was too tired even to bother making supper; besides, I suspected I was out of groceries. I would just go to sleep and blot out the miserable world for a time.

In this black mood I was rummaging in my rucksack, when by the feeble light of my torch I noticed something. Before I left Ellesmere, the school matron, a very beautiful and gentle woman called Mair, had asked to borrow my old rucksack. When she returned it, I saw that as a present she had sewn onto one end the Ellesmere College crest, an appropriate design as it depicts a crow with a ring in its bill – my own ship's flag, in fact. This I had known about and thanked Mair for, but what I had never noticed until this dreary, dreary night was that on the inside of the rucksack, on the reverse side of the school badge, she had embroidered in golden thread a message. By the light of my torch I examined it curiously. It read: *Sandy, may all that is good watch over you and keep you safe. God bless.*

With those simple words, my mood lifted. I had carried that secret blessing with me for a year, and as I thought back over the last twelve months, I realised how much I had indeed been blessed by all that is good – by friends and strangers, by birds and stars and clouds, by fine winds and the world's poetry, and by adventure and song. With that sudden lifting, I remembered that deep in the bows there was a bottle of red wine to finish off, and some Austrian salt-bread to be eaten, and even a little cheese. I slept that night in my iron labyrinth more soundly, more sweetly, than at any other time of the journey, and sent a silent blessing back to Mair in Shropshire, over all the sleeping leagues of Europe that lay between.

*

The wind was a contrary gale as I set off the next morning down river. The skies were grey and Wagnerian with bluster and flung rain. I was in fact in the Wachau region, the land of the Nibelung, and the Valkyries on their storm-steeds rode me down like a fleeing warrior. I came in the early afternoon to the town of Melk on the right-hand bank, and having had more than enough, pulled into a side arm of the Donau and trudged damply off to find a dry bed for the night.

Melk is famous for its great abbey, Stift Melk. It occupies the whole flat top of a loaf-shaped hill overlooking the river, and is possibly the finest example of Baroque architecture in the world. A tour leaves one feeling as though one has just devoured several crates full of caramel meringues. Each individual room, sure enough, each chamber, each ceiling, each nave, taken one by one with good doses of plain fare in between, is splendid. But taken all together, piled one upon the other like some toppling confectionery extravaganza, it left me wanting to lie down in a darkened room for several weeks.

It was in the baroque chapel that the ornamentation reached an opulence and tastelessness sufficient to dissolve any last lingering opposition to the Puritan aesthetic. Here the two most striking features are a pair of skeletons preserved in glass cases on either side of the main aisle. Instead of reclining decently in the usual manner of the dead, these two have been dressed and posed in a ghastly imitation of Life. One is reclining coyly propped on one elbow, his skeletal hand tucked under his chin, and one leg crooked as though he is posing for a fashion shot for *Cleo* magazine, pouting invisible lips at the camera. The other is clad in beetle-green silk pantaloons and is sitting clasping in his bony hand a quill pen and a little diary, recording the day's excitements:

Friday, September 4th (Quarter Moon)

Weather: *Cloudy, intermittent showers.*

Appointments: *None.*

To do: *Moulder a little.*

Comments: *Still dead …*

Several days later I reached the Wienerwald, the famous Vienna Woods, and on an afternoon of sunshine and rain in equal measure, slid over green-silver rapids like a yellow willow leaf and came to the marble splendour of Vienna itself, greatest of all the Danubian cities.

Vienna was an important stop. Beyond it I would be travelling into lands relatively unknown, leaving behind Western Europe and sailing into the former Eastern Bloc countries: Slovakia, Hungary, Croatia, Serbia, Bulgaria and Romania. Unknown indeed! As I stamped around the hot summer streets of Vienna to the different consulates, it soon became clear that my waterways map was as out-of-date as a map of the Prussian Empire. What had once been Yugoslavia, for instance, was now several different countries.

All consulates are pretty grim places at the best of times but the Yugoslavian Embassy (more accurately the Serbian Embassy) was a nightmare especially. There were queues of angry young women with squalling children, and older head-scarfed women standing despondently munching garlic sausages out of greaseproof wrappers, and as far as I could tell they were one and all being refused their requests to travel by the officials behind the grille. I gathered from the young woman behind me in the queue that the country was in such a state of flux that even long-term resident citizens were being refused re-entry. She herself had her Yugoslavian passport, she had lived all but the last year of her life there, and now was unable to go to Dubrovnik to visit her sick father. The mood in the waiting-hall was one of resentment and despair, and I am almost embarrassed to admit that in order to distract the woman's little girl I started doing some magic tricks. Soon the whole queue was watching in grave silence, some were beginning to smile – at the little girl's wide-eyed reaction, not the tricks, I must add – and the mood lightened a little as we made our way up the line. Ahead of me, one by one, people were being turned away with a curt refusal. By the time I got to the window, I was convinced that if all these people were being refused visas into their own country, then as an idle adventurer I would not stand a chance. And indeed, when I put my request to the hard-faced man behind the grille, his first reaction was a contemptuous snort. The borders were closed. The Kosovo situation had made things impossible. I was better to travel elsewhere.

'Ah,' said I, taking a deep breath, 'the thing is, you see ...' and I launched into an explanation about *Jack de Crow* and the Black Sea and the concept of rowing and how very tricky it would be to row elsewhere across the Carpathian Mountains. Under his stony stare I grabbed a couple of visa application forms and drew a little map on the back of them, and a rather natty picture of *Jack de Crow*, my fellow applicants leaning over my shoulder in a cloud of garlic fumes and murmuring their astonishment and approval. I came to a halt eventually and looked at the official, and fifty pairs of eyes looked at him too, all alike asking a silent, 'Well …?' The garlic-sausage munching stopped and the hallway was quiet. From the look in the man's eye and the bead of sweat on his brow, it was clear that this application was not on his clear-cut list of reasonable requests to be unblinkingly refused. In fact, it probably didn't appear on any list near at hand, so with a roll of his eyes off he went, vanishing through a doorway to consult with a superior office about how the iron rules applied to dinghy-sailors. The minutes passed and I was given a large hunk of sausage to pass the time. This was likely to take hours and meanwhile, there were fifty more deserving former Yugoslavians being held waiting. I should just leave …

To my astonishment the official returned only minutes later with a visa application form, a tight smile and look in his eyes that spoke volumes about the stupidity of the regulations. There was a soft but heart-warming cheer from the crowd as I turned to go, and I could see a dozen hopeful faces wondering where they could get a dinghy from at short notice. A precedent had been set and a wave of optimism rippled through the room. The man behind the grille saw this too and it was good to see an expression of exasperation cross his flinty features as he turned back to the no-longer-straightforward task of keeping apart a sick man in Dubrovnik and his daughter.

*

In Vienna I stayed with Alfons and Uli, two of the most civilised people one is ever likely to meet. I had met this couple on a walking holiday in the Alps some years before and we had kept in touch. We met for dinner, but then I was taken to their elegant flat, pushed into a hot shower and gently but firmly told that I was staying with them until further notice.

It was rather like being entertained by two slim, immaculate, well-bred Siamese cats. Alfons made it clear that anything of his was at my disposal: the new racing bike for getting around Vienna, the fridge stacked with the entire contents of a gourmet delicatessen, the slim-line phone for making international calls ('That is what it is *for*,' he explained when I started to wave aside the offer) – in fact, everything. In return I would have to help him sample the latest acquisitions in his collection of fine malt whiskies.

I responded to this extraordinary kindness by clod-hopping my way through the three-day stay, demonstrating in person the utter boorishness of all non-Austrians. When I loudly applauded the fact that Vienna had seen fit to provide free travel on the trams I had been riding over the last few days and what a jolly good thing that was, Alfons and Uli pointed out quietly that no, this was not the case, that it worked on an honesty system which no right-minded citizen would dream of abusing; tickets were available at the booths I had failed to notice on every street corner. When somebody mentioned *Kristallnacht*, I exclaimed merrily how I would love to have seen that and what a jolly sight it would have made. Somewhat surprised, Alfons gravely explained that *Kristallnacht* was Vienna's greatest night of shame when the citizens of Austria turned upon their Jewish neighbours, breaking their windows and humiliating them in the streets, and so therefore, no, not such a jolly sight after all. In vain did I try to explain that I had always assumed *Kristallnacht* to be some Christmassy festival involving lots of tinsel and icing sugar and sparkly crystal decorations and ... oh, never mind. When we went off to a nearby pub in a rainstorm and Alfons lent me an old plastic mac, the only item of clothing in their possession that didn't look as though it had been tailor-made, I slung it onto a coat-hook in the vestibule of the pub before charging ahead into the bar to buy a round of beers, later to find that Alfons had discreetly snuck back to re-hang it properly on a proper coat-hanger provided by the establishment for the proper care of one's vestments.

Lastly, I had been warned about the lift in the apartment block, an alarming contraption of brass and mahogany and wire cables with iron grille doors that scissored back to open and shut. Alfons had given me a careful demonstration that the lift was fine, just fine, as long as you didn't open the grille doors too soon, in which case the lift would jam irrevocably. Clear? *Ja* ...

Not long afterwards I found myself waiting on the ground floor for the lift with a breathless and slightly worried young lady who had rushed in from outside. As we entered the lift, she explained in good English that she had just left her two-year-old in the car in the street with the engine running while she ran upstairs to grab her forgotten purse. But all was well, she would only take thirty seconds, and what could happen in that interval, *ja?* We laughed merrily at her groundless worry, and as we approached her floor, I, ever the gallant gentleman, stepped forward to pull back the doors to speed her on her way.

Too soon.

The lift jerked to a halt, just six inches short of the fifth floor, and the grille doors stuck fast. I tugged at them. Apart from an alarming creak from the cables, there was no movement. We were stuck, stuck in a metal cage halfway up a deserted midday apartment block, and it was remarkable how quickly our recent international bonhomie and bridge-building evaporated. In a very short time, the emotional temperature in the lift became arctic, the woman's contempt for the stupid foreigner alternating with vivid images of how young Hans in the car had probably by now found the handbrake-release and was even now taking his first, and possibly last, joy-ride along the Frederikstrasse. I, in the meantime, was jabbing at buttons, rattling the grille, jumping up and down to try and dislodge something, anything, but to no avail.

Eventually, after several ice-ages, we were rescued by an elderly cleaning lady, and my now near-hysterical companion raced out to hurtle down the stairs to check on the infant. She quite forgot to say goodbye, but perhaps she had other things on her mind.

When not insulting Alfons and Uli and their fellow citizens, I spun around Vienna on the bike seeing the treasures of their marvellous city. There was the Belvedere, where most of the paintings by Gustav Klimt and Egon Schiele are displayed. There was the Orangery, with its Gallery of Grotesques and Messerschmidt bronzes. And there was the Hundertwasser House, one of the most bizarre and beautiful works of architecture anywhere in the world. Hundertwasser believed that as nature abhors a straight line or a plane surface, so too should the designer. He created buildings where there is scarcely a right-angle or a flat surface to be seen. The Hundertwasser House is actually a block of residences, built almost like a steep craggy hill in the midst of the city. Not one window is the same as any other; some are round portholes, others old-fashioned shuttered oblongs of flashing glass. Wide ledges and crannies all the way up hold saplings and trees in groves, so that in autumn the building is hidden beneath a shower of gold and scarlet and the spindly skeletons of birches. What surfaces can be seen ripple with mosaics of broken tiles in sea-blues and china-whites, cut here and there by ceramic oranges and greens. The courtyard on the ground floor holds a tinkling fountain of similar shattered tiles, but that is its least unusual feature, for the cobbles that pave the yard swell gently in rolling dips and curves, making a walk across them a 'symphony for the feet,' as Hundertwasser put it.

There was the great holy gloom of St Stephensdom with its crimson and azure Western Window blazing like a chrysanthemum of fire on high, and the sheer marmoreal splendour of the city buildings themselves. I had never seen such a wealth of marble, of gilding, of civic statuary: fountains swimming with Tritons, monuments scrambling with horse-hooves and manes, squares, columns and palisades, architraves and porticoes, each doorway upheld by a pair of giant, muscular caryatids, and in every little town square or park or courtyard a statue of yet another famous person: Liszt, Mozart, Freud, Klimt, Bruckner, Strauss. There seems to be a statue of everyone that ever existed. There is probably one of me somewhere, though I never found it.

The last thing to love in Vienna were the cafés. I spent blissful hours in a gloomy coffee-house all in dark brown with an immense gilt mirror soaring up into the darkness of the ceiling; the largest mirror in Europe, I was told. Another favourite was Santo Spirito: this was tucked down a side-alley and was furnished with polished bentwood chairs, lit only by candles and playing nothing but classical choral works: Pergolesi, Vittoria, Tallis, Byrd, Scarlatti, pure as candleflames themselves.

And what of poor *Jack de Crow* all this time, you may ask. How was she included in all this? Well, to tell the truth, she wasn't. I had abandoned her in a modern marina on the shores of the Danube. In my week in Vienna I went out to visit her only once, trusting that she was being well looked after by the gods and the Hafenmeister.

A week of blustery weather and squalls began to clear, all my jobs were done, my visas in order, my letters written, and the whisky collection of Alfons was looking distinctly thinnish. Ahead of me, and only half a day's sail, was the border of Slovakia and the end of Western Europe. I knew nothing about the lands ahead, apart from hazy apprehension engendered by the fact that every evil mastermind in any thriller always talked to his pet cacti or piranha with an Eastern European accent. I also had vague doubts about the trouble brewing in Serbia, wherever that was. I consulted my map but couldn't find it. Ah well. No doubt I would bump into it somewhere along the way.

Alfons and Uli came down to the marina to see me off. When they saw just how small *Jack de Crow* was, they blanched. Being accustomed to my stories, they had assumed that I exaggerated her size and were expecting a middling-sized yacht. Nevertheless, they soon rallied and produced a large bottle of wine, some stores of salami, bread, fruit and cheese, and a mysterious little package that clinked. This last item Alfons told me to keep closed until I was in need of some serious cheering up. Before a gentle breeze I hoisted sail, moved out onto the broad grey river and set off into the East and the Unknown.

Wilderland and War

Oh, East is East and West is West, and never the
    twain shall meet,
Till Earth and Sky stand presently at God's great
    Judgement Seat ...
             —KIPLING, *The Ballad of East and West*

Jack did not lightly forgive me for my callous abandonment in
Vienna. The next day she abandoned me and, like naughty Albert at
the zoo, was nearly eaten by lions. It happened like this.

My first night out of Vienna was spent in a grim shipyard outside
Bratislava, a cheerless place full of rusting tankers and oily water.
Without any desire to footslog through industrial wasteland into
town, I stayed on my dinghy that night, not even getting off to
stretch my legs. After an early night I woke at dawn and set off
down the river. As the morning progressed, the day became wilder
in all respects. The breeze stiffened to a following wind that sent me
churning down the river at a cracking speed. The river, too, was
fierce here; even in the early morning stillness, the placid-seeming
mirror of the surface would sometimes boil up in a great lazy swell,
suck at my oars and send me insolently spinning in a couple of circles before sending me on my way with a little pat on the behind like
some corporate manager goosing a very junior typist. Such moments
served to remind me of the power of this cold-handed god with
whom I was consorting.

As the miles passed, so the river widened until the banks blurred
into the distance. Where I could still see them, they were as straight
as a die, shelving parapets of rust-dark gravel and beyond them a
landscape so featureless and bleak that it is difficult now to recall.
Was it bare earth? No, for that would imply some richness, some
potential for fertility. Flat fields? But no, there was no living thing,
no hint of softness, nor the bleak beauty of dead winter pasture. An
expanse of concrete perhaps? But that would suggest some mighty

purpose, some monumental work of Man. No, the landscape was like one seen in a dreary dream, too unimportant to be sketched in by the dreaming mind, or like the unfinished background of a poor painting not worth the finishing.

Such thoughts were not in my mind at the time. All my attention was concentrated on controlling the dinghy as she rocketed along before what had become a gale. The wind blew straight from the north out of a sky that was as raw and bitter as frozen iron, and the river had widened until I was now on a vast lake. I could not in the increasing murk see any banks at all – occasionally I would see a lonely beacon post standing high out of the water, and then another, and then another, and these I followed for want of any other guidance. Sometimes far, far away I caught sight of what might have been a series of low bunkers or an electricity pylon, but otherwise I felt that I had stumbled onto a vast lagoon just off the North Sea, or the North Bering Strait for all I knew. I certainly had nothing like this marked on my map. In fact, from this point on, my precious map of Europe's waterways became pretty well useless.

Yet, as always happens when the conditions grow rough, I found I was enjoying myself. I was well rugged up and the dinghy was moving almost as fast as I had ever known it. The wind had rolled up the water into big smooth waves, as big as those on the open sea, and I was riding each one in smooth, powerful succession. *Jack* had a spurt of foam at her prow, a bone in her teeth as the sailors say. But I still felt as though I was sailing in a grey limbo, neither foggy nor clear, neither sea nor river. And then, ahead, there really was nothing. It was not a matter of fogginess or obscurity of sight. I could see perfectly well what lay ahead, but it didn't make sense. The vast lagoon seemed to stop in mid-air, and an uncanny nothingness to lie beyond.

Soon I drew near enough to see the explanation for this sudden cessation of landscape. The lake lapped right up against a low parapet that stretched from east to west across my whole forward horizon, and this was just the top foot or so of a great reservoir-wall. I was later to see that it dropped two hundred feet on the other side to a flat plain, but to a small boat on the lake it appeared that the water simply ended in a grey sky, and that this low concrete rim was the dreary World's End. With only a few feet to go and the wind blustering me onwards from behind, I realised the danger and heeled hard to the left. For the next few minutes I skimmed at high speed along the top of the wall, only a foot or two from the concrete lip, nearly shaving the wall with my gunwales. The tiller was hard over to the right as I desperately tried to steer further from that massive drop, but for some reason *Jack* wasn't responding. Any minute now and she was going to touch the wall, here only a foot above the slopping waves, and the wind was going to swat her sideways and tip me out and over the edge. I was going to die.

Then I saw what the problem was. The centreboard was not fully down. For the last three hours I had been sailing downwind and the centreboard had been half up, not needed when running before the wind. Now *Jack* had little steerageway and was simply skidding sideways across the top of the water despite the best efforts of the rudder. I leaned forward, placed my hand on top of the centreboard and pushed down with all my might.

Oh God, don't jam now.

Don't … jam … now …!

From where I was sitting in the stern, I could not get fully over the centreboard to plunge it further down; but if I squirmed forward to do so, I could not keep the tiller jammed over to the right. I was close enough now to the wall to look over the edge of the dam to the plain two hundred feet below. My rocketing passage was sending a bow wave swooshing up and over the wall. The wind was gusting harder still and I had to do something. Jamming my foot against the tiller to keep it in place, I lunged my body forward like an otter in the final stages of electrocution and body-slammed the centreboard down into its slot. Ah-ha! Jack responded immediately, turning up into the wind so swiftly that I very nearly went about and lost control altogether, flailing in a series of 360-degree turns. But no. I was safe and steadily moving away from that dreadful drop and towards the safety of the farther end of the dam.

Along to the eastern end of the dam wall was a concrete tower now familiar as the control-tower of a lock, and it was at this tower that I aimed. With the waves side-on, the sailing was less comfortable but infinitely safer than launching into mid-air at a height of two hundred feet above the landscape, so we bore up well, *Jack* and I. It was with a wholly false sense of approaching safety and calm that I approached the concrete complex of piers and wharves directing shipping into the huge double locks that would let us continue on the river far below. For once we sailed around into the relatively narrow jaws of the lock-approach, the waves went berserk. Until

The Jaws of Gabcikovo

now they had been big enough but regular and rolling. Between the sheer concrete walls of the piers, however, they shot up in savage vertical turrets of water, rebounding and interfering with one another to make a vicious chop the like of which I had never encountered. Even in the Thames Estuary, even in the Channel, the water hadn't behaved like this; in fact, I had only seen anything similar on film-footage of underwater mines being detonated. All about me, explosions of water shot up in six-foot high towers, now here, now there, as though a hundred depth-charges had been triggered by my arrival.

It was with great difficulty that we made it to the pier and an iron ladder up the side. Stowing the sails in their usual wrapped bundle

about the gaff and boom, I hoisted them up out of the way where
they swung murderously from side to side. *Jack* was still battering
helplessly against the concrete wall with every new wave, but there
was little I could do about that except to set off to see the lock-
keeper about getting into the lock as soon as possible.

The lock-keeper was less than happy. This, he explained in a mixture of Slovakian and German, was the notorious Gabcikovo Lock,
and the very presence of small craft on the reservoir or in the lock
was strictly *verboten*. He told me that a yacht had arrived here two
years back. It had been around the world several times. It had survived storms off Cape Horn; it had weathered typhoons in the Car-
ibbean; it had run the gauntlet of the Torres Strait reefs. But here,
here, he smirked with a perverse pride, here at the Gabcikovo Lock
it sunk with all hands. One of the crew they never found. Nevertheless, as I had presented him with a *fait accompli* by my arrival, he
grudgingly agreed to allow me through along with a barge that was
due in the next half-hour. I was to wait until it had passed into the
further of the two parallel locks, and row in afterwards. Meanwhile,
ja, I was welcome to wait here out of the Arctic wind until it was
time to go.

Eventually through the murk we saw the barge approaching and
I buttoned up warmly and trudged the five hundred metres to the
end of the pier ready to cast off and follow her in. She was half a mile
away and approaching steadily. It was only when I was close by *Jack*
that I thought to myself how odd it was that she was no longer lying
facing into the wind, as all boats do when tethered at the bow. Three
seconds later I realised that she was no longer tethered at all. The
blue painter was still tied firmly around the bollard, but with the
sawing of *Jack* up and down against the pier in the dreadful waves,
the rope had frayed right through. *Jack* was adrift!

Normally this would not have been too disastrous. A dinghy
adrift tends to blow aimlessly and quite slowly directly downwind,
and this would have brought *Jack* bumping along the pier wall until
she fetched up against the closed lock-gates of the nearer lock, in a
sort of cul-de-sac. At the worst I might need to fetch a boathook to
reclaim her and so miss the chance to go through with the approaching barge. But I had underestimated the free spirit of *Jack de Crow*.
She needed no skipper aboard to guide her on a properly steered and
purposeful course. The rudder was down, the tiller was held firmly
by an elastic cord, and the hoisted bundle of canvas and gaff was

enough of a sail in this wind to send her skipping across the waves on a course all of her own. She was sailing solo. The only problem with this jaunty show of independence was that the course she was on would end in a collision with the open lock-gates and the approaching barge. She was, in fact, racing to get there first, and from the look of it, would arrive at the lock-gates at precisely the same time as her rival.

In the serious world of Slovakian industrial river transport, the locks are the size of hydro-electric schemes and the barges could sit squarely in the middle of two football pitches end to end and not leave a lot of room for players around the edge. These iron giants have names like 'Bratislava Hulk Haulage' and are not to be trifled with. They are captained and crewed by grim-eyed, unshaven Romanians in grimy overalls who live on vodka, deep-fried pig's blood sausages and any dinghy sailors they can run down and gut.

This particular barge would fit into the Gabcikovo lock like a truncheon into a sheath. There was barely any room between the iron precipice of the hull and the concrete precipice of the lock's walls. There was certainly no room for a wooden dinghy off on a bid for freedom. In other words, in about three minutes' time there was going to be a keel-crunching, hull-splitting collision between a two-thousand-ton, unstoppable industrial barge the size of Wolverhampton, a small thirty-year-old plywood dinghy and the concrete mouth of a lock that had been there for the last thirty years and wasn't going anywhere. It was not hard to guess who was going to come off worst.

For three daft seconds I considered diving into the freezing choppy soup, clad in waterproof over-trousers, cagoule, fleece and several more layers of heavy winter clothing, in order to swim after the truant *Jack* and steer her to safety. Cowardice and sanity prevailed, however, and I set off haring down the pier in an attempt to reach the collision point before *Jack* did. The lock-entrance she was headed for was beyond the nearer one, and I needed to run the full length of this, across a bridge at the further end, and all the way back up the other side – about the same distance as two laps of a football pitch. The clothes I was wearing were about as suitable for a swift sprint as a Santa Claus suit. Nevertheless, I had no choice but to try.

I arrived blinded with sweat and too late. The giant barge was halfway into the lock and there was no sign of *Jack*, not even a yellow smear of paint on the ironwork of the barge's hull. I stood there numb with shock. Not only was all that I owned – passport, wallet, rucksack – now at the bottom of the lock, but the great journey had come to an abrupt end. The Gabcikovo Lock had claimed another gallant vessel. There would be no going to the Black Sea after all.

I sat down on a bollard and watched the last metres of the barge creep inexorably into the lock. The gates were closing. The crew were busy with mooring lines, and sure enough, appeared to be the rough Romanian crew I had envisaged. They seemed so unconcerned that it was clear that they hadn't even seen *Jack*, let alone noticed her demise. At least I would not have their angry recriminations to face.

Or would I? One of them was calling out and beckoning in my direction. Ah well, time to face the music. I rose from my perch and trudged bleakly down to the stern of the huge ship – and there, bobbing at the back, jaunty as ever, was *Jack de Crow*. I gaped. I gawped. I could not possibly imagine how she had been saved. Some crew were tying a tow-line to her, and others were leaning over the stern examining her for damage. Somehow, I gathered, the sharp-eyed crew had seen the imminent collision while I was running blindly down the lock, had deftly nipped forward to the bows, hooked *Jack* with a boat-hook, and dragged her to the stern as the barge churned in through the lock-gates.

Dazed with relief, I climbed down onto the barge into the midst of the unsmiling crew and went into my usual mime-routine, explaining that I had come from England. Beneath their unblinking gaze, I then faltered into stammering thanks and apologies, and more apologies, and thanks, and apologies, and went to untie the bow-line and disappear as quickly out of their lives as possible. At this point the grimmest of them all said, '*Nyet*! No! *Kom*!' and pointed down into the bowels of the ship.

Ah. Why? Was this the reckoning? Was I to face the stern Romanian *Kapitan* and an incomprehensible, enraged lecture on the folly of mixing footling pleasure craft with the serious Romanian barge-industry? Or perhaps to turn out my pockets and cough up my last Slovakian *krona* as a ransom before reclaiming my sorry little dinghy? Or perhaps this ugly crew were in need of a cabin-boy after the last one expired, and I would fit the bill nicely all the way to Odessa?

Well, no, not exactly. I was sat down at a table with ten other men, all of them swarthy and smoking what smelt like tarmac, and was poured a large tumbler of schnapps. A bowl of hot soup appeared, and a platter of bread; the soup was a broth full of root vegetables, white fish, black scaly fish-skin, paprika and black pepper. Then there followed another schnapps, burning like fire in my throat, and a sizzling plate of fat rissoles, chopped tomato and salad appeared through the haze of blue smoke in front of me, and I fell on it with tears of joy and exhaustion. All the while some of the crew were getting up from their dinners and moving outside to fix something. When I followed, I saw that they were rigging up a portable pump to sit in *Jack*'s waterlogged bottom to rid her of all the water that had washed aboard. Another man was handing out my sodden rucksack, my sleeping bag and my mattress in their sacks, and a third was inspecting some minor damage to the prow where the perspex bow-plate fitted by Peter in Coblenz had splintered into two. I moved to help but was ushered back down into the galley and poured a third schnapps by a man who, I realised, was speaking a thick guttural French and plying me with questions.

The next few hours passed in a tarry, schnapps-bright haze, and it was some twenty miles down the river again that they gently helped me into my dinghy, untied me from the stern and cast me adrift to make my own way again. The day had cleared, the river had narrowed down to a manageable size, and *Jack* and I were left alone to continue on our journey together. After a sheepish silence, *Jack* apologised to me for the truancy that had come so near to disaster that afternoon. I in turn did the right thing and said how sorry *I* was for abandoning her in Vienna and going off to art-galleries and coffee-shops without her. With a little shake of her sails, she made it quite clear that all was now well between us. To change the topic, I pointed out how well we had done that day, breaking all previous personal records. We had come just over one hundred kilometres in a single day. And so it was with a surge of mutual pride, the best of friends again, we sailed at dusk that evening out of Slovakia and into the land of Hungary.

*

'*Season of mists and mellow fruitfulness ...*'

Having got the whole of *The Eve of St Agnes* under my belt, I had turned back to some of Keats' shorter works to memorise, and as before, I found that day by day the words took shape around me in the landscape I was passing through. The land was flat but mellow with old golds and purple copses, and a haze of wood-smoke hung in the bright air from morning to dusk. Two more days of steady rowing brought me to the town of Esztergom, the ancient spiritual heart of Hungary. In my ignorance, I had never heard of it, but the very name conjured up something Byzantine and mosaic. You never see it written in any way other than this:

ESZ✝ERG⊕M

and it gave me an inexplicable thrill. High over the town loomed a rounded hill, and this was capped by the green-domed Dom. I wandered up through the massive fortifications of the Burg one morning. A wet night had left the ground soggy with large, sad leaves which lay like soiled paper bags on the unkempt grass and slippery paths. The place felt very Eastern Bloc, with cracked concrete and damp stone, and the Dom was cavernous and cold. I paid a small sum to climb up to the top of the dome and from there could see the whole length of the river, the Duna as we must call it now, sweeping backwards to the brown haze of Slovakia and onwards to the Great Bend a few miles ahead. Here the river, after so many hundreds of miles forging eastwards, turned sharply south to Budapest and beyond. Where it did so, gentle hills on either side were clothed with fruit trees and orchards, vineyards and little homesteads; here was a place where Keats could well have written his *Ode to Autumn*, especially as here still, as in the poet's day, cider-presses ooze the slow hours and reaping-hooks still spare the last twinèd wreath of flowers. But not in Esztergom itself. Here the distant yapping of dogs in back lanes, the faint pervading smell of open drains and the soggy trees argued a poverty very different from the well-brushed landscapes of Austria.

Wandering back down through the ramparts and the 400 steps to the river, I was bailed up by five dogs. Three were snarling about my ankles and another two were on a parapet engaged in a frenzy of barking and teeth-baring at the level of my head. Alarmed, and with nowhere else to go, I thumped backwards into an old wooden door set into a corner tower. To my surprise the door swung open and I fell through into the darkness beyond. As I slammed the door shut, I heard the satisfying thud and yelp of a dog hurling itself at me, but finding six-inch oak instead. When I had let out a shaky but triumphant 'Yippee!' I was startled all over again to realise that an ancient crone was sitting less than two feet away, hidden in the shadows. After gazing at me intently from hooded eyes, she made a sweeping gesture with her arm towards a hanging curtain and cackled something like 'Enter, kind master, and gaze upon your doom,' though I may have imagined this. Pushing aside the curtain I found myself in a large circular room which had been converted into a temporary photographic art-gallery. My mind full of *Macbeth*, I had been expecting a torture chamber at the very least. I am neither very knowledgeable nor interested in photography, but these were extraordinary because not one of the exhibits had been produced on ordinary commercial film. The artists had instead used a bizarre variety of materials – hessian, corrugated iron, bleached wooden slats, muslin – and had somehow projected their images onto these surfaces. The images were grainy or patchy, coarse, splashy, brush-stroked or mottled, depending on how the materials had been impregnated with light-sensitive chemicals, and the effect had the power of anything that is primitive. To see a derelict wasteland of winter trees and frozen puddles projected onto a sheet of rusting tin, or to see the figure of a Bosnian refugee mother and child caught in the fibres of a piece of dusty sacking like some latter-day Turin Shroud, was a strangely moving experience.

An hour later the dogs had moved on to terrify some other poor traveller and I was free to go. Despite the dogs, despite the decay, I found myself suddenly liking Esztergom and its people.

*

Now that I had left western lands behind, the river was rather wild in appearance. Towns and villages were far and few between. Instead there were watery forest groves, lonely islands in mid-stream, swampy backwaters and the odd ramshackle hut swathed in fishing nets on poles. Strange splashes and gurgles from the banks caused me to wonder, not entirely idly, about the possibility of 'gators. The river was wide and empty enough to set the sails in the faintest of breezes, tie the tiller and doze on the foredeck for an hour at a time. I wrote letters while drifting, I read, I dozed off again, and so came slowly down the great river to Budapest.

If you had taken Christopher Wren, injected just a little Turkish blood into him, gave him some warm siennas and umbers to work with rather than the blue-greys and sooty hues of the Thames, and then let him get on with it, he would have come up with something like Budapest instead of London. From the river the similarity was striking. It was like a condensed version of London with all the best bits left in, St Paul's, the Houses of Parliament, Big Ben, the Tower, but all the long grimy concrete-and-glass stretches left out. On the morning that I left it, four days after I arrived, that was what I was thinking, along with how much I admired the place. As for the four days of being there, well, that was another story.

Firstly, it rained torrentially for the entire four days. The weather sent me scuttling to a Youth Hostel where the first night was spent fighting for possession of the bunk that I had paid for with a drunk Irishman who was so blotto on vodka that he kept forgetting that he had checked out the night before and was meant to be on a train to Warsaw by now. For the next few days I managed to get a single room in a hotel, but was alarmed to find myself woken three or four times a night by a mysterious flash seeming to come from somewhere in the room itself. It was as though a spontaneous crackle of lightning was filling the room with a brief but highly charged flash. It was of the same intensity that you see on overhead lines as a tram passes, but it had nothing to do with the light-switch or the bulb as far as I could make out. It didn't do any harm, nor make more than the tiniest of fizzling pops, but it left the whole room feeling charged and potent each time, and me wide awake and staring. I never did find out what it was. Static? St Elmo's fire? Whatever it was, it was better than the Irishman.

Secondly, I found myself all at sea with the language. Hungarian belongs to a class of languages entirely unconnected with anything Indo-European, and the only people likely to make a stab at understanding the Hungarians are the Finns. Was it purely coincidental, then, that when I went to a bar and tried to strike up a conversation with the lively group at the next table, they turned out to be a party from Finland? Having not the faintest idea about the language gave me a small insight into what it must be like to be illiterate. How do I find a bookshop? Look in all the windows as I pass. How do I order food in a restaurant? Point to an item and pray that it's not pig's liver. What's the sign for *Metro Station* in the city underground system? Not a clue, so follow the people.

This brings me to my third reason for disliking Budapest. On the way back from a bar one night I found myself on a tube-train that at every stop filled up with more and more football fans. At each station they would swirl off and on the train in high spirits, chanting and pushing and shoving. Finally, at one Underground station below Deak Square, the central plaza of the city, the commotion became riotous and among the milling fans I could see the green uniforms of the police. There was an almighty bang. The fans who had swirled off the train so eagerly suddenly turned and attempted to scramble back on again, jamming the doors and preventing the train from pulling out. There was a lot of shouting and a good deal of pushing and shoving, and springing unbidden to my eyes were great stinging tears as though I had just cut a dozen onions.

I found that the whole cabin-load of passengers was crying along in sympathy and realised what was happening. The police had thrown a tear-gas canister. The cabin was filled with choking, acrid fumes, as though someone had splashed a vat of ammonia or bleach down the stairwell. By now my eyes were watering copiously and every gasp I took seared my nostrils and throat, and for a moment I could not think of anything else but getting out of there. But how? To step out onto the platform was impossible – the hooligans were still scrabbling in the doorways, and besides, I didn't fancy running through the incomprehensibly signposted tunnels of the Metro like an illiterate rabbit in a gassed warren. Another bang exploded and I saw through the crowd someone collapse on the platform. There was another more panicky surge of people determined to clamber aboard and finally the doors were clear enough for the fume-filled carriage to pull away from the platform.

When the gas had cleared a little, I turned to the animated group of fellow travellers next to me and asked in croaky pidgin English what had happened. To my surprise they ignored me but continued to chatter in fume-strangled voices among themselves. Again I asked, and a second time I was ignored, even though they had lapsed into teary silence by this time. Perhaps they were Finns. A third time I spoke, loudly and directly, and then saw what the problem was. They were a small party of deaf-mutes and hadn't heard a word I'd been saying. Once they realised, they signed and mimed their apologies and what I assume was their shared wonder and bewilderment at the adventure we had been through. I understood little of this, but one gesture was universal enough for anyone to understand. The leader of the group raised a fist, pointed his forefinger at me, cocked it and pulled an imaginary trigger. The bang I had heard had been one of the rioters being shot dead before my eyes.

After that I didn't need to know the Hungarian word for *Metro*: I rather preferred to walk.

I dined one afternoon on roast goose, something I had always wanted to do; it came roasted in plums and apples, which was much nicer than it sounds, and dripping with hot fat which I greedily licked up on the excuse that I would need a layer of blubber to keep off the winter chills over the next few months. I then dutifully climbed up the endless steps to the top of the Citadel high above the river. Here there were huge statues with that blend of muscularity and monolithic drabness that only Soviet sculptors seemed able to achieve, and fine views of a bunch of paratroopers leaping out of a plane and parachuting down to a pontoon in mid-river that was letting off a plume of scarlet smoke. I have no idea why. It was all part of the incomprehensibility that dogged my stay in Budapest. Finns. Deaf-mutes. Hungarian street signs. Sharing my room with lightning. Tear-gas and random death. It was time to move on to somewhere that made more sense. Instead I went to the former Yugoslavia.

Proud Hearts and Empty Pockets

> Alas, poor country!
> Almost afraid to know itself. It cannot
> Be call'd our mother, but our grave; where nothing,
> But who knows nothing, is once seen to smile;
> Where sighs and groans, and shrieks that rend the air,
> Are made, not mark'd; where violent sorrow seems
> A modern ecstasy ...
> —SHAKESPEARE, *Macbeth*

My first stop in Yugoslavia was at nightfall where I came to the border-control of Bedpans. I don't think it was actually called that but it may as well have been, as it was both clinical and foul at the same time. There, in a dismal and monumental building, I spent an hour doing the passport shuffle between ill-lit offices where lounged dangerous criminals armed with rubber stamps. The cracked floors seeped with water, the light-bulbs, where there were any, were of a peculiar Yugoslavian five-watt kind, and in the main office the strip-light flickered on and off like an irregular strobe for the entire hour I was there, until I felt my brain seeping out through my maniacally blinking eyes.

There was no pontoon to moor *Jack* to, so I hitched up to a midstream buoy, and, too dispirited even to put up my awning, slept under the night sky. The stars were brilliant that night, but with the beauty came the cold, and I lay in an aching shiver of wakefulness, too cold to sleep, too cold to get up and do anything about it. When dawn came and the sun poured warmth and life into my bloodless limbs, I felt as a dragonfly must, when first emerging from the cocoon he feels his wings shiver and spread as the life-fluid pumps through cell and fibre and gauze. I didn't even wait to perform my daily routine. I simply unhitched and floated away from Bedpans on the current in my pyjamas and sleeping bag, feeling more like Huck Finn than ever.

By lunchtime I had reached Apatin, where I intended to replenish my scanty funds and stock up on bread and tomatoes and salami and perhaps a bottle of plum wine. The only place to moor up along the steep rocky bank was next to a huge glistening pile of cow's intestines, silver-black with buzzing flies. A professional soothsayer may have been able to read the augury. I did not wait to try. Besides I would know soon enough. A visit to a large gloomy bank elicited the following interesting facts.

1. The handful of Hungarian forint I had brought with me out of Hungary were not exchangeable for Yugoslavian dinar. Indeed, the very thought caused a ripple of mirth around the otherwise joyless staff. Forints? Pah.

2. Yugoslavia was, it seemed, the one place in the galaxy that did not accept Visa, Mastercard, American Express, or indeed any credit card at all. This was despite the fact that the banks and shops uniformly displayed large signs in several languages saying 'VISA WELCOME HERE.'

It took me a little while to establish with the lady behind the counter that these two facts were indubitably true. Having done so, I stepped out into the street, stopped dead beneath the plane trees and contemplated with horror my present situation. I had about twelve dollars' worth of useless Hungarian forint, my credit cards were invalid, and I had about three hundred miles of slow river travel across Yugoslavia to accomplish without starving to death.

I walked back to the dinghy, half wondering if cow's intestines could in any way be rendered edible. On the way I passed a large and glossy building, the only glossy thing besides the intestines that I had seen in the country so far. I thought at first that it might be a smart hotel, and I had an inkling that the very smartest of hotels might be able to do things with a Visa Card that couldn't be done by common banks. I asked the clerk behind the counter if I could see the manager, and soon a smartly dressed businessman came and without any questions ushered me along a corridor and into a beautifully furnished office. It could have been the heart of Paris or Frankfurt. He spoke excellent English and courteously asked how he could assist me. A little abashed, I blurted out my story and then asked whether his hotel could allow me to use Visa to withdraw some much-needed cash for the weeks ahead. He spoke into an intercom and then beamed at me. 'I am sorry to tell you, my friend, that this is not a hotel. In any case you would not find a hotel in all of Yugoslavia to help you, alas. Perhaps one in Belgrade, I don't know. You see, for the last few months, we have been under an embargo laid down by NATO and much of the Western world, to which, alas, it appears we no longer belong.' He smiled sadly and shrugged his shoulders. 'Your country and America feel it necessary to interfere with the way we are running our country and have seen fit to punish our people for the follies of our President. We are all but cut off from the rest of Europe now, and I fear there are dark days ahead.'

He was putting into words facts of which I had been only vaguely aware on my media-free trip down the river. It was late September 1998, and over the next few weeks NATO was to begin its threats of air-bombardment in response to the Kosovo crisis. When a year on I saw the news coverage of shattered bridges and bombed towns along the Danube, I recognised every one of them, and saw in my mind's eye the ghost of a little yellow dinghy threading between the twisted girders.

'But meanwhile,' my host was continuing, 'not all is bad. This is not a hotel, but it is something better! It is a brewery. And, my friend,' he whispered, 'it is the best brewery in Eastern Europe!' A clerk entered bearing six bottles of Apatin beer. 'I have a little job for you,' said the manager, beaming. 'I need an impartial taster to try out our latest brew,' and with that bottles were opened, glasses produced and the rich dark foaming beer was poured out. A good while later, after we had compared and sipped and commented on colour and taste and texture, it was time for me to go. But before I did, my host said, 'You mentioned something about forint? It is true that one cannot exchange forint here for dinar, but I? I go across the border to Hungary three times a week. Let me exchange your money for you.' He pulled out his wallet and counted out a wad of Yugoslavian dinar. I now had at least twelve dollars and need not scavenge those cow's intestines after all. What is more, just as I was leaving, he said, 'But wait! I have not paid you for your tasting advice,' and put three large bottles of Apatin beer into my hand and led me to the foyer. 'Good luck!' he called and waved, and I walked off down the dusty road.

When I got back to the dinghy, I encountered another side of the country. There was a small crowd gathered around the boat and two policemen in generalissimo outfits of slate blue. Before I could stow my belongings, I was ushered into a battered car and driven off to the police station. There a balding officer with hooded eyes like a vulture questioned me about my presence. I showed him my visa duly stamped, and the papers that I had had signed in triplicate the night before in Bedpans, and he reluctantly accepted that I was legal. I should, however, have reported to him instantly on arrival. On the wall behind his desk was a large and detailed wall map showing the next forty miles of river. My own map being too small-scale to be useful, I tried making out what lay ahead: towns, splits in the river, the Croatian border on the right-hand bank. He saw me looking at it and angrily tore it off the wall. 'No! This is my map,' he said, 'not yours.' Then I was turned out and had to walk the mile back to the river.

There I was met by quite a different character: a tall man in black peasant dress with snowy white hair, a hooked nose and bristling eyebrows, looking for all the world like Gandalf the Wizard, who begged me in a mixture of German and very sketchy English to join him and his family for a midday meal in a nearby cottage. His name was Slobodan, 'like the President, *ja!*' and his daughter was Violetta. In their tiny front room, gay with brightly knitted peasant shawls and bead curtains, she brought lentil stew with pork, hot and salty, and black coffee as rich and gritty as river-silt. Slobodan the Serb talked fiercely and continuously in German, being under the impression that I was fluent in it, and I understood about one word in a hundred. It was mostly about politics, I think. The only two names I recognised were Milosevic and NATO; each time either was mentioned, he turned and spat resoundingly out the door. He put me right on one thing: I was not in Yugoslavia at all; I was in Serbia. Yugoslavia no longer existed. Finally I took my leave with many thank yous and smiles, and headed for a third time to the dinghy, where I was at last able to leave. As I set off down the wide and sun-lit river, I was unsure what lay ahead, but I was pretty sure it wouldn't be boredom.

*

One night I pull in under the overhanging boughs to a tiny fishermen's camp: a timber hut under the dank trees, and a small cluster of long wooden canoes tied to poles. Each one seems to have something resembling a seven-pronged Jewish candelabra attached to the stern. Some men are cooking a rich and scaly fish stew in a cauldron over an outside fire of red-hot coals. An old man with a face like a long walnut, the keeper of the hut, lets me eat my supper of bread rolls and tomato at his rough wooden table by the light of a smoky kerosene lantern. As I eat, he keeps silently bringing tidbits from his own cupboard to supplement my meal: a boiled egg, some mustard, some smelly cheese, and then the inevitable schnapps. A large black Polish hound called Nox begs for scraps. Around the walls is jar upon jar of pickling paprika, buckets and tubs and basins of the stuff, glowing as scarlet in the lamplight as the embers outside. Afterwards the three fishermen come inside smelling wonderfully of woodsmoke and take out a much-thumbed deck of cards. These are not the usual suits: diamonds, clubs, hearts and spades, but antique symbols: acorns, staffs, leaves and baubles, all in curly greens, scarlets and golds. They look to my unfamiliar eyes as ancient and enchanted as the first set of Tarot cards out of old Romany. The men keep filling up my glass with more schnapps, but otherwise ignore me, as though I am a daft old grandfather with whom they are completely familiar. That night I fall asleep in a rough bunk under coarse grey blankets that the old man has set up for me. I explain as best as I can that I have no money, but he waves that aside with a grunt. The only toilet is a hole off in the woods with a single sign over it saying TELEFON.

*

As I row on the next day, a daring and ridiculous plan forms in my mind to procure much-needed funds. Soon I am to come to a point where the right-hand bank will be not Serbia but Croatia. It is just possible that:

a) Croatia will not be under the same embargo as Serbia.

b) That I might be able to withdraw some money from a bank there using my Visa card.

c) Question: Do I have a visa for Croatia?

d) No.

e) Even if I am allowed into Croatia, my visa for Serbia is a single-entry one, and it is unlikely that I will be allowed back in after having set foot on foreign territory.

f) Assuming I *am* allowed into Croatia, I will have to withdraw deutschmarks, of course, or US dollars, as the Croatian krona is even less likely to be accepted in Serbia than the much-sneered-at Hungarian forint.

g) If they let me back into Serbia, that is. (See point e.)

h) Which I very much doubt.

i) This is assuming they let me into Croatia in the first place, of course.

j) Which I very much doubt. (See points c. and d.)

In short, I must somehow persuade someone official in the next town coming up on the Croatian side (called Vukovar) to let me enter Croatia illegally, withdraw large slabs of German currency from a local bank, tip-toe out of Croatia once more without being officially stamped, and then merrily go and spend my money in an enemy country. What is more, I have to explain all this using only the five words I know that might be understood by a Croatian (*pasaporte, visa, problema, banca* and *nema* meaning *not*) and possibly a good deal of vivid mime.

It will, of course, be impossible, so I decide to give it a go.

To the great credit of the Croatian police in Vukovar, who must play an awful lot of charades in their spare time, the white-haired Kapitan to whose office I was marched as soon as I set foot on Croatian soil seemed to understand the whole thing perfectly. He didn't speak a word of English, but sat patiently while I conducted my carefully thought-out little mime. I mimed a river running down the middle of his office with many a gurgle-gurgle noise. I mimed a little boat sailing down the middle of the carpet river, and leapt jauntily from the desk (Serbia) to the window (Croatia) and back again. I mimed being penniless with much rubbing of my stomach and turning out of pockets, and then did several masterful impersonations of strict, unsmiling Serbian immigration officers and their reaction on finding no second-entry visa in my passport. So carried away did I become at one point that I think I found myself miming being stood up against a wall and shot. Never has being a drama teacher, that most dilettante of all trades, been so useful. All this was of course accompanied by an improvised script of *problemas* and *nema visas* interspersed at crucial points: hardly Shakespeare, but the best I could manage. Finally, after a bow, I stood awaiting his verdict.

Which was for the Kapitan to call a guard and rap out some instructions. Five minutes later I was being driven around Vukovar in a decrepit police jeep looking for a bank. We found one, but it could not help me. It seemed that a bank fifty miles inland might have been able to, but no one in Vukovar itself was able to process my card. Despite the anti-climax I was thrilled by the kindness and understanding of the Croatian police who, as I had requested, omitted to sign me either in or out of the country so that the Serbs would not know I had ever left. I gathered that my uncomplimentary portrayal of the Serbian officials I had encountered so far was the main factor in winning over their Croatian counterparts.

Some years ago Vukovar had been the focus of Serbian bombardment, and many buildings were still shell-shattered and blitzed. Children played noisy games in rubble-filled lots and I saw one block where half of the apartments sported bright curtains and washing hung out to dry from high windows, and the other half gaping holes and twisted iron reinforcement rods sticking from demolished walls. The physical damage was still there, and, as I was to learn over the next few weeks, so too was a hatred between these neighbouring countries as intense and scalding as it had ever been.

After sailing away from Vukovar and my failed international money-laundering scheme, I found myself almost by accident floating down a little side-channel on the Croatian bank. Trees covered in vines shaded the water and gave to the river an almost Amazonian feel. After several hours I passed an island where a single white shack stood, and some fishermen cooking. Excitedly they beckoned me over, and when I rowed over to moor up, I recognised two of the men. One was the young guard who had driven me around looking for a bank, and the other had been witness to my vivid mime in the Kapitan's office. They were now off duty and had come down to join their friends in an evening of schnapps and grilled fish. I spent the next hour sitting in the late afternoon sunshine enjoying their hospitality while the two policemen reduced their friends to stitches of laughter. I could not, of course, follow what they were saying, but I suspect I was the main topic of conversation.

It struck me that this was the second time I had been on Croatian soil, both times illegally, and both times with the connivance of the police. These were my sort of officials. I was not to meet many more like them as I sailed onwards into the heart of the still-vex'd Balkans.

*

As I journeyed on, the sun shone warm and bright with September gold, flaming in the poplars and willows that lined the banks and silvering the threads of gossamer that now filled the air each morning, drifting in airy swathes across the river to festoon my rigging with fairy-pennants. The low, level light made the river always a molten shimmer of silver haze, and at times it felt as though I was rowing into Paradise, or the album cover for a Handel Oratorio. Still the endless trees marched on either side, at times thick and tangled where I was delighted to see wild pigs rooting at the river's edge, unaware of my gliding presence yards away. At times the air would turn even hazier and yellower than the autumn sun could account for, and stink of sulphur – a distant factory chimney above the trees would provide the unromantic explanation.

As I neared Belgrade, the forest ended and sandy cliffs reared high on the southern bank, the home of thousands of sand martins and swifts. Cormorants were common too – they kept surfacing near the boat in a casual manner, glancing around to see *Jack* a few yards away and diving in pop-eyed panic. Near lunch-time I was hailed by two fishermen in a grassy meadow at the foot of the cliffs: Jan and Estovich. Jan was fifty-ish, Estovich was a hundred-and-two. They plied me with beer and peanuts, and though their English was as non-existent as my Yugoslavian, we seemed to communicate with ease. Later they lit a fire and made a pot of coffee, the same river-silt which I found hard to like but drank gamely. Then I showed them a magic trick as thanks. Jan was so overcome with excitement that he did three somersaults in the long meadow grass like a gleeful child. I was tickled pink. When I finally indicated that I must sail on, they solemnly presented me with a large glass bottle of something they called 'Paradijo.' It was a gorgeous, rich orange-red, opaque, with countless golden-yellow seeds suspended in it, and made, I think, from tomatoes and paprika. Over the next four days I savoured every mouthful; the taste was a little like tomato-juice but with a rich, burning afterglow that went right to the belly. I could not work out whether it was alcoholic or not – I think on balance not – but it had the same warming effect as did my memory of the middle-aged Jan tumbling for glee in the green grass whenever I swigged that precious stuff.

Belgrade had a huge number of bookshops, but most of the books were on the occult. It had a marina called the Dorcol, meaning 'four corners' – it was where they used to quarter people using four horses all going in different directions. The marina was shabby but exceptionally friendly – I kept being given plum brandy by different people on old boats, poured out of coloured glass bottles shaped like St Nicolai, the patron saint of sailors. The Hyatt Hotel, though hugely luxurious, would not give me cash but allowed me to use my Visa card for services. I had a hugely luxurious afternoon tea and sat and wrote letters while Handel's Trio Sonata tinkled in the background. I made long, expensive calls to England. I had a large dinner. I made it my personal mission to trudge around every bank in Belgrade, telling them to bloody well take down their Visa signs if they were not going to cough up. I climbed the great park-like hill of Kalemegdan and watched the junction of the River Sava and the Dunav glow under a post-thunderstorm sky of orange and rose and purple. While I was spending a penny behind a bush near the marina, a large brown snake glided away through my legs, and I was not in a position to do anything about it. The subsequent instinctive clenching did something to my bladder that made it difficult to pee for several days afterwards. Now that I was back in a country where the language had some tenuous connection with Latin and Anglo-Saxon, the alphabet had capriciously changed to the Cyrillic one. For example, the perfectly guessable word RESTORAN for restaurant was now transcribed as PECTOPAH, which sounds like something you boil jam in. I remained as baffled as I had been in Hungary.

Over the next three days, as I travelled on, things began to get desperate. I had run out of food, and the supply of people to dole out provisions when needed was suddenly thin. So was I. The landscape slowly changed from pretty vineyards and orchards on gentle slopes (where I was sorely tempted to steal some grapes and apples) to a harsher, drier landscape as I neared the Carpathian Mountains and the Iron Gates. This was where the Dunav carved its way through the last great obstacle before the final run to the sea. It did so in a great gorge, sheer-sided and tortuous, the grim gateway into old Transylvania. But whether I would make it there before starving to death, I was not sure.

The need to get to Bulgaria and to a bank pressed me on, past the leaning fortress towers of Smederevo, past the fortress of Ram, through unfriendly Jugovo where in the dark streets men sat and played dominoes and chess with the grunting and jeering and raucous noise more associated with wrestling matches; through a smart little riverside resort where a hugely fat man bathing with his family shouted out things in a purple rage at the sight of my two Union Jacks. It had not occurred to me that my little dinghy flying the British ensign could enrage or offend the people whom Britain was on the point of bombarding. The point was driven home when I slept aboard in the town of Veliko Gradiste and woke the next morning to find that someone had slashed both my Union Jacks to shreds. I was furious. What did they think I was? A scouting party for some imminent invasion by the Royal Navy? But then a thought sobered me. Sleeping just three feet lower, I was lucky not to have been slashed to shreds myself.

One day a doleful-looking Serb called Branko came along, introduced himself and invited me back to his mother's house for lunch. He looked as lugubrious as a bloodhound that had been in a philosophical conversation with Eeyore, but his English was good – good enough to enquire tactfully whether I might like a hot bath first. The grubby ring around the bath when I had finished would have grown root-vegetables. Roast pork, potatoes, paprika (I really was a little tired of the paprika), vodka, damson-cake and wine, and then a cycle-ride out to a local beauty-spot. On the way we ran over two snakes and saw three more. I told Branko of my experience in Belgrade, and he replied that yes, there appeared to be a plague of them this summer. There were two possible explanations, he said. One was that it was a plot by the CIA, an experiment in biological warfare before the main bombardment began. The second and more likely one, he said with a perfectly straight face, was that God was punishing the Serbs for their wickedness. That opened the way for a long talk about Serbia and its problems, which were legion. Chief of these was corruption. Every town, every village had its local Mafia boss. Extortion on even the smallest, most local scale was rife. No one owned a business, not an apple-cart, not a newspaper stand, without paying a large cut to the thugs of the resident Mr Big. Those who resisted met with violence and terror tactics. Much of this stemmed from Milosevic and his ministers; the Kosovo problem was just one symptom of the sickness in the land. The poverty I was seeing everywhere – and I was, often worse than I had seen in Africa or Laos – was a recent phenomenon. Yugoslavia had been a rich and prosperous country until ten years ago, when the first blockades were imposed. Oh, it had never been as rich as Germany or Austria, but its farms had been productive, its orchards tended, its vines fruitful. Now everywhere there was filth and waste, and the people were confused and angry. That was the problem with the embargoes and blockades, Branko said. They drew the people's anger outwards to the United States and Britain, muddying the issue. It was so easy for the politicians to blame the country's woes on the evil superpowers and deny responsibility for their own policies.

'Why do the people not rise up against Milosevic if it is clear that it is his actions bringing about the embargoes?' I asked.

'Because,' he said with a sigh, 'Serbs watch only Serbian television. You don't think Milosevic allows any truth to creep into the news-coverage, do you? No! NATO is blockading us because they are jealous of us, or because they are afraid of us, or because they want to steal all our fruit. Not because of anything our glorious leader has done – dear me, never! Hence the CIA and the snakes,' he added, looking more doleful than ever. 'It is all very sad.'

When I continued on my way that afternoon, I did so with a huge bag of apples, a clove of garlic and a great jar of home-made honey, a present from Branko's mother. I also took with me a new insight, a new thoughtfulness – I understood a little, just a little, about my slashed flags now.

That night I met the local Mr Big, I think. Just ten miles downstream I moored up in a tiny inlet overlooked by a large, isolated restaurant. It was spanking new, with the bulldozers still lurking in the shrubbery, freshly laid gravel and plastic white umbrellas at each beer-garden table. The place seemed deserted, but when I sat and munched on my last bread roll at one of these tables, a man looking exactly like Danny de Vito came out and, after some sharp questioning in broken English, invited me into the front bar for a drink. Two young and sexy barmaids were sent off with a cheeky pat on the bottom each to fetch us food and more beers while the manager smirked at me, asking me what I thought of them, eh? Eh? Over the next hour he too discussed politics. Kosovo? Too right there was a problem. The Muslims ought to be shot, every one of them, sneaking into Serbia with their dirty ways. The only problem was that Milosevic wasn't being allowed to get on with the job quicker. Sure, he was no saint, but to run this country you need to take a firm hand. Now look at me, people whinge and moan about the economy, but with a bit of initiative, a bit of push, you could make ends meet. More than. Two Mercs. A town-house up in Belgrade. The wife doesn't know about these little crackers, of course – Sofi, another beer here, darling! – but what can a man do, eh? It'd only make her miserable.

Outside the evening was turning colder and damper, the expanse of river lonely and wild – but infinitely preferable to the warm geniality and leering confidentiality of my host. *Come, friendly bombs,* I thought

> *And get that man with double chin*
> *Who'll always cheat and always win,*
> *Who washes his repulsive skin*
> *In women's tears.*

> *And smash his desk of polished oak*
> *And smash his hands so used to stroke*
> *And stop his boring dirty joke*
> *And make him yell.*

On an irrational impulse I took out my last ten dinar that I had been saving and insisted on paying for the drinks and the meal. It probably wasn't enough, and my host waved it aside with a laugh, but I left it on the bar before I departed. Hard cash for the one Serb I had met so far who clearly had no need of it. I had not rowed very far that day, but felt the need for a bath all over again.

*

At last the Carpathian Mountains came in sight. They lay across a great grey expanse of water where the Dunav spread out into a lake. On the further shore were the high, bare hills of Romania, dusty grey and scored with ravines and gullies, a hostile and forbidding terrain. On the nearer shore, the right-hand or southern bank, the hills of Serbia seemed greener and gentler. But today there was nothing gentle about the expanse of water that lay between the two. It had been whipped into a savage frenzy by a wind blowing straight out of the jaws of the Iron Gates Gorge, a mere notch in the hills seen dimly through veils of blowing spray and squalling rain five miles away across the lake. For hours I had been battling into this headwind, tacking to and fro, and I was exhausted. The dinghy was three-quarters full of water and seemed to be taking on more than when she was out at sea. After two more hours I realised that I was not going to make it to the Gorge, and so ran into shore where sat the little town of Golubac. There I changed into dry clothes, retired to a hotel, and penniless though I was, begged for a corner to sit and write. Three days later I was still there.

For three days the fierce north-easter blew straight out of the Gorge. Three times I fooled myself into thinking that the wind had eased off, and three times got a hundred yards out before having to turn back, soaked to the skin once more. Normally I would have been no more than mildly frustrated by the delay, but with no money, no food and the nearest Visa outlet in Bulgaria beyond the mountains, the weather seemed to me infused with spite.

The weather was so foul that it was impossible to see the other side of the lake, and it felt as if I was on the shores of a great sea. Grey waves crested with yellow foam pounded the rocky shore, tossing the flotsam of plastic detergent bottles and polystyrene lumps to and fro onto the shingle. The marine effect was heightened by the sight of fishermen casting nets into the shallows. Each net was small and circular, no bigger than a round tablecloth that you might spread for afternoon tea. Around its perimeter were hundreds of little lead weights and strings like the strings of a parachute, but instead of the strings being attached together below, where the paratrooper would be, they ran back up through a hole in the centre of the net to a drawstring.

The fisherman stood on the shore and with a pretty twirling twist, halfway between a bull-fighter and a discus-thrower, cast the net into the water. Barely had it settled than the fisherman pulled the drawstring, the net furled itself up like a shrinking jellyfish, and out the whole thing came again. The astonishing thing was that each and every time the net was thrown in and pulled out, an operation that took about ten seconds, it would come up with fifteen fish at least. These were only small things, about the size of playing cards, which would be dumped onto the bank and quickly picked over by hand, some being thrown back, some going into the fisherman's bucket, indiscriminately it seemed to me. But I was amazed that every six cubic feet of water could yield so much life. It was as strange as if every random sweep of a butterfly net through the air should catch fifteen butterflies.

I turned into a rough little taverna on the other side of the village. Here I walked in on a group of burly boar-hunters who were so far gone on schnapps that they seemed to think I was one of their party and plied me with hunks of roasted boar and schnapps while calling me Vlad. The taverna owner kept winking at me as if to say, 'Just humour them, they're always like this, and besides they've got knives,' so I did, and retired to my dinghy that night replete.

My third day in Golubac was spent listening to a breathless, five-hour lecture on Serbian history by a young piano player called Alen, who clearly had been waiting seventeen years to try out his English on someone. His English was flawless, his delivery engaging in its sheer enthusiasm, and the subject matter fascinating, though readers will forgive me if I do not recall it all here and now.

Alen had come to Golubac to play the piano in his Serbian folk band; there was to be a big dinner dance that evening in the hotel, and he asked me along. The night featured folk-dancing in full costume, including a lovely moment when the dancers stood in a line, arms linked, and suddenly all stiffly leaned to one side in perfect synchronisation, like painted peg dolls on a line. In among the feasting and the drinking, the jazz solos and the slow waltzes, the band-leader stood up and announced the news: NATO was going to bombard the country in twenty-four hours unless Milosevic capitulated. Immediately the band to whom Alen had introduced me gathered around and expressed their concern ... for me. Was I alright? Couldn't I perhaps leave the little boat here in Golubac and flee the country before the bombing started? The saxophonist had a van – he could have me to Bulgaria by the next morning if we left now. Surely I wanted to ring home at least.

Their country in ruins, maligned by the world, under threat of immediate attack by Britain and the States, nevertheless they were busy worrying about the safety of a chance traveller from those very countries threatening them. I was astonished and moved.

*

By the next morning the gale had blown itself out, the lake was a blue dream, and the Iron Gates stood to welcome me across the water.

High craggy precipices of white limestone rose straight out of water as deep green as bottle-glass. At times the sky was nothing but a thin blue ribbon far overhead against which occasionally an eagle could be seen soaring. Often I could see no more than a hundred yards ahead, the view blocked by yet another crumbling buttress of the gorge wall or a free-standing pinnacle of rock in mid-stream.

The current was not as fierce as I had been expecting. Had I been doing this trip fifty years earlier, I would have been swept down through the Gorge on a turbulent mill-race of white water, which would have been rather fun, if fatal, but a huge hydro-electric dam at the far end had turned the torrent into one long and serpentine lake, allowing the safe passage of river boats in both directions.

At times the gorge would widen into pockets of Swiss-style scenery: hay-ricks in shaven meadows backed by steep pine-woods, and little red-roofed farmsteads, all held between the white knuckles of savage limestone rising to the sky. Then around another bend and the echoing stone would close in and the cold shadows lie across my shoulders. Sometimes around a particularly tight bend, the breeze would grow skittish and I would have to watch for sudden side-swipes, but on the whole *Jack* and I were laughing our way through.

> *Let us roll all our strength and all*
> *Our sweetness up into one ball,*
> *And tear our pleasures with rough strife*
> *Thorough the Iron Gates of Life*

I misquoted merrily to *Jack* as we bowled along, children in a giant's kingdom.

Towards dusk, after a long stretch through a broader section of woods and gentler slopes, we entered a further section of canyon. Again the walls closed in, and again I felt that I was entering some story of adventure. Round a bend we came across a place where the river ran between two sheer cliffs of stone and the current quickened. On the left-hand bank stood out a great column of stone, a natural tower some four storeys high, and this had been carved into a great brooding face, like the Mount Rushmore Presidents. This face, however, was no George Washington or Lincoln. It was a monstrous Apache face, hawk-nosed, heavy-browed, primitive and watchful.

Opposite this great guardian of stone was something smaller but more remarkable. Set into the cliff, just above the level of the river, was a plaque of white marble, beginning to gleam in the faint moonlight that was now suffusing the blue dusk. This was the Tabula Trajana, cut by the Emperor Trajan himself almost two thousand years ago and set here to stamp the presence of Rome even in this, the wildest part of the wild East. Here it still stood; no road or path passed it by, no buses of tourists crowded from their coaches to snap photographs. Even the great busy barges hurried by, I suspect,

Guardian of the Iron Gates

keeping to the safer northern bank, and never close enough to read it. I might have been the first to read those ancient words in a thousand years, there in the twilit dusk.

Since my Union Jacks had been slashed in Veliko Gradiste, I had flown as a flag my beloved red-and-white spotty handkerchief. That night it saved my life; that and the fact that I had read *Swallows and Amazons*. Soon after sailing away from the Tabula Trajana, the breeze died to nothing and I rowed on for another two hours in deepening darkness. The moon rose over the high cliffy hills, a single perfect puff of cloud sculptured in silver and blue shadow by the moon, and a solitary star, very bright and clear, hung at the moon's ear. Under such a sky, I came in sight of the lights of Tekja, a small town on the right-hand side of the valley, and pulled hard for the distant twinkle that spoke of warmth and company and a place to tie up for the night. Even as I pulled hard at the oars, one of them slipped, sending the rowlock tumbling into the darkened bottom of the dinghy amid the debris of ropes and sponge and bailer. I cursed, turned around and bent to grope for it. Boating at night is something I had learnt in the past to be a foolish thing to do – it is impossible to see what you are doing, impossible to judge distances, difficult to make out what lights are on land and what are those of shipping, and you yourself are well-nigh invisible to others unless you have proper navigation lights. I had none of these. And as I scrabbled around for the invisible rowlock, I realised that the lights twinkling across the black water ahead were not those of the pier or the town, but of a moving vessel, and one that was a good deal closer than I had thought. It was one of the barges, an iron monster churning silently through the darkness, only about thirty yards away and heading straight for me. The lights told me that last fact; I could see three in a row – green, white and red from left to right – and even I, who am spatially dyslexic, could work out in three agonised seconds what that meant. Unable to row out of the way and without showing a light, I had no chance at all. My torch was still handy, and grabbing it and yelling into the darkness I shone it straight at the wheelhouse of the barge.

But hang on! A boat showing only a single white light is a mystery to another vessel. If anything, it is the stern light of a retreating vessel and therefore no cause for altering course. I should be showing a red light, a port light to show that I was directly ahead but moving across their bows to their left, warning them to steer to starboard with all speed. I was, in fact, in precisely the same predicament in which the Swallows found themselves in *We Didn't Mean to Go to Sea* when they were adrift in a yacht on the North Sea and about to be run down by a liner. There the resourceful children had shone a torch straight through a red Woolworth's plate and avoided disaster. I had no Woolworth's plate, nothing red except – my hanky. There it hung, limply drooping from the port stay. I lunged across the dinghy, jammed the torch into its folds and shone the now reddened light at the great hulk of the barge, now only yards away. Would it see it? Would it respond? Still the green-white-red pattern showed, doubly reflected in the curling black bow-wave of the approaching monster. It wasn't working. I would be run down in about fifteen seconds. There was no time to find that bloody row-lock, no time to don a life-jacket.

But then ... ah, at last ... the green winked out and left only the white and red lights dancing, and then just the red. The skipper had automatically steered to starboard at the sight of a red light, and the great barge thundered by less than ten feet away. I was safe.

Even so, the passing wake knocked me off my feet and into the bottom of the dinghy, and from the barge, a hastily activated search-light swivelled and pin-pointed me like a moth on a board. Someone on a megaphone shouted something incomprehensible but clearly apoplectic out of the darkness and I was for a moment glad that I did not speak Romanian, or whatever it was. But I lay there sloshing in the bottom of the dinghy blessing the hanky and the Swallows over and over again before re-fixing my oar and rowing to the safety of the shore.

At the great dam-wall of Derdap I had to wait for several hours the next morning before the first of two locks was operated. I whiled away the time by washing all my clothes in the river and spreading them to dry in the warm sunshine. A young security guard called Nenad, as graceful as a deer, came and chatted to me all the while, telling me facts he thought might be of interest. During Ceaucescu's dictatorship in Romania just across the river, many hundreds had tried to flee the country; the most obvious route was here across the Dunav to Yugoslavia where the river was narrow and isolated. Many Romanians had attempted to swim the gorge unaided and had been shot by the border-patrols from the cliff-tops as they floundered in the water. Their bodies had drifted down and fetched up where I had been washing my socks. The Romanians disclaimed any knowl-edge of the pitiful corpses, and they had been buried in the little graveyard full of unmarked tombs up the hill from where we sat. Ceaucescu had in his later days of power, Nenad told me, decreed an edict banning curtains in restaurants, so paranoid was he that peo-ple might be plotting against him in public places. I couldn't help thinking that if you need to make laws like that, you should know you're getting something wrong.

*

The last run of a hundred miles to the border took three days, the chief feature of which was hunger. I spent the last two dining on nothing but honey from the large jar given to me by Branko's mother and the small clove of garlic. This I peeled carefully, piece by piece, and munched raw. With the honey it was not too bad. This was, after all, Transylvania, though vampires seemed thin on the ground. The Romanian pastures were wide and empty, with occasional scenes recalling a Children's Illustrated Bible: shepherd boys tending flocks, wicked-eyed goats, dry cliffs where the sand-martins breed, the occasional tall moustachioed patriarch with a black crook. In the final two days, the weather came in, a thick chilling murk so that I could barely see the passing landscape. Hatless and freezing, I took my red-and-white spotty handkerchief and tied it tightly over my head as a scarf, in the manner of headmasters' wives standing on the touchline of a House Rugby Tournament. In my moment of deepest misery, I remembered the little clinking package given to me in Vienna. It was somewhere tucked away in the forelocker. When I unwrapped it with numb fingers, I discovered five little bottles of something called Barenliquor, or Bear's Mead. It was wonderfully warming and reviving, burning into my veins and fingertips and restoring my feeble spirits as though made by Loki himself.

My last night in old Yugoslavia was at Prahavo, a dismal deadend of almost disused railway-sidings, a container port, some big factories and a solitary grimy bar. There I went, starving and wet and cold, and for the first time brought myself to beg for a little bread. Here at the most miserable spot in the country, two factory workers pooled their funds and bought me a bowl of paprika soup. I squirrelled some of the bread away for later. I slept that night in a deserted waiting-room in the railway station just by the river – it was too cold and wet for sleeping aboard – and kept stirring uneasily in my sleep at strange, furtive rustlings and whisperings. They seemed to be emanating impossibly from beneath my very head, propped on my little knapsack as a pillow, and I put them down as delusions caused by fatigue and an overdose of paprika. It was only on the following day when I went to fetch out the bread-rolls I had stored there that I discovered there was nothing left but a few gnawed crumbs and a large rat-nibbled hole right through the bottom of the knapsack. Judging by the size of the hole, they were the size of dachshunds. I was very glad that I had not woken fully in the night.

And so at last a final day of headwind slogging, revived faintly by the last of the Barenliquor and the honey, and over into Bulgaria. I was stopped at the border by a grey patrol boat that shot out from behind the river-bank bushes and accosted me in mid-stream. I was not worried. The Australian Consulate in Vienna had assured me that I did not need a visa for Bulgaria. The border-guards saw it differently. I could not enter.

'I cannot go back,' I pointed out, too exhausted and wet to be diplomatic.

'You have no visa.'

'No.'

'Where have you come from?' they asked, guns cocked.

'England.'

'No, no, where have you come from in this boat?'

'England,' I repeated, and showed them my map.

There was some discussion.

'You may continue to Vidin, twenty miles down the river. There you must report immediately to the police. Do you understand? Immediately.'

'Yes.'

And they put their guns away and roared off.

Welcome to Bulgaria.

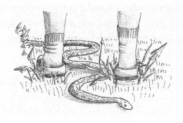

Bad Times in Bulgaria

> When I sally forth to seek my prey,
> I help myself in a royal way:
> I sink a few more ships, it's true,
> Than a well-bred monarch ought to do …
> For I am a Pirate King!
> Hurrah! Hurrah! For our Pirate King!
> And it is, it is a glorious thing
> To be a Pirate King!
> —W.S. GILBERT, *The Pirates of Penzance*

There was no way I was going to report immediately to the police. I arrived in Vidin after dark, cold, damp, starving and exhausted. The last thing I was going to do was sit in a draughty police-station for a couple of hours, only to be told at the end of it that I must leave Bulgaria immediately. I needed a hot shower, a square meal and a good night's rest, preferably without rats banqueting in my pillow as I slept. And for all this I needed money.

And that meant finding a cash-machine.

I found one soon enough. It was right next door to the police-station. Right.

Right!

I put on my large shapeless cagoule without putting my arms in the sleeves, pulled out my red-and-white spotty handkerchief, tied it in a headscarf over my head, persuaded myself that I looked just like a Bulgarian peasant woman out doing some late-night shopping, and marched up to the machine under the eye of an idle policeman. There I gave him what I hoped was a coquettish wink and extracted a great wad of glorious money. Then I marched into the nicest hotel I could find and proceeded to spend it all.

Next morning I mailed letters, phoned England, phoned Australia, did a ton of laundry, went back to bed until midday, and did all those things that are not possible to do while being deported for not having a visa. Having got that out of the way, I marched off to see the police, a winning smile on my lips. Four hours later I was being granted a visa. It was simple after all; they just needed a lot of money for the paperwork. And it needed to be in US dollars. Unmarked. In a brown paper bag.

Back I went to the bank and discovered the first of the many things about Bulgaria that are designed to baffle or repel visitors. See if you can work it out.

Me: *(walking up to the bank teller, a girl behind a grille)* Do you speak English?

Her: Yiss, of course.

Me: Super. Can I change some money into US dollars here?

Her: *(she nods)*

Me: *(highly relieved)* Oh, thank goodness, you've no idea what it's been like. I've been living on raw garlic for a week now, sorry about the smell. Now, I'd like to change this to dollars then. There's about four hundred and ...

Her: Ne, ees problema. Ees ne okay. Ne.

Me: *(somewhat taken aback)* Oh. Well, can I change less? Two hundred leva, yes?

Her: *(nod, nod)*

Me: Here you go then. *(I push it across to her. She doesn't take it.)* Sorry, is there a problem?

Her: *(she shakes her head)*

Me: Oh, that's a relief. I need it quite desperately, you see. Isn't it a lovely day outside?

Her: *(she shakes her head again)*

Me: Ah. Right. Right. Sorry. Yes, bring back the rain, that's what I say. None of this ghastly sunshine, no indeed! ... Er, you do understand me, don't you?

Her: *(shake, shake)*

Me: I'm sorry, I thought you said you spoke English. Do you?

Her: *(shake, shake)*

Me: Oh. Is there anyone else who does? Sprechen zie Englisch? Parlez el Anglais? Speaky Engleski?

Her: *(nod, nod)*

Me: Could I see him? Her? Speak to someone who speaks English? Please? Before one of us dies?

Her: I tell you, I speak the English. It is good I speak. There is no one else.

Me: So you *do* speak English?

Her: *(shake, shake)*

… and so on.

Can you work it out? It took me three more days. In Bulgaria alone of all the nations of the earth, a nod of the head means 'no' and a shake of the head means 'yes.' Over the next week I found this unique trait of the Bulgarian people incredibly frustrating, even when I had tumbled to it. The visual signal of a nod or shake is so much stronger than the verbal cue that I was often left baffled by the simplest exchanges. 'Can I buy some bread?' I'd enquire, and at the shop-keeper's shake of the head I'd be out of the shop and down the road sadly looking for another place before I remembered that I'd just been told 'yes.'

There was an awful lot to dislike about Bulgaria. I don't wish to appear churlish, but my enthusiasm for foreign travel hit an all-time low in that sad, dark land, the Bowels of Europe. Perhaps it was the large bowl of stewed pig's intestines, the speciality of the region, that I ordered one night by mistake. Perhaps it was the sultry, surly, gum-chewing girls in banks and shops who thought they ought to be parading the catwalks of Paris and not serving riff-raff like me. Perhaps it was the three separate attacks by small dogs, manic and filthy poodle-like creatures that hurtled out of open drains and sprang slavering at my ankles. Perhaps it was the patently crooked river-police who never missed an opportunity to demand a seventy-leva breathing tax at each place I came to. (I never paid, by the way.)

The landscape was utterly flat and hazy with pollution. I sailed by Europe's most dangerous nuclear reactor. I sailed past the notorious prison-island of Belene, a mosquito hell for political prisoners. I sailed past the chemical works at Nikopol, where the broad river turned a nitrous yellow-brown and dead fish floated in archipelagos on the surface amid cappuccino scum. I sailed past the entry of the river where a year later thousands of tons of cyanide and toxic waste would pour into the Danube, killing everything in it for hundreds of miles, all the way down the Delta. I looked forward to getting to a place called Lom, because I vaguely recalled a Saki short story in which a man on a park-bench talks lyrically of his home-town of Lom, far to the east. He talks of the almond-orchards in spring, the little wooden bridges arching over snow-melt streams tumbling down the hill-sides in white torrents, the apricots sunning against an old stone wall. I was looking forward to seeing it. When I got there and saw the usual cracked and filthy concrete, the yellow-eyed poodles, the sixties communist cement tower-blocks, I remembered several things: the village in the story was called Yom, not Lom; it was in Afghanistan, not Bulgaria; and the whole point of the story was that the narrator was a professional liar.

My hatred of Bulgaria took on a new intensity.

A few facts to consider. Even from antiquity, their neighbours have disliked the Bulgarians and attributed to them all sorts of unsavoury practices, a view I came to share after the third police interview. There were no children in Bulgaria, or at least none that I could see. All the way from Shropshire to Serbia I had been accustomed to urchins lining the river-banks, fishing, whistling, spitting, playing hooky, climbing trees, tormenting puppies and other healthy pursuits of the young, but not once in Bulgaria did I see anyone under the age of seventeen.

In the midst of all this dreariness I was lucky to have a contact in Sofia, the country's capital, two hundred miles from the river. Someone I knew worked as head of the Raffeisen Bank and had invited me to look him up, so I left *Jack* tucked up in the grimy river-port of Orjahovo and headed off on the bus. For a bizarre but comfortable few days I was translated from the primitive world of river-travel to the giddy life of high finance: a businessmen's lunch with the new British Ambassador; a newspaper interview for the Sofia papers in the upholstered luxury of the Sheraton Hotel; a gypsy and his dancing bear with tiny sad eyes and blistered snout who revolved drearily for pennies in the Square; hot baths and washing machines in a comfortable flat, and a chance to explore the city.

I learnt that of all the Eastern Bloc countries, Bulgaria had been the most fervently communist and the most reluctant to let the regime go. Stories abounded of poisoned umbrella assassinations, of the Security Police occupying secret headquarters in the great central dome of the city, of ex-agents and redundant spies still feeding the muscovy ducks in the damp parks and dreaming of carnations and catch-words. As I sat in the Sheraton tea-rooms writing letters, the music from *Schindler's List* played and the rain came down in solid sheets outside. The sad, sad music; the never-ending rain; I remember Sofia entirely in old black-and-white.

Then things improved. As I neared the eastern end of Bulgaria, my spirits revived, the people and the weather became sunnier, and I was attacked by pirates. For what more could one ask?

I had spent a lazy few days sailing down the broad stretches of river, stopping in villages that were less marred by the heavy Soviet style than upstream. The town of Ruse was unexpectedly pleasant, almost Parisian in its wide boulevards, its plane trees, its pavement cafés, its classical statuary. And God bless McDonald's: the hamburgers were as lousy as ever, but you can't fault the toilets. In Ruse I sat in a sunny square and scribbled a postcard to a friend in Holland. This is what I wrote:

> Voyage nearly over now. Another week or so will see me to the Black Sea, I guess. All jolly good, I suppose, but rather dull, looking back on it. I would have liked just a few more adventures; discovering the princess of a lost island-kingdom, perhaps, or being captured by pirates. Still, mustn't complain, I suppose. Speak to you soon.
>
> Love
> Sandy

They say that the gods destroy us by granting our wishes. They are right, and I was soon cursing the whim that led me to voice such an ill-made wish.

*

Romania now lay along the northern bank, Bulgaria along the south. The river here was very wide and empty, and scattered along both banks were countless islands, tangles of dense reeds and willows and osiers. All morning the breeze had been blowing gently from the west, a perfect following wind, so I had been able to set the sails, put the tiller on auto-pilot (a carefully propped shoe) and lie back in the dinghy propped up on cushions and read. I had done my daily memory exercises, this time saying the whole of *The Eve of St Agnes* in different accents for each part. The narrator's part ranged between Edinburgh Academy Miss Jean Brodie and Radio Sports Presenter. I was happy but – as is probably clear – partially insane.

The gossamer, I mused, had become a nuisance. It was all very well at first seeing it as a magical hint of autumn, drifting through the air, floating above the river's surface, borne on the slightest of breezes, airy silver strands of finest silk festooning the rigging with fairy-pennants. It was all very well musing that in the brilliant October sunshine, *Jack* was an enchanted barge out of Elf-Land,

> *a ship of leaves and gossamer*
> *With blossom for her canopy*

sailing along, trailing clouds of glory, straight out of an Arthur Rackham illustration into the world of Mortals.

Yet the great poets who have dealt with gossamer had failed to mention one or two salient points about the stuff, such as its stickiness, its tendency to drape over and around anything in its way, its habit of clogging and clotting together in one's ears and eyes and mouth, the way that every swipe of the arm to clear the stuff from tickled nostrils simply brings more fibres floating in to drape themselves in great swathes across the face and eye-lids; and perhaps most importantly of all, the fact that it comes out of spiders' bottoms and is therefore accompanied by tiny pin-head baby spiders in their thousands. These lose no time in crawling into every facial orifice, nesting in one's hair, no doubt eating their way deep into the middle ear there to rear their horrid brood and colonise the human cranium.

Such thoughts as these occupied my restless mind as I sailed along, all unknowing. Romania on the left-hand bank looked wilder and more attractive than dreary denuded Bulgaria, but it was forbidden territory as I was not yet ready to use my single-entry visa. Once I set foot on Romanian soil, I would not be allowed to return to Bulgaria. As much as I longed to leave the latter, I was still dependent on its riverside towns for the next hundred miles, as the Romanian bank seemed to offer nothing but trackless forest and the odd bevy of rummaging swine.

There were several long wooded islands in mid-stream, and the only channel where the wind was blowing steadily was along the left-hand stretch of water between the islands and the Romanian shore. I was halfway down this strait when from out of the reeds and willows appeared a Romanian fishing-boat manned by two fishermen. They beckoned me over with a wave. Not feeling like stopping I gave a cheery but hello-and-goodbye sort of wave, called out 'Engleski' and turned my attention back to the sailing. I was startled a minute later by their appearance alongside my boat – they clearly wanted to chat for a bit.

Ah well, so be it.

One of the fishermen was short and grizzled, with a smiley clownish face and a filthy beanie jammed down over his head. The other, manning the outboard in the stern, had a broad face, a gentle rueful smile and crinkled eyes. Both were quite indescribably filthy. They were jabbering away in Romanian, and before I knew it had grabbed my bow-painter and lashed me alongside their boat. Smiles. Laughter. Handshakes all round. The offer of some lethal dark-purple murky-looking liquor out of a lemonade bottle (declined) and before I knew what was happening, we were heading for the Romanian bank.

Puzzled, I tried to indicate that I didn't want to go there – indeed, was not allowed to go there – but the man at the helm stolidly ignored my pleas and we chugged on. Very soon they had me jammed up against the Romanian bank, the hoisted sail tangling dangerously in the overhead branches, and I was getting cross. They indicated with gestures and another burst of Romanian that I should take down the sail. I pretended not to understand. Again they jabbered and pointed, and though their meaning was very obvious, I continued to play the idiot. It seemed to me that the hoisted sail was in their eyes the one obstacle preventing them taking me where they liked; perhaps they felt that to tow me with it up was dangerous or conspicuous. At this stage all was still confusion. They were smiling away, offering me the purple murk and, for all I knew, waiting to take me to a surprise party they had prepared in the woods. But after almost half-an-hour of stalling, they began to lose patience. Over and over I had asked them to let me go on my way; in turn they kept mentioning Giurgu, a Romanian town some twenty miles back upstream. I was damned if I was going to let them take me there. The sail, I said firmly, stays up.

Finally the short one picked up a large brown catfish from where it was lying in the bottom of the boat and drew a large, purposeful knife from his belt. Carefully, deliberately, watching me all the while, he slit it from chin to tail, reached in and pulled out a handful of dark red giblets and hurled them at my head. I ducked, and they splatted into my sail. Then he held up the knife, pointed to me and drew a finger across his throat.

Now this … this … I recognised as an unambiguous threat.

'Oh, the *sail*? Take it *down*? You should have said …'

And a minute later I had bundled the now stinking sail, boom and gaff together and hauled them out of the way. The quiet one started the decrepit little motor and off we headed up the river.

Even now I was more puzzled and angry than frightened. But as we chugged up the channel, several things began to alarm me. When I went to loosen the rope that was lashing us together, the short one raised a black paddle above his head threateningly and I quickly desisted. When I decided that if he was going to have a knife, I might as well have mine, and reached down to unpack it, he again barked a threat and I turned the action into a harmless tidying up of twigs and debris fallen into the boat. But between whiles, all was so friendly, so matey: smiles and laughs and drinks all round. To try to lighten the mood I played my tin-whistle, a Mozart medley, which they loved. I even let them have a go on it. I offered them half a chocolate bar each. They grinned and accepted, but any move to free myself and the short one raised the paddle once more.

After a while we chugged out from behind the long island and into the main shipping channel, and there, oh joy! oh salvation! was a huge Danube barge half a mile away across the water. Surely if now I stood up and shouted for help, the two fishermen would be unable to prevent me. But too late. They too had spotted the barge, read my mind and quick as a flash had wheeled around and we were racing back behind the sheltering screen of the island. My fears were confirmed. Whatever it was they were up to, they did not wish the world to see.

For the next hour we hugged the Romanian shore, out of sight of any traffic on the main river. I spent the time considering my options, every one of which was impossibly melodramatic or impractical. One involved something I had read in *The Day of the Triffids* where the hero disabled an engine by pouring a jar of honey into the petrol tank. I had half a jar of honey but could not think of a plausible way of getting it into the outboard. Or could I drop the hoisted boom on the short one's head and ...? No, no, I had it! The motor was started, I noticed, by a detachable rip-cord. If I could do some of my magic rope tricks, ask to borrow the rip-cord and then fling it overboard so that ... that what?

The truth was that I could not bring myself to do any of these things. There is a strong and unshakeable conviction in most people that as long as one can keep things on a civil level, a friendly, reasonable level, nothing dramatic can go wrong. This, more than impracticality, is what ultimately prevented me from carrying out any of my plans, which would have involved *me* being far nastier and more dramatic than my captors had so far been: oars through skulls and so on.

Such thoughts were tangling in my mind as the two boats zoomed on through the water. But they were clarified a little when the short one leant over and rubbed his fingers together. 'Dollars? Deutschmarks? Leva? Krona?' He pointed at me, and at himself again.

'No, I'm afraid I don't have any money,' I said in a voice a little too loud. My two captors looked at me in amused certainty that I was trying it on. But at least now they had shown their colours. They were pirates of a sort. Not, I admit, the sort I'd been hoping for, with a parrot, a peg-leg and a penchant for lace at cuff and knee. These two were hardly likely to break into a G&S chorus of *Pour, Oh Pour the Pirate Sherry* and let me off for being an orphan. In fact I was sure that they were usually fishermen, but today had decided to indulge in a little piracy. Where it would end, I did not want to think.

I decided on a much simpler plan. I would push both men overboard with a swift one-two of the oar, leap into their boat and take off at top speed until I was thirty miles downstream, only then stopping to cut myself free and carry on my way. Yes. That was it. That was what I would do.

Only of course I couldn't.

To this day I do not know whether I would ever have plucked up the sheer primitive indecency to do this, but suddenly the decision was taken out of my hands. The two men had for some time been searching the near bank for something – an inlet, a comrade? – and now at a shrill whistle from the shore it seemed that they had found it. A horseman had emerged from the thick woods and was hailing them across the water. Any action I might take was now impossible – the man had a gun held at the ready.

Within minutes we were ashore. The horseman was the coldest, cruellest-looking man I had ever seen. In a face grained with dirt and sunburn, two lazy black eyes, cold as sloes, eyed me casually. He was clad in tatty khaki, but wore a bandanna of dirty crimson. His horse too had a red gypsy-knot tied in its bridle and a hundred jingling brass charms winking on its harness. This was quite clearly the King of the Gypsies, and my two friends bowed and scraped before him. A long argy-bargy followed, the rider smiling lazily all the while and looking me up and down in cold amusement. If it were not so ridiculous, I would have said that he was mentally undressing me, or picturing with idle pleasure how I might squirm if presented with a pointed stake, a leather strap and some anatomical diagrams. I began to feel very uneasy indeed. Questions and answers were flung to and fro, and at one point my bag was grabbed from the dinghy by one of the fishermen and handed to the horseman. He looked through it slowly – Keats poetry book, passport, tin-whistle, wallet: all were examined with the same smiling scrutiny. Then a decision was made. The horseman gave an order and they towed my dinghy round into a nearby creek, screened from the main river by willows and a half fallen poplar. There it was tied, and the fishermen pirates were dismissed. There was some grumbling about this at first, but the horseman stared coldly into the mid-distance and the whining petered out. They climbed in their filthy little boat and motored away.

Once they had vanished, the horseman – Gypsy-King, robber-chief, mercenary thug, whoever he was – motioned that I should walk into the forest ahead of him. I then did the only brave thing that day, and ignoring his obvious signal, walked down to *Jack* to tie her up properly – the fools had simply looped a line over a log and already she was drifting loose. Then straightening up, on an impulse I took out of the boat a single oar and walked back up to where the man and horse were waiting and we commenced our march into the forest.

Fear is a most peculiar thing. The body that scuffed its way through the yellow leaves clutching its ridiculous oar was sweating and nauseous and shaking like a jelly. It badly needed to evacuate its bowels and bladder. It was also wondering what on earth it was supposed to do with the oar. Trip up the horse? Deflect the bullets with a flashing twist of the oar's blade? But none of this mattered a bit, because it wasn't the real me at all. The real me was, I am almost ashamed to say, enjoying himself enormously. I was fizzing with daring ideas, to do with magic tricks and throwing dust in my captor's eyes, none of which my incompetent body would have been capable of putting into action. That didn't matter, though. The leaves are so yellow here, and smelling deliciously of plum-cake, rich and earthy. The horse is a noble beast. How could people ever eat them? Or break their legs with oars? I was alert and vibrant, almost gleeful – and intensely, excitedly curious.

I was excited because I thought I would soon know what became of people after death. I was sorry, of course – sorry for my parents and sorry too for whomever found my corpse, if anyone. Please do not think that I am boasting of a bravery that I did not possess. I was scared, very scared, or rather the unimportant puppet with the shaking legs was scared, leaving the real me to be curious. No. Even that doesn't get it quite right. The puppet *was* important, and I had to look after it, and it was, after all, *me*. I was feeling fear as I suppose it normally happens to anyone, but it was wholly different from what I had expected.

After several miles of walking through the forest – leggy nettles, swampy willows, dead brittle grey branches – we came to an impasse. Across the rutted muddy path lay a side-arm of the hidden creek. My captor, who had been riding behind me, gun at the ready, reined up and ordered me to wade across with him. But when he rode through, the murky water came up to the horse's thigh, and would have come up to my neck. This was as far as the road went for me. Ridiculous though it seems, and although I was sure I was about to be dispatched, I didn't want to get wet and muddy, even if it meant that the time had come for me to turn around and face a tree. This, I was sure, was it.

There is a moment in one of C.S. Lewis's Narnia books when the children are about to go into great danger, from which it is likely that none of them will come out alive. 'Let us go now,' says one of the characters, 'and take what adventure Aslan sends us.' An adventure! To see Death in this way seemed an admirable and comforting way of viewing things. If only my bowels and bladder would come on side, I thought, all would be well. Meanwhile, time hovered at the brink.

And now having built all that up, though as honestly as I can, let me now confess that this is where the anti-climax starts. I trust readers will not be too disappointed with the outcome. For on my refusal to cross the ford, the sneering horseman looked at a loss. After some thought he held up three fingers, said something that might possibly have been 'kilometros,' another thing that might have been 'Kapitan,' and indicated that I should wait there. Then he turned back across the ford, spurred his horse and trotted off up the rise into the trees.

'Righto!' I called after him. Then precisely seventeen seconds after I had watched him disappear from sight, I turned and ran like blazes back down the path. Twenty metres down the path I stopped short, changed my tactics and ran straight off the path and into the trackless forest. Ten metres and two blackberry swathes in I changed plan again and bolted out of the thicket and back to the ford where I stood quivering like a jack-rabbit, wondering what the hell I had been playing at. It was a purely animal reaction, the bolting to and fro of a released creature fuelled by pure adrenalin and few brain-cells. Now that the adrenalin was leaching out of my system, I was at a loss. I collapsed into a drift of leaves and began to think.

My theory that the cruel-eyed horseman was the King of the Gypsies and intending to rob or kill me seemed a little shaky. True, he had my bag and all my valuables, but his cavalier abandonment of me in the forest with the expectation that I would calmly await his return was puzzling.

I thought again. If I bolted back to *Jack* and took off down the river, I would do so without passport, wallet or money. So be it –my captors were welcome to them. But what if I had been mistaken? I still thought that the horseman was a cold-eyed killer, but what if this Kapitan he spoke of was a more genial man, a sort of Robin Hood of Romania, who after a fire-lit meal of venison pasties would return my possessions with a mocking bow – minus a small dona-tion for the widows' and orphans' fund, perhaps – and send me on my way again to tell the world of his magnanimity? Or something along those lines?

I decided that my best course was to adopt the age-old strategy of schoolboys and princes alike and climb a tree. There was a very good one just by the ford, a sturdy oak well screened from the path by broad leaves. There I would hide, wait until I had assessed the situ-ation further when the horseman returned, and either reveal myself or continue hiding as I thought best. Yes. That is what I would do. So up that tree I climbed still clutching my oar and sat down to wait in my leafy bower. As my heartbeat slowed and the blood stopped chugging in my ears, the silence of the forest stole over me and with it came a sort of calm. Far off I heard the life of the forest going on around me: some largish animal – a deer or a wild boar, perhaps – was scuffling a quarter of a mile away, and something unseen was working its way along the bank of the muddy creek in a rustle of grass and reeds. So quietly did I sit that a nuthatch, its plumage in neat cashew and slate grey, came pecking its busy way up the oak, creeping up the trunk to within a foot or two of my hand and would

Man Up Tree With Oar

have started on my oar if I had not swiped at it viciously to just bugger the hell off out of there.

Clearly my nerves were still scraped raw.

Half-an-hour later I was so intent on peering through my screen of leaves at the ford in front of me that I was oblivious to all else. Then there came a polite cough from behind and below me and I nearly fell out of the tree in pure shock. A small party of men had approached from the opposite direction to the ford – they were within ten yards of my tree, and I was in full view of them. One was in the smart green uniform of a police officer, while the others were in various items of khaki. They were looking up at me with the sort of gaze you too would use if you found a man up a tree with an oar. 'Humour him,' the looks said. 'He is possibly confused.'

I turned in alarm, nearly fell once more from my perch, caught myself in time and clambered hastily down, brushing twigs and leaves from my hair and attempting to rub moss-stains from my trousers. At a word from the officer, one of the men stepped forward warily and took the oar. Another helped me down the last five feet. The game was up.

To my relief the officer looked not only competent but kind. He was a man of about my age, with a tanned face, fairish brown hair and clear grey eyes. The neat uniform suited his grave and courteous air – this was no tin-pot generalissimo running a racket. And to my relief, after one or two false starts we made the discovery that we both spoke French.

The fact that he spoke French was reassuring. His first intelligible words, on the other hand, were not.

'I must arrest you for espionage,' he said kindly.

The rest of the story is swiftly told. I was taken a little way through the forest to a bend of the creek where was moored a speedboat, surprisingly new. This took us up the log-jammed creek at a terrifying speed to where it petered out on the further side of the forest. Here a lonely police outpost stood surrounded by pigsties, and an office was quickly cleared of a small piglet and three recruits playing chess. Strong black coffee was ordered, my horseman was sent for to join us, and my interrogation as a spy began.

The police-chief – his name was Florian – was as good as he seemed. Very slowly, very clearly, he questioned me about that afternoon's movements. Very slowly, very clearly, I told my tale. When I had finished, he told me that there were one or two discrepancies he would like to clear up. The two fishermen, he said, claim that they found me on Romanian soil, that I am a spy. Is this true?

No, I explained calmly but very clearly. I was certainly in the channel between the island and the shore – this is not a problem, the river is free to everyone, he reassures me – but I was certainly nowhere near the bank and had no intention of landing.

Ah. He smiled. They, the rascals, have told the horseman (who is, by the way, a border-patrol policeman, not a Gypsy-King despite his dress) that they found me on Romanian soil and knew at once that I was a spy. For the love of their country and as good honest citizens, they had taken the first opportunity to seek out the police and hand their spy over to the proper authorities. There would, perhaps, be a small reward?

No, added Florian to his narrative, but there might be a small fine. The two opportunists would be found and punished. Bit by bit we pieced together the events. We came to the conclusion that the two fishermen had hoped to take me somewhere quiet and rob me – hopefully nothing worse – but that their plan had been foiled by the appearance of the patrol-rider who had come along and seen them towing me and the distinctive *Jack*. Knowing that if there was any trouble, they would be the first to be questioned, they had quickly changed their plan. They knew that I had no visa and that I spoke no Romanian. Thus they quickly concocted a story about a captured 'spy' and spun it to the rider, hoping for a reward. (At this time of trouble over the border in Yugoslavia, the notion of spies was not as fanciful as it may now seem.) The rider accordingly had taken charge from that point on, perhaps over-zealously, and decided to bring me at gun-point to the Kapitan. It was ironic that I had in fact been perfectly safe from the moment the horseman had appeared – the appearance had been quite the opposite.

But now the ordeal was over. We had another coffee – as gritty and black as ever, but oh! how I enjoyed it – and Florian handed me my belongings and accompanied me back to the speed-boat. Then there was another nightmare speed-race through the floating logs and low boughs of the secret creek until *Jack*'s bright buttercup hull and furled red sails came in sight, tethered where I had secured her several lifetimes ago. Then they kindly towed me out into the main river, now a burnished gold in the late westering sun, and cast me off. The nearest town was Tutrakan on the Bulgarian side, some twelve miles down the river, they explained, before zooming off into the golden glare.

Those last twelve miles were spent driving my boat along across a molten river under a molten sky with oar-strokes still fuelled with adrenalin. As the miles passed, the sky deepened to apricot, then carmine, and then dying-ember crimson until starry darkness covered the heavens from West to East. Slowly my pace slackened, steadied, and I fell to singing every deep, glad, solemn hymn I knew to keep time to the strokes. The lights of Tutrakan crept nearer and nearer, and I passed the last two miles improvising an anthem-like tune, Byrd or Palestrina in style perhaps – it was hard to tell. But the words were those of my favourite prayer, one that I knew from boyhood.

Bad Times in Bulgaria

Lighten our darkness, we beseech thee, O Lord,
And by thy great mercy,
Defend us from all perils and dangers of this night
For the sake of thy dear Son,
Our Lord, Jesus Christ,
Amen

Amen, and again I say Amen!

The Wings of the Morning

He who does not know his way to the sea should take a
river for his guide.
                                        —PLAUTUS, *Poenulus*

Round the cape of a sudden came the sea,
And the sun looked over the mountain's rim:
And straight was a path of gold for him,
And the need of a world of men for me.
                        —ROBERT BROWNING, *Parting at Morning*

And so the long journey drew near its end. I calculated that there
were 376 kilometres to go, or half that distance depending on which
route I took. About forty kilometres down the river, a canal cut away
to the right, heading straight for the Black Sea and emerging at
Constanza on the coast. The longer route would take me further
north before swinging eastward into the Danube Delta, where the
river spread out into a maze of channels, any of which would take
me down to the Black Sea. I was in serious doubt as to which of the
two routes to take. The spirit of adventure, which should have cried
out for the mazy wilderness of the Delta, one of the world's greatest
wetlands, was now nearly extinguished. I was tired and grubby, on
the verge of madness from the sheer tedium of my own company,
and I think the events of the past few days had shaken me more than
I cared to admit. The straight canal to Constanza would have me
finishing within three days, and I could be back in England by the
weekend, sitting down in clean clothes among good company and
never having to recite *The Eve of St Agnes* again. I decided to take the
shorter route.

Signing out of Bulgaria with the Silistra Police Chief that first
morning was a surreal experience. Yes, the visa was in order, yes, I
would have no trouble entering Romania, but the problem was with
the boat. Where were her Ship's Papers?

Her what?

'Her Ship's Papers, Kapitan. Every vessel has Ship's Papers and without seeing them, I cannot let you continue.'

'Look, she's only a dinghy,' I explained, and led him out of his harbour-side office to peer over the jetty at the little tub floating below. 'There isn't even a motor.'

He was unmoved. 'As I say, every vessel has a set of Ship's Papers, and I must see them. Otherwise,' he added with a challenging stare, 'how do I know that you have not stolen this boat?'

What, and rowed it three thousand miles just to escape? I muttered under my breath. *There are easier ways to acquire a boat.* But I didn't voice my thoughts out loud. The police-chief was a fat, smug man who looked content to sit there chewing tooth-picks for the next few decades if needs be, waiting for the Ship's Papers so that he could stamp them for his records.

After half an hour I had an idea. I dug out my pencil case and a clean sheet of paper from my sketchbook. I sat down on the sunny steps at his door and drew as a letterhead a rather nice heraldic crow entwined with an anchor. Then I wrote neatly in black ink:

Name of Vessel: *Jack de Crow*

Class: Mirror dinghy

Reg. No.: 180463 (my birthday, by coincidence)

Ship's Owner: Alexander James Mackinnon

Insurance: Oh, surely ...

Cargo: Tin-whistles, watercolour paintboxes, parrot-embroidered cushions, honey-pots, magic tricks, silken handkerchiefs, gossamer, autumn leaves.

I did this while the Police Chief watched me through narrowed eyes, even getting up out of his chair to suggest a couple of curly mermaids at the top to flank the nautical crow. He nodded with approval at my artwork and went and resumed his seat behind his desk. I finished off, blew the document dry and went over to him once more. 'Oh, Ship's Papers?' I said. 'You mean *these* Ship's Papers. Yes, here they are, sorry, wasn't with you for a moment there.'

He said *'Ja,* Ship's Papers. I told you they'd be somewhere.' Then he took them as though he had never seen them before, stamped them, copied the details, signed the copies three times, gave one to me, put one in a file, lit his cigarette with the third, stamped my passport and bid me farewell. 'I'm a busy man,' he said, and went back to his toothpick jar and his desk. I returned to *Jack*, showed her the proof of her new official status, and we sailed off down the river into Romania.

SHIP'S PAPERS

Name of Vessel: Jack de Crow
Class: Mirror Dinghy
Reg. No.   ...er... 180463
Ship's Owner: Alexander James MacKinnon
Insurance: Oh, surely...
Cargo: Tin whistles, watercolour
                    parrot-embroidered cushion
                    honey pots, magnifying
                    silken handkerchiefs
                    Autumn leaves

*

> *Two roads diverged in a wood, and I,*
> *I took the one less travelled by,*
> *And that has made all the difference.*

In my case those roads were actually watery streams, and they ran down either side of a little island in mid-stream, clustered with thick yellowing trees. I took the left-hand channel on a whim – a white egret had flapped slowly off down that side – and discovered twenty minutes later that what I thought was an island was in fact a peninsula, splitting the Danube into two. The branch I was on was the Borcea River, and it ran another sixty miles in a meandering course before it re-joined the main Danube – thirty miles beyond the Constanza Canal turn-off. It looked as though I was going to the Delta after all.

I was not entirely unhappy about this. The lesser Borcea wound between sandbanks and green pastures where herds of fine-looking horses grazed. Tall clumps of poplars raised their golden towers like steeples over the landscape, and it reminded me vividly of my first days on the little Vyrnwy in the pleasant pastures of North Shropshire. Every now and then I saw the rising smoke of some settlement off in the trees, or closer to the bank large round conical huts made of larch-poles all leaning together to an apex, the gaps stopped with moss and grass. Everywhere was a great and spreading silence. Along the banks were fading sedges, bone-white and buff-coloured, and the only sound was the thin hiss and rattle of the breeze sifting through their stiff stems. Far, far overhead I could see three huge black and white birds, legs and necks outstretched in three great crosses. They were storks, sailing eastwards to the Delta. It did not seem far now.

I moored one night on the outskirts of a dark and almost lightless town next to a rusting barge. The owners, Niko and Georgi, invited me to bunk down in a cosy cabin on board. We set off after dark into the town to find something to eat, Niko and Georgi each taking a stout club. I wondered why, but soon found out as we reached the outskirts. Two snarling dogs launched themselves out of the darkness in attack, but were sent yelping into the darkness by savage blows of the clubs. It was quite unnerving. Even more so was passing by an open concrete drain, one of the huge cylinders of concrete that you see forming culverts under roads. From inside a light was flickering, and as I stooped to glance in I saw a family living there: a mother wrapped in rags, two thin children and a baby, huddled against the curving concrete walls to avoid the slimy trickle of dampness that ran down the middle of this, their home.

In the darkened town nothing was open, so we returned to the barge and I was plied with brandy. Communication was limited, but to my surprise Romanian was easier to guess at than any other language so far between France and here. I learned later that the Romanians proudly claim direct descent from Rome, the purest line there is, and their language reflects this. Here at the utter end of Europe we were back to Latin roots and a recognisable alphabet. By some accident of geography and history they had become islanded in a sea of Slavs, with whom they did not deign to mingle. They were a good-looking race, tanned and straight-nosed and clear-eyed with brown curling hair and frank grins – what could be discerned under the grinding lines of poverty, that is. For there was no doubt about it, Romania was crippled by poverty of an extremity I had not guessed at. It was hard to believe that they shared a continent with glittering Vienna or prosperous Frankfurt.

One night followed sleeping on *Jack* under a rookery full of incontinent rooks, another in an almost identical cosy barge cabin on the invitation of another Georgi – I thought for a minute that I had gone in a large circle. A day of racing winds and bright skies had me hurtling down the river through two large and surprisingly modern towns with gleaming white apartment-blocks, and I came at last to the very apex of the Delta. Tomorrow I would be in its wild heart, and the next day it would all be over.

Jack and I stopped at dusk in the middle of a wild part of the forest. Here a gnarled willow tree thrust out old roots into the river to form a natural mooring spot, a promontory of earth and grass and fallen trunks behind which *Jack* could nestle. That night I gathered together great chunks of rotten wood and kindling, built a fireplace of stones and lit a fire. Soon I had a great blaze going, red against the blackness of the forest beyond, and over it I toasted some bread and cheese. It was not terribly successful – the chunks kept dropping off or charring – but I also opened the bottle of wine that I had been saving since Vienna. Alfons and Uli had given it to me, and I thought of their exquisite and spotless flat as yet another cheesy lump adhered to my shirt-front. They would be very polite, I thought, if they were here, and offer me a linen napkin. Vienna seemed a long way away.

Soon I was finished with supper and sat enjoying the fall of glowing coals, the crackle of the tinder-dry wood and the sparks rushing up into the night sky. A night breeze sprung up and breathed cold on my back, but my front, my face, my outstretched palms were warm and glowing. I wondered that this was the first time I had made an effort to do this on the whole trip, now that it was so close to finishing. I pictured myself on a map of Europe, sitting alone in the forest on the very eastern edge, and marvelled at the fact that I was here. As I gazed into the falling caves and glowing grottoes of ash and ember, I saw the pictures of that day: an Orthodox priest in a church that morning with a long grizzled beard, reading from a great book while headscarfed women knelt and fingered the hem of his robe, weeping and crying, the whole scene a set-piece for Titian. The coals shifted and I saw another scene: a young man poling a reed-boat across the river, bare-chested even in the blue wind, leading a herd of swimming horses across the deep, broad river. Their rolling eyes and snuffling nostrils were close enough to be seen, an inch out of the water like a line of water-kelpies led by a naked brown Pan. A log fell and ashes flew up. I saw in them a great swirling dark cloud against a red sunset, which as I drew nearer resolved into a myriad of winged specks: a swarm of rooks flocking homewards to roost in a clamorous rookery, a thousand strong.

The bottle was half gone now and the fire was dying. It was getting cold. I placed another log on the fire and stoked it up, but then went and climbed into my little boat. The mattress was laid out on its decking, the awning was up, but its open triangle was facing towards the fire. As I fell asleep, I could gaze out into the night and see my toes in the sleeping bag silhouetted against the rosy glow of the heaped fire. I wiggled them to get them warm, and listened to the gurgle and chuckle of the water around the willow roots. I was as happy as a king. No, I was as happy as Ratty and Tom Sawyer and Doctor Dolittle all rolled into one, and that is something better.

I awoke the next morning to a grey ghostly mist over the river. It was as thick and blinding as wet wool, and it struck me that in a year's travelling, this was the one classical story-book hazard I had not yet encountered. It had been saving itself for the one part of the trip where I was not following a single river-course but must find my way through a network of channels in the Delta's maze.

I set off rowing, hugging the southern bank so as not to miss the channel to Sulina, the small port at my journey's end. If I ended up traversing the northern part of the Delta, I would pass into the Ukraine, and I had had enough of illegal frontier crossings. Phantom ships loomed up out of the fog, gaunt, rag-rigged things crewed by scrawny skeletal pirates jeering raucously as they approached – and then turned into drifting felled trees, their dead branches smothered in cormorants. My determination to stick to the southern bank soon led me down a side-arm, a very graveyard of ships and barges all rusting, derelict, broken-windowed, caved in, half-sunk under the overhanging boughs of the crowding forest – but not abandoned entirely. A chained dog, a draped line hung with grubby dishcloths, a flicker of an oil-lantern from behind yellowed glass showed that some at least of these hulks were inhabited. It was an eerie place, a Sheol of ships and their ghost masters, gibbering and squeaking in the mist.

Soon the graveyard arm re-joined the main river, and the mist began to lift, burning off the water in spectacular wisps and curlicues of steam. A wind sprung up, on the nose this time, but it was such a splendid day, such a sparkling stretch of river, that beating down the river was sheer delight. Yet though the channel to Sulina runs through the very heart of the Delta, I must confess to being a little disappointed by it. I had expected reedy channels where the wild-fowl nested in their thousands: geese and ducks, storks and ibis and egrets, and the croak of a million bullfrogs. I expected houses, if there were any, to be perched on long poles above the marsh and have nets drying on frames. I was fully prepared to put up with a constant swarm of midges and mosquitoes, gnats and flies, and horse-flies that could sting through leather. I was half hoping to contract malaria.

As it was, this stretch recalled one of the drearier corners of Essex. There was the odd farmhouse, neither decrepit enough to be a gypsy hovel nor luxurious enough to be the ex-king of Romania's shooting-lodge. There were a few villages, more ordinarily middle-class than anywhere else I had seen in Romania, and the most rustic thing I saw was an ox-cart being driven along the top of the dyke, but it was loaded with used tyres. There was not even the opportu-nity for a last camp-fire vigil that night, communing with the dark-ness. I arrived at a village called Maluc at dusk and could go no further, feeling suddenly rather dispirited and dreary.

*

But when I woke the next morning, I was excited and apprehensive, nervous even. I knew that today I would reach the Black Sea. I put on clean clothes and shaved properly with soap and water, as though I were due to meet with royalty: the Dark Queen, the Mare Neagra herself.

The morning was grey and still, even with the odd drizzle, very light and fine. The banks continued flat and dull, but as the day pro-gressed gave way to reed-beds where the sedges grew almost mast-high. They rattled like sabres on either side. The famed wildfowl were conspicuous by their absence; the only birds were an ugly spe-cies of hooded crow and the odd heron. As I rowed, I pondered again a long-considered question: what would I do about *Jack de Crow* when I got to the end? Reluctant though I was to admit it, this would certainly be the end of our long acquaintance. I could not possibly arrange to take her back with me. Various plans had come and gone in my mind over the last year. The wildest and loveliest of these was to give her a Viking send-off. I had visions of standing on the edge of the Black Sea and loading her with cedarwood and sandalwood, and dousing her with scented oils. Then, gently, I would set her sails and her tiller and push her from the shore, letting the west wind fill her sails and take her out to sea. At the last minute, before she gathered speed, I would fling a burning brand into her from the shore and she would sail into the east all afire, blazing like a comet until she dwindled from sight.

This vision had always in my dreams been swiftly followed by a vivid picture, however, of the burning *Jack* bumping straight into a Russian oil-tanker bound for Odessa, igniting it in one titanic explosion and precipitating World War Three. Perhaps I could do the whole thing without the fire, simply setting her off on a captain-less last voyage to sail to the land of the Golden Fleece, the far Caucasus.

Another idea had been – and I am not joking – not to stop at all, but to keep sailing down the coast, round to Istanbul, across the Aegean, on and on and on, a restless Odysseus sailing on until the boat fell to pieces under him. Sometimes I still dream of that, and someday I may do it. But in fact *Jack* had already reached the falling-to-pieces stage. Her decks were flaky with old varnish, her gaff was splitting and she was no longer as dry and watertight as she had been. There was hardly a fitting on her that was not working loose; they had all been screwed on and re-tightened so many times that the wood was rotting away around them. She had done extraordinarily well, covering 4900 kilometres, traversing 282 locks and visiting twelve different countries, but I had been no careful, loving master, and she had suffered breakages and bumps, rough handling and bodily dragging, frayings and chafings and scrapes. Mentally I was in a similar state, beginning to fracture at the edges and splinter into insane giggles every now and then. It was time to retire.

The last six miles before Sulina saw a new idea creep into my mind. The sight of two small boys on the bank, their faces alight at the sight of me and *Jack*, and their excited waving and calling made me wonder whether I could not hand *Jack* back to the children. She had after all spent most of her thirty years as a teaching vessel for the young. There must be a school in Sulina, surely, and stuck between the river-marsh and the sea the inhabitants must lead a fairly waterlogged existence. Was it possible that *Jack* could end up as she had started? The more I pondered on the idea, the more I liked it. Even if *Jack* was used for nothing more exciting than allow-ing the local school-teacher to get to outlying regions of the Delta where untaught children lived, she would serve a noble purpose. It was a splendid idea, and when I told it to *Jack*, she heartily agreed. She hadn't wanted to hurt my feelings before, but she now confessed that she had never been too happy about the Viking funeral-pyre send-off. (Who would be?)

In the mid-afternoon of that gentle grey day, the 26th of October, 1998, we sailed into the little town of Sulina on the Black Sea. It was pleasant: there were few Soviet-style buildings around and many of the older ones remained intact. There were classical edifices with pillars and curly architraves, including a beautiful domed church built by none other than our old friend King Ludwig who, for all his sanity, had clearly thought that he owned the entire Danube.

I stopped at the river wharf in the centre of town a mile before the harbour and found the Harbourmaster, ready to see what he thought of my scheme to donate *Jack* to the local school. But I had reckoned without the cold hand of bureaucracy, deadening all in its grip, not only here but across Europe and Britain and the civilised world. The Harbourmaster was a fatherly man, a sort of avuncular dugong in looks, but his first response was much rueful head-shak-ing. 'No. This is not possible. What about Import Tax?'

I stared at him. 'Import Tax? On the boat? What Import Tax?'

'You bring a boat here, you say you want to leave it here? Then you have imported it. On this, there is a tax. It is simple,' he said.

I gaped.

'And,' he went on, warming to his theme, 'what about insur-ance?'

'Insurance?!'

'Yes, my friend, insurance. Who will pay that?'

I didn't know.

'This is the law in our country, my friend. All boats must be insured. I am sorry.'

'I really think that – '

'And another thing. You say you leave your boat here as a gift. Perhaps you change your mind, eh? You come back. In six months' time you come back and you say, where is my boat, you thieves? What then?'

'Look, I can assure you that I won't be coming back, either in six months' time or ever. I – '

'Ah, my friend, my friend. You say you are a school-teacher. Hah! I believe you. You are clearly not a businessman!'

Having remained polite for fourteen months and across twelve countries, even when being threatened by pirates, I now allowed myself a moment of terseness.

'Look, I'm sorry,' I said, 'but tomorrow I am walking out of here and not taking my twelve-foot dinghy in my rucksack with me. For me, a very simple solution to *my* problem is to get up early tomorrow morning, cut her adrift and walk away. But that I think is where *your* problem will start, with a vessel adrift in your main channel, a hazard to shipping and God knows what else besides. I won't be here to fix it. *You* will be. Can't we be sensible about this?'

The Harbourmaster sat back in his chair and looked at me for a long, long time, his moustaches drooping. Then he came to a decision. 'You are right. These laws are stupid, but I see a way around them. As Harbourmaster, I have certain ... exemptions ... from these laws. If I say I need a dinghy for my job, then I need a dinghy. No import tax, and the insurance is covered by the Harbour authorities. Even if I then decide in my wisdom to lend it to the local school, you understand? Which,' he added, looking at me sternly, 'I am not saying I will do. Maybe, maybe not. That is the best we can do, I think. Yes?'

It seemed the only solution. I was in no position to argue. So a piece of paper was brought out, typed up to his dictation but translated into French for me, and then duly signed by me. It read something like this:

I, Alexander James Mackinnon, owner and master of the sailing vessel Jack de Crow, *do hereby give her unreservedly as a gift to the Harbourmaster of Port Sulina for his use in carrying out his duties, as of this day, 26th October 1998, and henceforth have no further claim on her or any part of her, nor expect any payment in hiring fees or purchase price from the aforementioned Harbourmaster.*

Signed this day, 26th October 1998, Sulina, Romania.

(I have no idea, by the way, whether the Harbourmaster later followed through on his hints that the dinghy would get to the school after all, no questions asked. I was sceptically aware that I had signed away my boat to an opportunist who had done rather well out of the deal – but then again, I had just spent an entire year proving

the extraordinary generosity and goodwill of ordinary people from
Shropshire to the Black Sea. He seemed a kindly man, after all. It
seemed not only churlish and grudging of spirit to take the cynical
view, but downright illogical to think thus. I saw no reason why the
unexpected goodness of people should suddenly stop here at the furthest edge of Europe. I like to think therefore that *Jack* was of some
use to the children of Sulina, but I am content never to know one
way or the other.)

Back in the Harbourmaster's office I signed the contract – and
then broke it immediately. I asked the Harbourmaster if I could
borrow her for the next few hours. There was still something to be
done and *Jack* and I had to do it together. We had not, after all, yet
reached the Black Sea.

*

Beyond the town, the land petered out into marshland and reed-
beds. The main river-channel, widened and deepened for shipping,
ran through this in a gently curving mile between built-up dykes of
rock and earth, the left-hand one of which continued right out into
the Black Sea itself as a long, sturdy breakwater. However, long
before I got to this point, I noticed, as I rowed, a little break in this
dyke, where the ruins of a stumpy little lighthouse stood overlooking a stunted willow. Beneath the very trailing fronds of this tree,
the waters poured away in a smooth funnel, and on an instinct I
allowed *Jack* and myself to go with them. There was a rush and a
gurgle, a brushing of willow-wands on cheek and sail, and we found
ourselves in a secret little world of reeds and pools and channels
behind the dyke-wall. It was as though we had slipped out the scul-
lery door of some grand house rather than out the front doors, and
instead of finding ourselves on the broad bland gravel of the coach-
drive, had found ourselves in the cabbage-and-nasturtium cosiness
of the kitchen-garden, smelling of dew and turned earth.

Here at last was what I had expected the Delta to be like. Tall
reeds hemmed us in on either side, rustling with little birds that
chipped and darted in their dry denseness. The channel we were
on was barely ten yards wide and split into two ahead. Which way
to take? Try the right-hand one. Ah, no, this was curving back
towards the sea-wall so … but wait, here was another branch, and
another. This one looked promising … but no, a few wiggling
bends later and it stopped in a wall of sedges. The next half-hour

The Black Sea

Reed Beds

Sea Wall

Main Shipping Channel

Old Lighthouse

The Willow

To Sulina

Back Door to the Black Sea

was a blissfully happy hunt through the maze of reed-beds for the channel that would take me out to open water. Soon even the sea-wall and the top of the lighthouse were lost behind the screening reeds and I was alone in a secret world under the mild grey sky. And then an opening showed ahead in the wriggling channel, a glimpse of clear horizon and open water, and a minute later *Jack de Crow* and I rowed out onto the calm waters of the Black Sea. The reed-marsh was behind us, and visible a mile away was the dyke and the stump of the derelict lighthouse, but before us the sea stretched to the horizon.

It did not look like a sea. It was so flat, so grey-silver, so calm that it looked more like a vast freshwater lake under the steely sky. I dipped a finger in the water to taste it. It *was* fresh. A good steady breeze was blowing from the north-east, so *Jack* and I decided to spend our last few hours together sailing out to find where the real salt sea began.

Well, we never found it, and I learnt later that such is the volume of water coming down the Danube that the Black Sea remains completely fresh for almost seven miles out from Sulina, but those last couple of hours were some of the happiest I have ever spent. We skimmed to and fro over the burnished water, this way and that, now skimming close to a reed-bed to investigate a likely coot's nest, now sailing out again to clear waters. It suddenly struck me that for the first time in a year I was sailing purely for pleasure. I had no course that I had to follow, no distant mark that I was trying to bring edging closer inch by inch, no hemming land to shift the wind at every turn. I could tack up into the wind purely for the pleasure of turning around and sailing downwind again. I could zig-zag here and there at a whim. For the first time in a very long time, I could sail on a reach – that is, across the wind rather than into or down it – and rediscovered that this is the pleasantest sailing of all. The boat is lightly balanced, the sails trimly set, and the tiller rests with a comfortable pressure from the fingertips.

And here at last were the birds. Battalions of geese gathered on the glass-grey waters and paddled gabbling away as I approached. A fleet of white swans dipped and glided among the fringes of the reed-beds and then took flight, oaring overhead with silver necks outstretched, wings whistling and creaking into the East. Smaller birds, sandpipers and dunlins, turnstones and knots, pattered and whirred on the mudflats in the distance and a marsh-harrier hawked over the reeds. And everywhere, commoner than all the others, were the homely ducks, bobbing like toy boats among the rushes.

After an hour or two the skies to the north and east had darkened to charcoal, but the west was watery yellow with the setting sun. A faint rainbow glimmered out in a far-off shower against the leaden sky; a brief thing, but as unearthly as they come. It was time to head back.

One last adventure remained to us. Finding my way back to the 'back-door' by the lighthouse was easy enough, rowing through the winding channels between the tall reeds, but when it came to passing through that doorway back onto the main river, the difficulties began. The current pouring down either side of the willow tree on its tiny island was far too strong to row against. Time and time again I would aim *Jack*'s prow for one or other of the gaps, row like smoke and at the last minute be deflected sideways by the onrush of the stream. Back I would go, spinning down the channel like a leaf on the flood. After half-an-hour of this weary business I was beginning to get tired and a little panicky. The dusk was deepening and rain was threatening, and unless I could get beyond this miniature Charybdis, I would be spending the night out here on the marshes, with the Harbourmaster convinced I had absconded with what was now technically his boat.

Finally with a change in tactics I managed to drive *Jack* up into the tiny triangle of quiet water in the lee of the willow'd islet, between the two torrents racing down either side. Then there was nothing for it. We were back to the Morda Brook all over again, here at the very end of our journey. I took down the rigging, lowered the mast, emptied her of my entire luggage, removed the oars and bodily dragged poor *Jack* up onto the knobbly roots of the tiny eyot. Clumsily and painfully I hauled her over the twenty feet or so, dragging her under and through the low, grabbing branches of her old enemy, the willow. Twigs and leaves rained down into her, branches clawed at her, roots rose up to batter her keel, but scratched and leaf-spattered we made it eventually to the upper side of the island. Our last problem was how to launch off into the main river again without instantly being swept back down through the doorway.

There was a good breeze blowing in from the sea and up the river. With oars and sail, we might just make it clear of this trap. But even here the willow-tree spread its branches out over the water, so that it was impossible to raise the mast and sail while still on shore. I would have to row clear of the island, and then somehow get the mast up and the sail unfurled before the current could sweep us back down past the willow-isle and into the marshes again. This would be an impossible feat in any ordinary Mirror ... to row *and* haul up mast and sail all at once ... but *Jack de Crow* was, after all, no ordinary Mirror. Blessing the day that I had dreamed up my Auto-Pulley-o-matic Ezy-hoist before even setting out, I realised that it was now, once more, about to pay its way. There could be no mistakes. This had to work the very first time.

Very carefully I set everything in place. The mast-foot was ready to slot into its step on the foredeck. The stays were untangled, the gaff and boom were slipped out of their tyers, ready to haul aloft at a second's notice, and the oars were in their rowlocks ready to do their job. I patted *Jack* on the gunwale, whispered 'good luck!' and tugged her down into the water. Then with an almighty push I sent her flying from the bank, floundered aboard and started rowing as hard as I could out away from that island and its encircling twin currents. I heaved and hauled at the oars with a strength developed over fourteen months of daily rowing ... but it was not enough. I was fifteen yards from the island but beginning to slip backwards, sideways, spun by the current. I abandoned the oars, threw myself at the forestay pulley and hauled, slotting the mast-foot into place with the other hand. Teeth and hand, teeth and hand, I pulled away and the mast rose upright and stood firm.

Ten yards to the gap ...

Seven yards ...

Like lightning I cleated the pulley rope and flung myself at the halyard.

Five yards ...

Four yards ...

I hauled at the rope and the gaff rose up the mast taking the scarlet sail with it. Never had she risen more smoothly or wonderfully to the task. The wind filled the sail, the boom swung wide, and with just four yards left before we vanished down the sluice again, *Jack* stopped her backward drift and began to inch forward. Setting to the oars once more, and now aided by the good sea-breeze, we made our way slowly back up the river to the lights of Sulina shining in the distance.

*

Earlier that afternoon I had had a vision. It was no mystic wonder, merely yet another fanciful flight of the imagination such as the thousand others that have filled these pages. It had been on the last stretch of river before reaching Sulina, perhaps five miles upstream from where I was now. As I had been rowing along, facing back up the river as usual, I had been struck by the powerful notion that there before me lay the whole vastness of Europe; it unrolled in my mind's eye like a map. Over there to my left somewhere the rocky-white promontories of Greece, deckle-edged and with the map-maker's Mediterranean blue coloured in up to each tiny crinkle. Over to my right the plains and forests of Russia stretching away, a blank paper wilderness, and straight ahead the little ridge of the Carpathian Mountains cut by the notch of the Iron Gates gorge, inked in tiny detail. Beyond that the great Magyar plain of Hungary and Yugoslavia, smudged and torn here and there by a careless hand, but dotted with the colours of plum and apple ripening on the tree. Then the Alps, tiny and perfect and sharp, like things seen in a globe of glass; the solemn temples, the gorgeous palaces, the cloud-capped towers of Austria and Bavaria. And so to the wavy line of the Rhine and the lesser line of the Moselle, wiggling up the map on a golden-green background, the colour of new wine – and so to France, scattered with woods and fields and the bright sprinkle of poppies. But the map does not end there. A narrow bar of painted sea and there is England as John of Gaunt saw it, a precious stone set in a silver sea. The White Cliffs are there, and London, and Oxford, every detail on the Magdalen Tower to be seen under the cartographer's glass. And there on the very furthest edge, where the paper is curling off the table, the green meadows and blue hills of Wales.

And through all this runs a single thread. At times it is the brandy-brown of country brooks; elsewhere it is salt-green flecked with white. Sometimes it is a thread of softest wool, dyed blue-grey. Sometimes it is stretched steel wire, scratched and harsh. In places it is a ribbon of midnight-blue, spangled with the sequins of stars, or a thread of pure gold that catches the light and runs it up and down its length like liquid in a glass. It is dotted with charms and trinkets along its length; the carved stones of cathedrals, or white quartz beads as cold as marble. There are rich gems strung there: garnets red as fire-coals, sapphires flashing like kingfishers, warm topazes set in gold. But in all its length it is unbroken, a single thread of water-green laid from one end of the map to the other.

As I sail the last mile back up to Sulina in the gathering dusk, I recall the vision of that afternoon, and then it fades again. There are things to do. As I sail along in the dusk, willow-twigs are thrown overboard, leaf-mulch and bread-crumbs and all the debris of the riverbanks that collects so easily in the boat's bilges. I straighten her lines, coil her painters and halyards, and sponge the worst of the mud off her decks and bottom-boards. She's not a bad little boat really. By the time we have arrived at the town pier, it is completely dark, but the job is done. *Jack de Crow* is ready for her new life, and I for mine.

The End

Acknowledgements

THERE ARE VERY MANY acknowledgements to be made, and these fall into two categories: first, of those who lent support and practical aid in the writing of this book, and second, of those, almost countless, who made the voyage possible in a variety of ways.

In the first category, I would like to express my heartfelt gratitude to Patricia Eve and all her associates at Seafarer Books, whose faith in the original product and cheerful rallying along the way were instrumental in bringing the first edition of the book to fruition. In a similar vein, I would like to acknowledge the professionalism and enthusiasm of the staff at Black Inc. in producing this second edition. I would especially like to thank Chris Feik, whose skill and patience as editor have taken an unwieldy vessel, trimmed its sails, offloaded ballast and shaped its lines to produce a swifter, lighter, more graceful craft than I could ever have imagined possible.

In the second category, the list is very much longer. It includes impromptu carpenters and boat-builders encountered at timely intervals, such as Phil Simpson, Alan Snell, Paul Stollerof-Zambinski, Peter Pohl and a host of anonymous donors of expertise, varnish and screwdrivers along the way. To this must be added the kind hosts, either known to me beforehand or complete strangers, only a fraction of whom could be included in this account. There were countless river-side dwellers across Britain and Europe who opened their doors and hearts to me; so numerous were they, and often so potent was their hospitality, that their names had vanished into an amnesiac haze by the next morning. To all these, I am immensely grateful.

For those whose names and deeds of kindness I have been able to record in the body of the book, there is the dubious privilege of seeing themselves portrayed in print. 'I Exaggerate For Effect' – my friends tell me I was born for that motto. Let those who find themselves parodied or lampooned in return for their kindness towards a stranger understand that here, more than ever, the motto is true. Indeed, the greater the caricature, the deeper runs my gratitude and affection.

A third category exists: those whose support made both the book and the voyage possible. Foremost among these are my family, and in particular my sister Margaret, my father and my mother. While I was enjoying the luxury of improvised voyaging in the realms of Fantasy, both my father and Margaret allowed me to sustain the illusion of eighteenth-century roving by tirelessly dealing with bank statements, credit-card payments and those elements of the modern world that don't really disappear after all.

My father has been doing this for years now, and can hardly be thanked enough for this labour of love. Margaret, during this voyage in particular, spent much of her spare time away from finding a cure for malaria, concentrating on what at the time seemed to me a greater priority: namely, forwarding mail and engaging in long reverse-charge phone calls from Eastern Europe when it had all become too much to bear. She was my anchorline to the real world, and occasionally to sanity when the Keats and the endless willows had begun to take over.

Lastly, I wish to thank my mother. Caricatured and gently parodied in these pages, she nevertheless typed the entire first volume from my handwritten pages and resisted (generally) the sore temptation to edit as she went. Her encouragement and enthusiasm for every aspect of both the voyage and the writing process has been characteristically boundless throughout – as has her love for sailing, falling in the water, coming up laughing and making a good story out of it for as far back as I can remember.

It is to her, therefore, that I dedicate this book.